DISCIPLINARY
CONQUEST

American Encounters/Global Interactions A SERIES EDITED BY
GILBERT M. JOSEPH AND EMILY S. ROSENBERG

––––––––––

This series aims to stimulate critical perspectives and fresh interpretive frameworks for scholarship on the history of the imposing global presence of the United States. Its primary concerns include the deployment and contestation of power, the construction and deconstruction of cultural and political borders, the fluid meanings of intercultural encounters, and the complex interplay between the global and the local. American Encounters seeks to strengthen dialogue and collaboration between historians of U.S. international relations and area studies specialists.

The series encourages scholarship based on multiarchival historical research. At the same time, it supports a recognition of the representational character of all stories about the past and promotes critical inquiry into issues of subjectivity and narrative. In the process, American Encounters strives to understand the context in which meanings related to nations, cultures, and political economy are continually produced, challenged, and reshaped.

DISCIPLINARY CONQUEST

U.S. Scholars in South America, 1900–1945

RICARDO D. SALVATORE

Duke University Press   Durham and London   2016

Printed in the United States of America on acid-free paper ∞
Typeset in Trade Scala Sans by Westchester Publishing Services

Library of Congress Cataloging-in-Publication Data
Salvatore, Ricardo Donato, author.
Disciplinary conquest : U.S. scholars in South America,
1900–1945 / Ricardo D. Salvatore.
pages cm — (American encounters/global interactions)
Includes bibliographical references and index.
ISBN 978-0-8223-6081-0 (hardcover : alk. paper)
ISBN 978-0-8223-6095-7 (pbk. : alk. paper)
ISBN 978-0-8223-7450-3 (e-book)
1. Latin America—Civilization—Study and teaching
(Higher)—United States. 2. United States—Foreign
relations—South America. 3. South America—Foreign
relations—United States. 4. Imperialism. I. Title.
II. Series: American encounters/global interactions.
F1409.95.U6S25 2016
327.730809'04—dc23   2015031549

COVER ART: Hiram Bingham's expedition staff with Peruvian natives at Machu Picchu, 1911. Hand-colored slide by Harry Ward Foote. Yale Peruvian Expedition Papers (MS 664). Manuscripts and Archives, Yale University Library.

This book is dedicated to my wife,

LAURA POSADAS

———

and to the memory of my parents,

Marica y Chili

CONTENTS

Contents

viii

ACKNOWLEDGMENTS

When Gilbert Joseph was in the process of organizing the "Rethinking the Postcolonial Encounter" conference, which would later become the edited volume *Close Encounters of Empire*, he asked me to contribute some ideas about the current status and possible direction in the study of U.S.–Latin American relations after the cultural-linguistic turn. The paper I presented at the conference (titled "The Enterprise of Knowledge"), hosted by Yale in 1995, launched me on a long journey into examining the formation of U.S. hegemony as a question of representation and power rooted in a quest for knowledge. Initially, my primary object of curiosity was how the nature and purpose of the U.S. empire in Latin America was represented and encoded into written texts. For a while, the U.S. informal empire and its "representational machines" stood at the center of my intellectual preoccupations. Yet with time my focus shifted toward the role of disciplinary knowledge in the making of U.S. hegemony over Latin America. Somewhat in between that conference and drafting this book, I discovered that "Pan-Americanism" in its various renditions was a force that tended to color much of the discussion about U.S.–Latin American relations since 1910, continuing to exert significant influence during the 1930s and 1940s.

My first thanks go to Gil for guiding me into this line of research, which has turned out to be so interesting and rewarding. And to Cathy LeGrand, who started the whole conversation about the communicative and discursive nature of imperial engagements and about the importance of culture in mediating the memory of past U.S. economic, military, and political interventions in Latin America. Since 1998, the year in which *Close Encounters of Empire* was published, my opportunities to discuss the American empire, its representations, and its forms of knowledge have multiplied exponentially. Consequently, there are many, many people I need to thank. My intellectual debt being so large, I am tempted to simply declare myself in default and be done with it. But that would be unfair. So I will mention a selected group of colleagues, librarians, and students who over the years have helped develop the ideas that are part of this book; at the same time, I extend my acknowledgment and gratitude to the many others who have given me the opportunity to present these interpretations.

It was at Princeton, during my stay at the Institute for Advance Studies (1988–1989), that I first discovered a close connection between mercantile activities and the available body of knowledge about overseas peoples. The extraordinary collection of "letter writers" and travel books I found at the Firestone Library helped me realize that, for merchants of the American Northeast, gathering information about other lands and peoples was a cultural imperative. In a paper I presented in 1990, at a University of Minnesota history workshop, I attempted to root the expansionist tendencies of the U.S. Northeast in the late eighteenth and early nineteenth centuries on both the curiosity awakened by travel and the mandate to register Otherness imposed by mercantile culture. The impulse to acquire transnational or global knowledge was constitutive of the notion of a "good merchant." By extension, one could expect that this intertwining between foreign commerce and knowledge would continue to influence U.S. expansionism in the late nineteenth century and early twentieth— only that now, after the War of 1898, the entanglement between business and knowledge would be projected into a foreign policy view (U.S. Pan Americanism) and re-elaborated by business experts, scholars, and diplomats.

Hence, I will begin by acknowledging the good work of the librarians and archivists who helped me find the wide range of materials needed to write this book, among them the librarians at Universidad Torcuato Di Tella, Yale University, Harvard University, Duke University, Georgetown University, and the Columbus Memorial Library in Washington, D.C. Without these resources and the librarians' advice, this project would have been more difficult to accomplish. As the reader will see, I was able to examine archival documents for three of the five scholars discussed in this volume (H. Bingham, C. Haring, and Leo S. Rowe). For the other two, my analysis is based on their works and memoirs.

Second, I would like to thank the institutions that funded my research. A Fulbright Advanced Research Fellowship allowed me to reside in Washington for two months, where I was able to research the papers and work of Leo S. Rowe and the Pan-American Union. A De Fortabat Fellowhip at the Rockefeller Center for Latin American Studies, Harvard, allowed me sufficient spare time to work with Clarence Haring's papers. Before that, I spent a semester at Yale

University, as an Edward L. Tinker Visiting Professor. There, at the university archives, I encountered abundant materials about Hiram Bingham and the Yale Peruvian Expedition. Back in Argentina, the Secretaría de Ciencia y Técnica (SECyT) provided funding for the assistance of graduate students. One of them, Juan Pablo Scarfi, helped me establish connections between the U.S. scholars and local intellectuals. Another group of graduate students worked on a database of U.S. publications about South America during the period under examination.

At various workshops, conferences, and symposia, I presented rough ideas about the nature of U.S. Pan-Americanism, the representational nature of the U.S. informal empire, and the multiple activities and processes that led to the establishment of Latin American Studies in the United States. Among these presentations were those I delivered at the annual meeting of the American Historical Association in Washington (1999); at a seminar on economic integration sponsored by the University of New Mexico in collaboration with my home university, Universidad Torcuato Di Tella (1999); at the international colloquium "Repensando el Imperialismo" at Universidad Torcuato Di Tella (August 2000); at a Duke–Di Tella workshop on "Globalization and the Humanities" at Buenos Aires (August 2001); at a symposium on "Cultural Encounters and Resistance" at University College London (June 2001); at a symposium on "Hybrid Americas" at the University of Bielefeld (2002); at a colloquium on "The Location of Knowledge" jointly organized by Universidad Di Tella and Duke University (2003); at the conference "Looking North" at the Universidade Federal Fluminense of Rio de Janeiro (2004); at the Social Science Research Council conference on "Empire and Dissent: U.S. Hegemony in Latin America" at Cuernavaca, México (2005); at a Harvard Global History Conference (February 2008); at a meeting of the Associação Nacional de Pesquisadores e Professores de História das Américas in Victoria, Brazil (July 2008); at the fifth global conference of International American Studies Association (IASA) in Rio de Janeiro (July 2011); and at the symposium on "Fugitive Knowledge" at the University of Rostock (September 2012).

I want to thank the organizers of these events for their efforts and kindness: Linda Hall and Gilbert Merkx of the University of New Mexico; Walter Mignolo, Grant Farred, and Cathy Davidson of Duke University; Nicola Miller and Christopher Abel of University College London; Josef Raab of the University of Bielefeld; Carlos Altamirano, Jorge Francisco Liernur, and Claudia Shmidt, my co-organizers of the Buenos Aires colloquium; Virginia Dominguez, Jane Desmond, and Sonia Torres, organizers of the Rio de Janeiro conference; Itty Abraham and Fred Rosen, organizers of the Cuernavaca workshop;

Sven Beckert, organizer of the Harvard conference; Antonio C. Amador Gil, convenor of the meeting at Victoria, Brazil; Patrick Imbert, organizer and commentator of the "Geography of Power" session of the IASA conference in Rio; and Gesa Mackenthun, organizer of the event at Rostock, Germany.

The reviewers who read this manuscript were very generous with their time and very precise in their criticisms. Their work certainly served to improve the coherence and persuasiveness of my argument. My friends Carlos Aguirre and Carlos Forment provided valuable advice in terms of the bibliography, as well as continuous support to this intellectual project. And so did Gil Joseph and Cathy LeGrand, already named. My colleagues at Buenos Aires have read drafts of various chapters or papers containing related ideas and responded with useful insights. Among them are Juan Manuel Palacio, Ernesto Boholavsky, Horacio Crespo, Hugo Vezzetti, Guillermo Ranea, Jorge F. Liernur, Irina Podgorny, and Karina Galperin. To all of them, I extend my thanks.

During the different stages of writing, the content and center of this volume changed. Indeed, three primary revisions were needed for this book to be as readable as it is. For this, I must thank my former editor Valerie Millholland, who provided early guidance, and Miriam Angress, who steered the project to completion. If the reader should notice that the book reads well in English, though written by an Argentine, it is due to the valuable help of the developmental editor Laura Helper-Ferris. My thanks extend also to the various technicians, correctors, and assistants who constitute Duke University Press and contribute to the excellence of its publications.

Though I was abroad for extended periods of time, visiting different universities, my academic home has remained Universidad Torcuato Di Tella. I thank my colleagues for making this work environment a precious refuge, isolated from the instability and rhetorical warfare that constitutes Argentine political life.

While writing this book, I encountered some unexpected life difficulties. The passing of both my parents between 2008 and 2011, after prolonged periods of illness, profoundly affected my emotional stability. My wife, Laura, helped me to navigate this difficult time, providing the support I needed to continue with my academic work. To her—and to the memory of my parents—I dedicate this book.

Disciplinary Conquest

———

From 1900 to 1945, well before the consolidation of area studies, U.S. scholars in the humanities and the social sciences delineated the contours of a recently "rediscovered" land: South America. Their publications provided comprehensive and empirically informed visions of the subcontinent that contributed to the United States' diplomatic rapprochement with the region. Parallel to business prospectors, Pan-American enthusiasts, religious missionaries, and travelers, a group of U.S. scholars came to the region in search of new data and fresh, direct observations to confirm or reject prior generalizations and stereotypes. Little by little, their authoritative representations began to fill the previous vacuum of knowledge, said to represent a major obstacle for more intense economic relations between the two Americas. Enhanced knowledge, the argument ran, would generate greater mutual trust in inter-American relations. These acts of knowing laid the foundations for a substantial apparatus of knowledge in the service of hemispherism.

I call these scholarly engagements "disciplinary interventions": disciplinary because they were rooted in scientific disciplines; interventions because they fostered U.S. economic, technological, and cultural hegemony in the region. In a way, these adventures in disciplinary knowledge constituted a continuation of U.S. hemispheric diplomacy through other means. In a region free from direct U.S. military and political intervention, information gathering and knowledge production constituted cumulative acts of possession, through which the United States apprehended, systematized, and rendered legible the realities of South America. Textual, scientific representations of the region, which later congealed into regional disciplinary knowledge, constituted the appropriate mode of engagement for a benevolent informal empire.

In the interwar period, scholars were increasingly engaged in Pan-Americanism, a movement that envisioned a hemispheric system of cooperation. Its promoters expected university professors and researchers to produce new knowledge that could reveal the "true nature" of the southern republics, ascertaining the similarities and differences in the region's cultures. By the time of the Second World War, U.S. scholars had established the infrastructure of Latin American studies: the institutes, the research centers, the experts, the university programs, and the library collections for sustained interdisciplinary research on the region.[1] Most of them were proud that the knowledge attained by their disciplines served to inform U.S. policies toward the region. Implicit in the design of Latin American studies was a constitutive connection with U.S. foreign policy. This connection gave meaning and substance to many of the research efforts deployed to "know" South America. In addition, scholars expected that, once disseminated to the U.S. population at large, this new knowledge would bring about feelings of sympathy and understanding for South Americans.

In this book I explore the engagement of U.S. scholars with distinct aspects of South America—its natural environments, human settlements, pre-Columbian cultures, colonial history, and contemporary social relations and forms of government—during the period 1900–1945. I examine the growth of academic knowledge about the region in relation to the building of informal empire. More precisely, I investigate the connection between the region's integration as an object of U.S. scientific inquiry and the "economic conquest" of South America. In *Disciplinary Conquest* I argue that knowledge enterprises could be considered ancillary activities in the making of imperial hemispheric hegemony. Scholarly visions of South America made the countries of the region more easily apprehensible, their "realities" more readable both to U.S. foreign-policy experts and to the U.S. general public.

My inquiry focuses on the works of five scholars: a historian (Clarence H. Haring), a geographer (Isaiah Bowman), a political scientist (Leo S. Rowe), a sociologist (Edward A. Ross), and an archaeologist (Hiram Bingham). While restricted, this selection of scholars and disciplines provides a panoramic overview of knowledge production about South America in the United States. In other words, the work of these five scholars could be considered as representative of the modalities of U.S. scholarly engagement with the realities of the southern republics. *Disciplinary Conquest* deals with the parallel and complementary expansion of the U.S. informal empire and the formation of regional knowledge about South America. Increased commercial and investment opportunities in South America motivated these scholars to extend disciplinary research into this new and unexplored territory. Interest in Inca citadels developed into a full-blown inquiry of Andean archaeology. A geographical survey along the 73rd meridian provided the initial step for the project of South American geography. Interest in the administration of the Spanish colonial system and in U.S.-Latin American diplomatic history served to configure the field of Hispanic American history. In areas as different as geography, government, social relations, economics and finance, education, and history, scholars made a concerted effort to survey, report, and interpret the complex realities of the region, comparing them with Europe, the United States, and former Iberian empires.

My claims refer specifically to the period 1900–1945, which corresponds to the construction of Pan-American institutions and ideals.[2] Before 1900, the very rarity of specialized regional knowledge made the interaction between knowledge and state power less frequent and effective. First proposed by Secretary of State James G. Blaine in 1881, the Pan-American ideal was envisioned as a loose cooperative union of the American republics.[3] Later, under President Woodrow Wilson, as the U.S. launched a rapprochement with South America, the notion developed into a full ideology, hemispherism, which centered on ideas of economic cooperation, cultural engagement, and collective security. By the mid-1930s, support for Pan-Americanism reached a peak of enthusiasm. Throughout the country, "Pan-American societies"—associations devoted to promoting inter-American friendship and understanding—received the broad support of U.S. functionaries, corporations, universities, and municipalities. Indeed, Pan-Americanism became a government-sponsored social movement. The Good Neighbor Policy of President Franklin D. Roosevelt, for example, served to deepen U.S. rapprochement with the subcontinent.[4] The era of Pan-Americanism was a particular conjuncture in which economic opportunities made knowledge of South America a special concern shared by U.S. businessmen, foreign policy makers, and scholars. Diplomatic efforts to gain the cooperation of the South American republics presented U.S. officials with many questions about the opinions of South American intellectuals.

This study focuses on South America, the region geographically located south of Panama. After 1900, diplomats, scholars, businessmen, missionaries, and other travelers delineated an enduring geopolitical division of the hemisphere. In the academic discourse of the period, "South America" stood for a region quite different from Mexico, Central America, and the Caribbean, where the U.S. exerted more direct forms of intervention. North of the Panama Canal were nations with frequent revolutions, with illiterate populations living under conditions of extreme poverty, and subjected, because of their proximity to the United States, to close and frequent supervision by Uncle Sam. South of this divide, in South America, were more politically stable republics, some of which had attained a significant degree of economic progress, particularly the so-called ABC powers, Argentina, Brazil, and Chile, as well as, by extension, Uruguay. In the U.S. foreign-policy community and in business circles there developed during this period a temporary fascination with—at moments bordering on perplexity at—the rapid progress attained by the ABC powers.[5] As a consequence, authors called for a differential treatment of the region relative to the rest of Latin America. For diverse reasons, the Washington establishment never considered these republics as possible targets of military intervention. Promoters of Pan-Americanism, such as John Barrett, presented the southern republics as "lands of opportunity" to U.S. investors and merchants.[6]

Once they had constructed the divide, U.S. scholars filled this construed geopolitical entity, "South America," with meaning. In this book, I examine several instances in which U.S. scholars presented this crucial geopolitical difference (the Great Divide) as a constitutive element of Latin American studies. In the works of geography, government, archaeology, sociology, and history I review, the specificity of "South America" resonated clearly and vividly. My inquiry traces the steps taken by U.S. scholars in making regional disciplinary knowledge, my central preoccupation being the ways in which this newly acquired knowledge helped diplomats and policy makers envision new U.S. foreign policies toward the region. I demonstrate that new knowledge about South America brought greater order and enhanced visibility both to U.S. scholars and to U.S. foreign-policy makers.[7] Scholars endeavored to order the great diversity of observed phenomena with concepts, methods of direct observation, and generalizations proper to their academic disciplines. By aggregation, these observations developed into general panoramic vistas of history, society, politics, culture, and the environment. These synthetic views condensed understandings about race, gender, nation, and power in South America. Certain aspects of these knowledge-producing activities were constitutive of Latin American studies: comprehensive visibility, the attempt to describe and understand regional and subnational diversity, and the prestige associated with scientific methods of observation.

In addition, these acts of knowing presented a purportedly scientific vision of the subcontinent that businessmen and foreign-policy experts deemed necessary for the United States as an emerging international power. The possibility of viewing the whole field from a distance and the authority to pronounce general statements about the region's past, present, and potential future constituted a pervasive and enduring form of power.[8] In relation to this, we can claim that there was an intellectual conquest of South America, in the sense of appropriating and incorporating the region within the field of vision and range of influence of U.S. academic knowledge. The institutional and developmental issues of the region would not have developed into "problems" without thorough regional disciplinary work in the social sciences and in the humanities. Regional knowledge was a precondition for the construction of hemispheric influence and power.

I present various instances of the production of regional knowledge: the exploration of Machu Picchu by the amateur archaeologist Hiram Bingham; the mapping of South America by the American Geographic Society under Isaiah Bowman's leadership; the social landscapes of Andean nations drawn by the sociologist Edward Ross; the comprehensive revision of Spanish colonialism made by the historian Clarence Haring; and the studies of government in colonial and neocolonial situations pioneered by Leo Rowe. These studies entailed a recurrent adjustment or calibration between preconceptions and realities, between national generalizations and subregional description. I examine the processes that created such new knowledge and the circumstances and relationships that made it possible. These scholarly interventions—together with others not discussed in this volume—generated new understandings of South America. The increased academic interest generated by these interventions caused U.S. diplomats and businessmen to reappraise the region's limitations and possibilities.

By studying these scholars' intellectual trajectories, research designs, and foreign-policy opinions, *Disciplinary Conquest* revisits the question of the origins of Latin American studies from a different perspective: an understanding rooted in the mutual constitution of disciplinary regional knowledge and the U.S. exertion of economic and cultural influence over South America. First, until now, the consolidation of Latin American studies has been erroneously dated to the early 1960s and understood as a by-product of the Cuban Revolution.[9] My position is that the fundamental intellectual apparatus of the Latin American field was already established prior to this—in fact, before the Second World War. Second, I emphasize the connection between U.S. scholarly engagements and U.S. foreign policy, arguing that the motivations for knowing South America "scientifically" were diplomatic, economic, and political. The disciplines' move toward regional knowledge cannot be separated from the discussions about the U.S. role in the hemisphere, the ideal of Pan-Americanism, and the cultural turn in inter-American relations implicit in the Good Neighbor Policy. Endowed with the authority of disciplinary knowledge, U.S. scholars intervened in foreign-policy debates, gauged the possibilities of further economic penetration, and argued for or against the convergence of Anglo-American and Spanish-American cultures. Whether they were staunch supporters of Pan-Americanism or not, scholars tended to envision the nature of the U.S. hegemony in South America as something to be wrought in the terrain of culture. In this regard, their views sustained and accompanied the transition from Big Stick diplomacy to the Good Neighbor Policy.

Disciplinary Conquest is intellectual history with a twist.[10] For although I am concerned with scholars' intellectual trajectories, influences, and interests, I do not separate the ideas and visions of these scholars from the social context and the material dimensions of their labors: their teaching, their travels, their editorial tasks, their networking activities, and their political and social interactions. In conjunction, all these activities contributed to shape U.S. academic visions of South America, which, in turn, were crucial for building the foundations of disciplinary regional knowledge in U.S. universities and learned societies. In this sense, my perspective follows the agenda, advanced in *Close Encounters of Empire*, of examining the postcolonial encounter in its multiple, ground-level manifestations and representations to ascertain the relationships construed and the positions claimed by U.S. representatives in Latin America.[11] This time, though, the object under study is a collection of disciplinary interventions, themselves a diverse assembly of knowledge-producing experiences and representations.

An empirical impulse guided these scholars, and their "findings" tended to emphasize differences internal to the object of study (South America). In the book, the reader will see the perplexity of scholars as they tried to account for an array of nations and negotiate the obstacles in collecting evidence, the satisfaction when they successfully carried the evidence to their home universities, the temptation to make great generalizations about the whole region, the pausing to consider the challenges that a certain piece of evidence presented to existing understandings. In this terrain, I greatly benefited from Bruno Latour's insights about the nature of scientific work: research is socially and institutionally grounded; there is a constant circulation of materials and concepts; and interpersonal networks of scholars matter.[12]

My argument is not reductionist, nor does it lend itself to a facile instrumentalist interpretation. The U.S. economic expansion and the diplomatic rapprochement that followed Secretary Root's visit to the region in 1906 opened up many questions about the nature and condition of South America. U.S. scholars posed these questions within their disciplines and realized that, to answer these questions, they needed field observations. This data gathering foregrounded the emergence of regionally based knowledge. Within three to four decades, initial regional subdisciplines came together as Latin American studies. *Disciplinary Conquest* shows that the content of the new regional disciplines was informed by several forces, among them the problems posed by foreign policy, the availability of library and archival collections, contemporary currents of thought, expert definitions and concepts, academic politics within universities and learned societies, technologies of observation and recording, and the interest awakened in the U.S. public about "South America."

U.S. scholars brought back to their home universities and learned societies new claims about South America's natural environment, population, history, politics, social relations, and antiquities that in time consolidated into formidable structures of regional knowledge. Their research constituted new subdisciplines, such as Andean archaeology, South American geography, and Hispanic American history. Inquiries into politics and government in the region did not generate a discipline called "South American politics," just as the interest of sociologists in social relations in South America did not produce a "South American sociology."[13] These intellectual contributions acquired meaning in discussions internal to U.S. academe, and also in dialogue with questions posed by U.S. foreign-policy makers. The common theme that connected scholars and diplomats was the role the United States had to play in the hemisphere.

In this book I consider scholarly interventions in South America in relation to the growth of research universities and disciplinary knowledge in the United States.[14] These were the expansive forces that accompanied the deployment of U.S. cultural authority and disciplinary knowledge in South America, at a time of unprecedented expansion of U.S. investment and trade in the region. During this period, there was a complementary relation between the expansion of knowledge capital and that of financial and physical capital. For this reason, it is quite difficult to separate neatly the economic and knowledge imperatives of informal empire. Many forces were connected in this period, including capital and knowledge, research universities and progressive ideals, a cosmopolitan, post-isolationist national outlook and the apparently insatiable quest for knowledge of the outside world.[15]

The "intellectual conquest" that this book examines cannot be reduced or subsumed to grand metanarratives of evolution and progress, Euro-American centrism, or the constitution of a permanent and well-delimited alterity.[16] While the different authors spoke to the preoccupations of their time and culture (race, gender roles, nation, tradition, modernity, economic progress), we cannot speak of a common discourse connecting the enunciations of their disciplinary endeavors. The claims I advance concerning the relationship between knowledge and informal empire should be read within the bounds of "situated knowledges."[17] They do not belong to the slippery terrain of great discursive formations or grand epistemes. To be sure, U.S. scholars betrayed in their writings some general notions of U.S-style Occidentalism, some condescension toward women, and even some overt racism.[18] U.S. scholars also tinkered with the idea of U.S. exceptionalism in relationship to South American development. But, by and large, their characterizations of South America were governed more by the evidence they gathered—and how they interpreted this evidence—than by any metaconceptions about humanity, races, gender roles, or national prejudice. For this reason, *Disciplinary Conquest* does not deal much with stereotypes and cultural biases, a usual focus of most literature on the history of inter-American relations.[19] In short, U.S. scholars "conquered" their fields by contributing data, new discoveries, and a bounty of interpretations about the realities of South America. The knowledge they produced was not so much trapped into "Occidentalism" or "Americo-centrism" as propelled by a voracious will to know, informed by the history of the different disciplines and by foreign-policy imperatives.

My argument about the origins of "regional knowledge" is rooted not in a wide-ranging critique of universality and Western epistemology, but in a pragmatic view of knowledge production as located within institutions, power networks, and the accumulation of cultural capital. It would take much imagination—and very little common sense—to reduce the contributions made by Haring, Bowman, Rowe, Bingham, and Ross to a complicity with metadiscourses of white supremacy, male domination, or U.S. superiority. Besides a common ascription to U.S. exceptionalism, the only discourse that united the different academic interventions was that of "useful knowledge," a rhetoric that connected the arguments of different disciplines about South America to the dilemmas of the U.S. role in the hemisphere.

Knowledge is, after all, an arrangement of elements, a deployment of arguments, that is always situated and material, in its production as well as in its circulation. As Bruno Latour has taught us, knowledge requires a vast circulation of objects, a constant negotiation with language, and innumerable skirmishes over what constitute "facts" and how they should be interpreted.[20] The pursuit of knowledge is not simply an altruistic endeavor; it is part of a process of construing academic authority, a process that tends to concentrate knowledge-power in certain locations, from where it radiates influence to the international scholarly community. Though certainly influenced by the work of Michel Foucault, my work in this volume advances a slightly different conception of power/knowledge. Instead of emphasizing that knowledge cuts across all exercises of power, I underline the instrumental value of knowledge in the construction of imperial hegemony. That is why I speak of "knowledge-power" rather than of power/knowledge.[21] Disciplinary knowledge is a particular form of knowledge, with boundaries and objects of study defined by experts or professionals, generally working within academic institutions.[22]

The formation of regional knowledge may entail the marginalization of locally based knowledges and peripheral intellectuals. Regional disciplines such as Hispanic American history or South American geography have tended to present themselves as superior to national disciplines such as Peruvian history or Colombian geography, the practitioners of the former often discrediting the works of the latter as unscientific, incomplete, noncomparative, or simply sloppy. The alleged superiority of regional disciplines over national ones is in turn related to important asymmetries in the accumulation of cultural capital.[23] The construction of academic fields of regional knowledge presupposes that libraries, archives, and museums hold specialized collections. It requires scholars to mobilize labor and financial resources to sustain wide-ranging research agendas on foreign lands.[24] Underdeveloped nations rarely possess such resources for generating knowledge about their own conditions, much less to study the industrialized centers of the world economy. This basic asymmetry is often dismissed as unimportant by scholars from the North.

Knowledge and cultural capital tends to concentrate in the center at the expense of the peripheries.[25] Institutes for the study of colonialism, development, slavery, and other themes crucial to the peripheries of the world economy are usually located at the center. Sixteenth-century debates about the condition of the American Indian and the proper form of evangelization took place in Spanish centers of high learning (Valladolid, Salamanca). Imperial history was born in England, though its subject matter was the colonies, more specifically "colonial India."[26] The same could be said of African studies in France or colonial studies in the Netherlands. Latin American studies in the United States do not depart from this centripetal logic: knowledge purported to be specific of peripheral regions and populations tend to concentrate into the hegemon's centers of knowledge.

Introduction

In addition to location, there is a question of usage. At the center, the findings of regional-based knowledge could be used to design policies that facilitated the exploitation of the resources of the peripheries while avoiding conflicts and resistance. I call this knowledge useful in the sense of knowledge oriented toward the needs of the central nation-state. Yet, to the degree that regional knowledge provided policy makers and businessmen at the center with enhanced visibility of the peripheries' problems, this knowledge was also imperial.

By and large, U.S. scholars measured the realities of South American nations against the model of "American modernity." This contributed to the process of "Americanization," the attempt to deploy the U.S. way of life as a model to be imitated or replicated by South American societies.[27] Edward Ross projected his own view of U.S. social modernity (the agrarian democracy of the Midwest) onto his portrayal of the Andean societies. In similar ways, Leo Rowe evaluated the condition of Southern Cone universities against that of U.S. college culture and measured Argentine federalism against U.S. constitutional theory and practice. Isaiah Bowman presented the exploitation of natural resources in the southern Andes in relation to U.S. corporate methods and rationality. Yet this book is not about U.S. modernity or its deployment in South America. It is about the forms of knowledge that emerged out of U.S. scholars' encounters with the realities of the southern republics. At the heart of this knowledge formation was an ethnocentric conception of knowledge and of the organization of higher learning that is not particularly "American."

This book offers an introduction to the intellectual conquest of South America. Notable U.S. scholars drew the fundamental insights and posed the most important questions about the region's nature, present condition, and future. Their work pioneered the road to a comprehensive knowledge of the region. As later acknowledged by practitioners of Latin American studies in the 1960s, these pioneers sought to understand the totality of "Latin American culture." By this they meant the interrelations among geographies, populations, governments, economies, and forms of society and culture. At the same time, they established the bases for disciplinary authority in certain locations within the United States: Cambridge, New Haven, Philadelphia, New York, Madison, Austin, Berkeley, and so on. In this regard, these scholars participated in the centripetal logic implicit in the accumulation of regional knowledge and disciplinary authority. New evidence "traveled" from the southern periphery to a selected group of academic centers in the United States to serve as raw materials for the generation of new knowledge about South America. By the late 1920s and 1930s, these centers were actively producing knowledge about South America and, at the same time, bringing business leaders, diplomats, state functionaries, and regional experts together to discuss "Latin American problems."

Unlike the business prospectors, casual travelers, or explorers, these academic observers came to South America to "conquer the field" for a given discipline. It is not that South America (its regions, or constitutive nations, or its populations) was literally conquered by the United States or by the universities that these scholars represented. Rather, the region was claimed as possession by the disciplines themselves—geography, political science, archaeology, sociology, and history—in the sense of being incorporated into the field of visibility and into the core problematic of each academic community. It was through disciplinary knowledge that the region's "problems" came to be a concern of universities and learned societies in the United States. The inclusion of South American politics, ancient cultures, geography, colonial history, and social relations as crucial elements of the research agenda and curricula of U.S. universities constitutes a form of imperial engagement.

If empires are a transnational form of possession (dominium) and sovereignty (imperium), then academic conquest encompassed and contained both constitutive dimensions of empire.[28] In the specific case of an informal empire committed to a policy of persuasion and cultural transfer, as the United States was after the First World War, imperiality acquires the form of technical and knowledge superiority, rather than of direct settlement on the ground. To this extent, the incorporation of the hinterlands takes place "elsewhere," in the classrooms, libraries, research labs, and professional publications of the hegemon. During this period, U.S. disciplines in the social sciences and the humanities extended their boundaries to include South America's diversity within their scope of vision. U.S. geographers, for instance, took possession of the knowledge of South American geography, claiming superior authority over this domain. By building the most formidable collection of maps of Hispanic America, the American Geographic Society transformed itself into a mecca for the future peregrination of scholars and businessmen.

The United States entered the Second World War period with an impressive accumulated knowledge about Latin America. Books and articles with the words "South America" in the title published before 1945 are too numerous to examine.[29] Scholars in the United States tend to minimize the value of the knowledge already gathered and to persuade their universities to make new efforts to study Latin America more intensely and completely. Almost ritually, they talk of the ignorance of the U.S. public about the culture, geography, and history of the lands south of Panama. However, from the perspective of South

America, the existence of a vast institutional apparatus of learning dedicated to the region in the United States is notable—and it is puzzling, to say the least. For there is no reciprocity. Latin American universities have not made a proportional investment in the development of United States studies (usually called American studies).

Disciplinary interventions are, by definition, forms of purposeful activity. They are constellations of initiatives and endeavors productive of specialized knowledge and very conscious of its purpose. Academic research is a goal-oriented, rational work process, which presupposes knowledge as the object of desire. In order for these intellectualizations to be communicative—that is, the knowledge produced is intended to be disseminated among scholarly communities, universities, and classrooms—they must produce textualities and, consequently, discourses. *Disciplinary Conquest* deals with the discourses produced by U.S. scholars in the construction of disciplinary regional knowledge. These discourses are quite specific: they concern racial and economic oppression, education, natural endowments, obstacles to economic progress, ancient civilizations, indigenous peoples, European immigration, and other related topics. In their characterization of South America, different authors singled out distinct sets of problems and causal factors.

Although U.S. scholars shared some progressive views, their enunciations varied from topic to topic. This was particularly so in relation to the question of imperial engagement. Each scholar had a different view about the role the United States should play in the hemisphere. Some suggested that the United States abandon the Monroe Doctrine, while others argued for making it multilateral or Pan-American. Some conceived that the key to hemispheric hegemony was the formation of an inter-American intellectual entente. Others argued for intensified technical assistance and cultural diplomacy. Toward the mid-1920s and 1930s, most scholars agreed that the United States needed to court and co-opt leading men in the most progressive southern republics in order to build a hemispheric commonwealth of peace, welfare, and security.

Among the regional disciplines here discussed, imperiality is embedded in the very definition of the object of study and its disciplinary boundaries. Moreover, U.S. scholars who built regional knowledge tended to articulate expert knowledge as useful for imperial hegemony. For example, Rowe thought that the empires of the past, because of their limited commitment to understanding the hinterlands, had failed to spread their own cultural identities into those regions. The British had built a commercial empire detached from culture and hence were not concerned with learning much about their colonial subjects. Germany, on the other hand, acted as modern empires should, providing education to those who lived in their hinterlands and building knowledge about the peoples with whom it interacted.[30] To Rowe, modern imperial sovereignty meant the capacity to relate more intimately to the peripheral nations' life and culture. This could only be achieved through knowledge. Forms of imperial hegemony more pervasive and enduring than those attained by commercial empires required a greater commitment to knowledge production. Thus, to truly sustain a "unity of thought and action" between North and South America, U.S. universities had to acquire and disseminate an understanding of "the significance and content of Spanish-American civilization" (Rowe 1909, 593).

Since readers in the United States have regularly taken exception to terms such as *imperial* or *imperialist*, I need to clarify my use of the term. I use the term *imperial* in the sense of hegemony, exemplarity, and purported cultural and technological superiority. Viewed from a long-term perspective, U.S. policies toward Latin America veered toward hegemonic influence through expertise, accommodating the modalities of rule of both formal and informal empire. (In chapter 9 I discuss more extensively the relationship between informal and formal empire.) It is true that the United States did not establish territorial colonies in South America. In strategic, legal, and political terms, the subcontinent was quite different from Central America and the Caribbean, territories subjected to close supervision, repeated interventions, and tutelage by the United States. Throughout the age of Pan-Americanism (1890–1945), the South American republics were able to preserve their territorial integrity and governmental autonomy. Though concerned about the economic power of the "Northern Colossus," South American governments did not consider U.S. invasion of their territories likely. Yet the experience of colonial government in the "American Mediterranean" influenced U.S. conceptions of hegemony in relation to South America.

Though free from military interventions, South America was considered a "land of opportunity" by U.S. manufacturers, merchants, and financiers. The region was the object of their recurrent textual and inquisitive interventions, through which they sought to discover and reveal its inner nature. During the period under consideration, for economic, political, and cultural reasons, the United States pursued a policy of enticement with regard to the South American republics. This policy included intellectual cooperation, scholarly exchanges, technical advice, translation of literature and history, and the promotion of Spanish education in U.S. schools. This cultural politics of Pan-Americanism was sustained by the belief that mutual knowledge and understanding between the two Americas would generate a better climate for business, diplomacy, and other activities.[31] These multiple engagements were not "imperial" in the same sense as India was part of the British empire, that is, as a territorial possession and administrative dependency. They were imperial in the sense that they represented the United States' desire for hegemony and cultural superiority. So this "imperiality" resembled the relationship of Britain to its former colonies: Canada, Australia, New Zealand, and South Africa were "settler colonies" on which Britain exerted overwhelming cultural influence. In similar ways, the United States imagined the Pan-American Union as a hemispheric commonwealth, a virtual terrain for the deployment of U.S. superiority, advice, and reform agendas. Scholars have shown how the Pan-American conferences and the Pan-American movement served as vehicles for different reform agendas, from childcare to *feminismo*, from forest preservation to the eradication of malaria and yellow fever. The idea of "Pan America" also served to mobilize the energies of literary figures and even artists.[32]

To the extent that regional knowledge participated in enterprises of cultural influence, it could be called "imperial." My argument goes further. I consider disciplinary knowledge itself to be imperial. Disciplinary knowledge can only increase its scope, consolidate its domain, and build comparative inquiries by extending its reach to incorporate the territory of the Other. There would be no anthropology without "the native," and there would be no "human geography" outside the notion of "settlements" and "frontiers."[33] Some degree of imperiality—the impulse to attain supranational sovereignty through enhanced and reliable visibility of the new peripheries—is implicit in the definition of disciplines. When practiced in advanced capitalist societies, the social and human sciences—geography, sociology, political science, and history—tend to transcend national boundaries, striving to establish generalizations valid for all societies. "South America" was such an object of knowledge. Once incorporated into the curricula of U.S. institutions of learning, it could radiate in different directions, enhancing the prestige of U.S. scholars. The knowledge thus produced could enhance the prestige associated with U.S. research universities, attracting students and researchers from abroad.

Disciplinary knowledge is also imperial to the extent that it appropriates and uses a series of local knowledges: generalizations, observations, and characterizations made by local intellectuals, collectors, and other informants. It is the role of centrally located scholars—scholars working at the center of Western modernity—to collect these diverse utterances, artifacts, and local doxa and transform them into a coherent set of principles and generalizations conducive to disciplinary knowledge. Local intellectuals may at times claim to belong to European science or to international scholarship, but scholars at the center often dismiss or discredit their activities as second-rate replicas of original North Atlantic thought. Hence, in studying the formation of "regional knowledge" it is quite important to pay attention to the interaction between international and local intellectuals, between foreign scholars and native informants.

Scholars have examined the relationship between knowledge and empire, chiefly within the context of territorial empires, showing that knowledge provides valuable services in the governability of colonial situations.[34] Less attention has been devoted to the formation of regional knowledge in neocolonial situations, where hegemony takes the form of economic, technological, and cultural supremacy. With regard to Latin America, the existent literature deals with Latin American studies' complicity with the politics of the Cold War.[35] U.S.-based social-scientific agendas generated some concern among Latin American intellectuals, the accusation being that U.S. social sciences extended abroad the espionage proper to the U.S. security state. On the imperiality of disciplinary knowledge, few studies have reached the depth and scope of Neil Smith's *American Empire* (2003). The author claims that U.S. geography, through the work of Isaiah Bowman, contributed significantly to envisioning and implementing the U.S. transnational agenda after the Second World War.

With *Disciplinary Conquest*, I contribute to the debate on the relationship between neocolonial expansion and imperial knowledge. Whereas different works have examined the influence of expert knowledge in creating opportunities for U.S. interventions in delimited fields of activity in South America, most notably in the terrains of medical philanthropy and economic advising, much needs to be done in relation to the early foundational texts of U.S. Latin Americanism.[36] Literary critics and philosophers have critically examined the question of U.S. Latin Americanism, and much has been said about the rise and demise of area studies.[37] But the origins of this grid of knowledge, and the important role played by Latin American specialists in it, still requires critical examination. Was Latin American studies the "tail" to the "politico-commercial kite" of U.S. expansionism, as Richard Morse claimed? Or was it, rather, a semi-autonomous force that participated in the construction of the various problematics and policies of informal empire?

This book can also be read as a contribution to debates about the origins of Latin American studies. In this regard, let me advance a few simple arguments. Before the dynamics of the Cold War came to influence the development of Latin American studies, the area had developed as a strong confluence of interests within the U.S. academy. In leading research universities were professors providing instruction in the areas of Latin American or South American history, geography, archaeology, literature, and other disciplines. Professors of political science and sociology used South American examples while examining problems of social order or political stability. The political fragmentation of South America, its weak central states, and its frequent revolutions had acquired already the status of research problems in the social- and political-science labs of leading universities. Round tables were organized across the country to discuss problems of democratic government in Cuba, petroleum rights in Mexico, military coups in Chile and Argentina, and indigenous life in the Amazon—well before the Cuban Revolution ignited interest in the region. In other words, before the consolidation of area studies as an interdisciplinary dispositive at the service of Cold War foreign policy, U.S. scholars had already inscribed South America within the domain and the field of vision of U.S. disciplinary knowledge.

By 1947, the pioneers in these fields had already established the basic questions to be addressed and puzzles to be solved. Resolving these questions involved disciplinary expertise and direct observation through travel. South America, upheld by business writers and promoters of Pan-Americanism as a "land of opportunity," became, almost at the same time, a vast reservoir of evidence for the development of original research in the humanities and social sciences. In *Disciplinary Conquest* I show that the scholarly push-forward (*avanzada*) on South America paralleled contemporary exploration of business opportunities, the landing of foreign direct investment, the increase in inter-American trade, and the establishment of more intense diplomatic relations with the region. The book presents the "rediscovery" of the subcontinent in the first four decades of the twentieth century as a harvest of useful knowledge that contributed to a better understanding of South American politics, societies, and culture *in the United States*.

ONE

South America as a Field of Inquiry

———

To U.S. businessmen and diplomats, South America had been a land of curiosity since the 1790s. Interest grew after the 1823 proclamation by President Monroe that the Americas should remain a continent free from European colonialism and should be governed by republican institutions. Early U.S. Hispanists (William H. Prescott, Henry W. Longfellow, George Ticknor, Washington Irving, and Mary T. Peabody Mann) expressed interest in the region, its history, languages, and literature.[1] But they failed to develop stable institutions for the study of Hispanic America. After 1873, stimulated by the effects of the economic depression, industrialists, statesmen, and naval strategists started to think of South America as a possible outlet for the overproduction of American industrial goods.[2] Yet, before the first Pan-American Conference in Washington (1889–1890), many U.S. scholars and citizens considered South America a "terra incognita." Here was a mass of territory containing important potential markets for U.S. commodities, as well as sources of valuable raw materials, a land about which little was known.[3] In the aftermath of the Spanish-American War (1898), new scholarship began to question the cultural similarities between Spain and Spanish America, calling for a separate study of the latter.[4] Starting in the early 1900s, the International Bureau of the American Republics contributed new information—chiefly statistics and maps—to make the region appealing to U.S. investors and traders. Yet professional study of the region took time to develop.[5]

Between the Spanish-American War (1898) and President Franklin D. Roosevelt's declaration of the Good Neighbor Policy (1933), South America became the object of scholarly interest and study in the United States. Historians have characterized this period as preparatory for a professional "Latin Americanism," itself part of an emergent area studies complex.[6] Rather than clumsy preparatory steps, these U.S. disciplinary interventions were comprehensive and enduring intellectual visions in themselves. From the first decade of the twentieth century, U.S. scholars visited, observed, and measured the subcontinent, raising crucial questions for future research. Geographers, archaeologists, sociologists, historians, and political scientists, among others, turned South America from a land of curiosities into a "field of inquiry," a virtual territory of science. Distinct individuals working within different disciplines collaborated to create a more intimate, profound, and reliable knowledge of the region's nature, problems, and possibilities of development. Theirs was not just a search for information about the societies south of Panama, but the beginning of an enduring academic engagement with South America, the branching southward of U.S. research disciplines.

In this chapter I start with a curious diplomatic exchange indicative of the extent to which scientific inquiry and diplomacy were intertwined. The incident reveals a persistent presupposition of U.S. scholars: that South America was a treasure of information waiting to be claimed by U.S. disciplinary knowledge. Next, I discuss the importance of knowledge in the period's business and diplomatic discourse, in particular in relation to cultural engagement. Then I turn to scholars' rhetorical interventions in favor of a comprehensive disciplinary study of the subcontinent. I close with a brief analysis of the relationship among scholarship, foreign policy, and the early origins of Latin American studies.

A Diplomat's Curious Proposal

In December 1940 the State Department received a curious proposal from Boaz W. Long, U.S. ambassador in Ecuador. In a memorandum entitled "Possibilities of Ecuador as a Field for Advanced Academic Studies," Long explained how U.S. researchers could take Ecuador as their field of study.[7] To the ambassador, Ecuador was a territory virgin to scientific inquiry, a land overflowing with intriguing questions and research possibilities. The language of his memorandum replicated the rhetoric of early promoters of inter-American economic cooperation with the promise of expanding knowledge rather than commerce and investment.[8]

Specifically, Long argued that Ecuador should interest U.S. scholars in several fields of inquiry: archaeology, ethnology, geography, economics, and sociology. To students of archaeology, the country offered almost unlimited research possibilities. The School of American Research's latest survey had found many unexplored sites in the country, and since the cost of excavation was low, almost any graduate student could afford to set up camp. Scholars might even investigate the connection between the great pre-Columbian cultures of Mesoamerica and the Andes (Long 1941, 3–6). The student of ethnology could expect to find indigenous groups relatively untouched by Spanish colonization. Though much had been written about the Jívaros, other groups remained unstudied, including the Capayas, the Colorados, the Otavalos, and the Salasacas (ibid., 9). Each of Ecuador's three major regions—the Pacific coastland, the Andean highlands, and the Amazonian jungle—afforded researchers many opportunities to study indigenous textiles, folk music, and traditional medicine.[9]

To the geographer, said Long, Ecuador was a "gold mine": a country with a diversity of climates, vegetation, and landscapes that remained almost unmapped and relatively unexplored. Its jungles, *páramos*, and highlands presented opportunities to investigate different types of land use, the effect of climate on agriculture, and the altitude at which farmers tilled the land.[10] Those interested in economics would find in Ecuador backwardness in its most "virulent form." Here was an underdeveloped agrarian economy with a preponderance of indigenous peasants. A racially divided society with three distinct standards of living (white, black, Indian) would be appealing to the student of economics. The sociologist could find in Ecuador examples of inbred cultures and sociabilities developing at the margins of Western law and civilization.[11] On the coast, a peasant mestizo society (the Montuvio) had developed on the fringes of Hispanic civilization, whereas in the Esmeraldas, African traditions seemed to have remained intact. In Ecuador's marginal and backward agrarian societies, Long argued, U.S. sociologists and economists could begin to untangle the mysteries of underdevelopment.

It was Long's intention to alert U.S. universities and scholars to the possibilities open in Ecuador. Pressing for further research in South America's least-noticed country, Long replicated an assumption typical of U.S. diplomacy in the Good Neighbor years: that a better understanding between the United States and South America depended on the production of cross-disciplinary knowledge. He viewed the small Andean country as a vast deposit of evidence useful for validating theories in the social and human sciences. Scientific inquiry in Ecuador itself was an underdeveloped field, and it was up to the United States to deploy U.S. intellectual capital to exploit all existing research possibilities. In short, Ecuador was a field ripe for the model of cross-disciplinary research pioneered by the leaders of the "university movement" in the United States (James B. Conant, Daniel Coit Gilman, William R. Harper, among others).[12] Long wrote, "Here is a rich interplay of the material introduced in departments of History, Anthropology, Sociology, Economics, Linguistics, and Political Economy. Moreover these studies have the two advantages, first, of being human, living studies, and second, of being of immense value to the development of the Western Hemisphere" (1941, 19). U.S. specialized academic communities could help to complete the work of explorers who had pioneered the study of the Andes, the Amazon, and the Pampas.[13] Long's proposal was clearly informed by the area-studies perspective, in which a group of disciplines, acting in conjunction, could better understand a region's peoples and problems. Though the area-studies complex is supposed to have emerged as a knowledge auxiliary to Cold War politics, it is clear that several departments of U.S. universities had established the bases for Oriental and Latin American studies much before 1947. In fact, by 1940, the State Department was aware of the need to promote economic development in the hemisphere. And several of the key promoters of this idea—among them, none other than Nelson Rockefeller, the coordinator of Inter-American Affairs—believed that such assistance could not be extended without further knowledge of the region's history, economies, societies, and politics.[14]

Why Promote Regional Knowledge?

A diplomat with a long expertise in Central America and the Caribbean, Long ended up advocating knowledge as the key mode of U.S. engagement with Ecuador. Early on in his career, Long had favored direct intervention and Dollar Diplomacy. In 1913, after ten years of traveling as a diplomat in Mexico, Central America, and Cuba, he was appointed head of the Latin American division of the State Department. In this role, he supported new loans to Nicaragua to expedite the U.S. acquisition of canal rights.[15] Indeed, in Mexico and Central America, Long sustained a position close to Dollar Diplomacy: where direct intervention proved neither possible nor desirable, the United States could exert influence and oversight through bank loans. Long's 1914 report on Honduras was typical of U.S. imperial views and policies in Central America: he argued that high illiteracy, substandard diets, and alcoholism provided the structural conditions for "chronic revolution." To overcome Hondurans' impulse to anarchy, the United States should assist the country's economic recovery with loans and technology. To this end, Long supported the railroad-and-loans scheme designed by agents of Minor Keith and the United Fruit Company (Baker 1964, 5). In 1918, at the time of a crisis in U.S.-Mexican relations, Long argued that the United States should loan money to Mexico in order to secure control over Mexican oil fields.[16]

While serving in Central America and the Caribbean, Long maintained his imperialist view of the region. In 1919, he was appointed U.S. minister in Cuba. In response to his reports on civil disorder and labor strikes in Havana that year, the United States sent the marines to the island. Long was the one who requested that a small corps of marines remain in Camagüey until 1922 (Schoultz 1998, 233).[17] After Cuba, he served in Nicaragua, during 1936 and 1937. Next, he was appointed U.S. minister in Ecuador, where he became interested in archaeology and ethnology, gathering a rich collection of native rugs and artifacts.[18] In 1943, after his memorandum on Ecuador, he was named ambassador to Guatemala.[19] Retiring in 1946, he went to Santa Fe, New Mexico, where he assumed the directorship of the Museum of New Mexico.

In Ecuador, Long learned to appreciate the importance of indigenous cultures to the country's social and cultural make-up and, in time, he became a collector and an amateur archaeologist. At the time, as the United States weighed whether to join the European war, education and scholarly exchange became the new frontier in the cultural war between American "democracy" and German "dictatorship." To counter German propaganda in Ecuador, Long cooperated with Galo Plaza to establish the American College of Quito.[20]

Beyond a response to the new international conjuncture, Long's 1940 memorandum was an assertion of the quest for hemispheric knowledge that accompanied the expansion of U.S. economic interests in South America. His gesture could be seen as a continuation of the scientific conquest pioneered by U.S. scholars between 1900 and 1930, in which the United States sought to affirm its supremacy over South America in science and education, and to learn to interact with its southern neighbors on the terrain of culture. In the heyday of the Good Neighbor Policy, scholars and politicians alike considered knowledge of the societies and cultures of South America to be crucial to American diplomacy.[21]

During the period 1900–1918, calls for enhancing knowledge of the region abounded; business prospectors, economic analysts, and diplomatic reformers all hungered to know more. For U.S. businessmen concerned with winning an increased share of the South American trade, opening trade and investment opportunities in South America required a better knowledge of the region. Such demands were instrumental. To capture these markets from traditional European traders, their sales representatives, diplomatic agents, and other commercial travelers had to be acquainted with the languages, traditions, and habits of South Americans.

Their demands for enhanced cultural competency were part of a more general discourse about how to gain South American markets, a discourse deployed in books of advice to merchants and manufacturers, in expert articles about U.S. trade and shipping, and in promotional literature published by the International Bureau of the American Republics.[22] This discourse emphasized the need to establish U.S. banks in the region, the convenience of direct shipping lines to South American ports, and the urgency of improving how exporters conducted their business. Attention to better packaging, greater information about customs practices, and a more nuanced knowledge of consumers' preferences completed the list of concerns of South American trade as construed by business rhetoric.

At first, business prospectors did not require academic knowledge to achieve their ends. They took on themselves the task of discovering the "real South America," advising traders on the practical obstacles they would face in the region. On occasion, business writers protested the "superficial knowledge" dispensed by travel writers and the unrealistic optimism of local consuls and Washington officials.[23] Often their main concern was that commercial travelers and agents lacked adequate training in languages and local culture. So they demanded that commerce schools and colleges do better at teaching Spanish.[24] As for learning "people's wants and tastes," they considered this to be their own mandate and were not ready to relinquish this to anthropologists, historians, or geographers.[25]

Occasionally, business experts entered into the discussion of U.S. commercial policy in relation to cultural awareness. In 1907 James Van Cleave took on the argument that German and British traders were well ahead of Americans in their linguistic training and cultural sensitivity.[26] If this was so, he said, a bit of cultural immersion in Hispanic America and better language training would help U.S. businesses win those coveted South American markets. But the competition for informal empire, Van Cleave argued, was chiefly a contest of productive forces among industrial nations. In the short-term, sales persuasion might require agents to possess some cultural background knowledge and good language skills, but in the long run, U.S. manufacturers would have to outcompete European firms in product cost, quality, design, and convenience.

The business community increasingly sought cultural knowledge as the 1920s began. In 1920, the National Convention in Foreign Trade (gathered in San Francisco) recommended equipping US business agents with "accurate knowledge of foreign markets, with practical knowledge of foreign languages and with a wide knowledge of the economic, social and political conditions prevailing in overseas markets" (Lord 1921, 167). Universities and colleges had taken on the challenge of training men in foreign trade, they argued, but the curriculum was too practical and lacked content in the humanities.[27] Greater training in the history and literatures of the world was required.[28]

A similar demand emerged from diplomatic quarters, calling for improvements in the U.S. Foreign Service. Almost ritualistically, reformers demanded entrance examinations as part of ending political favoritism. These examinations would test language competence as well as a general knowledge of the history of the areas where the United States was involved. This discourse was also instrumental and specific: the knowledge demanded was considered a requisite for better job performance. In 1896, trying to overcome British and German dominance of foreign trade, the world traveler and writer Charles Dudley Warner demanded that consular officers have both business training and a command of the local language.[29] Their appointment should be by examination only. In addition, he urged U.S. manufacturers and exporters to imitate British and German training: Germans sent quite educated agents abroad to study foreign markets, while British business agents carried with them catalogs of manufactures and were prepared to accommodate the demands of local merchants.[30]

The government agreed with the reformers. Executive orders of 1905 and 1909 required applicants to pass examinations to enter the; U.S. Foreign Service. Regulations demanded that they know international law; diplomatic usage; modern languages; U.S. history and institutions; histories of Europe, South America, and the Far East; as well as composition, grammar, and punctuation. Though the salaries of consular officers remained quite low and the numbers of positions small, examination requirements improved the quality of the U.S. Foreign Service.[31] By 1915, sixteen well-known universities and colleges were offering courses tailored for these exams.[32]

Apparently, the demand for more comprehensive academic knowledge did not come from policy makers. Though Secretary of State Elihu Root advocated

South America as a Field of Inquiry

greater understanding between the intellectuals of North and South, his rhetoric echoed that of other promoters of hemispheric friendship and co-operation. Root came back from his 1906 South American tour filled with enthusiasm about economic opportunities.[33] Speaking at commercial clubs in Kansas City, Saint Louis, and Cincinnati, he talked about the economic and cultural complementarities between South America and the United States.[34] Mainly he spoke about the products that U.S. businesses could sell, the need for agents who spoke Spanish and Portuguese, the importance of opening branches of U.S. banks in the region and improving maritime transportation, and the imperative to treat South Americans with respect. But like the speeches of other business promoters, his "South American Address" (reprinted by the *American Exporter* and later distributed among manufacturers and merchants) contained nothing to suggest the beginning of a scientific conquest of the sub-continent (Jessup 1938, 490–91).

Building Fields of Regional Knowledge

To conquer a new field of study, one must first envision the field in terms of a problematic core and draw, however tentatively, its disciplinary boundaries. Next, one must disseminate interest among potential practitioners of the field, highlighting the importance of certain paradoxes, unanswered questions, or puzzles about the region's geography, antiquity, history, political regimes, and societies. To sustain interest over time, efforts must be made to translate the initial intellectual curiosity of a few scholars into teaching subjects, for it is through courses and class interaction that this interest is passed on to students. As practitioners grow in number, they seek to form professional associations that, in turn, sponsor disciplinary journals, conferences, and specialized collections. At a certain point, with the assistance of government and philanthropic foundations, a further step will be taken: the setting up of research centers, institutes, and graduate programs.

This succession of events is not far from the process by which scholars constituted Latin American studies in the United States.[35] Every step of the process required enunciatory acts: invitations to visit the region; calls to conduct research in certain areas or problems; discussions as to the propriety of gathering evidence in foreign lands; propositions about the need to teach the subject in colleges and universities; and demands for concerted actions to recruit professors, finance research, launch journals, and organize conferences. Thus, the invention of a new study area composed of various subdisciplines entailed a collective process of construction mediated by discursive interventions.

After Root's visit to South America (1906), South America came to be considered a region in need of further exploration, knowledge, and understanding. Not only was it a provider of raw materials and a market full of potential consumers of U.S. manufactures, it was now a field of interest for the U.S. social sciences and humanities, that is, a repository of evidence that could corroborate generalizations stemming from the emerging disciplines.[36] Scholarly curiosity about South America grew contemporaneously with economic and financial interest. During the period 1907–1930, academic visits to South America increased significantly, and as a result, a rich harvest of new data and interpretation reached universities and learned societies in the United States. New contributions to the fields of sociology, geography, archaeology, anthropology, politics and government, constitutional law, economics, finance, and international relations began to appear in various academic journals in the United States.[37]

Gradually, the region started to acquire greater visibility and significance within research universities. The First Pan-American Scientific Congress gathered at Santiago, Chile (from December 1908 through January 1909), was perhaps the event that triggered closer intellectual connections between the two Americas. Here began the process of constituting Latin American studies in the United States.[38] Well before Ambassador Long, that is, other U.S. scholars and statesmen had envisioned Latin America as a "field of research," an empty territory of inquiry open to the gaze of U.S. explorers and researchers. The impetus for this change came from scholars' minds, rather than from the workshops on foreign policy. The Pan-American Congress set in motion a series of reconnaissance expeditions that delimited U.S. research interests in South America. An influential group of experts attended this congress as U.S. government delegates, among them Archibald Coolidge from Harvard, Bernard Moses from California, William Shepherd from Columbia, Paul Reinsch from Wisconsin, Leo Rowe from Pennsylvania, and Hiram Bingham from Yale (Karnes 1979). Before the congress started, Bingham went on an expedition from Buenos Aires to Potosí, trying to map the old royal road. This trip put him in contact with people and information that later led to the discovery of the ruins of Machu Picchu. Other scholar-delegates also engaged in exploration travel, trying to personally inspect certain aspects of South America for future research.

Root believed that the scientific congress at Santiago would "bring together the best scientific thought of this hemisphere" and make possible "the scrutiny of many distinctly American problems." In his view, intellectual cooperation between men of North and South America was necessary for scientific and practical reasons. The "common understanding and free exchange of opinion upon scientific subjects is of great practical importance," he wrote, because many

South America as a Field of Inquiry

specific relations could arise that were "incident to our expanding trade, our extending investment, and the construction of the Panama Canal" (quoted in Holmes 1909, 442). In other words, scholars would act as ambassadors of U.S. economic interests, trying to tone down the criticism of the United States by Latin American intellectuals. Yet scholars encountered in South America much more than Yankee-phobia; they found a wealth of information for the development of regional or comparative studies in their own disciplines.

Envisioning a new field is itself a labeling operation, one that assigns a name to a series of problems, questions, and information about a particular area. Just before he was appointed assistant professor at Yale University, Hiram Bingham (1908b) published an influential paper that promoted research in South American history and politics.[39] Bingham assumed that U.S. scholars shared a distinctive "interest" in understanding the southern republics, and that study should concentrate first on history and politics.[40] In his initial argument, two reasons justified Bingham's initiative: economic interest and the availability of sources. He noted the ample economic opportunities open to U.S. firms in the subcontinent and the interest of Yale students in those opportunities.[41] He was confident that graduate students would find enough library resources in the northeast to conduct research on the South American topics.

In 1910, invited by President Porfirio Díaz, Leo S. Rowe visited Mexico City for the inauguration of the new National University. Besides observing the progress of Mexican universities, Rowe envisioned intellectual cooperation between U.S. and Mexican scholars and universities. He returned to the United States convinced that anthropologists from Mexico and the United States could work together to solve the problems presented by Toltec, Zapotec, and Maya antiquity, leading perhaps to the establishment of a binational school of archaeology. After this, cooperation could extend to studies in the natural sciences, the social sciences, and the humanities (Leo S. Rowe 1910a).

During his work with the Yale Peruvian Expedition (YPE), the geographer Isaiah Bowman defined the "Southern Peruvian Andes" as the area in which to concentrate multidisciplinary research efforts. Later on, in 1914, his observations about geographical accidents, climate, patterns of settlement, and natural regions extended to a wider area: "South America." The new subdiscipline—South American geography—would concern itself with the relations between humans and the environment in the territory extending south of Panama. Bowman's volume on South America was part of Rand McNally's series Lands and Peoples, which included other "geography readers" on Asia, Europe, and Africa.[42]

The work of the YPE opened up for research questions about Inca history and culture. But the YPE was hardly the definitive blueprint for the archaeology of Andean South America. Other U.S. archaeologists did a better job in drawing the contours of this regional science, calling attention to important pre-Inca cultures such as the Chimu, Nazca, Chavín, Tiahuanaco, and Diaguitas, among others. Philip A. Means's *Ancient Civilizations of the Andes* (1931) was perhaps the compendium work that helped to establish "Andean archaeology" as a disciplinary subfield.[43] Nevertheless, the publicity that the discovery of Machu Picchu and the launching of the YPE attracted set the precedent for further academic adventures in the Andean region.[44]

To generate interest in a new field, scholars usually presented the area as an unexplored territory, empty of knowledge. In 1932, in a proposal for the study of the Caribbean region, Clarence H. Haring described Latin America as a "terra incognita" of scientific knowledge: "Latin America is from the scientific standpoint, and especially in the Social Sciences, still a virtually unexplored territory. South of the Rio Grande these disciplines, and above all the science of political economy, are still in an embryonic stage. There is little adequate instruction and virtually no research."[45] The backwardness extended not only to the new social sciences, economics and sociology, but also to the more traditional disciplines of law and history. The challenge was, then, to extend U.S. research efforts into these uncharted lands. This entailed a further specialization within university departments. In history departments, for instance, Latin American experts had to persuade their colleagues of the importance of the new field in relation to the existing concentration in European and U.S. history.[46]

Demands for greater emphasis in under-researched areas often led scholars and universities to extend existing fields. This was the case of Brazilian history in relation to Hispanic American history. When in 1933 William Shepherd asked his colleagues at Columbia University to expand the study of Brazilian history, he deployed a battery of arguments. Among these were the lack of comprehensive treatises on the subject, the availability of documentary sources in U.S. libraries, and the growing economic importance of Brazil, a country then in the midst of industrialization.[47]

Adding Latin American courses to the curricula of colleges and universities was a crucial part of constructing subdisciplinary fields of regional knowledge. In December 1926 the Hispanic American History Group gathered at Rochester to discuss ways to encourage the interest of students in their particular branch of history. Much of the discussion pivoted on the question of where to locate the new subject within the existing history curricula. Some suggested teaching Hispanic American history in the "foreign affairs" section of regular U.S. history courses. Others thought it more convenient to discuss the Spanish and Portuguese empires within courses on the expansion of Europe. A third proposal was to open up new courses on the comparative history of the Americas.[48]

These scholarly interventions illustrate the complex process of construing a regional discipline and its relationship to existing fields. Some of these interventions built the infrastructure of new disciplines devoted to regional study, among them Andean archaeology, South American geography, and Hispanic American history. Others transformed the discussion within established disciplines, as in political science and sociology. To most U.S. observers, the political and social condition of the peoples of the southern republics did not constitute an autonomous field of inquiry. In spite of this, scholars built an area of interest around crucial questions of politics and government. In sociology departments, experts kept talking of "social problems" in the region, often relating them to economic and political problems, instead of hatching a new subdiscipline called "South American sociology."[49]

Scholarship and Foreign Policy

U.S. scholars usually presented their knowledge-seeking adventures in South America as beneficial to the "mutual understanding" of the two Americas. This lofty ideal was in tune with the rhetoric of foreign-policy makers, particularly those who promoted the cause of U.S. Pan-Americanism. During the 1920s and 1930s, many authors published works about South America as contributions to the better understanding with the "southern neighbors." For example, in the introduction to William Spence Robertson's *Hispanic-American Relations with the United States* (1923), the economist David Kinley wrote,

> Among the things desired by all patriotic Americans, north or south, are a better acquaintance with one another and more intimate relations. Our people need to be better acquainted with our neighbors in Central and South America and they with us. This is desirable not only for reasons of mutual economic benefit, but in the interest of international peace, in the interest of the influence of the American continent on world affairs, and in the interest of securing that advantage which comes from the reaction of the culture of one people on another. (Robertson 1923, iii)

Kinley and others expected that better knowledge would help the United States influence Latin Americans and their markets. Crucial to this rhetoric was the idea that the average U.S. American would somehow familiarize herself with South American ways of life and problems. But in time scholarly publications distanced themselves from such business rhetoric, claiming to be in pursuit of truths that were more permanent, objective, and reliable.

After the Second World War, Leo S. Rowe, the director of the Pan-American Union (PAU), came to be persuaded that extensive intellectual cooperation was the only path to an enduring mutuality of sentiments and interests between the United States and Latin America. An important policy in his plan was the exchange of students and professors. By bringing Latin American students to U.S. universities, the policy would expose them to the "American-way-of-life." Rowe also emphasized the importance of creating interest among U.S. scholars about Latin America.

> It is also important that students and investigators in the U.S. should more fully realize the opportunities for study and research in Latin America. The countries to the south of us afford great opportunities for scientific inquiry to students from the U.S. and the prosecution of such inquires tend to strengthen the intellectual currents between the northern and southern sections of the hemisphere. (Rowe 1927b)

To the director of the PAU, academic research had a political potential. Taking over Latin America as a field of study facilitated the policy of inter-American cooperation.

Geopolitical forces influenced the development of regional knowledge. At the time of the First World War, scholars had mobilized in response to anti-American propaganda, seeking to interpret the "Latin American mind" (Perry 1920). In the 1930s several universities cooperated with promoters of Pan-Americanism, establishing institutes, centers, and programs devoted to Latin American studies.[50] Harvard University founded a center for the study of Latin American economies and also a council for translating the best literature from Latin America (Doyle 1936). The University of California, Berkeley, made important efforts to institutionalize Latin American studies (LAS), as did universities such as Texas, Duke, Columbia, and Wisconsin.[51] It is difficult to disentangle the establishment and funding of these LAS programs from the imperatives of U.S. foreign policy. For example, when Julian Steward (1943), the chief of the U.S. Bureau of Ethnology, tried to define the direction that "acculturation studies" were taking, he recognized that U.S. government "action programs" had initiated and sponsored much of the new work of U.S. anthropologists in Latin America since the Second World War. Similarly, when the British geographer J. A. Steers tried to entice his colleagues to enter the study

South America as a Field of Inquiry

of Brazil's geography, he could only point out the success of the American Geographic Society and the U.S. government in spreading U.S. influence among South American geographers (Steers 1957, 330). Some scholars, threatened by government-supported research, sought to establish a balance between scientific and political objectives.[52]

The creation of specialized fields of regional knowledge, though stimulated by the government and assisted by the generosity of private foundations, was by and large carried out by scholars. This complex work included inviting scholars to join in the study of the region, promoting interest among students, discussing the state of the field and discerning its most important questions, identifying funds for research, organizing conferences, launching specialized journals, and interlinking the activities of the government, businesses, and scholars in the region. Moreover, though, scholars working on the field did more than merely forge "intellectual bonds" with the South American intelligentsia; they delimited the internal divisions of what constituted the hinterlands of the United States in the former Spanish colonies. By the early 1960s, three areas were clearly established: Mexico and Central America; the Andean or Bolivarian nations; and southern South America.[53]

Placing South American Knowledge in Context

There was a complementarity between the new knowledge formations and the export of financial and physical capital to South America, and to understand these new scholarly interventions and knowledge projects, one needs to place these individual and institutional initiatives within the context of certain expansionist forces. What forces generated such complementarity? Four of these expansive forces are noteworthy: the rise of professionalism in the U.S. academy; the spread of progressive ideas; the consolidation of the research university; and the expansion of U.S. financial and commercial capital into the territory of South America.

First, the expansion of U.S. disciplinary knowledge to the South American borderlands appears as an overflow of energies emanating from growing research universities as they attempted to outdo their European models. Clearly, this period coincides with revolutionary transformations in U.S. universities, a process that produced the departmental division of knowledge, the expansion of research-dedicated faculty, the creation of graduate programs, and the intensified use of labs, museums, and libraries in the provision of university instruction. Though envisioned by a few pioneers, the "university movement" produced tangible results only because sufficient funds, provided by businessmen and foundations, were available to acquire the needed human and physical capital.[54]

Second, this was the period of the progressive movement, an intellectual and policy-oriented conjuncture that expressed a new confidence in the powers of expert knowledge for the resolution of social, institutional, and economic problems. In particular, scholars and professionals began to openly support organized labor, black education, the women's movement, and other social reforms. They fostered active government policies to control Big Business. To an extent, the progressive movement reshaped the nature of U.S. democracy and government or, at least, promoted a kind of professional-civic involvement hitherto unknown.[55] Thus, U.S. scholars carried to South America many of the concerns of the progressive agenda and measured the achievements of the southern republics on the basis of this standard.[56]

Third, this period coincided with the emergence of professional associations that affirmed the prestige of specialized knowledge as a new force claiming for greater participation and influence in the formulation of government policy.[57] In the terrain of the social sciences and the humanities, the Progressive Era generated a proliferation of new associations that defended the autonomy of expert knowledge, among them the American Historical Association (1884), the National Geographic Society (1888), the American Academy of Political and Social Science (1889), the American Sociological Association (1905), and the Society for American Archaeology (1934), among others.[58] These scholarly associations promoted the extension of research into the United States's new areas of influence. Their publications brought to readers the new knowledge about Central America, the Caribbean, and South America.

A successful institutional development (the research university), an ideological mind-set (progressive ideas), and the consolidation of an ideal social status (the middle-class professional) combined to generate the autonomy of thought, the prestige associated with academic positions, as well as the responsibility for public service that facilitated the expansion of departments, fields of study, and academic subdisciplines. But the extension of disciplinary knowledge to other areas of the world cannot be explained by these expansive forces alone. Underneath the efforts to better understand "South Americans" were the expansionist drive of U.S. technology and capitalist enterprise. This constituted the fourth most important force of expansion southward.

This was the time in which American corporations ventured into South America, after gaining experience in Mexico and Canada. In the late nineteenth century, U.S. entrepreneurs had conquered the tropics, building in Central

America an emporium of trade based on the production and commercializa-tion of bananas. Also during this time, U.S. firms competed with their British and Chilean counterparts for the control of nitrate fields, later entering into the mining of copper for export. Yet interest in and exploration of petroleum deposits in Mexico, Venezuela, and Peru was a phenomenon of the twentieth century, as was the investment of Chicago meat-packing plants in Argentina and Uruguay. If Secretary Root's visit to South America in 1906 stimulated the search for closer cultural relations and a better understanding of the southern republics, it was the First World War and its disastrous effects on European–South American trade that provided the impetus and the opportunity for an expanded economic and financial engagement in the region. Complaints about the lack of U.S. shipping lines to South America or about the lack of U.S. bank branches in the region subsided in the 1920s, as American businessmen invested in these and other sectors of activity. In the first two decades of the twentieth century U.S. companies renewed their efforts to increase the pro-ductivity of sugar *ingenios* in Cuba, built electric tramways in Rio de Janeiro, and developed new oil fields in Colombia and Peru.[59]

The impulses to seek sources of raw materials and new markets in South America, and to invest in agriculture, mining, and manufacturing varied ac-cording to time. In the 1870s and 1890s Southern manufacturers in particular expected the opening of South American markets to provide a solution to their problems of overproduction. During the Mexican Revolution, many Ameri-can investors suffered wartime destruction of property, while others com-plained that the different factions of the revolutionary government imposed on them excessive taxation. These investors and entrepreneurs were willing to move their capital elsewhere in the continent, particular after the enactment of the 1917 constitution in Mexico, which declared the subsoil to be the inalien-able property of the nation. However, much before this happened, the Gug-genheims were investing in Chilean copper mining, Swift and Armour moved their meat-packing activities to Argentina and Uruguay, and the National City Bank of New York started to establish branches in the most important capitals of South America. The availability of natural resources, the potential for high profits in relatively undeveloped markets, and technological superi-ority must have stimulated the expansion of U.S. business activities in South America. Though these investments were carried out on the bases of minimal information about the destination countries, the difficulties encountered soon made U.S. investors aware of the need to better understand the culture and sociability of the southern republics.

As it is often the case, it was a combination of circumstances that made for the emergence of specialized fields of knowledge about Latin America in the United States. Among them the expansionist forces of U.S. American capital and technology, the emergence of the research university, the rise of professionals, and the spread of the progressive movement. Still, the enthusiasm and dedication with which U.S. scholars undertook the building of the new fields of regional knowledge indicates certain personal involvement that cannot be reduced to contextual circumstances or underlying factors. Moreover, the extension of scholarly interest from a specific and local research question into problems of international relations demands a study of particular intellectual trajectories and academic interests. The debates over the U.S. role in the international arena, its "responsibility" to the Caribbean and Central American nations, and the pertinence of the Monroe Doctrine to South America were issues that naturally could have been taken on by international relations experts. But, in actuality, these issues were taken on by scholars working in a variety of fields, from archaeology to literary studies, from economics to political science.

During this period, the scope of certain disciplines extended to include South America. This expansion was related to previous available knowledge, the ways scholars envisioned the new study fields, the methods of observation employed, and the generalizations derived from them. Knowledge-generating activities can only be studied in their located materiality. New knowledge about geography in the Central Andes, federalist government in Argentina, Inca culture, racial oppression in Peru, and the effectiveness of the Spanish commercial monopoly emerged from the interaction between U.S. scholars and local informants, on the occasion of field trips or participation in academic conferences. Local circumstances were quite important for the development of knowledge projects of transnational scope.[60] That is, particular circumstances shaped by the local context influenced the way the evidence was constructed, as well as the set of problems that were considered crucial for each research program.

Latin American Studies

During the first four decades of the twentieth century, an important accumulation and processing of information and knowledge took place within research universities and learning societies in the United States. This accumulation delineated the contours and content of U.S. scientific interest in the subcontinent. Scholarly discussions in U.S. journals about the human, economic, and cultural potential of the Southern Andes, of Chile and Argentina, and of the Amazon and Patagonia were developed into "problems" and "interests" well before Fidel Castro and Che Guevara appeared in scene. Though the Cold War in general, and the Cuban Revolution in particular, gave a great impulse to the extension of Latin American studies in the United States, the basic structure of this multidisciplinary knowledge arrangement was already in place by the early 1940s.

In fact, the interwar period witnessed an enormous advance in setting the foundations for the study of Latin America. The central themes and programs of the discipline had already coalesced by the 1930s. In 1937 Clarence H. Haring spoke before Latin American historians about the need for a comparative history of the Americas. At the time, he said, there were 160 colleges and universities in the United States teaching the history of Hispanic America. Haring's estimate was conservative: ten years earlier, a survey by the PAU had established that there were 175 colleges and institutions teaching courses on Latin American history in the United States.[61] The accumulation of this teaching and research capital accelerated during the Second World War, and the U.S. government stepped up the exchange of professors and students with South America as well as U.S. programs in Latin American studies. By the end of the war, the United States had built a substantial and integrated knowledge about South America. Libraries at universities such as Harvard, Yale, Texas, Michigan, Wisconsin, North Carolina, Duke, and Chicago and the Library of Congress and other public institutions had amassed impressive collections on *Latinoamericana*.[62] Large foundations offered subsidies for travel and study in the region. Great bibliographic enterprises were underway, the most important of which was the *Handbook of Latin American Studies*.

In 1947, Miron Burgin, editor of the *Handbook of Latin American Studies*, published a list of universities and colleges teaching subjects on Latin America in the United States. He estimated that 600 colleges and universities and over 2,000 teachers were involved in this type of undergraduate instruction. In 1948–1949 the PAU studied the curricula of 1,500 institutions of higher learning, finding that 875 of them offered 3,346 courses dealing with Latin America (Delpar 2008, 120–31). Clearly, the intellectual capital accumulated in Latin American studies was not small or negligible. The idea that it might be is one of the myths that I attempt to undo: the idea that, before the Cuban Revolution, Latin American studies was a neglected field of inquiry, sustained by a small community of experts, relatively autonomous from the State Department, suffering from a perennial lack of funds. This was not the case.

In the fields of history, geography, and archaeology, scholars and universities took significant steps to develop a regional comprehensive knowledge. Studies in government and sociology lagged, but interest was growing. Ambitious bibliographical projects had reached maturity, and as a consequence, a researcher working in a leading U.S. university could acquire a comprehensive vision of the main research problems related to Latin America. After the war, funding declined for a while as other areas required priority (Korea, Japan, and Russia).[63] But Latin American studies maintained a strong presence in U.S. universities. In 1956 Haring visited Puerto Rico to address a round table on the question of intellectual cooperation in the Americas. He noted that the average U.S. American was still quite ignorant about Latin America, but that area specialists had done much to gain knowledge about the region.

> Most of our colleges and universities offer courses in the history of the Latin American republics. Some universities have professorial chairs devoted solely to that subject. Courses of a more general descriptive sort on Latin America also appear in many of our secondary schools, especially on the Pacific coast which has a Spanish heritage of its own. The literature of the Latin American countries is likewise studied and taught in most departments of Romance languages. . . . The geography, anthropology, and archaeology of the Latin areas of America are also represented on our faculties by distinguished specialists. In some of our universities so-called Institutes have been organized which offer special programs in Latin American civilization and culture, including history, literature, law, anthropology, economics, sociology, and leading to the bachelor's or higher degrees. Several North American learned journals devote their pages solely to the history and literature of Latin America.[64]

Latin American studies was consolidated in U.S. universities and learned societies, and by the time of the Cuban Revolution, it was already prestigious and long-standing. It had established a series of characterizations, problems, and peculiarities to define the region, constituting the armature of a large scholarly enterprise. When John J. Johnson surveyed the state of Latin American studies in 1960, he found the field to be a complex teaching and research apparatus already immersed in the practice and identity of research universities in the United States.[65] It was part of the consensus that courses on Spanish and Hispanic American history and literature were part of the "liberal education" that colleges provided.[66] The field had clearly evolved from an intellectual curiosity of the few to an educational force teaching thousands annually.

Conclusion

From the time Secretary Root visited South America, in 1906, the State Department had been courting the South American intelligentsia through educational exchanges. It is not surprising that Ambassador Long would try to set up an American college in Quito and present Ecuador as a field ripe for U.S. research in the social sciences and the humanities. Like many of his contemporaries, Ambassador Long believed that the expansion of U.S. influence in Latin America hinged on the development of specialized regional knowledge. Only the study of the different countries and subregions of Latin America would provide a comprehensive understanding of the subcontinent's problems and their causes. This comprehensive view would enable statesmen and scholars to rearticulate the idea and project of the Western Hemisphere. Under Roosevelt's Good Neighbor Policy, the United States had set up education, technical assistance, and scholarly exchanges in South America. By extension, supremacy in science and education came to be considered central to the exertion of hemispheric influence.

To an extent, the idea of a "soft empire," energized by exchanges in the areas of culture and higher learning, was predicated on the relative failure of early Pan-Americanism (the economic type promoted by Secretary Blaine). A "loose union" of republics without a unity of purpose, the PAU had failed to realize the expectations the United States held for the region at the end of the nineteenth century. The Panama Canal did not, after all, open immense commercial possibilities on the western coast of South America.[67] And it was clear that the cooperation of leading countries in the region—such as Argentina and Chile—was never reliable. Yet the potential harvest of new knowledge continued to inspire scholars to engage with the region.

Local embassy officials learned to deal with U.S. researchers. As Lewis Hanke recalled later, it was unusual in the 1930s for U.S. embassies in the region to be visited by U.S. university professors; ambassadors were unprepared to deal with scholars' requests. Writing in the mid-1960s Hanke stated, "Such days are definitely over, and the academic presence of the United States in most Latin American countries today is an important and even pervasive force" (1967, 48). It is possible to infer from this anecdotal evidence that the gradual occupation of the field by scores of U.S. scholars—archaeologists, ethnographers, geographers, geologists, economists, historians, and others—had by the 1940s transformed a curious intrusion into a normal activity.

Foreign-policy and disciplinary concerns had converged, so that U.S. scholars felt entrusted with a mission to survey and understand Hispanic American civilization. New trade and investment opportunities had opened in South America starting in the 1890s, which the United States translated in the early 1900s into a policy of rapprochement toward the southern republics. U.S. foreign-policy gestures—such as Secretary Root's visit to South America in 1906, or the presence of the United States at the Pan-American Scientific Congress in 1908—motivated scholars to immerse themselves in research on the sub-continent to an extent unknown before. While "rediscovering" South America through closer observation and disciplinary methods, they thought to contribute to the understanding of the new position of the United States in the world. Gradually, their scholarly visits rendered visible and legible a region that had remained a "vacuum of knowledge" until 1900.[68]

TWO

Five Traveling Scholars

———

Why did these different disciplines undertake the task of understanding Latin America? Why did U.S. scholars engage in the laborious work of building regional knowledge? The answer lies perhaps at the intersection of intellectual trajectories, travel experience, and disciplinary rules. As Adam R. Nelson (2005) has convincingly argued, the significant transformations in the structure of higher learning in the United States rested on the very transnational work done by scholars of emerging research universities. He suggests, indeed, that disciplinary knowledge itself would have been difficult to establish in the absence of these traveling experiences.

> As a group, the men and women who created the first United States' universities spent time in virtually every part of Europe (including Russia) and travelled extensively in North Africa, the Middle East, South Asia, Australia, South America, and the Pacific Islands. . . . They forged ties with countless institutions overseas and pursued in an impressive variety of disciplines, from geology, mineralogy, botany, zoology, and other fields of the natural sciences (and medicine) to comparative philology, history, archaeology, theology, political economy, and law. In the process, they developed new approaches to knowledge and used these approaches to

reshape their sense of the United States' place in an increasingly competitive world system. (432–33)

That is, traveling scholars were the very expression of a profound transformation of higher learning in the United States. Yet geopolitical and historical conjunctures are also crucial for understanding why U.S. scholars felt entrusted with "the mission" to survey and understand Hispanic American civilization. There was, in this regard, a convergence of interests between foreign-policy and disciplinary concerns. Between 1890 and 1914 new trade and investment opportunities made Washington reconsider its relationship with the South American republics. This in turn created the context in which various information-gatherers, from both the business and the scholarly communities, started to explore the natural resources, societies, cultures, and histories of South American nations.

The amateur archaeologist Hiram Bingham, the geographer Isaiah Bowman, the historian Clarence H. Haring, the political scientist Leo S. Rowe, and the sociologist Edward A. Ross achieved national and international recognition for their pioneering work on South America. Through their publications, teaching, institution-building, and particularly through their travel, they contributed significantly to the building of academic interest about South America in the United States. Arguably, they created the first professional arenas for the incorporation of "South America" within the field of vision of U.S. social sciences and humanities. Their interventions in their respective disciplines provided the foundation for what later became the field of Latin American studies. In addition, they left powerful and enduring characterizations of the region that informed contemporary U.S. policies. This chapter provides the general background of the five scholars, their travels, and publications.

Travel implies a physical displacement that stimulates observation and reflection. For U.S. scholars—at least, for the ones I study in this book—travel to South America confronted them with a new reality: with poor, indigenous, and premodern nations in the Andes; and with modern societies and economies in the Southern Cone. Though the five scholars I examine traveled in pursuit of different objectives, most of them took advantage of these travels to observe and report on the condition and progress of the "southern republics." Whether they wrote about colonial history, contemporary social and racial relations, geographic regions, or political culture, the displacements produced by traveling were sources of productive comparisons and profound reflections about comparative development, foreign policy, and cultural difference. Writing about the "novelty" of South America, they were able to pose important comparative questions that later became foundational to their respective regional disciplines.

Hiram Bingham

Hiram Bingham was a history professor, a politician, an aviator, and an amateur archaeologist.[1] He first garnered public acclaim in 1911 with the discovery of Machu Picchu, the famous "citadel of the Incas." As Anthony Brandt writes, "He is remembered for one thing, and one thing only. He was an explorer who found the most famous ancient ruins in the Western Hemisphere: the lost Inca city of Machu Picchu" (in Hiram Bingham 1922, xi). This finding alone granted him a prominent position among world archaeologists.[2] After the discovery, Bingham obtained financial support from Yale University and the National Geographic Society to conduct long-term explorations in the southern Peruvian Andes. The Yale Peruvian Expedition, a multidisciplinary enterprise he conducted between 1912 and 1915, advanced knowledge of Peruvian archaeology, geography, and geology, as well as of botany and zoology. That is, Bingham's discovery brought the attention of world archaeologists not only to himself but to Machu Picchu.[3] Three of his books, completed long after the exploration, relate to this discovery: *Inca Land* (1922), *Machu Picchu: A Citadel of the Incas* (1930), and *Lost City of the Incas* (1948). In these works Bingham advanced various hypotheses about the function of Machu Picchu: a refuge for the last Inca emperor; the cradle of Inca civilization; a sacred site where Inca virgins were secluded.[4] After the discovery of Machu Picchu, his attention turned to his archaeological findings—bones, bronzes, pottery, and textiles—which presented him with multiple riddles about the civilization of the Incas. Through his activities as a book collector, historian, geographer, and archaeologist, Bingham helped build scholarly interest about South America in the United States.

A man of multiple trades, Bingham never attained the degree of specialization that other scholars did. Being financially independent, he was free to be a generalist. He worked on history, geography, and archaeology, occasionally weighing in on U.S. foreign policy. He helped build the first collections of Latinoamericana at Harvard and Yale Libraries.[5] He believed that business and humanistic instruction could be profitably combined in the education of university men doing business with South America; his students at Yale, if they were to pursue business in South America, had first to learn about the region's geography, history, archaeology, and government.

Bingham was a "gentleman scholar" with no financial limitations on traveling overseas. (Before starting graduate studies at Harvard, he married Alfreda

Mitchell, heir to the Tiffany fortune.) In 1906–1907, accompanied by the Amazon explorer Hamilton Rice, he traveled to Venezuela and Colombia to retrace the route from Caracas to Bogotá followed by Simón Bolívar during the wars of independence. He wanted to test the difficulty of this epic march on the terrain itself.[6] His account of this journey, published in 1909, was an unremarkable adventure narrative punctuated by encounters with "wild Indians," mules that refused to advance, dramatically changing natural scenes, diverse animal life, and every now and then, traces of Spanish colonization.[7]

In November–December 1908 Bingham undertook a long trip overland from Buenos Aires to Lima with the explicit purpose of following the historic route used to transport supplies to the rich silver mines of Potosí. This resulted in a second book, *Across South America* (1911), a travel narrative that—unlike his previous book—provided interesting insights and historical background. Traveling on modern railroads from Buenos Aires to Tucumán, he witnessed the dramatic change in the landscape from the fertile pampas to valleys cultivated with sugarcane. Moving on to La Quiaca, Bingham found himself on a cold, dry plateau where nothing grew without irrigation. In Bolivia, Potosí attracted Bingham's historical curiosity. Here was the "largest city in the Western Hemisphere" in the seventeenth century, now in decay: houses, churches, and convents stood as silent witnesses of a colonial glory, long past (Hiram Bingham 1911b). The local prefect received the U.S. party with red-carpet treatment. Celebrations in his honor lasted a week, including bullfights, dinners, balls, fireworks, and illuminations.

After attending a scientific congress at Santiago, Chile (1908–1909), Bingham and other delegates visited Cuzco.[8] It was probably there, at the museum of Incaica built by the merchant Cesar Lomellini, that Bingham became interested in Inca civilization and history. He was dazzled by the large walls of Sacsayhuaman (Cohen 1984, 83–85). In conversations with local informants Bingham learned of sites alleged to contain Inca ruins, as well as how to find them; Prefect Núñez and other *cuzqueños* pointed him toward the ruins of Choqquequirau (Hiram Bingham 1910b).[9] The visit awoke a curiosity in him about Inca fortifications, burial rituals, and the route followed by the Incas escaping from the Spanish conquerors.

Subsequently, Bingham made three major archaeological expeditions to Peru. In the first, in 1911, he discovered Machu Picchu. With the help of local informants (among them hacienda owners who interrogated their Indian tenants and peons), Bingham was able to find the "hidden citadel of the Incas." Assisted by six other men (the explorer Herman L. Tucker, the topographer Kai Hendriksen, the naturalist Harry W. Foote, the geographer Isaiah Bowman, the physician William G. Erving, and the college senior Paul B. Lanius), Bingham was able to find in the valley of Vilcabamba another Inca ruin, which he identified as the monument of Victos referred to by the Spanish chroniclers (Baltasar de Ocampo and Antonio de la Calancha, in particular). He then marched down the valley trying to find Old Vilcabamba, again following the traces provided by the Spanish missionary Calancha.[10] This was another historically driven trip. If before he had followed the steps of Bolívar, now he was tracing the steps of the last Inca rulers, Manco Capac and his three sons.

The second (1912) and third (1914–1915) visits were part of the Yale Peruvian Expedition (YPE). Financed by the National Geographic Society and the Kodak Company, these expeditions attempted to clear the bush that covered Machu Picchu and excavate the ruins, to survey a wider area in search of additional ruins, and to investigate issues concerning the geology, ethnography, physical geography, and biology of the region. Photography and popular magazine articles were among the most salient results of these expeditions. But in Peru the Yale team met the opposition of traditionalists and early *indigenistas*. The YPE brought back to Yale an important "scientific harvest," measured by the number of scientific publications it generated and by the collection of bones, pottery, bronzes, and textiles from Peru (later donated to the Peabody Museum at Yale and to different scientific schools in the Northeast). After 1915 and a bitter experience in Peru during the YPE, Bingham ended his exploration and field research in South America. After 1924, he abandoned university teaching for a career in politics: he became lieutenant-governor, governor, and then senator of Connecticut. In the 1930s and 1940s his U.S. foreign-policy concerns shifted from Latin America to China and the Pacific, and he wrote occasionally about aviation and U.S. defense.

Isaiah Bowman

The geographer Isaiah Bowman, one of the members of the YPE, used the results of his South American explorations to build a solid reputation in the field of geography, and from there won positions of power in both government and the academy.[11] In 1919 Bowman was appointed head of the geology and geography division of the National Research Council. He advised President Woodrow Wilson in the aftermath of the First World War, going on to serve as science advisor to President Franklin D. Roosevelt, as head of the National Research Council, as president of Johns Hopkins University, and as vice president of the National Academy of Sciences. As president of the American Geographical Society (AGS), he helped develop professional geography in the United States.

In *The Andes of Southern Peru* (1916), Bowman presented a synthetic and comprehensive view of Peru's main natural and human regions. He wrote up his explorations in northwest Argentina and the Atacama Desert in *Desert Trails of Atacama* (1924), a book that enhanced his credentials as a regional geographer. At the beginning, he defined geography as the science that studied the relations between humans and their environment. Later, in the 1930s, he advocated for geography to become a "science of settlement" concerned with world agricultural frontiers. Over this whole period, Bowman supervised the compilation at the AGS of the Millionth Map of Hispanic America, a work named for its unprecedented detail and published between 1922 and 1945. The new map proved of invaluable assistance to mining prospectors, geologists, road constructors, land developers, and other geographers.[12]

After serving on the U.S. delegation to the Peace Conference in Paris in 1919, Bowman emerged as an expert on world politics. He was among the founding members of the Council on Foreign Relations (CFR), a group established in 1921 to foster the vision of liberal internationalism. Within the CFR, he chaired study groups on U.S.-Latin American relations.[13] It was Bowman who secured the funding for the first issues of *Foreign Affairs*. After 1926, he began studying pioneer settlements, a research program he extended to various world regions with funding from the National Research Council and the Science Advisory Board.[14] Out of this research came two important volumes: *The Pioneer Fringe* (1931) and *The Limits of Land Settlement* (1937).

Believing in the power of science to resolve issues of public policy, Bowman upheld geography as the discipline that could make "world order" possible. At the Paris negotiations, Bowman had learned about the tensions in the European colonial world and was able to anticipate its demise. He thought, however, that Dollar Diplomacy was better than protectorates, mandates, and other forms of direct intervention. He was perhaps one of the first U.S. scholars to articulate a defense of economic supremacy over older forms of imperialism. He had been in close contact with President Wilson since 1918, admiring the president's internationalist idealism, his notion of "scientific peace," and his vision of a world in which colonial possessions or military might no longer dictate international supremacy. He was quite disappointed about the Senate rejection of the League of Nations and the electoral defeat of 1920.

Bowman first traveled to the subcontinent in 1907, as the head geographer of the South American Expedition. He made a second visit in 1912, when he accompanied Bingham's YPE. He was in charge of traveling south from Cuzco to the Pacific to survey the 73rd meridian. In these early trips, he observed the physiography, the topography, the settlements, and the economic activities of northern Chile, western Bolivia, and southern Peru (Bowman 1914). In 1913, under the auspices of the American Geographic Society, he conducted geographical reconnaissance in northwestern Argentina and southern Bolivia.

Early on, attracted by the extreme variation of climate and relief in the Central Andes, Bowman decided to study the adaptation of settlers to distinct natural environments. By the time of his third trip to South America, his disciplinary approach was already established: he was to combine "anthropogeography" with observations of physiography. Though still working under a Davisian framework (using geological evidence to focus on long-term relations between human settlements and their physical environments) his interest shifted toward the relationship between humans and physical geography. After 1915, administrative responsibilities at the AGS prevented Bowman from returning to South America for a while. In 1930–1932, in the midst of the Depression, he resumed fieldwork, this time to study farming frontiers in the United States. With his son, he traveled by car to Montana, central Oregon, western Kansas, and Nebraska. He discovered that the U.S. "pioneer frontier," despite Turner's prediction, was alive and well (Martin 1980, 114–15). In 1941 he finally revisited the Central Andes, this time as advisor to President Roosevelt during the latter's goodwill tour to Colombia, Ecuador, and Peru (ibid., 162). His advice, it was reported, was crucial for settling a long-standing boundary dispute between Ecuador and Peru (Wrigley 1951, 47).

Clarence H. Haring

Clarence H. Haring was a Harvard professor fully devoted to the development of the field of Hispanic American history. He was a founding member of the *Hispanic American Historical Review* (1918) and a leading scholar on studies of Spanish colonialism. Harvard served as the resonance box for Haring's concerns about Hispanic American history and about the promises of Pan-American cooperation. He brought to Harvard the problematic of Pan-Americanism, lending prestige to a doctrine expressing U.S. hegemonic ambitions in the region.

From Harvard, through round tables and workshops, he articulated a network of economists, businessmen, scholars, and policy makers interested in the "problems" of Latin America. He used historical generalizations and these connections to activate policy thinking about Latin America. Over the thirty years (1923–1953) that he taught there, Haring mentored graduate students who later became prominent members of the historical profession.[15] He promoted the formation of Pan-American societies, monitored political developments in South America, and advised the U.S. government about the emergent field of Latin American studies. He occasionally collaborated with the State Department, providing intelligence and advice.

Haring's historical publications dealt mostly with the history of the Spanish empire. His two most salient contributions were *Trade and Navigation between Spain and the Indies in the Time of the Habsburgs* (1918) and *The Spanish Empire in America* (1947). In between these two books, he published many essays on the economic and institutional history of the Spanish colonial system. These works criticized the Spanish commercial monopoly, the systems of coerced labor it imposed on indigenous peoples, and the lack of participatory political institutions. He was particularly interested in the similarities and differences between Spanish colonialism and the modern U.S. empire. Earlier than Herbert E. Bolton, Haring conceived a thesis about the "parallel but distinct" paths of historical development of the two Americas.[16] His works on the Spanish empire contain the basis for a project on the comparative study of the Americas, now back in fashion.[17]

In addition to historical works, Haring wrote two notable interventions in the field of inter-American relations: *South America Looks at the United States* (1928), and *South American Progress* (1934). In matters of U.S. foreign policy Haring was a progressive thinker; in his writings he anticipated positions close to Roosevelt's Good Neighbor Policy. He opposed U.S. interventions in the Caribbean, being particularly critical of U.S. policies in Nicaragua. Haring was the academic ambassador par excellence. To him, expertise in the field of Latin America implied responsibilities in the promotion of U.S. Pan-Americanism. He was appointed U.S. delegate to the most important scientific conferences involving Latin America, acting in some of them as organizer. Haring and Leo S. Rowe were the chief U.S. representatives to the Second Pan-American Financial Conference, held in Washington in 1920. In 1935 Haring chaired the U.S. delegation to the General Assembly of the recently founded Pan American Institute of Geography and History. In 1940 he was appointed U.S. delegate to the Eighth American Scientific Congress at Washington, under the chairmanship of Secretary of State Sumner Welles.

Haring did not travel extensively across South America until the mid-1920s. Ten years earlier, he had visited Spain to complete the research needed for his B. Litt (bachelor of letters) at Oxford, spending some time at the archives in Seville and Simancas. His early professional publications dealt with silver and gold shipped from Peru and Mexico to Spain, a theme central to colonial economic history. Interestingly, these articles appeared in economics journals. In 1926–1927 he obtained funding from the Bureau of Economic Research to study South American attitudes toward U.S. investment, products, and foreign policy. He visited Rio de Janeiro, Buenos Aires, Santiago, and Lima, where he found that South American intellectuals and newspapers shared a deep "distrust" of the United States. His 1928 book, *South America Looks at the United States*, contained an insightful report of the emerging forces of nationalism and anti-Americanism in the region.

From 1930, when a series of military revolutions interrupted the constitutional trajectory of several countries, Haring gathered intelligence for the Council on Foreign Relations about changing political conditions in South America. He endeavored to show that these "revolutions" were the result of social progress and new demands for political participation, rather than a return to personalist and authoritarian government. In 1937 he headed the U.S. delegation to the Second Congress on the History of America, held in Buenos Aires. There, he delivered the keynote speech, "Race and Environment in the New World," telling local historians that Anglo-America had become more prosperous than Latin America, but that the possibility of converging trajectories was there, spelled out in comparative history. He also met leading Argentine representatives of the historical profession, among them Ricardo Levene and Emilio Ravignani.

After Pearl Harbor, the State Department encouraged scholars to contribute to the cause of inter-American cooperation. Harvard granted Haring a leave of absence to undertake a tour to South America that included visits to Peru, Chile, Argentina, and Brazil. After attending the Lima assembly of the Pan American Institute of History and Geography, he was to survey the conditions of democratic politics in the region for the Council on Foreign Relations. During this trip, Haring gathered intelligence about Nazi activities in the southern republics. In 1941 he published a pamphlet on the relations between Argentina and the United States. In this study he denounced the presence of German Nazi propaganda in Argentina and examined Argentine public opinion about the European war. His book *Argentina and the United States* (1941) contains valuable information about Nazi organizations in Argentina.

Edward A. Ross

Edward A. Ross was one of America's foremost sociologists. A progressive thinker and disciple of Richard Ely, he developed new concepts and methods for the study of societies. He is well known for his defense of selective immigration and of academic freedom. Although his theorization went beyond any particular region, his observations about and valuable examples from South

America infused his social theory. His sociological tracts are full of "South American problems": elite exclusionism, racial prejudice, labor oppression, and the colonial legacy. Much earlier than structuralist Marxists, Ross discussed the question of the "feudality" in Andean South America's and Mexico's contemporary social relations. Rather than working toward a regional science, Ross strove to build a comparative social theory, made from observations gathered in different world regions.

Ross was one of the last "system builders" in U.S. social theory. His intellectual ambitions compare with those of the great European sociologists Max Weber and Émile Durkheim. His books *Social Control* (1901), *Foundations of Sociology* (1905), and *Social Psychology* (1908) helped lay the foundations of U.S. sociology (Weinberg 1972, chap. 4; Page 1969, chap. 7). In addition, Ross wrote educational books for the general reader, in which he appears as a public intellectual committed to the resolution of U.S. social problems. Some of these books addressed the demographic, social, commercial, and cultural transformations of U.S. society, including, for example, *Changing America* (1912). Others, like *The Social Trend* (1922), cautioned U.S. Americans about world changes that were bound to affect the United States. In *Roads to Social Peace* (1924) he discussed the question of social conflict and the need to endeavor for social peace.

Two of his books contain superb social portraits of Latin America: *South of Panama* (1915) and *The Social Revolution in Mexico* (1923). From these works, Ross built the theoretical architecture for a comparative "worldly sociology," a science of society informed by observations made around the world. A progressive social reformer, Ross participated in important public debates on immigration, workers' protection, family reproduction, the emancipation of women, and corporate influences on universities and the media (McMahon 1999, chaps. 4 and 6; Weinberg 1972, chap. 4). His progressive views, displaced into the territory of Andean South America, led him to severely condemn social and racial oppression in the region. Despite his progressive stand on other social issues, his opposition to Asian immigration based on racial arguments gained him a reputation as a racist. He coined the term *race suicide*, later popularized by President Roosevelt.

Unlike the other scholars I examine, Ross was a world traveler in search of the basic organizing patterns of societies. His 1913–1914 South American journeys appear as one moment in a series of travels around the world. He visited South America and Mexico, but also Russia, China, Japan, South Africa, the Pacific Islands, India, and most of Europe. These travels allowed him to compare social trends in different countries and to observe social upheavals

Five Traveling Scholars

in the making. Few U.S. scholars could claim, as he did, to have witnessed the Mexican Revolution, the Russian Revolution, and the 1910 Chinese uprising.

Ross spent the second semester of 1913 on the west coast of South America. On his way, he spent a few days in the Canal Zone, where General Gorgas explained how he had eradicated infectious disease in the area, malaria and yellow fever. In this colonial enclave Ross first "saw" the contrast between Spanish backwardness and U.S. modernity. He spent sixteen days in western Colombia, traveling on horseback from Cali to the Cauca Valley. He visited all the ports down to Guayaquil, then traveled to Quito and Riobamba. Next, he visited Peru, where he stayed for six weeks; he spoke at the University of San Marcos in Lima. He rode from Cuzco to see the ruins of Machu Picchu, accompanied by the "vagabond traveler" Harry Franck. In Bolivia he spent a week in La Paz, taking from there a train to Antofagasta. In Chile he spent a month traveling north to south, reaching Lake Nahuel Huapi, on the Argentine border. Returning to Santiago in January 1914, he took the Transandine Railway to Argentina, where he visited the cities of Cordoba, Tucumán, Salta, and Rosario (Edward A. Ross 1977 [1934], 136–37).

Ross went to South America to observe society. In preparation for the trip, he learned Spanish and read historical materials about the different countries. In addition, he was well read in the history of religion, the Middle Ages, ancient empires, and traditional systems of hierarchy. To evaluate South American societies, Ross interviewed Chilean landowners, sugar planters in northern Argentina and Peru, managers of smelting firms in Chile, and university administrators in Arequipa, Santiago, and Buenos Aires. He also talked to U.S. and European residents, paying special attention to foreign missionaries' reports. The University of Wisconsin and U.S. progressive organizations financed Ross's travels (his first trip to Russia in July–December 1917 was funded in part by the American Institute of Social Service). In the 1920s and 1930s Ross became fond of Mexico and accepted invitations to give conferences and participate in academic meetings there.

Leo S. Rowe

From 1920 to 1946, Leo S. Rowe, a political scientist at the University of Pennsylvania, served as the director of the Pan-American Union (PAU), the institution that channeled U.S. views and policies in matters of hemispheric integration and that was the precursor of the Organization of American States. He was a scholar-statesman, a promoter of Pan-Americanism, and a knowledge-gatherer on a hemispheric scale (Salvatore 2010a). His obituary (1946) presented him as the foremost advocate of inter-American friendship, understanding, and solidarity (Welles 1947; Hill 1947). During his early contact with South America (1906–1908), Rowe acknowledged the progress made by Argentina, Brazil, and Chile in constitutional government and economic growth. He thus combated the U.S. misconception that the countries south of Panama were lands of recurrent revolutions. Well before the advent of the Good Neighbor Policy, Rowe promoted U.S. cooperation with the "southern republics" in culture, law, and education. Indeed, he was the first scholar to articulate a coherent strategy of "intellectual cooperation" with them.[18]

A progressive thinker, Rowe was interested in improving the quality of municipal and state governments in the United States, freeing local elections from the corruption of "machine politics." He was active in the formation of the National Civic Federation, an association directed toward those goals (Cyphers 2002, 38). Believing in the power of public opinion to control the abuses of government, he tried to share his concern for "American democracy" with South American intellectuals. Rowe's administrative experience is itself interesting. He moved from positions in colonial government in Puerto Rico and Panama to serve as head of the PAU. Under his tenure, U.S.-Latin American relations improved significantly. He is credited with presenting practical solutions to end the U.S. intervention in Haiti, with finding an amicable solution to the U.S. dispute with Venustiano Carranza in Mexico, and with arbitrating long-standing border disputes among South American nations.

Rowe's policy of "intellectual cooperation" anticipated FDR's Good Neighbor policies by more than a decade. Under his leadership, the PAU enacted a policy of collective hemispheric defense, a multilateral version of the Monroe Doctrine. In collaboration with James Brown Scott, Rowe promoted a common system of inter-American law and was instrumental in the establishment of the Central American Court of Justice (Scarfi 2009).

Rowe's early works dealt with the comparative history of constitutional government, urban improvements, taxation, and higher education. Before he assumed the directorship of the PAU, he published two books: one about his own experience in colonial governance (*The United States and Porto Rico*, 1904); the other about the problems of municipal administration (*Problems of City Government*, 1908). His last important book, *The Federal System of the Argentine Republic* (1921b), was a comparative study of Argentine and U.S. federalism, where he reconsidered his earlier prejudice against Hispanic political culture.

Rowe first visited South America in 1906. In June of that year he sailed from New York to attend the Pan-American Conference at Rio de Janeiro. From Rio he traveled overland to Argentina. This allowed him to observe farming communities in Santa Fe and Entre Ríos before reaching Buenos Aires. He established an academic connection with the University of La Plata, where he spent six months at a residential college, interacting with students of veterinary, agronomy, and law. During the Pan-American Conference at Santiago (1908), he and various other delegates traveled to Argentina. In November of that year, accompanied by Ambassador Rómulo S. Naón, Rowe visited the northwest provinces to survey educational institutions. The results were published as "Progresos educacionales en la República Argentina" (1910). He then returned to Santiago, where he embarked on a ship that took him from Valparaíso to Guayaquil.

In September 1909, invited by President Porfirio Díaz, Rowe traveled to Mexico City to attend the inauguration of the National University of Mexico (UNAM). In his lecture, he praised the progress made during the Porfiriato, without anticipating that a great social upheaval was in the making (Leo S. Rowe 1910a). Though there were some disturbances, Rowe assured U.S. reporters that no revolution was to be expected. Contemporary political unrest was, rather, a sign of an increased demand for political participation. When he returned to Mexico in December 1911, the revolution was in full swing (Leo S. Rowe 1911). In 1914 he visited Argentina for a third time, this time staying five months. In Buenos Aires Rowe delivered a series of conferences about the state of U.S. democracy. There in South America's most modern city Rowe interacted with intellectuals with European manners. The dramatic contrast between Caribbean colonial outposts and Belle Époque Argentina impressed him greatly, affecting his views as a constitutionalist and political scientist. After the start of the First World War, he promoted the doctrine of "the rights of neutral nations," looking for allies among the southern republics.

As a top-level representative of the U.S. government in the field of inter-American cooperation, Rowe received red-carpet treatment across the hemisphere during his travels from 1907 to 1909. Everywhere he went, he was treated as a celebrity: banquets were organized in his honor; his addresses were printed in local newspapers; and scholarly societies granted him honorary membership. Before assuming the directorship of the PAU, he was granted honorary degrees by the universities of La Plata in Argentina (1906), Católica de Chile (1907), San Marcos, Lima (1908), and UNAM (1910). His success also had much to do with his message. He spoke about the United States' willingness to intensify commercial and cultural relations with the southern republics, and about the need for closer intellectual cooperation between the two Americas. Years before, President Theodore Roosevelt had stated that personal ties with elite, university men were crucial for a greater cooperation with

"Latin nations." Rowe carried this advice into practice with great effectiveness. After taking office at the PAU (1920), his opportunities to visit South America multiplied. Rowe used these occasions to evaluate the state of democracy and development in the subcontinent, and to spread his gospel of good will and intellectual brotherhood. To Rowe, travel was an instrument for building inter-American connections. He believed that private tourism could help to build Pan-American cooperation. In 1934 he established the travel division of the PAU with the explicit mandate of promoting tourism among the Americas (Leo S. Rowe 1945).

Conclusion

These five scholars traveled to South America to report on the new conditions and possibilities of a region recently incorporated (or in the process of being integrated) into the sphere of U.S. economic influence. It is significant that they made their direct observations of the "southern republics" during a period in which the United States was redefining its relations toward the subcontinent, from a position of Caribbean policeman (Big Stick policy), to one of financial enticement (Dollar Diplomacy), to one of hemispheric friendship and cooperation (Good Neighbor Policy). This important transition in foreign policy stimulated them to examine a central question: the modernity and civility of South America in comparison with the achievements of the United States.

In a way, the changing language of the hegemon (from "dependencies" to "neighbors") opened up possibilities for a growing field of transfer of advice and knowledge (North to South) that by itself promised the continued interest of the United States and its institutions of higher learning in the "newly discovered" region. This motivated U.S. scholars in several fields of inquiry in the social sciences and the humanities to pose questions, gather data, and present preliminary syntheses that later served as the basis for the construction of regional subdisciplines, such as Hispanic American history, South American geography, and Andean archaeology. Though the building of disciplinary fields of regional knowledge took place in U.S. research universities, South American travels delimited the boundaries of the research designs, posed the core questions constitutive of each subfield, and advanced, however tentatively, the relations that these inquiries had with the extension of the U.S. informal empire in South America.

THREE

Research Designs of Transnational Scope

———

U.S. scholars built comprehensive regional knowledge by gathering information about South America. The programs of research imagined by the
scholars Hiram Bingham, Isaiah Bowman, Clarence H. Haring, Edward A.
Ross, and Leo S. Rowe transcended the boundaries of the nation—they were
transnational—and called for the intellectual collaboration of various branches
of knowledge. Grand research designs in geography, archaeology, history, political science, and sociology accompanied the period of diplomatic rapprochement with South America. And this development in turn was fueled by the
expansion of U.S. direct investment and trade in the region. The vast scope
of these undertakings facilitated imperial visibility, at a time when the United
States sought to understand its South American neighbors. Some of these
research designs made explicit their allegiance to U.S. foreign-policy visions,
such as Pan-Americanism and the Good Neighbor Policy. Others invoked lofty
ideals—mutual understanding and inter-American cooperation—to rationalize
the southward expansion of U.S. knowledge. Either way, by building research
projects of hemispheric or transnational scope, U.S. scholars laid the foundations of a comprehensive knowledge that could help diplomats and politicians
formulate U.S. foreign policies for the region.

The historian and explorer Hiram Bingham and the Yale Peruvian Expedition carved a space for other scholars to negotiate future U.S. archaeological

expeditions to South America. The geographer Isaiah Bowman persuaded U.S. investors, statesmen, and researchers of the need to thoroughly survey and map the subcontinent. The historian Clarence H. Haring proposed a comparative history of the hemisphere, which would make it possible to distinguish nations that converged toward the U.S. model from those that did not. The political scientist Leo S. Rowe pioneered the study of South American government in comparison to Caribbean dependencies. The sociologist Edward A. Ross in turn presented regional "social panoramas" as a way to synthesize and simplify the complex realities of South America.

All these paths to knowledge aimed to create a comprehensive understanding of the subcontinent. Research projects of macro regional scope were "designs" for the construction of orderly visions that rendered legible the chief phenomena and attributes of a given region. The disciplines themselves (archaeology, geography, history, political science, and sociology in our case) contributed the organizing principles for the chaotic and diverse realities of South America. In this chapter I discuss the concept of "imperiality" of knowledge as key to understanding these disciplinary interventions. By examining the research designs of our five scholars, both to understand their explicit objectives and to ascertain the imperiality implicit in them, I connect the formation of regional knowledge to broader expansionist tendencies of U.S. capital, technology, and culture. At the center of this process stood the U.S. research university, a constellation of fields of knowledge, cultivated by scholars working under a new organizational structure (departmental units, research labs, great libraries, academic journals, graduate programs, and so on).

On the Imperiality of Knowledge

Knowledge-producers create research designs. These are blueprints containing the set of problems to be investigated, the methods of inquiry, the instruments of measurement, and the scope or extent of the research. A research program can take as its object of study a locality, a province, a nation, a region, or a continent. The scope of the field transforms the nature of the inquiry. The passage from national to transnational history (or geography, or political science) presupposes an expansion in the will to know. Disciplines that contemplate projects of knowledge of transnational scope are commonly associated with universities and learned societies located in the advanced, industrialized nations of the West. It is these institutions that have the finances, the human resources, and the academic ambition to undertake the appropriation of local knowledge in order to build comprehensive, transnational, imperial knowledge.

Research Designs

To the extent that all knowledge seeks to overcome a previous vacuum of information and understanding, to illuminate an uncharted terrain of inquiry, or to conquer new territories for the assertion of expert authority, all knowledge can be deemed "imperial." In exploring the expansion of informal or soft empire, based on cultural influence and economic and financial supremacy, knowledge is one of the expansive forces that we need to consider, in particular expert, disciplinary knowledge stemming from research universities and learned societies. Economic flows and expert regional knowledge are two interacting forces, whose expansion is mutually reinforcing. That is, efforts to gain access to needed raw materials and markets or to favorable conditions for overseas investment are often accompanied by an expansion of regional knowledge—not just of "commercial intelligence," but also disciplinary knowledge in the natural sciences, the humanities, and the social sciences.

In colonial situations officials produce imperial knowledge under the auspices or mandate of an imperial government, as when the East India Company in India instructed Warren Hasting to collect and translate Sanskrit legal manuscripts or when the U.S. occupation government in the Philippines ordered local officials to take a census.[1] In these cases, the knowledge gathered was instrumental to the administration of colonial territories. Maps, censuses, legal texts, and land surveys gave colonial authorities direct instruments of government. The anthropologist Nicholas Dirks writes,

> Colonial knowledge both enabled conquest and was produced by it: in certain important ways, knowledge was what colonialism was all about. Cultural forms in societies newly classified as "traditional" were reconstructed and transformed by and through this knowledge, which created new categories and oppositions between colonizers and colonized, European and Asian, modern and traditional, West and East. (Cohn 1996, ix)

In the case of an informal empire, the relationship between knowledge production and expanded hegemony is not so direct and transparent. The imperiality of knowledge does not stem from the colonial nature of government and its requirements. It is predicated instead on the very discourse of expert knowledge, which promises economic and political power a more accurate and simplified representation of the areas of influence. In other words, the authority rests on the prestige of specialized disciplines and the scholars who enunciate truth claims about the hinterlands and their populations. The knowledge produced renders similar services in terms of expanded and comprehensive visibility, but is not immediately useful to the routines of government. In neocolonial situations, rather, scholars make the effort to link their inquiries to the greater problematic of establishing hegemony.

One of the central features of imperial knowledge is extraterritoriality: information is gathered about outlying regions that are to come under the influence of a more powerful economic, technological, or political center. Expanded visibility is a second important aspect of imperial knowledge. The new disciplinary knowledge has to generate ways to enhance the capacity to observe in simplified terms the complex phenomena of areas of influence or hinterlands. Simplification is a crucial function of imperial knowledge; through various representations (charts, maps, tables, narratives, and hypotheses), scholars place the diversity of territories and populations under observation in a platform of comparability.[2] Expert knowledge that does not clarify or simplify the main problems affecting the hinterlands could hardly be called imperial. A third feature of imperial knowledge is usefulness. It is necessary that knowledge-producers orient their research toward solving problems of governance or influence, as construed by the hegemon. To this extent, imperial knowledge contains always a dose of *empiria*: data needs to be gathered, classified, and interpreted at the center's workshops of knowledge. Purely theoretical or deductive work does not render much service to empire.

Imperial knowledge always entails a centripetal circulation of objects.[3] Statistics, artifacts, manuscripts, ethnographic notes, photographs, measurements, surveys, and so forth are constantly flowing toward centers of knowledge. There, scholars attempt to build synthetic and general understandings of a given region and its population. Peripheries, to an extent, function as great repositories of evidence to the center. The imperiality of this centripetal circulation is underscored by the impossibility of a reciprocal relationship: the periphery cannot accumulate the voluminous evidence that the center already has, nor does it have the ambition to do so. To the extent that this constellation of objects-evidence is already displaced and accumulates in the center, it is difficult for the peripheries to imagine or conceive fields of study of transnational scope. The transnational scope of knowledge is, then, derivative of a prior concentration and accumulation of evidence, which is itself tributary to colonial and neocolonial relationships.

Imperial knowledge is not formed simply by an assemblage of "heterologies," the name given by Michel de Certeau to a set of practices of writing and knowing that center on the study of "the Other": the mystic's search for God; the discoveries of curiosities found in travel narratives; psychology's exploration of the mind; the inscription of savages, barbarians, and cannibals by

Western philosophies; as well as studies of folklore, street poetry, and a variety of other practices.[4] Rather than illuminating the marginal or repressed side of Western modernity, U.S. disciplinary discourse about South America sought to describe the totality of a region. Individual subalternities or characters—the Boricua, the Peruvian "tapada," the Chilean "roto," the Argentine "gaucho," and so on—could not be rendered legible without the understanding of this totality. Instead, the disciplines aimed to form an orderly and synthetic understanding of South America in relationship to "American" models of governance, history, society, and culture. Thus, the resulting regional knowledge contained a balance between homogeneity and diversity, between difference and similitude.

Moreover, central expert authority cannot be built simply from expressions of total alterity. Claims that the center possesses a "superior" or "exemplar" society and culture can help construct the position and perspective of the observer. But an absolute and complete alienation of the areas under observation from the center would not do the trick. Scholarly work about a newly incorporated region should be able to translate this alterity into the national self in order to sustain reasons for primacy, tutelage, or guidance. In other words, the central and the peripheral, the "superior" and the "inferior," should be put in connection, so as to construct credible pronouncements about the center's mission in relation to its peripheries.

More generally, the discourse of U.S. expert knowledge should place the given object of knowledge (Peru, the Amazon, South America) in relationship to certain notions of self ("Americanness," U.S. traditions, U.S. history, U.S. social organization, U.S. mass culture, etc.) in order to transform it into useful knowledge. Traveling scholars created a discourse about South America centered on the region's obstacles to economic progress, political stability, democratic governance, and cultural modernity. Yet, committed to contribute truthful and reliable representations of the condition of the "southern republics," U.S. scholars also underscored the differences separating the various countries, regions, and populations. Because of its internally differential nature, U.S. disciplinary knowledge on South America was not another type of Orientalism, that is, an invented other around which a series of study areas emerge, or, as Said put it, "a way of coming to terms with the Orient that is based on the Orient's special place in European Western Experience."[5]

The problem with the emerging field of Latin American studies was therefore not its excessive generalizations and lack of attention to difference, but its constant projection of U.S. understandings into the territory of the other. U.S. experts had to examine the possibility that a region's economies, societies, politics, and culture might converge with the model of the U.S. center, while also raising doubts about the feasibility of such convergence. Questions about the backwardness of Latin America vis-à-vis the United States were, therefore, constitutive of the field of Latin American studies. Implicit in this formulation was an imperial gesture: the necessity for a continued transfer of institutions, culture, and ideas from the United States to Latin America. It is when the "problems" of the periphery are integrated as areas of research of the center's academy that we may characterize a given research design as "imperial."

Earlier, we discerned three conditions for disciplinary knowledge to be considered imperial: (1) when the scholarly work collaborates with, gives support to, or otherwise advances the cause of supranational hegemony or control; (2) when the discipline itself provides the methods, the measurements, the concepts to attain a comprehensive visibility of the region under influence; (3) when the scholar makes extra efforts to bring his or her own inquiry in line with a given foreign-policy vision or principle. Extraterritoriality, expanded visibility, and utility for expansionist designs are the standards for considering academic designs "imperial." Now we can see that there is a fourth feature or condition. The most imperial of all predicaments is to take the "problems" of the hinterlands as the center's own. Here, there is a double responsibility: the collective "we" of scholars taking primary responsibility for solving the puzzles of South American civilization, and also the responsibility of the United States for the region's development and modernity. In this regard, regional expert knowledge is imperial not only because it provides economic and political capital an expanded and comprehensive visibility, but also because it imagines the possibility for an endless transfer of the center's ideas, culture, and technology to the periphery.

Studies in Colonial and Neocolonial Governance

The political scientist Leo S. Rowe pioneered the study of government in colonial and neocolonial situations. His writings reveal the pursuit of two grand research designs: one concerning questions of legality, constitutional guarantees, and congressional review in the government of insular dependencies; the other directed toward the comparative study of U.S. and South American forms of federalism, which entailed a reflection on the evolution of democracy in the southern tip of the continent.

Early on, in the last years of the nineteenth century, Rowe had been studying financial and political issues related to municipal government. His appointment to administrative positions in Puerto Rico (1900–1902) and Panama (1912–1913) afforded him a unique opportunity to study government transitions in colonial situations. During these years, the political scientist tried to answer a set of four related questions: How does the transition from military to civil government proceed in overseas dependencies? Are U.S. constitutional prescriptions valid to occupation governments? How much of local traditions and legal principles should be incorporated in the legal structure of occupied territories? Are U.S. conceptions of property and rights to be extended to overseas dominions?

We know the answers Rowe gave to these questions. Almost without exception, U.S. military occupations gave way, sooner or later, to civil governments. At first, all three powers were concentrated on military governors, but in time these officials began to delegate judicial and legislative powers to local authorities. Transition to self-rule was gradual; U.S. authorities first built a municipal government, then established a national congress, and only later relinquished control of the executive. Though appointed by the U.S. president, military governors of the newly acquired colonies were responsible for their actions before Congress. To this extent, congressional review of the executive was maintained in colonial situations.[6]

From his experience in Puerto Rico and Panama, Rowe drew insights about Spanish-American political culture. In drafting local legislation, it was wise to pay attention to local traditions and inherited legal principles. Otherwise, the cost of inculcating new legal principles in local populations could override the benefits of "American government." Local *cabildos* were forms of political participation that could be used to modernize government in the former Spanish colonies. Thus, the organization of city government—the laboratory of self-government—should be attentive to and aware of Spanish political institutions and culture (Leo S. Rowe 1902d).

The U.S. Caribbean dependencies proved an experimental laboratory for the adaptation of U.S. political ideas and standards of government to colonial situations (Leo S. Rowe 1902b). From his analysis of the "insular cases," Rowe concluded that the Supreme Court had given colonial authorities a free hand to experiment with hybrid forms of government (Leo S. Rowe 1901). Hispanic political culture, however, could degrade the character of democratic government in colonial situations. Inherited ideas of paternalism could lead to widespread corruption and the colonization of the state by private interests. Consequently, transition governments needed to teach colonial subjects the true meaning political democracy (Leo S. Rowe 1914d).

Out of his experiences in the Caribbean, Rowe delineated an impressive research program. Governing colonial situations necessarily implied a legal transfer from center to periphery, a process whose legal and constitutional implications had to be studied. Legal reforms in the colonies required the hybridization of Anglo and Hispanic legal traditions. The Supreme Court had given colonial governors the freedom to implement flexible, hybrid variants of "American government." These experiments needed to be monitored in practice to test whether individual liberties and republican government could work in cultures dominated by the Hispanic legacy.

Rowe's engagement with South America turned his attention away from colonial administration and into the new politics of scholarly brotherhood and cultural engagement. His intellectual production between 1909 and 1919 reveals this shift. In publications of this period, Rowe underscored the great economic transformations and newly acquired modernity of the ABC countries (Argentina, Brazil, Chile). He became a reporter of South America's progress in matters of urban improvement, municipal government, and education reform (Leo S. Rowe 1908a; Leo S. Rowe 1908b; Leo S. Rowe 1910b). This provided a new working hypothesis to his research design: the ABC republics tended to approach "American standards" of governance, civility, and progress.[7] Later on, Rowe collected evidence for testing whether Argentine federalism, in its peculiar incarnation (centralized and presidentialist) could be considered compatible with U.S. notions of democratic government. In other words, he posited the possibility of a convergence of U.S. and South American democratic government, a position that favored a direct and more equal relation with the ABC nations.

Due to his responsibilities as head of the PAU, Rowe never had the time to write a synthesis of his views on "American government" in colonial and neocolonial situations. Nevertheless, his grand vision of politics, constitutions, and republican government in Latin America contributed to shape U.S. foreign policies toward the region. Quite clearly, his implicit research design participates in the features of imperial knowledge: it was transnational in scope; it entailed an enhanced visibility to the question of the transfer of "American government"; and it was certainly a type of useful knowledge, providing principles of foreign policy and guidance in colonial and neocolonial situations.

Transdisciplinary Implications of Machu Picchu

Hiram Bingham's research program in Peru developed out of the organization of the Yale Peruvian Expedition (YPE). At the beginning, the expedition's center of interest was the reconnaissance of archaeological sites, particularly those relating to Inca culture. During the first year of exploration, the expedition focused on archaeology, geology, and topography. Bingham, assisted by the naturalist Harry W. Foote and the engineer Herman L. Tucker, identified and described sites of archaeological interest, among them Machu Picchu, the temple of Yuracrumiu, Vitcos, Vilcapampa, and the ruins near Cuzco.[8] They located the sites, drew plans for each building, and reflected on the possible antiquity and use of each construction. The geographer Isaiah Bowman took samples of soil and gravel to determine the age of each subterranean layer and searched for traces of past glaciations. The topographer Kai Hendriksen drew up maps of the area and plans of the ruins.[9]

In January 1914, after the first stage of the YPE had been completed, Bingham announced plans for expanding the research that transcended both disciplinary and geographic boundaries.[10] The area of research was no longer the Urubamba Valley, but the whole southern Peruvian Andes.[11] The expertise to be tapped included all disciplines that could contribute to a comprehensive view of the region's problems. Understanding of Inca culture was still the central issue, yet the expedition now incorporated a curiosity about "living Indians." Bingham's quest turned to questions of geological formations, natural resources, indigenous cultures, and geographic accidents. With regard to archaeology, his plans were exceedingly optimistic. He expected that interdisciplinary collaboration could "unravel the puzzle of the ancient civilization of South America" (Hiram Bingham 1914d, 677). The newly discovered sites led him to imagine an ambitious and expansive research design. He was now intrigued by questions of Inca agriculture, building methods, metallurgy, roads, tax collection, forms of conquest, and so forth. In this, he was trying to outdo the work of William Prescott or Sir Clements Markham.

By 1915, the YPE had become a large multidisciplinary research enterprise that had overstepped the original interest in Inca ruins and archaeology. At the end, when Bingham decided to abandon the excavation work, he left a researcher in charge of making anthropological and linguistic observations in the selvatic region east and south of the Urubamba Valley. The original archaeological interests expanded into a multiplicity of disciplinary questions. As explained by Bingham, to understand the culture and way of life of the Incas, the archaeologist would require the assistance of geographers, biologists, linguists, historians, and architects. The whole area was now conceived as a reservoir of new evidence for a variety of scientific disciplines. The YPE program now embraced topography, archaeology, geographic reconnaissance, zoology and botany, pathology and anatomy, meteorology, anthropology, linguistics, and economic geology.[12]

Ambitious and interdisciplinary, Bingham's research vision entailed a temporary occupation of the field—the Urubamba Valley—by U.S. researchers. Unlike other disciplines, archaeology is a territorial science that demands prolonged settlement near the "sites." Once discovered, the ruins needed to be uncovered. Territorial occupation and labor demands were bound to present troubles to the YPE. Most of the work of the archaeological branch of the YPE consisted of excavations to uncover "archaeological treasures." There followed activities of classification, labeling, and packaging. In addition, Bingham and Foote photographed indigenous peoples and ruins on a daily basis. These two activities must have appeared quite intrusive to local inhabitants.

For several reasons, Andean archaeology, as conceived by the YPE, was the most imperial of research designs. It entailed the occupation of land in the Urubamba Valley. The clearing of the Machu Picchu buildings demanded months of arduous work, which took laborers away from the surrounding haciendas. The presence of the YPE team disturbed traditional interactions between hacendados and peons, and triggered the reaction of local indigenistas and other cultural nationalists. What the YPE wanted—that is, to incorporate Machu Picchu as a free territory for international science—was clearly an overt form of colonial intrusion, one that transferred the enunciatory authority about Peruvian antiquity to university centers in the U.S. Northeast.

Mapping Latin America

Isaiah Bowman's geographic projects were ambitious in scope and dimension. He moved from topographical and physiographic recognition of the central Andes to sponsoring the drafting of a massive collection of maps of Hispanic America. Then he engaged in collaborative work destined to identify frontiers of recent settlement around the world. All of these projects underscored the power of geography to present large amounts of information about regions and resources in an orderly fashion. He had carried into the southern Peruvian Andes a preconceived approach—William M. Davis's theory of geological cycles—yet, in the field, his research changed in the direction of geographical anthropology.

Bowman's first work in the Andes of southern Peru (1907–1913) proved that geographical diversity could be simplified by dividing the country into regions, according to land use and type of settlement. He divided Peru into four regions: the forest, the highlands, the coastal desert, and the eastern valleys. Applying geographical survey techniques, Bowman claimed to have captured the realities of Andean South America in a comprehensive and synthetic fashion. In particular, he claimed to understand the enduring relationship between natives and their natural environment. In the Atacama Desert, the diversity of soil conditions, climate, and land use could be used as a microcosm for a general study of human adaptation to harsh environments.

His early undertaking, the survey of the area along the 73rd meridian, convinced him of the necessity of a map of continental scope. The mapping of Hispanic America was a massive enterprise undertaken by the American Geographical Society (AGS), under Bowman's directorship. They set a goal of drafting a series of maps on a 1:1 million scale (collectively called the Millionth Map), which required much research and data gathering. Cartographers at the AGS used maps contributed by local geographical societies on the subcontinent, as well as new survey materials collected by U.S. firms in the region. For example, the "Caracas Sheet" (North C-19) was made possible by a donation of surveys and published materials from the petroleum companies. Missing information was completed with the help of aerial photographs provided by the Aeronautical Chart Service of the U.S. Air Force ("Caracas Sheet of the Map of Hispanic America" 1945, 312). It took the work of seven to eight compilers and drafters, working over twenty-five years (from 1920 to 1945), to complete the Millionth Map. The whole operation cost half a million dollars (Martin 1980, 72).

The maps of Hispanic America provided comprehensive visibility of the region and were useful instruments for U.S. investors, foreign-policy makers, and researchers. Promoters of Pan-Americanism considered them essential tools for the arbitration of border disputes. Bowman found that the arbitration of border disputes in South America required the same type of information as that used at the Paris Conference: historical background, legal claims, population settlements, and a map that could reflect these three elements. In addition, Bowman expected the map collection to foster the development of regional studies. Deposited at the AGS Library, the maps would attract the attention of geographers across the continent. Bowman wrote in 1946, "It was the promotion of scholarly studies in Hispanic America on the part of students everywhere on the Western Hemisphere that was the grand objective, and the map was one instrument of such study" (Bowman 1946, 320). By building a unique map collection, Bowman helped lay the foundations of Latin American studies in the United States.[13]

In 1935, at a meeting of the Pan American Institute of Geography and History, Bowman proposed the elaboration of a Pan-American atlas, a project of Humboldtian dimensions. He presented it as a cooperative undertaking of North and South Americans scientists that reflected the politics of Good Neighbor-hood: "It was not a proposal to learn how to use science to 'conquer' Latin America after the fashion of the German geopolitikers, but how to work together for common ends, and specifically how to do so through cultural exchange, trade, and general economic improvement" (Bowman 1942b, 649). The Atlas would be a gigantic inventory of hemispheric resources for development, cataloging plant and animal life, population, mineral deposits, water resources, and climatology. "With the millionth sheets for a base, comparable data on meteorology and climatology, water resources, economically important mineral deposits, soils, rock structures, culture and landscape, archaeology and anthropology, plant and animal life, population and the like, can be assembled on a comprehensive map of uniform scale" (ibid., 650). The AGS completed this atlas in 1941. That year, the New York chapter of the AGS presented the finished Atlas to the Pan American Institute of Geography and History at Lima, a gift from U.S. geographers to their poorer southern neighbors. The Atlas covered all the Americas; it was the accomplishment of Pan-American intellectual cooperation in the field of cartography. Only now the idea of a "hemispheric shell" was used to combat German geopolitics, a science at the service of Nazi international aggression.[14]

These ambitious cartographic enterprises—the Millionth Map and the Pan-American Atlas—were clearly instrumental to providing U.S. policy makers and investors with a comprehensive visibility of Latin America, its natural resources and economic potential. The practical utility of this type of knowledge was commended repeatedly by scientists, investors, and foreign-relations experts. Through these disciplinary interventions, U.S. geography expanded its influence to the whole territory of Latin America.

Assessing the Impact of U.S. Influence

In 1925 Clarence H. Haring presented a "Plan for Research on Economic Internationalism in the Caribbean Region" to Harvard's Bureau of International Affairs.[15] The plan contemplated interdisciplinary research in economics, history, diplomacy, and law in order to assist U.S. foreign policy in the region. A policy-oriented and cooperative inquiry, involving various departments of intellectual labor, could bring about more effective policy options for the Caribbean.[16] The research entailed putting a comprehensive type of knowledge at the service of empire. The object of study, "economic internationalism," referred to the economic penetration and consolidation of U.S. capital in the Caribbean. In a sanitized fashion, the term recuperated Woodrow Wilson's liberal internationalism together with Theodore Roosevelt's concerns about the region's perennial political instability and fiscal irresponsibility. Haring was candidly explicit about this. At the center of the research program were questions of property rights and the availability of natural resources required for the expansion and reproduction of U.S. economic interests in the Caribbean. The recommendations of the committee that approved this research plan are worth quoting.

> The members of the committee believe that scientific research on certain aspects of economic internationalism in Latin America, particularly in the Caribbean countries, will yield valuable results. The utilization of undeveloped resources, the control of raw materials, the protection of foreign investment, are only three of the numerous significant aspects of what may be called economic internationalism, but they are probably enough to indicate the commanding importance of this general topic, and to suggest its close relationship with problems of diplomacy, law, and government. The research calls for an intensive study of the economic, diplomatic, legal and historical aspects of this subject, in the area of most immediate interest to the United States.[17]

The research areas chosen were consistent with the strategic and economic interests of the United States: Mexico, Cuba, the Caribbean nations. In their effort to assert themselves, these nations might attempt to expropriate the assets of U.S. companies or to default on their external debts. To preempt these dangers, Haring proposed regional interdisciplinary research functional to the formulation of U.S. foreign policy.

Haring's concerns about U.S. investments in the Caribbean and Mexico were later projected onto South America. By 1927, he was working on a project entitled "Grounds of South American Attitudes towards the United States," which contemplated the study of three issues: (1) competitive trade methods in South America; (2) negative attitudes of South American merchants and officials to U.S. products and businessmen; and (3) the influence of foreign investment on commerce, with specific studies of Argentine railroads, the Peruvian Corporation, the American Packing Company in Argentina and Brazil, the United Fruit Company's investments in Central America, and oil companies in Colombia and Venezuela.[18] By studying foreign trade and investment in South America, Haring expected to understand better the interconnection between widespread anti-American feelings and the expansion of U.S. investment. The research program entailed collecting statistics about U.S. investments in South America and conducting interviews among managers of U.S. corporations in the region.

These two research designs—South American attitudes toward the United States and economic internationalism in the Caribbean—were to be the foundation for the Harvard Bureau of Economic Research on Latin America (1930–1932).[19] At the time, European industrial powers (England, France and Germany) were endeavoring to recover markets lost during the First World War, including those on the subcontinent; they used anti-American propaganda that damaged U.S. prestige in the region. So it was crucial to understand and overcome South Americans' "distrust" of the United States.[20] Haring's research designs were clearly targeted to the problems posed by the U.S. economic expansion in South America, at the expense of European traders and manufacturers.

Not All Revolutions Are the Same

The Roosevelt Corollary to the Monroe Doctrine stated clearly that the United States reserved the right to intervene every time that a small country, through its "misconduct" (whether fiscal disorder or revolution), brought about the possibility of European intervention.[21] In the Caribbean, revolutions were such a common feature of political life that they came to serve as a justification for U.S. interventions.[22] Many in the United States considered Haiti and the Dominican Republic, for instance, to be "lands of revolutions," where the transition from one government to another usually entailed a military coup engineered by power-hungry individuals. Having spent time discussing problems of government in subjugated territories, the political scientist Leo S. Rowe thought otherwise. Some revolutions in the region were not the result of the personal ambition of local dictators, but reflected the population's expectations for social and political change.

> There is a deeply rooted belief in the United States that there has been no such thing as orderly constitutional development in Latin America. We seem to accept, almost without question, the idea that the political history of these countries has been a long succession of revolutionary movements, and that there has been no continuity, no real orderly progress in the growth of political institutions. *Nothing can be farther from the truth.* It is true that there have been uprisings, all too numerous, due to personal political ambitions, but practically all the important revolutionary movements have had as deep a social and economic significance as our own Civil War. (Leo S. Rowe 1917a, 274)

By placing "Latin American revolutions" within U.S. misconceptions about the region, Rowe was reopening an important research question: whether the political cultures of Central and South America were in a transition toward democracy. To the extent that true revolutions reflected deep-seated demands of workers, peasants, and the middle sectors, these upheavals were indicators of underlying democratic aspirations.

Rowe called for a reexamination of Latin American revolutions in a comparative perspective. Political science needed to find out the details about underlying causes of revolutions, identify some basic regularities in government, and advance generalizations about the region's political development. He reframed the end of caudillo government in the Argentine Confederation (1852), the struggle between congress and the executive in modernizing Chile (1890), and the Mexican Revolution (1910–1917) as signals of important expansions in political rights and political participation. Political unrest, previously an argument for taking control of small Caribbean states, could become a window into a vast research program about the development of democratic government in Spanish America.

> It is a matter of very great importance that students of political science analyze with greater care than has hitherto been the case the causes of political unrest in certain sections of the American continent and we distinguish clearly between violent changes that have a deep social significance and those revolutionary movements that represent nothing more than the selfish ambitions of a few unscrupulous leaders. (Leo S. Rowe 1922, 7)

The Mexican Revolution, in particular, had given Rowe and other U.S. observers the distinct impression that underneath its violence and political instability were demands for greater political participation and for labor and social reforms. The revolution was the expression of genuine popular feeling against the misguided policies of Porfirio Díaz (Leo S. Rowe 1912). Díaz's authoritarian program of progress and order had caused widespread discontent among industrial workers, peasants, and middling rancheros. Industrial progress had created a militant working class, while the strengthening of police forces (the *rurales*) and of local *jefes políticos* increased the repressive powers of the state. By 1910, the Mexican people were no longer as ignorant and submissive as they had been in 1877. Therefore, autocratic rule ceased to be regarded by the Mexican people as necessary for the nation's progress (ibid.).

Understanding the differential political development of Spanish America could illuminate a more informed U.S. foreign policy in the future, Rowe pointed out. It was one thing to meddle in the domestic politics of small Caribbean and Central American nations; quite another to intervene in South American politics. These nations had experimented with republican government for at least fifty years. Improvements in education, public health, and municipal government constituted evidence of important institutional and social change in the ABC nations. Consequently, it was crucially important to ascertain whether revolutions were part of a learning process leading toward popular government, or if they were symptoms of a pathology affecting small and unstable republics. Political science had to go beyond the study of law and constitutional government, and concern itself with the existing variety of governments in relation to community ideals of good government. The topics that interested Rowe about South America were various, including municipal government, taxation, education reform, and urban sanitation. He saw these topics as indicators of the modernity of their political and social formations.

Rowe never formulated a full blueprint for the comparative study of revolutions in Latin America. His reflections, though, highlighted the importance and true dimension of this research problem. By stressing the difference between small local uprisings and large rebellions aimed at structural social and political reform, he shifted the problematic of government in Latin America, from teaching for self-rule to a more comprehensive understanding of the peculiar national dynamics of sociopolitical change.

Opportunity for Transnational Race Research

The sociologist Edward A. Ross was interested in processes of social change in comparative perspective, and traveled to a number of countries to gather evidence. His study of Andean societies (*South of Panama*, 1915) provided him with key concepts to contrast modern and premodern sociabilities. In Andean South America he encountered great landed estates, racial oppression, and vestiges of colonialism that he dubbed "medieval." In Argentina, by contrast, he found a society blessed by European immigration and in the process of rapid social and cultural modernization. These social panoramas helped him envision a transnational research agenda on questions of social hierarchy, social control, and—mostly unlike the other scholars here—race. In 1924 Ross contributed to the *Journal of Social Forces* a note titled "The Greatest Research Chance in the World." The paper argued for the need for international, cooperative research on "race crossing." To counter contradictory assertions about the degrading or strengthening effect of race mixture (usually based on flimsy evidence), Ross recommended a comparative survey of miscegenation. This work, too, would necessarily be transnational.

> As never before the world needs a great anthropological survey of the results of race crossing in those regions where it is going on or has recently

occurred. The enterprise would require a board of anthropologists, eth-
nologists and sociologists to work out the questionnaires which the field
workers would strive to obtain answers to, the measurements to be taken,
and the data to be sought. Then field expeditions should be sent into the
most instructive areas of race crossing, such as Hawaii, Tropical South
America, Brazil, Mexico, the South Seas, South Africa, the American
South, the West Indies, Egypt, Portuguese Africa, the Sudan. (Edward A.
Ross 1924, 550)

Though global in scope, the survey Ross had in mind concentrated on colonies, dependencies, or hinterlands of informal empire.[23] The colonial and the
neodependent world would provide the main laboratories of a racially informed sociology. The great universities should divide among themselves the
different world regions (ibid.). Ten years of sustained, cooperative, comparative survey research should render conclusive results about "race crossing" and
finally put to rest propositions based on stereotypes or elite prejudice.

Making Hispanic American History Your Own

After 1918, the U.S. historical profession witnessed the emergence of a group of
scholars who considered the comparative study of Hispanic American history
to be their own field. This extension of the spatial frontiers of what until then
was considered "American history" was clearly a response to the economic, political, and cultural expansion of the United States over Latin America. While
at the beginning the Hispanic American history group was mainly concerned
with revising the history of the Spanish empire, their project later extended to a
long-term comparative history of the Americas, a project that had two leading
figures: Eugene Bolton and Clarence Haring.[24] This project was extraterritorial
and comparative by design; it was conceived to provide a useful contribution
to foreign policy; and it was supposed to supply a *longue durée*, comprehensive
understanding of the region's history, a history that would overcome the limitations of national historical traditions.

In May 1937 Haring arrived in Buenos Aires to participate in the Second
Congress of the History of the Americas. He delivered the keynote address
before hundreds of historians from Argentina and Latin America. Titled "Race
and Environment in the New World," the address defended the project of a
parallel and comparative history of the Americas. The project, pioneered by
Herbert Bolton in his 1932 address to the American Historical Association, was
not popular at the time.[25] Haring explained how Anglo-America and Spanish

America had passed through similar experiences of colonial subjugation, independence wars, nation-building under republican principles, and modernization processes (urbanization, industrialization, universal education, etc.). He characterized this evolutionary progress in differentiated terms, arguing that the ABC republics had reached further, leaving their Andean neighbors behind.

At the center of Haring's 1937 address was the idea that similarities and differences between Hispanic America and Anglo-America stemmed from race and environment. Within Hispanic America also, these variables served to explain different historical trajectories. In the Andean nations race and environment conspired against rapid development and progress, whereas in the ABC nations convergence with the United States was a real possibility. But political developments in the early 1930s contradicted this expectation: the progressive South American nations fell back into old traditions of dictatorship and populism. The crucial difference between and betwixt the two Americas was to be found in the colonial period. To Haring, the Spanish colonial legacy held the key to understanding contemporary developmental differences. An institutional setting that provided colonial subjects with no experience in self-government made all the difference in explaining Hispanic America's contemporary backwardness.

Before presenting his essay, Haring explained to fellow historians why U.S. historians had identified and developed the field of Hispanic American history.[26] The reasons had to do with the politics of intellectual cooperation, with the common historical roots of the two Americas, and with the role of history in U.S. research universities. A comprehensive and cooperative history of the Americas promised to build connections among historians of the hemisphere. With time, historians would contribute to a commonwealth of knowledge that would help promote good will and cooperation among the peoples of the Americas. Moreover, U.S. historians recognized that the United States and the Hispanic American republics shared a common heritage: the influence of Spanish discovery and colonization. And their interest in Hispanic American history was also related to the expansion of historical studies in U.S. research universities. Harvard University had forty-six scholars providing instruction in all fields of history, including Europe, Hispanic America, and the Orient.

The interest in South America extended to the whole territory of the humanities. The object of desire was not just history, but the understanding of "Latin American culture." By the early 1930s, achievements in this area were significant. U.S. scholars were engaged in research in areas of archaeology, anthropology, and geography, from the Rio Grande to Patagonia (Haring 1937).[27] Bringing together the intellectual powers of various disciplines was essential to

Pan-American cooperation. In 1935 a permanent central Committee on Latin American Studies had been established in the United States to further cooperative research. Haring reported, "The ideal of this Committee, and the chief purpose of the Handbook of Latin American Studies, is to integrate research in adjoining, marginal areas to lower the barriers which separate their conventional, academic fields of scholarship, and to emphasize the *unity of the study of Hispanic American culture*" (ibid., 3; emphasis added). To Haring and other promoters of intellectual cooperation—clearly Leo S. Rowe, but also historians such as Herbert Bolton, Arthur Whitaker, Charles Hackett, J. Fred Rippy, John Tate Lanning, and Irving Leonard, among others—only the cooperative efforts of various disciplines could produce the complementarities needed for understanding the true location of Latin and South America in the historical development of the hemisphere.[28]

To the historians gathered at Buenos Aires, Haring proposed a continental history committed to finding the similarities and differences in the trajectories of the two Americas. This comprehensive history had to be a collaborative endeavor. In such a project national historians residing in South America had a role to play: that of providing the raw material for the grander narrative of the history of the Americas. Implicit in this communication was a division of labor that subalternized (marginalized and made subsidiary) local and national histories.

Grand Designs: Business Expansion and Interdisciplinarity

Interdisciplinarity was basic to the research programs of all of these Hispanic Americanists.[29] Haring, Rowe, Bowman, and other U.S. scholars made efforts to build a multidisciplinary apparatus for the study of the region. To an extent, they created the institutional infrastructure and the motivating forces for Latin American studies, perhaps one of the first "area studies" to emerge in the United States. This development accompanied and reinforced the expansion of U.S. direct investment and trade in the region.

Yale University and the National Geographic Society joined to launch a vast, multidisciplinary research program in the southern Peruvian Andes. Yale historian and archaeologist Hiram Bingham's research design entailed taking over the Urubamba Valley and its surrounding area in ways that affected Peru's sovereignty over its archaeological sites. His program of research was both interdisciplinary and imperialistic. In his view, the hidden citadel of the Incas held the key for correcting the inherited history of the Spanish conquest and, indirectly, for better understanding the origins of humanity in South America. Harvard historian Clarence Haring directed his efforts to build a comparative history of the two Americas. His project focused on the historical forces that accounted for the convergence or divergence in the developmental paths of Anglo-America and Spanish America. To him, South America's most advanced nations (the "ABC powers") were converging toward the U.S. standard of living and modern culture. This was not the case with the Andean nations, whose economies and cultures remained impaired by the colonial experience.

Political scientist Leo Rowe delineated a vast field for the study of colonial governance. From the design of government institutions and legislation in new colonial situations, he moved to the question of the adaptability of "American government" to Hispanic American political culture. Later, his encounter with South America presented him with new issues and problems: among them, economic progress, municipal government, public opinion, and federalism. Revolutions, Rowe suggested, held the key to ascertaining whether the Latin American republics were making progress in their political evolution toward democracy. From his first visits to the region (1907–1909), geographer Isaiah Bowman thought of the Andes of Southern Peru and the Atacama Desert as two great laboratories or great reservoirs of information for the study of the relationship between humans and their environment. He pioneered a method of survey that allowed him to detect differences in land use in large portions of the Peruvian Andes. Data about climate, irrigation systems, plant life, and human settlements could be summarized and used to produce ideal regions. By defining homogeneous subregions according to a typology of human settlements, geography could provide a comprehensive understanding of the western countries of South America.

How did these great designs relate to foreign policy? Implicit in the researchers' formulation of research objectives and the transnational scope of their inquiries were questions that preoccupied the U.S. foreign-policy establishment: the role the United States should play in relation to the "southern republics," the contemporary relevance of the Monroe Doctrine, and the degree to which the South American nations might absorb U.S. economic and technological modernity. Sometimes the connection between policy objectives and research designs was more explicit and direct. In Haring's research proposals we find an attempt to interweave knowledge, foreign policy, and business enterprises. His program on "economic internationalism" was a clear example of multidisciplinary studies at the service of U.S. foreign policy and U.S. economic expansionism.[30]

The arguments these scholars used to "sell" the need for interdisciplinary, regionally based research to foundations, university authorities, and business leaders are worth examining as further evidence of their import to foreign policy. The structures of knowledge implanted in the aftermath of the First World War persisted after 1939, though the Second World War and then the Cold War presented a quite different scenario and motivation for research. When Haring, as director of the Bureau of Economic Research on Latin America at Harvard, wanted to show the importance of doing comprehensive research on the economics and history of Latin America, he underscored three things: (1) the field as a vacuum of knowledge; (2) the absence of a comprehensive hemispheric history and economics; and (3) the intersection between academic and business interests in the making of regional knowledge. So far, neither political economy nor sociology had advanced in studying business activities in the region. In this territory, where national economic interest—in particular, the conditions for the expansion of U.S. business interests in South America—and academic curiosity converged, there was much work to be done.

> The business interest of the U.S. in South America has of recent years vastly increased. *We have advanced from the period of adventure to that of permanent and extensive commercial and financial relationships.* Yet in view of its importance to us, in both the political and the economic sphere, it is surprising that today in this country there is virtually no specialized study of economic relations. Such things as the observation of business cycles in Latin America, and the construction of economic barometers, have never been given much attention; and the number of economists who know anything at all about Latin America is negligible.[31]

To Haring interdisciplinary research in law, economics, and history should follow the path of economic flows. In this way, new knowledge of the societies recently incorporated into the sphere of U.S. economic influence might facilitate the expansion of informal empire. Though the necessity of further knowledge was predicated on existing and continuing "economic relations" between the United States and Latin America, at the basis of such academic design was a discourse about the absence of scientific research in the region and the corresponding superiority of interdisciplinary expertise in U.S. universities. By design, this argument rested on the assumption that local knowledge was lacking in both scientific methods and modern library resources.

Conclusion

In the aftermath of the First World War, U.S. scholars imagined vast research projects, whose scope comprised the Andean region, South America, the hemisphere, even the world. The grandiosity of these projects reveals a comprehensive, imperial vision. Implicit in these designs was the notion that U.S. knowledge-producers could acquire hemispheric or global visibility and, as a result, make the hemisphere more understandable and legible. Their research designs, rooted in established scholarly disciplines, tried to generate useful knowledge for the formulation of U.S. foreign policy. Some of them (Haring's and Rowe's) were directly interwoven with the cultural machinery of Pan-American cooperation. Others (Ross's and Bowman's programs) aimed for a more global visibility.

Bowman's geographic studies were perhaps the most ambitious, in terms of scope. He started with physiographic studies of the southern Andes, moved to the production of a map collection of Hispanic America, and then to an atlas of continental scale. By interconnecting studies in economics, history, law, and diplomacy, Haring expected to create a new configuration of knowledge adapted to the needs of the new U.S. Caribbean empire. For South America he designed a research program focused on the attitudes of local inhabitants toward the United States and the behavior of U.S. corporations in the region. In addition, he envisioned a program in the comparative history of the Americas that privileged questions of convergence and divergence in historical trajectories.

Edward Ross's social panoramas of the Andean nations highlighted a few important research questions that would later become central to Latin American studies: indigenous oppression, landlordism, race, and the persistence of unpaid labor. His views about the Andean nations showed important similarities to those of geographer Bowman, underscoring problems of economic backwardness, political fragmentation, and the enduring legacy of Spanish colonialism. Rowe's early works established the bases for an inquiry into the constitutional, legal, and cultural aspects of U.S. colonial governance. The reality of "South American progress," however, shifted his interest toward questions of democratic sociability, the tension between political ideas and social formations, and the role of city government in transitions toward "American democracy."

Four of the five scholars made clear gestures toward interdisciplinarity. Bingham, a historian-geographer turned archaeologist, felt that only the joint effort of various disciplines could unravel the mysteries of the ancient civilizations of the central Andes. Interdisciplinarity seemed to have developed in the field—in team discussions at the camp in Ollantaytambo. The deployment of U.S. researchers in the southern Peruvian Andes promised results in various branches of knowledge. The same could be said about geographer Bowman. His "science of settlement" called for the coordinated mapping of world regions, and this required the cooperation of demographers, agricultural engineers, geographers, and ethnographers. Similarly, historian Haring proposed a strictly hemispheric research in which historians would cooperate with linguists, anthropologists, geographers, legal experts, and economists,

The research designs examined shared the features—extraterritoriality, expanded visibility, and foreign-policy usefulness—that make scholarly undertakings "imperial." Regional history could be used as a platform to argue about the advantages of informal, indirect influence versus territorial dominion. Regional geography provided the maps, the regional subdivisions, and the characterizations that made "South America" readable—not just according to expert expectations, but also in relation to Washington's ideas of governability. Regional archaeology presented the possibility of an extensive research into the resources and history of the Peruvian Andes. A political science at the service of hemispheric visibility should look at the important economic and social changes that created new political actors, new sensibilities, and new demands for reform. These academic designs produced hemispheric and global visions that tended to concentrate the resources needed for understanding inter-American affairs in U.S. universities and learned societies.

FOUR

Yale at Machu Picchu: Hiram Bingham, Peruvian *Indigenistas*, and Cultural Property

―――

The ruins of the city of Machu Picchu are situated on a plateau at an altitude of 2,000 feet. We discovered it by following some Peruvian Indians up a narrow goat path. . . . I believe that *we were the first white men to gaze on the city of Machu Picchu since Pizarro went there 400 years ago.* The white granite stones used in the foundation of the temple measured 8 by 12 feet, and were well chiseled and beautifully joined without mortar in Egyptian style. —HIRAM BINGHAM, interviewed by the *New York Times*, 11 December 1911 (emphasis added)

In 1913 *National Geographic Magazine* trumpeted the news of the "discovery" of Machu Picchu in 1911 by professor Hiram Bingham of Yale University. Newspapers large and small across the United States spread the story. Due to the sagacity of the Incas, Machu Picchu had remained hidden from white view for almost four centuries. Hence, the headline adopted by Bingham and the newsmen: "The Lost City of the Incas." Editors and columnists framed the event as part of the imperializing impetus they attributed to scientific endeavors overseas. Quite often, the word *discovery* appeared near the word *conquest*. Implicit in the reports of the discovery of Machu Picchu was the understanding that a U.S. American, a man of science, a professor at Yale University, had begun a *second conquest of South America*. Made possible by the association between business and science, the discovery promised to reveal the secrets of an ancient Peruvian civilization, misunderstood by prior white conquerors.

Newspapers reported Bingham's achievement in terms of race, gender, and nationalism. Bingham was the first *white man* to have seen the marvelous granite walls of the "lost city" since the times of Francisco Pizarro, his mere gaze transforming the event into a "scientific discovery." The fact that "natives" knew about the existence of such ruins carried little significance. Also important was the fact that when Bingham had climbed Mount Coropuna, the "second highest mountain of South America," he got there before the female mountaineer Anny Peck from Harvard (Hiram Bingham 1912a). And by planting the Yale flag on Mount Coropuna, Yale University symbolically took possession of a new field of study—the Southern Peruvian Andes—from European men of science.[1]

The story and the images of Machu Picchu fired up the U.S. imagination. The story seemed to reopen the old question of the Spanish conquest from a completely different perspective. Here was an ancient American civilization that had resisted Spanish colonialism until the end, maintaining a whole city hidden from the gaze of the colonizer. Projected into the landscape of mass-consumer capitalism, the second conquest of Peru attracted a wide variety of interests. News companies wanted to send reporters to Peru. Book publishers wanted to include pictures of Machu Picchu in geography textbooks. Hunting clubs and naturalists suddenly developed an interest in collecting mammals in South America. Shipping companies started to plan for an increase in the number of travelers to Peru. Mining companies tried to decipher the riddle of "Inca metallurgy." Surgeons began to inquire about Inca cranial trephinations. And the U.S. Department of Agriculture developed an interest in Inca roads and terrace farming.

In Peru the reception of the Yale Peruvian Expedition (YPE) proved problematic. A group of local amateur historians and archaeologists managed to disturb and slow the advance of this project of knowledge, questioning the legitimacy of Yale University's presence in the Urubamba Valley. Between 1912 and 1916 *cuzqueñistas* and indigenistas waged a battle for the control and ownership of cultural assets. Peruvian antiquity, they claimed, belonged to Peru and should be under the strict supervision of the Peruvian state. With the support of the press and a wink from the central government, the local intelligentsia created an unfriendly environment for the Yale group, which translated into delays, red tape, and lack of cooperation.

In this chapter I examine Bingham's subsequent YPE—a vast enterprise focused on the Southern Peruvian Andes—as a way to understand the cultural apparatus of informal empire. Like the U.S. newspapers, Peruvian media rumors framed the expedition as an imperial intrusion, associating Bingham's scientific endeavors not with triumph but with colonial pillage and mining imperialism. The rumors disrupted the initial cooperation between the Yale scientists and the cuzqueño intelligentsia—a small number of amateur archaeologists, university students and professors in Cuzco—and young indigenistas. (Indigenismo was a politicocultural movement that attempted to improve the condition of contemporary indigenous peoples while claiming pre-Columbian civilizations as part of the nation's heritage).[2] In spite of the impressive armature supporting the expedition, Bingham was ultimately unable to counter local opposition.

The Armature of Scientific Conquest

The YPE was an impressive scientific endeavor, unprecedented in its scope and ambitions. Other scientists had been part of the enterprise of knowledge in South America. There was William C. Farabee, an ethnologist from Harvard, collecting materials for the Philadelphia Museum in the Peruvian Amazon. Adolphe Bandelier, the famous Harvard ethnographer, had previously worked in Lake Titicaca, Bolivia. In 1906–1909 Max Uhle had collected artifacts for the museums of Berkeley and Berlin. But the YPE set out to map all the archaeological sites in the Urubamba Valley, comprehensively survey the geology and topography of the Southern Peruvian Andes, photograph and measure "natives," study local botany and zoology, and set up meteorological stations. As Bingham explained to the Yale president Arthur Twining Hadley in 1914, "It is not only archeology, but also work on topography, geology, meteorology, biology, anthropology."[3] The YPE shared with U.S. expansionism an insatiable desire for knowledge.

Indeed, both the newsmen and the Peruvian opposition were right: YPE was an enterprise of conquest, a moment when business and scholarship united in the construction of the U.S. informal empire. First, the project incorporated Peru and the Andean region into the U.S. sphere of scientific observation. At one point, for example, Bingham entertained the idea of establishing an "International School of American Archeology" at Cuzco. U.S. archaeology, already contending for primacy in Greece, Rome, Jerusalem, New Mexico, and Central America, could now conquer a new frontier: Andean South America. Like the international schools of Athens and Rome, Bingham thought, Cuzco would attract the attention of intellectuals from around the world.[4] This would be a golden opportunity for Yale University to establish a branch in the Andes, with the financial support of U.S. business. As Yale would not support this idea, Bingham tried to sell it to the Archaeological Institute of America, a Washington-based institution that shared Bingham's view about the need for U.S. archaeological expansionism abroad.

Second, the YPE acted as a multinational corporation with regard to its object of study. U.S. scientists saw the Peruvian Andes as simply a reservoir of knowledge, a treasury of facts, they might profitably exploit. In the same way that promoters of Pan-Americanism or U.S. mining companies talked about the natural resources of South America, the members of the expedition referred to Peru as "their" field of study. Reading to what Aleš Hrdlička (a member of the YPE) had to say about Peru, one wonders about the separation between the rhetoric of business and knowledge.

> The country is *a vast store-house of facts as well as specimens*, and I should like to see at least some of *our institutions engaged there.* . . . Should you ever decide to go back and send some archaeologists, I should be glad to give exact information regarding a number of localities easily accessible where *good collections could be made at moderate expense.*[5]

Good collections at low cost of extraction, vast deposits to be exploited, an opportunity for U.S. presence: if we were to substitute *minerals* or *natural resources* for "facts and specimens," we would get the same discourse that John Barrett had been promoting since the early 1900s and that U.S. business interests shared. South America was a good "field of opportunity" for business and science alike to conquer.

Third, this scientific mission shows the interconnection between business and knowledge in the age of informal empire. The YPE was facilitated by the prior penetration of U.S. capital in the region (in transportation, petroleum, rubber, mining, etc.), while new technologies (especially photography) enhanced the observation and surveying capacity of U.S. explorers. But the collaboration between scientific discovery and business enterprise went well beyond that. The YPE was a scientific venture supported by the business community. Though the principal funds came from the National Geographic Society, corporate interests contributed equipment, know-how, and publicity. Kodak Company supplied the expedition with photographic cameras, film, and development equipment. Waltham Watch Company provided chronometers and astronomical watches. Winchester Repeating Arms Company supplied small weapons. Once on Peruvian soil, the expedition received intelligence, manpower, and social connections from W. R. Grace and Company, the largest U.S. trading firm in South America. Rubber prospectors contributed information about the Southern Peruvian jungle, while U.S. "railroad men" were essential in negotiations with the Peruvian government.

Chapter 4

Moreover, the infrastructure of foreign capital paved the road to Cuzco. The members of the expedition traveled in United Fruit steamships, at subsidized cost. Personnel from W. R. Grace & Company transported equipment, clearing it through customs, and took care of monetary arrangements in Lima. The Peruvian Corporation provided scientists with free train tickets from Arequipa to Cuzco and later contributed an agricultural expert to collect plants. The Inca Mining Company, which had helped to establish the Harvard Observatory in Arequipa, provided the team with valuable meteorological information. The managers of W. R. Grace and of Cerro de Pasco Mining supplied intelligence about political conditions in Lima.

Indeed, the interpenetration of business and science was remarkable. In the preliminary stages of the expedition, the geographer Isaiah Bowman suggested installing a line of meteorological stations in the Peruvian Cordillera to map the region's temperature, barometric pressure, winds, and rainfall.[6] U.S. and British mining companies shared his interest in this data and persuaded the Harvard College Observatory to send meteorological equipment to Peru. The equipment went to the "Inca Mining Co." and the "Inca Rubber Co.," two firms that helped to set up the equipment and later took responsibility for the measurements.[7] The observatory at Arequipa would centralize this information and distribute it among the users. U.S. and British capitalists, Yale and Harvard, all cooperated to create a thorough meteorological knowledge of southern Peru.

The question of "Inca metallurgy" is another instance of business-knowledge cooperation. In 1914 Bingham tried to disprove the preconception that Inca bronzes were "accidental."[8] He needed to show that copper and tin were rarely found together in a natural state and that, consequently, the bronzes must be the product of Inca metallurgy. To prove his point, Bingham drew on the expertise of U.S. and English mining engineers. Edmond Guggenheim wired Bingham's question to his company's experts. Representatives of the Braden Company in Chile got interested, initiating an inquiry among the region's foreign engineers and mineralogists. So did Cerro de Pasco Mining. In response, Bingham received letters dated in mining towns of Bolivia (Corocoro), Southern Peru (Chuco), and northern Chile.

The information sent by the Braden Company expert in Chile, the engineer Alfredo Sundt, helped Bingham to solve the enigma. Copper-tin amalgamation was common to Bolivia, he said: first indigenous peoples and then the Spaniards had used it to make everything from church bells to cooking utensils. But it was not natural. Nobody had ever found minerals in which copper was allied with tin.[9] Therefore, Inca bronzes were "artificial" amalgamations.

Yale at Machu Picchu

More than that, said the engineer Tarnawiecki, from Cerro de Pasco Mining at Chuco, after analyzing the samples: Inca bronzes were a metallurgical miracle.[10] Working with minerals containing tin in a concentration of 5 to 1, the Incas were able to get a bronze with only 6 percent of tin. Inca command of metallurgical techniques was admirable.

Cooperation was essential to this enterprise of knowledge.[11] At the request of Bingham, U.S. business firms mobilized their personnel to solve the problem of Inca bronzes, a technical puzzle about Peruvian antiquity. A Yale mission helped Harvard to establish a chain of meteorological stations that, in turn, provided accurate information to road builders, mining companies, and rubber tappers. Bowman's morphological and geological survey of the 73rd meridian contributed an inventory of natural resources in the central Andes.[12] Two additional instances of cooperation proved crucial to the YPE: Kodak provided the expedition with key technologies for recording ancient Peru, while the National Geographic Society helped the expedition disseminate its results among the U.S. reading public.

Photography, Ruins, and Advertising

Kodak had pioneered the use of advertising to create markets. Its success in the marketplace owed much to its campaigns persuading the U.S. public that photography was a "pleasurable and necessary component of modern life" (West 2000, 19–35). The primary message of Kodak advertisements was that everybody could use a Kodak camera to capture almost all aspects of quotidian life. Advertising modernity as an attainable, democratic good had made Kodak the leading firm in the trade. Advertisements portraying explorers, however, were not common before the YPE.

Kodak supported Bingham's exploration for reasons related to product development and marketing. Executives took the YPE as an opportunity to experiment with new cameras and film-developing methods in the adverse conditions of "the tropics." They wanted to know how their newest equipment performed in damp, tropical valleys or at high altitudes. In three expeditions to Peru (1911, 1912, and 1914–1915), Bingham tried successively the A3 and the A3 Special, the Panorama, and the Cirkut cameras. Members of the expedition tested also the Kodak "tank developer" to develop film on the spot, and quite naturally, they used only Kodak paper for their prints. Results were adequate but not remarkable.[13]

Images of U.S. explorers carrying Kodak cameras into their "fields" could also be used for advertising purposes.[14] If consumers could see that Kodak cameras functioned well in inaccessible regions of the world (such as the North Pole, in the Amazon jungle, or in the Peruvian highlands), much value could be added to these products. And Bingham himself took care to disseminate his archaeological and historical finding using photographs, giving Kodak a reputation as a firm supporting U.S. scientific exploration. In an article in *Harper's Weekly* (1912), Bingham mentioned that he had used a 3A camera at an altitude of 21,000 feet. A subsequent article in *National Geographic* (1913) contained 200 photos, "all taken with the Kodak," and was a publicity hit.[15] That issue of the magazine, entirely devoted to Machu Picchu, sold at least 126,000 copies. Because of this success, Kodak included the Peruvian panoramas in its own promotional campaigns. In July 1914 the company added these pictures to its "touring exhibition" across the United States.[16] Later, in 1915, the company contributed these photographs to the Panama-Pacific Exposition at San Francisco, a quite popular event. The advertising returns were certainly greater than those garnered from product experimentation.

The supply of cameras, film, and development equipment reduced the cost of production of images for the expedition. Photographs were an important YPE objective. It was expected that pictures circulated later among other research centers could help to decipher the mystery of Peruvian antiquity. According to a catalog published in 1915, more than 12,000 photographs were taken during the three Yale expeditions. Of those, 3,000 were of ruins, 4,000 dealt with the physical or geographical features of the region, 1,000 depicted Indian types, and 1,000 portrayed customs and social life (Hiram Bingham 1915). Without exaggeration, the YPE became a machine producing mass images of Peru. Back in the United States, these images would have multiple uses.[17] They helped the public visualize Peru and its ruins; large photographs would be exhibited in the National Geographic Museum, in the Hispanic Society of America, and in the Pan-American Exhibition. Bingham himself used Peruvian photographs to illustrate his classes at Yale and his lectures to numerous scientific societies in the Northeast. Other members of the expedition used these photographs to illustrate articles about Andean geography, archaeology, ancient medicine, animal and plant life, and geology.

Dissemination: The National Geographic Society

The National Geographic Society (NGS) was the most important financial sponsor of the YPE. Its publications provided ample publicity to the discoveries of the expedition, elevating Bingham to the status of popular hero. Because of its role as mediator between science and the U.S. people, the society was a central component of the armature of scientific conquest. *National Geographic Magazine*, with its plainly narrated articles and colorful pictures, presented the discovery of Machu Picchu and the work of the YPE as an extension of the desires of U.S. Americans.

The objectives of the NGS in supporting the expeditions were clearly stated in the contract signed with Yale University in May 1912. In exchange for financially supporting the expedition, the NGS acquired the "exclusive rights in the first popular story of the Expedition." When the NGS and Yale University signed a second contract, in 1914, the same clause applied. Against its financial contributions, the NGS would receive "a *popular article* of 6,000 to 7,000 words, written by the Director of the Expedition, describing in a *popular form* the results of the expedition."[18] The repetition of the word *popular* underscored the importance of translating the results of scientific exploration into the language of the people.

A "popular story," that was all the NGS wanted. Not just any story—a story with pictures about early man in South America. Visualization was central to the aims of the NGS. The U.S. informal empire was not only a social formation dominated by "print-photo capitalism," it was also a democratic sort of empire, in which people needed to connect visually with the lands recently "rediscovered."[19] The legibility and translation of its new informal hinterland was done in the name of the "American public." Gilbert Grosvenor, director of the NGS, contributed to the overall design of the YPE. It was Grosvenor who persuaded Bingham that "ruins, lost cities, and bones"—rather than geological surveys and geographical descriptions—were what the public wanted.[20] The discovery of Machu Picchu had touched a chord in U.S. sensibility and created a venue to exploit. The U.S. people, according to Grosvenor, were interested in ancient humanity in South America.

> What we particularly want is "meat," *facts and information* rather than personal movements of various members of the party—as much information as you can give *on these ancient peoples and of the new cities* which you have discovered. I don't care particularly for a detailed account of mapping, etc., but want *everything that is of human interest*. Be sure and tell us as much as possible of Machu Picchu and your surmises as to the manners, life and civilization of the ancient people who built this remarkable city.[21]

Grosvenor talked of South America as "the New World," in the same way colonizing Europeans had spoken of the Americas four centuries before. Now it was the turn of modern America to discover its southern neighbors. The modern United States was a mass society demanding information. Readers wanted to know about ancient peoples, their temples and cities; they were in search of their own antiquity. The United States deserved to have within its orbit of influence its own Rome or Athens.

The NGS played a key role in the popularization of the expeditions and also contributed funds for the publication of the scientific papers that derived from it. Publication was the main business of the society. In fact, as accurately described by Grosvenor, the NGS was a busy printing factory of popular geographic knowledge: "Six big, and most modern presses working night and day, week in and week out, are not able to take care of the job."[22] Popular demand for curiosities about faraway lands in visual form kept the machines of *National Geographic Magazine* running.[23]

Skirmishes over Cultural Property

Between 1911 and 1915, the relationship between Hiram Bingham and the local Peruvian intelligentsia dramatically deteriorated. Early partners in the discovery of Peruvian antiquity soon turned into adversaries contending over the ownership of cultural assets. Though other factors prepared the terrain for the emergence of cultural nationalism—in Cuzco, at least, these included the reform of the university, the modernization of the city, and the crisis of the wool trade—it is clear that the YPE helped to congeal a regional and national opposition against U.S. scientific explorations. The strong reaction of the cuzqueño and Limeño intelligentsia against the "pretensions" of the Yale mission contributed to create a consciousness among Peruvian readers of the need to preserve "national antiquities." In cooperation, local antiquarians and early indigenistas pressed the Peruvian state to assume a new role: that of broker between universalizing science and local-regional knowledge.

The partnership had begun auspiciously. In June 1911 *El Comercio* (Cuzco) gave Bingham and his group of researchers an unconditional welcome.[24] The objectives of the expedition—performing topographical, astronomical, and archaeological observations—seemed transparent and innocuous to the nation. The members of the expedition—Bingham, Bowman, Kai Hendriksen, Harry Foote, and William Erving—were outstanding men of science, whose impeccable credentials left no doubts about their motivations. They were altruistic men who had come "to resolve enigmas of science."[25] More important, argued the paper, the work of the YPE would contribute to the "cause of progress," integrating the local intelligentsia into its project.[26]

The same reception awaited the group at Lima. When Bingham delivered a lecture before the Sociedad Geográfica (5 December 1911), "well-known

Peruvian professors, university students, and students of the Normal School for Men" gathered to welcome the Yankee discoverer.[27] Bingham explained to this cultivated audience Yale University's interest in Latin America, what he believed he had found in Machu Picchu, and the group's future research plans. His lecture, assisted by lantern slides, presented the audience with a comprehensive project of knowledge. Bingham spoke of the need to study all aspects of the Urubamba Valley, from paleontology to geology, from hydrography to osteology. In particular, there were two things he wanted to know: how far the Incas had gotten in the mountainous region, and whether the Ucayali River was fully navigable. His objectives, however grandiose, seemed "scientific" and nonintrusive. At the end of the talk, as it had happened in Cuzco, Limeño intellectuals felt they had been invited to participate in this project of knowledge. The gestures were clear. Bingham praised Machu Picchu as the "proof of the greatness of the Ancient Peruvian civilization" while Bowman credited two local scholars for their mapwork.

At the beginning, the Yale group also enjoyed the support of the Peruvian government (under Augusto B. Leguía) and the patronage of "good society." Bingham brought with him letters of recommendation to important notables in Cuzco and Lima (judges, physicians, clerics, military), preannounced the arrival of the expedition through local newspapers, and hired an influential lawyer (Cesar Lomellini, a counsel for the Peruvian Corporation and a cousin of President Leguía) to obtain the permit for the excavations.[28] At Lima, the NGS was so enthusiastic about the project of the YPE that they provided Bingham with a complete set of maps drawn from the Raimondi's Atlas. Meanwhile, at Cuzco, Albert Giesecke, the U.S. American rector of the university, assisted Bingham in drafting a map of the Cuzco Valley and interested his students in visiting the ruins of Machu Picchu. And the local intelligentsia gave Bingham a big welcome. The University of Cuzco asked him to deliver a lecture about Machu Picchu and the YPE. At a ceremony with all the signs of an international-relations event, Bingham delivered a speech, praising the progress of Cuzco and presenting his "discovery" as an advancement of science and humanity. After this, the local university granted him the honorary degree of Doctor in Letters. Bingham reciprocated, extending to Giesecke, now the president of the university, the Yale bronze shield.[29]

In the background of these public ceremonies, there was a growing discomfort about the presence of U.S. American scientists. The second expedition (June–December 1912) involved a greater degree of excavation work and, consequently, was more likely to attract public scrutiny. Increased notoriety also surrounded the concession that the Leguía government had granted to Yale

University, permitting excavation.[30] As the Peruvian congress and the new president failed to approve this concession, the work of the YPE proceeded in an environment laden with suspicion and debate. Soon, a disrespectful comment, attributed to Bingham and exaggerated by the local press, started to erode the initial enthusiasm.

In May 1912 *El Comercio* (Lima) reported that Bingham had warned foreigners about Cuzco's bad smell. *El Sol* (Cuzco) immediately published derogatory remarks it attributed to Bingham: "To walk along the streets of Cuzco, [the traveler] needs to make efforts to keep the balance and has to either carry various perfumes or close his nose with his fingers" [Para andar por las calles de Cuzco hay que hacer equilibrios y taparse las narices e ir pertrechado de pomos de esencias].[31] Apparently, the source of such information was Bingham's recently published book *Across South America* (1911), in which the author had portrayed Cuzco as "one of the dirtiest cities in America" (262). The alleged remarks produced great indignation among the Cuzco and Lima elites.[32] With a bit of irony, *El Sol* demanded that the municipal government make a greater effort to clean the city; otherwise, "neat North-American tourists" would start canceling their travel plans. While sharing Bingham's views that indigenous peoples were not up to U.S. American standards of cleanliness, the newspaper presented Cuzco as the Rome of South America. It was a city already installed in the imagination of the modern scientific traveler: a city holding treasures of ancient civilizations.

Between July and October 1912, the political situation turned around. Guillermo Billinghurst, a populist politician who seemed ready to confront the oligarchy, was elected president, raising the hopes of workers and indigenous peoples and signaling problems ahead for the YPE. The new president thought it a "disgrace" that Peruvians were unable to investigate "their own" ruins.[33] During Billinghurst's short period in office, some indigenistas and cuzqueñistas rose to prominent government positions in areas of culture and education. (Cuzqueñistas were intellectuals and publicists who asserted the importance of Cuzco in the history and politics of Peru, in part by valorizing local music, dance, theater, and literature.) This created a hostile environment for the Yankee explorers. So Bingham's petition for permission to excavate went down the bureaucratic ladder: from the congress to the Ministry of Education and then to the Instituto Histórico de Cuzco. Here, the YPE encountered its first clear opposition. The members of the institute wanted to supervise the activities of the YPE.[34]

To no avail Bingham tried to use the former president Leguía and the minister of justice as leverage. But his old allies were now suspected of corruption, and this placed Bingham in a difficult situation. Though the scandals of the former Leguía administration were chiefly financial, the question of cultural patrimony was also in the public eye. It was rumored that Max Uhle, a German archaeologist, the last director of the Museo Histórico at Lima, had "smuggled out of the country nine tenths of his discoveries." Hence, the members of the YPE came under suspicion of wrongdoing. (Bingham wrote, "All foreign archaeologists are in bad odor and we are probably no exception.")[35]

To counter the public perception that government paid no attention to the protection of "Peruvian antiquities," the new president appointed agents in different departments to act as custodians of national cultural assets. In Cuzco the appointment went to the people of the Instituto Histórico. The indigenista journalist and writer José Gabriel Cosio supervised the activities of the Yale mission and found no wrongdoing.[36] But he insisted that the YPE was working without the corresponding government permit, as established by the 1911 decree. For Bingham this meant only additional government red tape. From July to October 1912, Bingham spent more time than he expected in Lima, lobbying government.[37] Local bureaucrats, not accustomed to direct talk, were difficult to deal with. "This is a queer place, honeycombed with subterfuge and suspicion," he wrote to President Hadley of Yale.[38]

What at first sight appeared to be indifference or inexplicable delays turned soon into outright opposition. Only after much insistence, the new minister of justice told Bingham that he was opposed to the exportation of archaeological finds. He considered these artifacts "part of the riches of Peru" that should remain within the country. In October 1912, after months of unproductive lobbying, Bingham came to realize the obvious: there was actual hostility against the United States among the new leadership.[39]

On October 26, Bingham persuaded President Billinghurst to agree to an intermediate solution. In a new meeting with Billinghurst, Bingham and his ally W. L. Morkill, of the Peruvian Corporation, used heavy artillery. Morkill threatened the minister of justice with international discredit: "How unpleasant it would be for Peru to have us return to the States and say *we have been robbed of half our collections on a technicality*."[40] To compromise, Billinghurst promised a new decree that would grant permission for the YPE to excavate for the rest of the year. But he did not immediately sign the decree. A campaign *El Comercio* launched against the Yale contract caused the new government to postpone the new resolution. The newspaper claimed that granting exclusivity to Yale University for twenty years would prevent other men of science from investigating Peruvian antiquity. By the end of the month, however, the decree was finally signed and went into effect.[41] Bingham would now be able to export the bones and artifacts collected, but under quite severe limitations. The decree prohibited any excavation work after 1 December 1912, placed all excavation under the supervision of José Gabriel Cosio, and stated that all materials sent to the United States had to be returned to Peru within eighteen months. What offended Bingham the most was the warning that the YPE "should not mutilate or destroy the architectural monuments of Perú," which sounded like an official accusation that the Yale excavations had damaged the Inca ruins.[42]

By January 1913, Bingham and the rest of his team were back in the United States. A shipload with thirty-seven cases of osteological and archaeological materials was on its way to New York.[43] The remaining boxes, detained by customs officers at Mollendo for no apparent reason, took longer to arrive.[44] Measured against the favorable impact of the expedition in the U.S. media—*National Geographic* published the article about Machu Picchu with two hundred photographs to great acclaim—the opposition found in Lima and Cuzco seemed like a minor discomfort. In the United States, Bingham soon found himself transformed into a public figure. In a commemorative ceremony at the NGS in Washington in January 1913, he sat for a publicity photo with Robert Peary and Roald Amundsen, who, respectively, "discovered" the North Pole and the South Pole (Alfred M. Bingham 1989, 291). Bingham's fame, enhanced by his lectures in scholarly societies and elite clubs and by press interviews and notes that presented him as the "second/scientific conqueror" of Peru, gave him a new platform from which to address issues of political interest, such as the current validity of the Monroe Doctrine.[45]

Emboldened, Bingham started to organize a more encompassing expedition to Peru for 1914 and 1915. For this third expedition, the budget, which was greater than those allotted for the preceding expeditions, allowed him to add to his team additional experts—two botanists, a zoologist, a second topographer, and a surgeon acting as a physical anthropologist—and to widen the scope of the research. While planning for the new expedition, Bingham thought his team could either bypass the Peruvian government's prohibition on the exportation of Inca artifacts or, alternatively, examine the artifacts in the field. He imagined the new expedition as a convergent series of research efforts, including botanical and zoological collections and more ethnographic studies. None of this new work demanded government permission.

The third expedition (1914–1915) was a success in terms of discoveries: Bingham and his team located a dozen new ruins, discovered a fifty-mile Inca road, and found new glaciers.[46] The excavations also yielded a great deal of evidence. Members of the expedition gathered "a few mummies, quite a number of skulls, and several boxes of sherds from various localities."[47] Trepanned skulls, mummies in full burial clothing, and the "Inca trail" constituted the true treasure discovered by the expedition. In spite of their success in the field, however, the expedition was unable to counter bad publicity from the local intelligentsia. The YPE was encircled and trapped by rumors and could not deal with them. A small provincial institution, the Instituto Histórico de Cuzco, led by indigenistas, and the local newspaper *El Sol*, helmed by the prominent indigenista, historian, and anthropologist Luis E. Valcárcel, managed to discredit the Yale commission, presenting its members as pillagers of Peruvian ancient treasures.[48]

Rumors circulated that the U.S. Americans were exporting national treasures, bypassing governmental controls. Disguised as men of science, the members of the YPE were engaged in a deplorable commerce of Peruvian antiquities. With the intimidating presence of gendarmes and for a few cents, they were purchasing objects of great value from local Indians. In Cuzco *El Sol* raised an alarm about the loss of "national treasuries," as did *El Comercio* in Lima.[49] One of these rumors stated that the expedition had brought a steam shovel from the Panama Canal in order to unearth Inca treasures more quickly. Popular gossip claimed that the Yankees had already accumulated five million soles in Inca gold and were shipping this treasure out of the country via Bolivia.[50] Another version had it that the Yale explorers had purchased a golden idol sixteen inches high for only thirty soles.[51] The number of boxes smuggled out of the country, as well as the value of the "treasury," varied according to the storyteller.[52] To complicate matters, an unconfirmed report said that two images of Catholic saints, San Jerónimo and San Francisco, had disappeared from Cuzco churches.[53] And landowners charged that the excavations were luring away their workers.

At this point, the Instituto Histórico del Cuzco, led by prominent indigenistas such as Luis Valcárcel, the Cosio brothers, and Vega Enríquez, entered into the debate. The institute appointed a commission to investigate the allegations. This commission determined that, although there was no clear evidence that the YPE was exporting gold and silver objects through Bolivia, the foreign group was excavating without proper authorization and, in some cases, jeopardizing the security of ancient ruins. Bingham tried to convince the members of the Instituto Histórico that his excavations had not damaged Inca ruins, that they had not diverted labor from productive activities, and that the expedition had collected only scientific evidence.[54] But his arguments fell on deaf ears. His interlocutors—local cuzqueñistas and indigenistas gathered around the institute—took the occasion as a golden opportunity to promote cultural nationalism.

Chapter 4

In fact, they converted their own supervising activities into rites of national affirmation. On 1 July 1915, members of the Instituto Histórico confiscated and inspected four boxes of materials at the YPE camp. As Prefect Costa Laurent read the government decree, the indigenistas opened and inspected the boxes, carefully annotating their contents.[55] Bingham and his assistant William Hardy had to stand and watch as bits of pottery were unpacked and repacked, their tags getting mixed up in the process. The scene resembled a ritual restoration of sovereignty. Through the newly appointed *interventores*, it seemed, the Peruvian nation was reclaiming its precious cultural assets. Dedicated to their new mission, the indigenistas sent a delegation to La Paz to further inquire about the rumor that the YPE had already smuggled some of the "Inca treasure" out of the country.

Although the boxes were later returned to Bingham, local suspicion persisted. In July 1915 the government put the whole YPE deposit of archaeological remains at Ollantaytambo—which the locals now called Yanquihuasi—under surveillance. Later that year, the Instituto Histórico took more steps to stop the YPE activities, applying for a judicial injunction against the exportation of Inca artifacts. The members of the institute believed that the YPE had continued excavating, against the government's order.[56] This was an intolerable affront to Peruvian sovereignty. Luis Valcárcel, the director of the Instituto Histórico, took the opportunity to gain control of what he considered "national historical resources." That year, he presented to congress a bill that would ensure national control of archaeological resources by prohibiting new excavations without government authorization, by putting all the activities of foreign scientists in Peru under the control of Peruvian experts, and by absolutely forbidding the export of artifacts from the Inca or pre-Inca period.

By November 1915, the tension between Bingham and the local intelligentsia (indigenistas and cuzqueñistas) had reached the breaking point. Facing increasing opposition from these cultural nationalists and unable to counter the press campaigns against him, Bingham decided to stop all further research in southern Peru.[57] His refusal to continue the project reveals a sense of frustration and incomprehension. Although he tried to counter rumors with lectures and newspaper columns, Bingham could not defeat his "enemies." After he left Peru, the local opposition managed to obstruct the exportation of the archaeological materials for another year, impounding the last harvest of the expedition (seventy-four boxes with Inca bones, pottery, and mummies).[58] To reclaim the boxes and get them out of Peru, Bingham had to acknowledge in writing that all these materials were "Peruvian property" and had to be returned to Peru on request.[59] Before the boxes were shipped, the director of the National Museum,

Gutiérrez de Quintanilla, examined them, noting the importance of the tre-panned skulls as proof of the sophistication of Inca medicine. On 17 August 1916, all seventy-four boxes finally arrived in New Haven and were carefully stored in Yale's Osborn Hall.[60] In spite of claims to the contrary in Bingham's *Lost City of the Incas* (1948), Yale University failed to return the bones until recently.[61]

Indigenistas and Cuzqueñistas

What was the nature of the opposition the YPE encountered? The activities of the YPE seemed to threaten two key actors in the regional scene: the local intelligentsia and the landowners. University students and amateur collectors became, after Bingham's "discovery," zealous competitors in the enterprise of knowledge. Already in 1911–1912 Giesecke's students were invading the Yale camp, trying to participate in the experience of discovery. They considered the Urubamba Valley their own field of study. The local subprefect visited Machu Picchu and hurried to print a report before the results of the YPE reached the press. (In 1915, a group of cuzqueños claimed for themselves the discovery of the Huayna Kenti ruins, unaware that Bingham had claimed the same discovery in 1911.)[62] Local landowners, hacendados and *gamonales*, complained to the prefects that Bingham was taking away "their peons."[63] The higher salaries paid by the YPE were threatening to local employers: the expedition offered $1 a day, while hacendados offered 40 cents a day. More important, the expedition paid wages in cash, while local landowners paid wages in kind. It is also clear that hacendados did not approve of the YPE giving free medical attention to Indian peasants. This eroded their prestige as patrons and showed indigenous peasants a side of modernity that local landowners were not ready to embrace. To the gamonales, Yankee visitors seemed a more immediate menace, for they raised wages, defied traditional social hierarchies, and engaged peasants in the search for Inca artifacts.

Bingham did not talk of indigenistas or of cultural nationalists. He simply referred to them as "anti-foreign elements" and as "our enemies." To him, opposition to the YPE came from an amorphous group made up of antiforeign-ers, students and professors at Cuzco University, and political opponents of the Leguía government. Bingham's simplified view of the opposition made him unable to read through the maze of Peruvian politics. In fact, he never questioned why the students of his friend and supporter Giesecke had turned, all of a sudden, into rabid cultural nationalists. Bingham blamed his "bad luck"—the sudden change in government—for the obstacles facing the expedition. But more was at stake than a political turnaround.

Among those who opposed the YPE, we can distinguish two groups: the "antiquarians" and the "early indigenistas." In different ways both groups defended a cultural-nationalist position against foreign scientists and museum collectors. The director of the National Museum, Gutiérrez de Quintanilla, an antiquarian, demanded that the state take a stronger position to preserve "national treasures," and the cuzqueño indigenistas wanted to prevent the YPE from exporting Inca artifacts. Early indigenistas were directly involved in controlling the activities of Bingham and his U.S. American colleagues. In 1912 Gabriel Cosio was the commissioner appointed by the government to inspect the Yale group and its collecting methods. In August 1915 two leading indigenistas—Valcárcel, then the director of the Instituto Histórico, and Angel Vega Enríquez, the president of the Centro de Arte e Historia de Cuzco—traveled to Bolivia to assess the validity of rumors that Bingham was smuggling Inca artifacts through this country. Their denunciations filtered into the newspapers in Cuzco, Lima, and La Paz, generating intense debate about the ownership—Peruvian or international—of cultural assets.

Early indigenistas criticized their government, foreign scientists, and dealers in antiquities. They accused the government of failing to protect the country's cultural assets. They denounced foreigners for clearing out Peruvian archaeological sites. And they blamed native informants and merchants for facilitating the work of foreign scientists, by selling them valuable collections of *Incaica*. In this campaign of national affirmation, the press again acted as a powerful ally. The local newspapers *El Sol* (radical, sensationalist) and *El Comercio* (liberal, moderate) provided indigenistas and antiquarians with a platform for their denunciations.

The day after the indigenistas first visited the Yale camp at Ollantaytambo, *El Sol* published a shocking news story: "The Criminal Excavation of Machu Picchu: The Members of the Yale Commission Take Away Our Treasures" (Alfred M. Bingham 1989, 307). Bingham and his group were treated as criminals. They had defied the restraining order of the subprefect and were robbing the Peruvian people of their past ("Quitarle al Cuzco sus tesoros que testimonian su grandioso pasado es labor criminal y el pueblo mismo no lo debe tolerar").[64] In Lima *El Comercio* condemned the extraction and exportation of "Peruvian antiques" as an offense against the fatherland. While supporting the strong position taken by the Instituto Histórico de Cuzco in defense of Peruvian national culture, the article blamed the continued exportation of valuable Inca treasures on *huaqueros*. (Based on the word *huacos*, which means delicate ceramic pieces often found in ancient burial sites or near temples indicating association with indigenous religious or ritual practices, *huaqueros* refers to those who excavate, extract, and hence, pillage ancient burial grounds.)[65] A group of "unscrupulous persons" who practiced an "inadmissible commerce" for the benefit of foreign museums were damaging "Peru's scientific interests." The Yale affair was only the latest example of a long history of illegal appropriation of national cultural treasures.

By 1916, cultural nationalism was rampant. In January *La Prensa* published an article denouncing the exportation of archaeological artifacts. The article supported the position of Gutiérrez Quintanilla against granting an exportation permit to the YPE.[66] The columnist used strong language: the YPE had come with the object of "extracting huacos, mummies, cloth, weapons, utensils, and other archaeological curiosities *belonging to the ancient dwellers of the Tawantinsuyo empire.*" The foreigners were taking artifacts that belonged by right to the Incas. And, since Inca heritage was protected by the Peruvian state, Bingham and his group were stealing "national property." The article presented state patronage of national culture as a mark of modernity. The columnist associated the possibility of writing a national history with the possession of a given cultural patrimony. The message was clear: Peruvians should have priority in the study of their own antiquity.[67]

For the cuzqueño indigenistas the defense of national culture meant nothing less than an Inca renaissance. In August 1916, in an "interview" published by *El Sol*, Valcárcel presented the Instituto Histórico as the vehicle for the affirmation of Peruvian cultural sovereignty.[68] The institute, he said, was committed to the revival of "Inca patriotism." It had recently celebrated the third centenary of Inca Garcilaso's *Comentarios Reales de los Incas* (1609), a critical rendition of the Spanish conquest and colonization of Peru and a defense of Inca civilization and government; a year earlier the city and the institute had observed the centenary of the Cuzco Rebellion of 1814, a key moment in which indigenous peoples participated in the independence struggle.[69] Valcárcel insisted that "Bingham y compañía" had extracted gold and silver objects and smuggled them out of the country, and he credited the institute's commission with forcing the Yale archaeologists to abandon all excavations and with preventing them from exporting Inca remains. The institute, Valcárcel affirmed, was engaged in a comprehensive study of the Inca past and present: a project involving language, history, theater, and anthropology. Valcárcel himself said he was studying *ayllus* (Indian communes united by family ties) and the religiosity of the Incas, as well as preparing a guide to colonial Cuzco. It was only natural that the members of the institute promoted a law declaring all Inca ruins "national property."

Limeño antiquarians, cuzqueño indigenistas, and local government had cooperated to stop (momentarily) a foreign project of knowledge. To pull this off, they had used a powerful weapon: rumors circulated through local periodicals. Newspapers disseminated and provided expert credibility to popular rumors about the activities of the Yale group. The campaign for the preservation of Inca artifacts on Peruvian soil touched a chord in popular sensibility; Peruvians were soon denouncing the wrongdoings of the Yankee explorers as if it were their patriotic duty. The press served also as a platform for the launching of alternative historical and archaeological projects. Antiquarians and indigenistas used the Bingham incident to articulate the need for a different type of knowledge. One of the groups insisted that the key was the study of the Inca past in the present (an archaeology of the present). The other group simply defended the position that Peruvians needed to control their cultural assets in order to write their own national history.

If in 1912 cuzqueñistas had been united in the enterprise of "progress," by 1915 antiquarians and indigenistas were deeply committed to the enterprise of cultural nationalism. Implicit in the local contestation was a new critique of Yankee imperialism. Opposition to the YPE was ultimately based on cultural arguments. This new kind of regional nationalism foresaw and reacted against a future of total cultural deprivation.[70] If Peruvians allowed their best archaeological ruins to leave the country now, in the future Peruvians would have to travel to New Haven or Berlin to study their own prehistory. At a time in which the indigenistas had not yet developed a full-blown critique of *gamonalismo* (the despotism of hacienda overseers, usually mestizo) or constructed the basis of the *utopía andina* (the utopia of a regenerated Indian culture and government), the defense of Inca huacos, mummies, skulls, and pottery was their only effective critique.[71]

The Bingham affair preceded the Indian rebellions (in Ayacucho, 1922–1923) by at least seven years. In the background of Bingham's correspondence and memoirs, signs of discomfort were already evident: Indian laborers who abandoned the camp without reason, peasants who refused to sell mules to the expedition, mestizo guides who kept Indian laborers away from the Yale camp, and commoners who denounced the wrongdoings of Yankee explorers to the press. Perhaps an underground understanding of the Yale mission nurtured the skirmishes over cultural property. Perhaps indigenous and mestizo peasants and laborers cooperated in the construction of a critique of Yankee imperialism that predated not only the rebellions of 1922–1923 but the mid- to late 1920s formulations of the indigenista intellectuals José Carlos Mariátegui, Víctor Raúl Haya de la Torre, and Luis Valcárcel.[72] Popular rumors equated scientific exploration with imperialistic expansionism. Connecting the YPE with the Panama Canal, the rumors warned of the power of the new empire, a mechanical-scientific power able to move mountains to open a water pass connecting the two oceans. Associating the expedition with treasure hunters, the rumors pointed to the reenactment of the colonial conquest. The scientists were like the old conquerors, blinded by the greed for gold. But modern conquistadors were more powerful: they had machines capable of tearing down "at one fell swoop" the buildings of past civilizations. The fear of destruction associated with the YPE excavations was not a mere invention of Bingham's detractors. It was implicit in Bingham's own explanations about his "discovery." The best tombs—those that had not been tampered with by grave-diggers—were to be found underneath the great religious temples. Excavations therefore seemed to threaten the stability of Inca buildings. In this context, the notion that a bulldozer from the Panama Canal might level Machu Picchu to reveal the "Inca treasure" was not so far-fetched.

The rumors also revealed hidden connections between foreign business enterprises and scientific knowledge. Rumors intentionally confused the activities of the YPE with those of a mining company.[73] Quite efficiently, great machines of the North were taking wealth from Peruvian soil and leaving the earth in ruins. Embedded in these rumors was a criticism of foreign enterprise's mode of operation (railroad builders, oil prospectors, and mining companies), as well as a critique of government. The permissiveness of the Peruvian government, or the corruption of government officials, enabled foreign technology to appropriate Peruvian nature.

The stories of "boxes of gold" smuggled through Bolivia made wealth and knowledge equivalent: "treasures" desired by foreign agents. Boxes with bones and pottery were transformed into boxes of gold, because both were equally valuable to the imperialist other. Bingham himself referred to his collection of "trephined skulls" as a sort of unique treasure for science. For the first time, scientists were finding evidence of sophisticated surgical procedures performed by ancient Americans. This evidence was pure gold. And if the boxes were taken out of the country, it was only thanks to the cooperation of corrupt government officials. In this regard, the rumors were not in error: the YPE managed to smuggle an important number of boxes with all sorts of treasures (books, bones, pottery, and a few "bronzes").[74]

The conflict between Bingham and the local intelligentsia was not about the exportation of bones and broken pottery. It was about the ownership and control of cultural property. Cuzqueñistas and indigenistas pushed the Peruvian state to take responsibility for the preservation of "national" monuments of past civilizations. At stake was the control of the "evidence" necessary for the writing of Peruvian prehistory. The public debate about whether the government should grant exclusive rights of exploration to Yale University or give permission for the exportation of Inca remains hinged on this issue. In the debate, sympathizers with and opponents of the U.S. explorers alike brought up the issue of the widespread commerce in "antiquities." While Bingham and his allies (including the local doctor, Cesar Lomellini) tried to separate their "scientific" activities from the commerce in antiquities, his opponents suggested that the members of the YPE were actually part of this commerce. Foreign and national merchants, motivated only by profit, were exporting to European and U.S. museums important pieces of Peru's rich colonial and precolonial past. If the loss of Inca and colonial artifacts to foreign museums was already a long-standing practice, the possibility that Peru would become a nation without a past was near.

Huaqueros and the Commerce in Antiquities

The third side of the story comes from subjects unwilling to take a position in the public debate: the "huaqueros" and the merchants of antiquities. Though without a public voice, these actors greatly influenced the cultural policies of the Peruvian state and mediated the relationship between the local intelligentsia and foreign explorers. Silently, they eroded the very cultural capital that was the basis of the dispute between foreign and local knowledge-producers. By unearthing and circulating ancient artifacts, they created anxieties about the exhaustion of the ancient Peruvian past. These anxieties were a powerful force in the forging of cultural nationalism. On the other hand, these merchants acted as facilitators. They contributed to the formation of antiquarian elite culture and assisted foreign explorers to acquire and export precious artifacts. Their services provided state museums with "antiquities" which could serve as the basis for educational, historical, and ethnographic projects.

During the years 1912–1915, the increasing fame of Bingham and the YPE attracted the attention of dealers and seekers of huacas. On several occasions, Bingham's quest for the origins of the Incas was sidetracked by exchanges with seekers and merchants of Incaica. Traces of embarrassing transactions crop up, here and there, among the papers of the YPE. From Lima and from small towns (Pisco, Guadalupe, Cerro de Pasco), collectors and merchants wrote Bingham tempting him with good deals in "antiquities."[75] They offered him huacos, books, gold and silver jewelry, paintings depicting pre-Columbian events and ancient rituals, expertise on detecting fake Incaica, and directions to great ruins. Apparently, the "treasures" Bingham was looking for had already been collected and were available at a price.

Bingham, like other archaeologists, was ambivalent about these deals. On the one hand, he needed the assistance of these native informants to locate Inca ruins. The purchase of collections was not to be discarded as an option at a time in which the Peruvian state was imposing restrictions on new excavations. On the other hand, grave-diggers badly damaged archaeological sites; by taking all the valuable pottery and jewelry, they stripped the remains of connection to locality, family, and place in the social hierarchy. Once treasure hunters had done their job, all the archaeologist could find were scattered bones and broken pottery. For this reason, Bingham had to be selective about these offers, accepting some, rejecting others.

The unearthing of Indian tombs was an old practice, which increased in the post-independence period.[76] The French explorer Count of Sartigés reported in 1834 that grave-diggers always accompanied archaeological expeditions in the expectation of finding the treasures of older civilizations. Treasure hunters were the most immediate competitors of the archaeologist: if they reached a burial site first, they would irreparably damage it. Bingham was quite aware of this competition. During the 1912 expedition, he and George F. Eaton, curator of osteology at Yale's Peabody Museum, had found skeletons in a cave near San Sebastián already tampered with by "treasure hunters."[77] These "competitors" took Bingham as a potential customer. In September 1912 Bingham received a letter from the huaquero Belisario Rosas. In this letter (dated in Cerro de Pasco), Rosas offered information for locating ruins that were much older than those of the Incas.[78] As a local expert (as well as a gold miner and photographer), he had a secret to sell: a place where two pre-Inca peoples, the Huancas and the Yungas, had purportedly fought a great battle, a place hidden from science. Furthermore, he was ready to inform Bingham about the business of fake Incaica being produced at workshops in Piura and Lima. With knowledge of how to detect fake artifacts, Bingham would be able to cleanse U.S. museums of fraudulent pieces.

Rosas was poor—he had no money to travel to meet Bingham—but he possessed valuable secrets. His knowledge came from his experience as a gold miner (previously a gold seeker, then a mine worker with an amateur interest in "Indian antiquities"). He was a prospector of huacos who had acquired special skills in identifying pre-Inca artifacts. His knowledge was essential to science. Without it, museums ran the risk of being stocked with fake artifacts, and foreign scientists were at risk of spending much of their precious time excavating in the wrong location. Yet for some reason, Bingham rejected Rosas's offer.[79] Perhaps he was not ready to study the Yungas and Huancas, peoples whose "history" did not relate directly to the question of Hispanic colonialism.

But the possibility of an exchange between the huaquero and the foreign explorer was there, and this possibility is quite revealing of the vortex of interests mobilized by the cultural-economic apparatus of informal empire.

We know that Bingham purchased some collections of Incaica, but cannot find details of these transactions. To protect his reputation as a scientist and to avoid further conflict with Peruvian cultural nationalists, Bingham left few paper traces of these operations. The purchase of books and manuscripts, on the other hand, was completely legal.[80] During the second expedition, Bingham purchased a valuable book collection from F. Pérez de Velazco, a Lima book trader and insurance agent. For two rooms full of books, Bingham paid 2,500 Peruvian pounds.[81] The collection was simply unique. It contained original royal *cédulas*, the *Listas de Toros*, viceregal *bandos*, and a good selection of rare books and pamphlets, many dating to the seventeenth century.[82] Bingham referred to this as a "magnificent" collection. Personnel of W. R. Grace & Company arranged for the shipping of the collection, which arrived safely to New Haven in January 1913.[83] Perhaps one of the most valuable "treasures" resulting from the expedition, the book collection arrived much earlier than the boxes with bones, and without so much publicity. This collection would form the basis of Yale Library's South American Collection, now hosted at Mudd Library.

Regional-ethnic history was also for sale. When the local historian Luis Ulloa found out of the purchase of the Velazco collection, he offered his own books and manuscripts for sale. A member of the Geographical Society of Lima, Ulloa had known Bingham, supported his research, and published some of his articles. As a representative of the Peruvian government in Spain, Ulloa had accumulated a mass of archival materials on colonial Peru. Back in Peru, he continued to build his library and archive, with the intention of writing a comprehensive history of South America. His involvement in politics led him finally to abandon this ambitious history project. So he decided to put his entire colonial collection up for sale, offering Yale University unique documents of the sixteenth century: *probanzas* (statements of evidence used in judicial settings) about Inca genealogy, legal conflicts over property between *encomenderos* (Spaniards entrusted with the usufruct of Indian labor), and materials from the Inquisition and the Franciscan missions to Lima. His "ethnologic collection" was, in fact, the basis of a new type of history, one that focused on Indian society and culture: an ethnic-regional history. In these documents, as Ulloa explained to his potential buyers, Indians themselves were telling the scribes that they all descended from Mama Ocllo and Huaina Capac. The whole question of ayllus (Indian communities united by family ties), property relations, and what would later be called *mentalités* (ideas and imaginaries shared by these communities) was accessible through these documents.[84]

Ulloa was selling Yale University not only colonial documents but also a local perspective on history. It is not clear that Yale was ready to pay his high prices or that Bingham was ready to understand the meaning of these sources. Bingham, the modern colonizer, had learned to read ancient Peru through the Spanish chroniclers and was more interested in topographical maps of southern Peru than in Indian genealogies or property disputes. Perhaps he was not prepared to venture into the field of ethnohistory. What is important about this small interaction is the possibility of the transfer, by a commercial transaction, of a whole perspective on history. The predicament of the amateur local historian—the impossibility of embracing a long project of history while trying to make a living—had much to do with this possibility.

During his stay in Peru, Bingham received various other business propositions from sellers who had a solid understanding of the U.S. American enterprise of knowledge. In July 1912 Bingham received a letter from Mariano Ferro, the alleged owner of the lands where Machu Picchu was located. In lieu of rent, Ferro proposed splitting fifty-fifty with the U.S. explorer the "*hutilidades* [*sic*]" or profits derived from the excavations.[85] Perhaps heeding popular rumor, Ferro assumed that Bingham was searching for Inca treasures. Another interesting proposal Bingham received in 1915 came from the amateur collector Carlos Belli. Since the government had prohibited the exportation of huacos, Belli offered to sell Bingham a collection of oil paintings of Nazca huacos. This form of representation, Belli explained, was specially tailored for exhibitions in geographical societies and museums in the United States. If people wanted to know "the true history of the American Continent," let them see paintings of it.[86]

How many of these men did Bingham encounter in his travels across southern Peru? How many of his "discoveries" were actually purchases? The letters sent by huaqueros and antiquity dealers reveal a new dimension of the YPE. The expedition's goal was to accumulate knowledge, ideally via exploration but also, as it turns out, via purchase. Perhaps the expedition was never able to clearly separate commercial transactions from scientific research and, in this way, provided ample ammunition to local critics. Rumors about Yankee professors purchasing and exporting "Peruvian treasures" thus contained more than a grain of truth, for the YPE carried back to New Haven invaluable treasures in books, artifacts, and bones, many of them acquired by purchase.

At this point, it is appropriate to remind the reader how the U.S. press framed the discovery of Machu Picchu. Headlines declared "Fifty Cents Finds Ancient Ruins," "Bingham Pays Half Dollar to Find Treasure," and so on.[87] These headlines referred to the original transaction between Bingham and an Indian guide which led to the discovery of the "Lost City." At the founding moment of the story of the lucky discovery was a transaction, in which local knowledge was purchased at a bargain price.

The actual appropriation by the foreign explorer of "Indian antiquities," historical sources, and local perspectives is not really the point. What is important is that the deployment of the economic and cultural apparatus of informal empire created the possibility for these transactions. What was at stake was the very possibility of creating a local and national history and archaeology in the face of a transfer abroad of local sources, information, and perspectives. This was the main question raised by local indigenistas and cuzqueñistas. This problem does not reduce a bit the ingenuity and creativity of local subalterns to get on the train of the U.S. "enterprise of knowledge."

What was the harvest of the YPE? At the end of 1915, the YPE had collected a vast amount of material: 12,000 photographs; between 90 and 100 cases containing bones, pottery, and mummies, as well as a few "bronzes"; two rooms filled with rare books; and several thousand plant specimens. In part, these materials would serve to fill the cabinets of natural history museums in the United States: the bones and pottery would go to the Peabody, the zoological and botanical collections to the Smithsonian, and some pieces to the American Museum of Natural History. There, resignified by scientists and museum personnel, they would become part of an "object-based epistemology" that supported and legitimized the narrative of progress (Conn 1998). Photographs would help disseminate the "discovery" of Machu Picchu and of Peruvian antiquity among the U.S. public. Kodak's advertising "touring exhibits" and the pages of *National Geographic* carried with them the fiction that the emerging empire was discovering ancient Peruvian ruins for the sake of the "American people."

To Bingham, however, the true harvest of the expeditions was an expansion of the frontiers of U.S. knowledge. This meant extending the gaze of the U.S. scientist to the Peruvian Andes, incorporating the region within the domain of "problems" to be solved by U.S. scientists. Bingham aimed at a comprehensive and ordered legibility of the southern Peruvian Andes. U.S. science needed to present Western civilization with an archaeological map of Peru, that is, to order "early man in America" in sequential stages. Discovering the riddle of Machu Picchu was just one step in a more comprehensive plan of discovery and conquest.[88] Bingham and the U.S. press viewed the "discovery" as a second and better (more enduring) conquest of South America. Like a religion, U.S. science was engaged in a quest for origins. In Bingham's words, the YPE would "unravel the puzzle of the Ancient Civilization of South America" (Hiram Bingham 1914d, 677).

What sustained this quest was ultimately the U.S. reader; hence, the need to obtain masses of reproducible representations of Peruvian antiquity. In the end Bingham understood the wisdom of Grosvenor's advice and directed the results of his expeditions to the U.S. people, the readers and spectators of South American antiquity. He was proud of having created "enthusiasm" among U.S. readers for the question of South American antiquity. Like the Spanish conquistadors, he felt that what really mattered was to bring news about the "marvels of the New World." Numbers of readers and the enthusiasm of spectators—measures of the emerging consumer mass society—justified the investments of the YPE.

Relations among the YPE, Kodak, and the NGS illustrate the interconnectedness of business and knowledge in the age of the informal empire. This collaboration was necessary, not only because the nature of the enterprise of knowledge required the most modern technologies for the production and reproduction of images, but also because "print-photo capitalism" could produce value out of circulating Peruvian antiquity. The imperative of businessmen and knowledge seekers was to incorporate the region (Andean South America) under the orbit of U.S. knowledge and influence. Representation was crucial to this enterprise. Without photography, museum exhibits, articles in popular magazines, and lecturing circuits, the discovery of Machu Picchu would have been largely ignored.

How deep and far was this project of knowledge supposed to go? Before we place "reality" or the "Indian-social question" on the indigenista side and leave for U.S. science only the distant and comprehensive vision of archaeology and geography, we must read Bingham's letters to Osgood Hardy, the ethnologist of the 1914 expedition. Bingham repeatedly insisted that Hardy should learn the language of indigenous peoples (Quechua), observe "native feasts," and take notes on their agricultural methods and lifestyle.[89] Hardy was "to learn folklore and local tradition," even if this entailed hiring an Indian as a permanent servant.[90] Bingham, the mountaineer-historian-archaeologist, had finally developed an interest in Indian South America. Language, traditions, manners, and customs were the "stuff" of the new science: anthropology. This was the discipline that in the future would extract the final secrets from South America, those still hidden in the memory of indigenous peoples.

Bingham was unable to lead this vast project of knowledge to its conclusion: the complete mapping of Peru's archaeological sites; the total topographical survey of the Southern Peruvian Andes; and the in-depth investigation of Peru's indigenous groups. In particular, the riddle about Machu Picchu remained unsolved. The discontinuity of the surveys made it impossible for Bingham to validate his two most daring theses: that Machu Picchu was the "cradle" of Inca civilization and also its "last refuge." In the cultural battles at Cuzco and Lima between the YPE and the local intelligentsia there was something close to a tie. In the United States, Bingham gained public acclaim as the discoverer of Machu Picchu, rapidly ascended the academic ladder, and soon became a recognizable name in the foreign-relations debate, a public man, and a successful politician. Yale University also profited from the YPE, accumulating materials about Peru in its natural history museum and its libraries. In fact, after the YPE, Yale became a recognizable site (like Berlin, Berkeley, and Harvard) in the field of Peruvian archaeology and South American history.

Indigenistas and antiquarians also made significant gains. Planting the notion in public opinion that foreign researchers were actually "treasure hunters," they managed to stain the purity of foreign scientific explorations and, at the same time, to legitimize their own claims as custodians of Peru's cultural property. For a moment at least, Ollantaytambo ceased to be a field open to international research. Clearly, cuzqueño institutions and research methods could not match the credentials of Euro-American science. As amateur collectors tinkering with "wild ideas" about the origins of pre-Columbian civilizations, they remained in a subaltern, marginal position, unable to finance large-scale excavations or wide-ranging topographical surveys. But they planted the seed of cultural nationalism and this proved instrumental for the control of key positions in Peruvian universities, museums, and historical institutes.

The YPE was able to ship its "boxes of bones" to New Haven, but the erosion of its credibility was so high that Bingham abandoned all interest in new Peruvian expeditions. In fact, according to his biographer, after 1916 Bingham returned only once to the area: in 1948, at the time of the inauguration of the Hiram Bingham Highway, in Cuzco (Alfred Bingham 1989, 178). Despite the popularity of the Peruvian articles, *National Geographic* also withdrew its support from the project. Back in the United States, Bingham continued to monitor the publication of popular and scientific articles about the expedition and, stimulated by friends and his publisher (Houghton Mifflin), he wrote a popular narrative of his expedition, *Inca Land*, published in 1922. But his encounter with "fabricators of rumor" left deep imprints in his memory. Reconciliation came with time, when the breeze of the Good Neighbor Policy reestablished the fiction of a continental friendship.

It is only fair to say that the same indigenistas who orchestrated the 1914–1916 press scandals came in the end to recognize the work of Bingham and the YPE. True, travel guides to Peruvian archaeological sites still put Bingham's discovery within quotation marks, underscoring the fact that he publicized only ruins that indigenous Peruvians already knew well. And for years, indigenistas made a point of presenting Max Uhle as the "true father" of Peruvian archaeology, placing Europe at the center of Andean studies. But by the late 1930s and early 1940s, prominent indigenistas had made peace with Bingham and forgotten the First World War incident. In his memoirs, Valcárcel downplayed the incident, crediting Bingham for having stimulated an interest for Inca culture among his generation (Valcárcel 1981, 186–87). The fact that Valcárcel himself became a discoverer—conducting large excavations in Sacsaywaman in 1934–1938, making important finds in Pukara and Tambayeque, and even coming to be recognized in the United States—may very well explain this suspension of conflict in the official memory of indigenistas.[91]

The Bingham affair constituted a formative moment in the history of Peruvian *indigenismo*. The conflict gave indigenistas public notoriety as custodians of Peruvian antiquities. It provided a platform that legitimated their claims to leadership in the remaking of modern Peru. Who could own and use the remnants of the Inca past was a crucial question constitutive of their domain. Other questions—regarding *gamonalismo*, the social condition of the *indio*, and the possibility of an Inca renaissance—would come later. First, cultural nationalists had to establish Peruvian sovereignty over its own antiquity. Only the fear of national cultural deprivation—the anxiety of losing control over their own prehistory—worried indigenistas more than the condition of the Indian.

Bingham's self-representation as a "conqueror" ready to commence the rediscovery of ancient Peru speaks of the imperial ambitions of U.S. science with regard to its novel object of study: Andean South America. He expected only admiration from the locals, the type of reception given by Federico Alfonso Pezet, the Peruvian representative to the 1915 International Congress of Americanists. Pezet recognized his country's inferiority in science vis-à-vis the United States: In order to belong to the continental union imagined by the architects of Pan-Americanism, Peru has to welcome scientific missions from the North. The gesture of subalternity is clear: Peru would agree to be just a repository of ruins with the expectation that, in the future, foreign science would locate Peru among the privileged sites of world antiquity.

The local intelligentsia, of course, had a different position. Speaking in the name of national culture, they also sought to "elevate" Peruvian antiquity to the level of other famous archaeological sites. Amateur historians and archaeologists from Cuzco and Lima liked to imagine themselves as part of the international scientific enterprise of discovery. Exclusion and neglect from the U.S. scientists made them resentful. Their aspirations for social and economic progress seemed suddenly questioned by a representative of Yale University. In the hegemonic project of Pan-American science there was little room for local intellectuals. Cuzqueño and Limeño intellectuals found themselves serving as mere providers of information and antiquities to archaeological and historical projects that emanated from U.S. universities. It was precisely this refusal of recognition that prompted the local intelligentsia to formulate an alternative enterprise of knowledge.

Perhaps nationalism is always a "derivative discourse" and indigenous histories are always condemned to obscurity by the hegemony of Eurocentric history.[92] But the local intelligentsia at Cuzco and Lima tried to present an alternative project of knowledge in archaeology and history. In the end perhaps, they failed. Overwhelmed by the center's epistemological apparatus, local archaeology and history tended to replicate the theories and methods of U.S. and European scholars. But between 1912 and 1916, they managed to put in doubt the credibility of an emerging center of knowledge (Yale University) and created the basis for the cultivation of regional-ethnic history.

In the skirmishes over cultural property, none of the main contenders made explicit the connection between U.S. archaeological discoveries in Peru and the increasing penetration of U.S. capital in oil, mining, transportation, commerce, and banking. Much less did they unveil the increasing symbiosis between modern capitalism and the mechanics of representation. The antiforeign rhetoric of the cuzqueñistas and indigenistas had a limit: the separation of cultural and economic spheres. The defense of Peruvian national antiquities was not linked to a critique of U.S. enterprise. The local intelligentsia questioned the YPE's exportation of bones and artifacts, but had nothing to say about the immense photographic collection that the expedition brought back to the United States. In the future, Bingham's photographs, presenting living Indians in front of Inca ruins, would fixate Peru as a land of a glorious past and miserable present: as a land of contrasts incapable of achieving full modernity.[93]

Only popular rumor—the anonymous voices that circulated the story that Bingham was collecting Inca gold with the most modern technology and smuggling it out of the country—alluded to the connection between foreign enterprise and scientific exploration. Only these stories seemed to uncover the

Yale at Machu Picchu

materialist and imperialist motivations of their explorations. Underlying the parade of knowledge deployed by the YPE was the same basic economic interest that motivated the prospecting work of mining and oil companies. Moreover, by assimilating the modern, scientific collection with the colonial persecution of "idolatry" and the pillage of huacos, rumors turned around the positive construction of the YPE as a scientific enterprise. Bingham seemed like Pizarro, in the sense that he reenacted the colonial project of cultural amnesia and pillage. At a time in which a new economic empire was forming in the Americas and a renewed Andean consciousness was beginning to surface in politics, this old denunciation acquired a poignant actuality.

The huaqueros and dealers in antiquities present us with yet another dimension of this story. Merchants in antiquities were morally condemned as treacherous agents, motivated by greed and money. In actuality, they provided a crucial intermediation in a business that grew alongside with the fantasies of National History and Informal Empire. Both projects of knowledge (the local and the global) necessitated their mediation. Much of the "discovery" of antiquity was based on the purchase of artifacts—simple commercial transactions. The huaqueros in turn were creators of value; they brought income to their communities and disseminated stories about the ancient indigenous past. Their stories magnified the myth of fabulous treasures absconded underneath Inca ruins. Moreover, they competed successfully with men of science in the "discoveries" and managed to supply fake antiquities to Euro-American museums and scientific cabinets. For doing this, they became the public enemy of cultural nationalists. Dealers in antiquities and huaqueros contributed to the vast transfer of "evidence" from Peru to European and U.S. museums and universities. Their function was to put the objects of dispute, Peruvian antiquities, into circulation as commodities. The huaqueros—subaltern seekers of Inca artifacts—knew the secrets of ancient Peru and were ready to sell them to the foreign men of science, for a price. But it was the responsibility of men of science and scientific institutions to fixate these elements of "evidence" into the bounded territoriality of nation, science, and modernity.

FIVE

Hispanic American History at Harvard: Clarence H. Haring and Regional History for Imperial Visibility

———

In this chapter I examine the construction of an enunciatory position within the U.S. academy: Hispanic American history at Harvard, a position from which a professor, Clarence H. Haring, was able to speak authoritatively about the history and contemporary condition of South America. I emphasize the role of an institutional location, Harvard, in the process of accumulation and dissemination of knowledge in the relatively new field of Hispanic American history. Looking at the classes, publications, conferences, and public addresses of this distinguished Harvard professor, I show how a single location—Harvard—influenced U.S. ways of apprehending Latin America.

While focusing on the career of one of the makers of Hispanic American history, I address a broader question: the parallel and mutually reinforcing relationship between academic prestige and imperial visibility. That is, Haring's cultural and social capital grew in proportion to his comprehensive understanding of Latin America. The Harvard professor was able to shape the formation of a subdiscipline and, at the same time, to influence contemporary debates on U.S. foreign policy.[1] Haring maneuvered within a network of social relations to build a locus of enunciation—Hispanic American history—from which he was able to speak about the challenges facing the United States in its commercial and cultural expansion over Latin America. His grand vision of the historical trajectory of Latin America was permeated by concerns accompanying the international position achieved by the United States after the First World War.

Haring's vision of Latin American history as an experimental field for the comparative study of governments, societies, and cultures helped the United States transition from Dollar Diplomacy to the Good Neighbor Policy. His scheme of two parallel histories with different temporalities and outcomes placed the United States as a more advanced neighbor ready to guide the southern republics in the road toward progress and democracy. While acknowledging the great economic, political, and social "backwardness" of the region vis-à-vis Anglo-America, his historical master narrative made feasible the expectations of economic progress and good government in South America.

In 1923 Harvard University hired Haring to be the Robert Wood Bliss Professor in Latin American History and Economics, a position funded by a former ambassador to Buenos Aires, Robert Wood Bliss, who was impressed by the economic potential of South America.[2] From this prestigious position, most of Haring's activities and contributions to the field of Latin American history were infused with a profound preoccupation with empire. His lectures, public addresses, academic publications, and policy advice always came back to a central question: the contemporary and projected hegemony of the United States in the American continent. In the parallel but distinct development of British and Spanish colonial America, Haring found the keys for understanding the present. His travels enabled him to adapt the Monroe Doctrine to the new situation of "South American progress" much as Bingham had suggested. At the core of his preoccupations in the mid-1920s were the disdainful and suspicious attitudes of South American elites toward the United States. In his grand historical narrative, Haring was able to reimagine U.S. hegemony as a benevolent force seeking to spill democracy and economic welfare over the sister republics of the south.

The Latin American Chair

Haring's academic work had started with an interest in Caribbean pirates. Soon he moved into the study of the Spanish system of navigation and trade. In 1918 he published *Trade and Navigation between Spain and the Indies in the Time of the Hapsburgs.*[3] But he did his most important work at Harvard, where he taught from 1923 to 1953, holding important positions along with the Bliss chair: he was chair of the history department from 1931 to 1939 and the Master of Dunster House from 1934 to 1948. His influence radiated in many directions. His students—Lewis Hanke, Howard Cline, Miron Burgin, and Arthur Whitaker, among others—were quite influential in the formation of the discipline. From Harvard, Haring organized and directed the Bureau of Economic Research on Latin America, and in collaboration with his assistants at the bureau, he prepared an important bibliography on economic matters (Haring 1935). In the mid-1920s, his interests shifted to political and foreign-policy analysis. He wrote essays criticizing U.S. intervention in Central America and others alerting the U.S. public to the discontent of South Americans with these interventions.[4] He moved from the question of imperial rivalries of past empires (Spain, Britain, and France) to the most urgent questions of when and how the United States should intervene in the hemisphere. Haring was a founding member of the discipline's most prestigious journal, the *Hispanic American Historical Review*, and promoted the largest bibliographic enterprise ever made in the field, the *Handbook of Latin American Studies*.

His publications connected well with the U.S. rapprochement with South America in the late 1920s and early 1930s. In 1928 he published *South America Looks at the United States*, followed in 1934 by *South American Progress*, a book more historical in outlook but also oriented toward foreign policy. These two books were the Harvard historian's most important contributions to the debate on U.S. foreign policy toward Latin America. It was during this period that he developed the idea of a comprehensive and parallel history of the hemisphere. In the 1930s, he served as chairman of the Committee on Latin American Studies of the American Council of Learned Societies. From this position of power-knowledge, he directed students' attention toward Latin America. In the 1930s and 1940s he helped found different Pan-American societies and clubs in the northeast, motivating students to promote the gospel of hemispheric cooperation through commerce and peaceful resolution of conflicts.

Throughout his career, Haring showed a sustained interest in the economic and institutional history of the Spanish empire. He published essays on the Spanish colonial exchequer, on sixteenth-century gold and silver production, and on the Spanish system of trade. His most celebrated book, *The Spanish Empire in America* (1947), was the result of more than twenty years of research and teaching. In the 1930s, as he monitored the politics of South America, he published essays that carried important implications for U.S. foreign policy. He reported about recent military coups resulting from international commercial paralysis and about the growing activities of Nazi sympathizers in the region.[5] Toward the end of his tenure at Harvard, he started gathering information for a book on Brazil, which later became a classic: *Empire in Brazil: A New World Experiment with Monarchy* (1958).

These interests shaped his teaching. He offered courses on colonial Spanish America, the history of the ABC countries (Argentina, Brazil, and Chile), and the history of modern Mexico, courses he developed in that order. Occasionally, he offered courses on Spanish-British relations in the seventeenth-century.[6] At the height of Pan-American enthusiasm (1927–1933), Haring offered a course at Radcliffe that covered the history of Latin America since independence, from Mexico to Patagonia. Titled "History and Contemporary Politics of the Latin American Republics," the course also included a great deal of commentary on U.S.-Latin American relations.[7]

Haring was probably one of the first professors in the country to teach a special course on the history of the so-called ABC powers. The history of the ABC nations (Argentina, Brazil, and Chile) was a success story. As he explained to his students, the ABC powers stood out from the rest, because of their size, population, and wealth, and also because they had achieved political stability. After overcoming great political instability and social disorder in the post-independence era, they emerged in the twentieth century as institutionally and socially stable nations. Their separate trajectory complicated the great divide between the United States and South America. Here were countries (the ABC nations) whose historical experience contradicted the U.S. view of Latin American nations as inherently unstable politically and incapable of self-government. Sooner or later, the ABC nations would resemble the United States in levels of political maturity, economic welfare, and cultural sophistication.[8]

What was history but a useful laboratory for the study of comparative development? By comparing the ABC nations to the United States, Haring was able to single out similarities and differences and to pose—much earlier than today's economic historians—the important question of why today's Southern Cone countries had "fallen behind" the United States. Argentina was, among other things, the most "European" of Latin American countries, for it had removed its indigenous population as successfully as had the United States. And, unlike other South American nations, Argentina lacked a substantial black population. Relieved of racial mixture, the country's economic progress could be attributed to the two chief forces: environment and institutions. Under "the environment," Haring included variables such as geography, climate, and natural-resource endowments. Under "institutions," he included political development.[9]

Of course, Haring's view about the preeminence of the ABC nations did not withstand the test of time. By the early 1930s, military coups and Nazi sympathies forced Haring to revise his views about the progressive southern republics. Haring thought of South America's military coups as temporary setbacks in the long-term trajectory toward institutional and social stability. In the midst of the Second World War, Haring still sustained that Latin American countries may have inherited a dictatorial tradition, but they were not ready to embrace European fascism (Haring 1944). After the end of the period covered by this book, Cold War politics put a halt to the idea of parallel histories and, for that matter, to the whole project of a history of the Americas.

Concern for Empires and Imperialism

Whether he dealt with European nineteenth-century history, with colonial Spanish-American history, or with contemporary politics in Latin America, Haring was concerned with the same set of issues: how empires maintained their power over time, how empires served as vehicles of cultural transfer, and what forms of imperial domination generated the least resistance.

Between 1912 and 1915, Haring taught at Bryn Mawr and at Yale, offering courses on English history and on modern Europe. The syllabus of his course "Europe since 1815" shows the importance he attributed to imperialism.[10] The course started with the French Revolution and ended with the Balkan Wars. Though traditional in many regards, the course included topics that were relatively novel, such as the French colonial experience in Algeria and the resistance it encountered (students learned about Emir Abdelkader and his promise to drive the French into the sea). Also nontraditional was the inclusion of the recent "Scramble for Africa" and the diplomatic conflicts generated by European nations' imperialistic ambitions

The question of late nineteenth-century imperialism (the Scramble for Africa) would turn out to be central to the course, for it was the origin of the First World War, a war that threatened European civilization. A second issue attracted Haring's attention: the French Revolution. He saw it as a tragic moment in European history, in which everything—governments, classes, manners, religion, beliefs, passions, and hopes—was thrown into the "melting pot." In the French Revolution Haring found a narrative model adaptable to post-independence Hispanic America. All the ingredients were there: social and political upheavals leading to prolonged wars, and autocratic regimes forming on the heels of anarchy. Haring's concentration on these two central topics—the French Revolution and the Scramble for Africa—speaks of his search for historical models to narrate aspects he considered central to the formation of Hispanic America: the tormented experience of self-government after independence, and the ever-present danger of European imperialism to the region.

Haring's interest in empires continued at Harvard. In his History 174 course he presented the Spanish colonial empire as an inefficient but admirable system.[11] Haring admired the fact that Spain could hold on to a vast empire stretching from California to Patagonia for three centuries. On the other hand, he was critical of the Spanish economic and political system. Monarchical absolutism and the commercial monopoly, he thought, were the ultimate causes of the empire's long-term decline after the seventeenth century. Unable to combat contraband or to control governmental corruption, the empire could not withstand the competition of European rival powers. The Spanish empire had given its colonies a long-lasting peace and the gift of Christian religion, yet it had failed miserably in elevating the standard of living for colonial subjects. This was Haring's standard for measuring imperial success: public goods and economic well-being.

Haring's Spanish colonial history contained the elements for a comparative history of empires.[12] He contrasted the Spanish commercial monopoly with the experience of British colonization in North America. Spaniards, having started the process of colonization from a situation of free trade and colonial manufactures, soon closed off all possibility of free enterprise by establishing a rigid commercial monopoly. The experience of the British Thirteen Colonies pointed to a different developmental path: colonization with small farmers, dispersed property rights, ample trade opportunities, and institutions of self-government. These divergent paths since colonial times opened the way to an analysis of Latin American backwardness and to the examination of the U.S. role in twentieth-century hemispheric relations.

Haring's intellectual trajectory shows a spatiotemporal displacement: from the Caribbean, to the Spanish empire, to South America and Mexico in the twentieth century. Not only the research sites but the researcher moved. Before the First World War, he went to Oxford to study inter-imperial rivalries between Spain and Britain in the seventeenth-century Caribbean. Then he did archival work in England and Spain, concentrating on the institutional and economic aspects of Spanish colonialism. And toward the mid-1920s he traveled from his perch at Harvard to South America, where he discovered a different perspective from which to examine U.S. twentieth-century imperial adventures in the Caribbean.

The Mistakes of the Spanish Colonial Empire

In *Trade and Navigation* (1918), Haring undertook a thorough examination of the institutional and economic aspects of the Spanish empire in America— its complex commercial, administrative, and fiscal machinery—in order to understand the decline of Spain's global power in the seventeenth century. A free trade versus state monopoly dialectic dominated his interpretation. Other mercantilist empires had used the forces of the market to sustain their accumulation of state power and economic dominance. Spain did not. Its commercial monopoly stifled the forces of free enterprise, bringing stagnation and poverty to the American colonies (Haring 1918, 24). Spain chose to become a monopolistic commercial empire, when it could have benefited from a freer and larger maritime empire.

Haring followed the development of the Casa de Contratación from its humble beginnings as a three-man office until it became, in the mid-seventeenth century, an "elaborately organized institution" in charge of regulating the commerce and navigation of the Indies (ibid., 28–45). The first bureaucracy in the Americas, initially oriented toward the control of royal interests, ended up suffocating the development of commercial capitalism in the colonies. The expansion of bureaucracy brought about increased levels of red tape with regard to relations with the American colonies. Growing deficits forced the monarchy to sell public offices to augment government revenues. Philip II's decision, in 1625, to sell to the Duke of Olivares the post of *alguacil mayor* of the Casa de Contratación was the "original sin" that corrupted the machinery of colonial government (ibid., 46, 53–54).

Like the British colonies in North America, the Spanish colonies had also enjoyed a period of "salutary neglect," but this period had been too short to generate economic development. Before 1600, the Crown had promoted the development of agriculture in the Caribbean islands, introducing wheat, sugar, vines, and olives. In addition, the Spanish Crown allowed and encouraged the production of manufactures in the colonies (chiefly silk and woolen textiles). This, combined with the resistance of local governors and viceroys to enforce royal regulations, permitted the early growth of a limited intercolonial trade (ibid., 124–28). But soon, pressure from the Council of Indies and the Seville monopoly caused the Crown to prohibit most of these activities, drastically curtailing the number of ships allowed to supply American colonial ports. Once the Spanish commercial monopoly was firmly established, the colonies were subjected to the tyranny of exorbitant prices and irregular supplies. These conditions stimulated the growth of contraband trade and corruption.

In the late seventeenth century, Spanish colonial policy was out of tune with the mercantilist policies of her commercial rivals (ibid., 129). The Crown's advisors did not understand that in order to maximize royal revenue and accumulate state power, it was necessary to grant concessions to chartered companies. Nor did they understand that it was illusory to keep bullion within Spain when the colonies were already dependent on England, Holland, and France for supplies of manufactured goods. American silver naturally tended to flow out of Spain, and no system of regulations could stop this outflow. To this failure in economic policy, the Spaniards added a new insurmountable problem: the creation of European aristocracy in America. The Crown transferred power to the Church and created a landed aristocracy in the Indies. This was perhaps the greatest blunder, for aristocratic privilege prevented the development of self-reliance, the work ethic, and social equality in Hispanic America (ibid., 130–31).

During colonial times, Haring argued, an alternative model was possible: the U.S. model (ibid., 131). Small-scale holdings, free trade, and greater social equality would have generated in Central and South America a society and economy similar to that of the Thirteen Colonies. Instead, Hispanic America developed into a hierarchical, aristocratic society with great landed estates and servile labor, a place where Indian peasants tilled the land with primitive methods and lived in the greatest ignorance. Overall, Spanish colonialism had had a negative impact on the welfare of the native Americans. To sustain the royal treasury and parasitic social elites, the Crown had failed to elevate the standard of living of indigenous peoples.[13] The Indian masses had accepted Christian evangelization, but this was all they had gained from "European civilization." Only in the towns, where Spaniards and Creoles dominated, were there clear signs of "civilization." Measured in these terms, the Spanish empire had not been a "progressive system" of transnational governance.

Three main factors were at the root of the decline of the Spanish empire, said Haring. One was the persistence of erroneous economic ideas: a trade monopoly with fixed ports, annual fleets, and a list of prohibited goods that discouraged local commerce and industrial enterprise. A second factor was the early establishment of aristocratic privilege and large landed estates. This reproduced servile labor and an aristocratic disdain for manual work. The third factor was corruption. The introduction of the sale of public offices undermined all possibility of responsible government (ibid., 150). The imperial bureaucracy, permeated by favoritism and bribery, proved unable to enforce royal regulations on navigation and trade. Contraband grew to alarming proportions, and hence, the royal treasury lost great amounts of revenue.

In the early eighteenth century, the Bourbons tried to revamp colonial trade, creating chartered companies and granting privileges to local and foreign merchants for the introduction of slaves, but it was already too late. Spain could no longer secure its supremacy over the seas. In this context, the American colonies became a liability to Spain. Its supplies came to be provided by foreign

Chapter 5

manufacturers, while Spanish industry declined. Trade regulations ceased to be enforced, exacerbating the problems of contraband. Underneath the decline of the Spanish empire were policies inconsistent with Spain's actual powers and resources. The ultimate folly of Spanish imperial policy was the attempt to keep a territory as vast as a hemisphere under the monopoly of one city (first Seville, later Cádiz) and of a single royal bureaucracy.[14]

Other forms of imperial engagement proved more effective over time. Haring explicitly mentioned British commercial hegemony in the nineteenth century as one of these new models. Controlling commerce through more flexible rules, enabling the participation of merchants from several nations, while patrolling the seas with a powerful navy, the British established a more productive and enduring empire. Haring's *Trade and Navigation* also dealt, albeit less explicitly, with the U.S. informal empire. Since colonial times, the U.S. economy had developed an expanding settler frontier, assisted by policies of free trade and salutary neglect in questions of government. Then, in the nineteenth century, the nation experienced an industrial and transportation revolution. Hence, the union evolved from a relatively wealthy colony into a large industrial power that, from the beginning of the twentieth century, contended for hegemony in the American hemisphere. Combining a British-style maritime empire with frontier development, the U.S. model was, in Haring's view, a superior mode of imperial engagement.

Haring's indictment of the Spanish trade monopoly needs to be understood within the framework of a comparative study of empires. He went into the treasury of Spanish archives to find faults in colonial policy and institutions—erroneous economic ideas, the transfer of feudal society, widespread corruption and contraband—that could explain the contemporary divergence between Anglo- and Spanish-America. That is, Haring's colonial history sought to understand two problems that intrigued the U.S. foreign-policy establishment in the twentieth century: why Latin America was lagging behind the United States; and, crucially, how the United States should expand its influence in Latin America in order to spread peace, progress, and mutual understanding. The Spanish empire stood as a negative example: something that the United States should not attempt to repeat.

Apparently a counternarrative of empire, Haring's criticism actually aimed to reconsider U.S. hegemonic politics. The same narrative that depicted the Spanish empire as a failed experiment also presented the possibility of another type of imperial governance: a benevolent empire radiating influence through university training, expert advice, consumer advertising, free trade, private property, and democratic governance. In this way, Hispanic American history became instrumental for differentiating and elevating the "American path" to exceptionality and exemplarity, a new mirror in which contemporaneous Latin American nations could see their future.

Why It Is Important to "Us": Teaching Imperial Reasons

When teaching the history of colonial Spanish America, Haring always started class by pointing out the importance that the subject matter had for "us." The collective subject invoked was, of course, Anglo-Americans. In his view, there were two reasons to study the subject. First, European colonization was one of the most remarkable phenomena of modern times. Over a relative short span of time, Europe, a small continent, had exported population, institutions, and cultures to other continents in ways that had radically transformed the world. The European expansion of the sixteenth to the eighteenth centuries, he thought, was a world transformation from which U.S. Americans had much to learn. Second, the history of the Spanish-American colonies showed remarkable parallels to that of the English colonies in North America. Similarities of environment, motivation, and historical experience rendered the comparison of the two Americas productive and enticing.[15]

Spanish and British colonies had both developed in environments far removed from their motherlands. Similar motivations—love of adventure, desire for wealth, longing for religious freedom—drove British and Spanish colonizers to the New World. The Americas were the refuge for individuals and groups whose difference Europe could not incorporate. Both colonies developed under "frontier conditions" that stimulated a spirit of personal independence and equality, contrary to European social hierarchies. Over time, both colonies developed social and economic restrictions that made colonials uncomfortable with European policies until, finally, both colonies revolted against their mother countries and obtained independence

Comparability was central to Haring's understanding of and interest in colonial history. Haring told his students that Hispanic American history was relevant to understanding the past and the present of the United States, because of its similarities (environment and history) and its differences (locality and race). Each spring, on the first day of classes, he told his "History of Colonial Spanish America" students that Latin American history was important to U.S. Americans not only because they were neighbors whose support was needed, but chiefly because Latin America and the United States shared a "common historical experience."[16] U.S. scholarly interest in Latin American history rested on a basic premise: the "two continents" had common and parallel histories. By this, Haring meant something more than coevalness. He meant similar historical conditions and potentially parallel trajectories, with deviations that could lead to different outcomes in government, economic growth, and societal development.

After independence, imbued with similar ideas of freedom, equality, and democracy, the Latin American nations tried to imitate the United States. But toward the beginning of the twentieth century a great gulf in economic welfare separated the Latin American republics from their northern neighbor. What caused the great divergence between the two Americas? Anarchy, race, and fortune.

> Moreover, while the recently emancipated Latin states were a prey of the disruptive forces of sectional jealousy and personal ambition in their domestic life, the U.S., much more homogenous in race, much more European, without the Indian element, than these other states, and much more fortunate in its background of political experience, forged ahead very rapidly in population, industry and wealth.[17]

The anarchical disposition inherited from Spaniards, the mixed racial experience of Latin America, and the greater "fortune" of the United States were the sources of the great divergence. If this was so, the obstacles for a great hemispheric union did not seem insurmountable. The great economic power of the United States had caused alarm and suspicion among the southern republics, but this was something that a well-informed diplomacy could gradually turn about. Regarded in the mirror of long-term American historical trajectories, Pan-American ideals did not seem ill-founded. Latin American nations had followed a trajectory similar to that of the United States, only to diverge temporarily in the late nineteenth century. The success of a Pan-American union could help Latin America reconnect with its post-independence historical trajectory.

By bringing the different into the terrain of the familiar, Haring caught the attention of his students. Spanish mercantilism could be understood in relationship to English mercantilism. Spanish absolutism made sense when contrasted with English constitutional monarchy. In addition, the Spanish colonial past provided useful lessons with which to interpret the present. In this regard, Haring made a clear connection with the current worldly ambitions of the United States. Starting with military conquest, Spain had created "*flourishing civilized communities*, with universities, government buildings and monasteries."[18] A colonizing power was also a civilizing power, a provider of public goods to colonial subjects. Without naming it, Haring was alluding to the United States and its imperial incursions in the Caribbean since 1898.

To persuade students of the importance of Spanish colonial history, Haring spoke of the importance of Latin American economies to the welfare of the United States. The region was a reserve of food supplies (corn, wheat, coffee, cacao, bananas, beef, mutton, etc.) and raw materials (copper, iron, tin, oil, hides, wool, etc.) crucial to the U.S. economy. (A similar discourse could be found in Leo S. Rowe's conception of "constructive Pan-Americanism.") To prove his point, Haring presented students with statistics that showed the importance of Latin American nations as global producers of commodities. A map with icons for export staples (dated 1889) helped to illustrate this contemporary phenomenon. The map and the statistics carried an additional message: the economic colonization of Spanish America remained an open project. The continent was still full of undeveloped natural resources, which presented a "vast field of opportunity" for U.S. capital.

South American Attitudes toward the United States

In his book *South America Looks at the United States* (1928), Haring assessed the attitudes of Latin American intellectuals, politicians, and publicists toward U.S. interventions in the Caribbean and Central America. This book, the product of his 1925–1926 tour of South America, reappraised the phenomenon of imperialism. Haring affirmed that the United States had to redefine the Monroe Doctrine according to the new geographical divide. Central America and the Caribbean were areas crucial to U.S. domestic security, where the United States had to exercise a permanent tutelage to maintain order and political stability. In South America, on the other hand, there was already economic progress and political stability. Consequently, the United States had to maintain a policy of friendship and commercial cooperation with its southern neighbors. Haring argued that the United States had much to learn from South America, presenting the region as the "natural complement" (in artistic talent and poetic ability) to U.S. mechanical civilization. Given South America's degree of economic development and the spread of anti-American feelings, he argued, a policy of persuasion based on the promotion of "American culture" was the most reasonable means by which to secure hegemony.

Haring thought of U.S. hegemony in Latin America as a type of "modern empire," one that bestowed public goods on its hinterlands. He considered Pan-Americanism as a sort of hemispheric commonwealth in which the wealthy and more experienced United States had to dispense advice and technical assistance to its less advanced sister republics. If the British had endowed India with railroads and a civil service, the U.S. empire should promote peace through international arbitration, assist sister republics with medical and economic advice, and provide forums for the discussion of common problems. Pan-American conferences that brought together experts of the two Americas in a wide range of policy areas—international law, journalism, child welfare, natural reservations, public health, and so on—were manifestations of such a form of modern empire.[19] In Haring's view, an empire committed to the improvement of the well-being of its hinterlands was a better empire. For this reason, South Americans' "distrust" of the United States was nothing more than a problem of miscommunication, something that could be dissolved with an intelligent cultural diplomacy.

Previously, Haring had believed that in the mechanics of trade, investment, and finance, one could find the answers to the expansion of a benevolent empire. His travels through South America in 1925–1926 changed this view. Now it became clear to him that the makers of public opinion in South America—intellectuals, politicians, the printed press, the radio, and so on—were spreading "anti-American feelings." The United States was confronting a problem of bad image in South America, not because of misinformation and innuendo introduced by European traders, but because of the emergence of an anti-imperialist movement in the southern republics. Even the traditional press carried articles critical of the United States: about U.S. interventions in the Caribbean, Prohibition, the rise in the divorce rate, and Ku Klux Klan lynchings. Haring was perhaps one of the first U.S. scholars to name the Latin American intellectuals who undermined the prestige of the United States, among them José Ingenieros, Rufino Blanco Fombona, Carlos Mariátegui, Manuel Ugarte, José Vasconcelos, and José L. Suárez (Haring 1928, chap. 7). Twenty years after the publication of José Enrique Rodó's *Ariel* (1900), a canonical text of anti-Americanism, South American intellectuals were uniting in defense of Latin American culture, *Hispanidad*, and anti-Americanism.[20] This reaffirmed Haring's belief that new research combining history and politics, public opinion and economic penetration, would be greatly beneficial to the field of international relations.

The Pan-Americanist Network

Between 1929 and 1933, in the midst of the Great Depression, Haring organized a series of Summer Round Tables on Latin America at the University of Virginia's Institute of Public Affairs at Charlottesville.[21] The round tables gathered prominent men in the "Latin American field": high-ranking officers of the administration; Latin American diplomats in Washington; directors of U.S. companies; publishers and editors of magazines and newspapers; international lawyers; members of academic societies; and university professors. Each summer the institute offered six to eight sessions, featuring two speakers each, with a discussion session at the end the day. Sessions included topics of actuality and relevance for those involved in policy and business decisions in the region.[22]

From the list of speakers and participants recovered from Haring's archives, we get a tentative impression of who the "Pan-Americanists" were. Some of them had administrative experience in U.S. protectorates in Central America and the Caribbean. Others brought to the Round Tables business experience or scholarly knowledge. There were men who had shifted from one area of expertise to the other. Among them were powerful lawyers such as Edgar W. Turlington (advisor to Ambassador Guggenheim in Cuba, assistant solicitor of the State Department, and advisor for the Mexican-American Claim Commission), leading financial men such as W. W. Cumberland (the U.S. general receiver in Haiti), executives of powerful multinational corporations such as William K. Jackson (vice president of United Fruit) or Robert H. Patchin (vice president of W. R. Grace & Company), important journalists and editors such as Wallace Thompson (author of popular tracts about Mexico and Central America, and the editor of *Ingeniería Internacional*), and famous members of the diplomatic corps at Washington such as Ricardo J. Alfaro (Panama's minister to the United States).[23] Academic authority was also well represented. Among the scholars were historians—Fred Rippy (Duke), William Robertson (Illinois), Dana G. Munro (Princeton), and Leland Jenks (Rollings)—with expertise not only in Latin American history, but also on current political conditions. There were also scholar-statesmen such as James Brown Scott, a lawyer of international renown who was at the time solicitor for the U.S. State Department; he was also secretary of the Carnegie Endowment for International Peace, the leading U.S. institution in the field of "intellectual cooperation" with Latin America.[24]

These were some of the connections Haring had forged from his base at Harvard, a network of men occupying key positions in academic institutions, government, business, and the press. Some of them were militant Pan-Americanists, while others were simply interested in the expansion of U.S. business in the region. Workshop participants constituted an informal network of relations that could be activated every time there was the need to debate issues crucial for the expansion of U.S. influence in Latin America.

The Round Tables were a common terrain in which experience in academic, business, and imperial government intersected. Aspiring and educated men used their experience in colonial administration, foreign-policy positions, and overseas investment to claim expertise in the "Latin America field." Having been in Mexico, Central America, the Caribbean, and South America gave them the authority of experience and a comprehensive vision of Latin American "problems." (Sixteenth-century chroniclers of European expansion in the New World used this very strategy to affirm the credibility of their accounts, no matter how fantastic.) Those who, due to their careers, had perambulated through the territory of the empire were able to issue generalizations about Latin America's great regions.

By uniting the experience and expertise of scholars, diplomats, and businessmen, the organizers expected to translate individual experience "in the field" into a collective policy consensus.[25] Charlottesville offered the opportunity to connect the practical knowledge gathered by administrators and businessmen with the academic knowledge of experts and scholars. At the workshops, well-known historians were able to discuss issues with representatives of United Fruit, W. R. Grace, and other major U.S. railroad or banking interests. At these workshops, "the field" was not restricted to academic knowledge. Gaining a clear and comprehensive understanding of the region's problems (imperial visibility) required scholars to be open to the suggestions and commentaries of producers of practical knowledge. Some voices, however, were excluded. In 1932 Charles Maphis, the director of the Institute of Public Affairs, wanted to invite the writer Waldo Frank, author of *America Hispana*. Haring strongly opposed this initiative.[26]

Participants discussed the most recent issues in U.S. foreign policy in Latin America and also crucial trends in economic, social, and political movements: from tariffs to railroads, from national debts to the national character, from geography to politics. Ideas, contacts, and information circulated at these workshops. Business representatives could get from scholars and diplomats a wider sense of the political, social, and economic aspects of inter-American relations. In return, businessmen contributed their own perspectives as to what constituted the "American interest" in each practical area. In the intersection between the general and the particular, between history and foreign relations, between business and politics, the field of "Latin America" acquired a thick presence, a concrete visibility.

But tensions between "practical" and "scholarly" knowledge were unavoidable at Charlottesville. The role of the scholar was to guide the discussion reminding participants to connect their contributions to the "big picture" of U.S. interests—namely, democratic governance, economic growth, international peace, and cultural exchange. In particular, the organizers, Haring and

Maphis, wanted the debates to center on crucial economic and political questions of the day. Businessmen, on the other hand, wished to deal with "practical matters," such as ocean transportation, road building, public utilities, the sugar industry, or the banana trade. In the end, the scholars had the upper hand, for they framed the questions under discussion and selected the participants. But the organizers first had the program checked by officers from the State Department and the Pan-American Union, as well as by some key financiers.[27]

The new territory of empire (formal and informal) produced authority: the right to represent and to speak for the dependencies and the hinterlands. To the "Pan-Americanists," the comprehensive visibility given by colonial situations provided the basis for regional knowledge. That is, the intersection of university power, colonial administration, and business experience made their observations and opinions appear to be "knowledge." Useful for boosting individual careers, regional knowledge also legitimated their policy opinions. "Pan-Americanists" had accumulated practical experience that, once included into an organized catalog of things observed, could function as truthful statements about "Mexico," "Central America," "the Caribbean," or "South America." All that Haring and Maphis did was to bring together this plurality of knowledge-producers to generate a productive interaction.

Keeping the Gates of the Subdiscipline

The organizers of the Summer Round Tables at Charlottesville absorbed all sorts of opinions, information, and testimonies to constitute a novel, collective, and experimental type of knowledge. Here imperial visibility required scholars to be open to the suggestions and commentaries of businessmen, journalists, foreign-service officials, and other producers of practical knowledge. In contrast, Haring and others defended the field of Latin American history as a bounded space for the deployment of scholarly knowledge, acting as gatekeepers of professional knowledge.

Since the creation of the *Hispanic American Historical Review* (HAHR) in 1918, a small group of scholars had dominated the field of Latin American history. By the mid-1920s, Haring of Harvard, Fred Rippy of Duke, Charles Hackett of Texas, and Arthur Whitaker of Pennsylvania were the key figures, controlling both the editorial board of HAHR and the Committee on Latin American History (CLAH), a division of the American Historical Association (AHA). In 1937–1938, when a group of new scholars wanted to open up the profession to a wider set of knowledge-producers, the established "Latin American group" stood together and successfully defeated the attempt. A proposal by A. Curtis Wilgus for establishing an Academy of Hispanic American History, separate from the AHA and open to nonacademic members, was rejected at the Philadelphia conference of the AHA in 1938. And so was the proposal to democratize the government of the CLAH and of the journal.

Had Wilgus's proposal for an academy been accepted, a growing number of amateur collectors and writers interested in the "history and civilizations of the countries of Latin origins in the Americas" would have shared the academic prestige conferred by the association and the journal. This was inadmissible. Haring, in a letter to Raúl O. Rivera, executive editor of *HAHR*, considered the project as a gate through which "third-rate scholars" could enter the subdiscipline and ultimately control its publications.[28] Here we see a network of scholars defending established positions of authority from challenges from outside. Why did they feel threatened by Wilgus's proposal? Opening the association to the amateur historian, to the explorer-adventurer, to the geographer could mean the debasement of "quality work," a situation which in the end, they thought, would destroy the new field. That explains why, in 1938, the "Latin American group" decided to remain within the AHA, voted against the proposed new academy, and agreed to change only the name of the section (from then on, the "C" of CLAH would stand for "Conference," not Committee).

Gathering Intelligence: Networks at Work

In the early 1930s Haring's prior predictions of a convergence between North and South America were suddenly invalidated by a series of military coups in Argentina, Uruguay, Chile, Brazil, Bolivia, and Ecuador. Haring wrote in *Foreign Affairs*, "A wave of revolutions has over the past six months swept over the Latin American world, from the Pacific to the Atlantic and from the Peruvian highlands to the prairies of Buenos Aires" (1931b, 277). In his efforts to understand this new development, Haring gathered fresh evidence about political conditions in the region using informants from various countries.

In 1932–1933 Haring provided the Council on Foreign Relations (CFR) with the names of several informants in South America. He had tried to involve true native informants, including the historian Jorge Basadre and Alfredo Alvarez Calderón, without success. He turned to U.S. businessmen who, due to their privileged positions, had access to sensitive political and economic information. Among them were Enrique Chirgwin, manager of the Banco Central of Valparaíso, Walter Van Deusen, from the Peruvian National Loan Committee, and William Scroggs, a member of the council traveling in Colombia.[29] These men were to write letters every three months reporting on economic and political conditions in the region.[30] Through the reports of these informants Haring, and through him, the influential CFR, came to know about the volatile political climate in Peru, Colombia, and Chile during the Great Depression. As their reports indicated, anti-Americanism played an important role in the new political climate.

In addition to economic intelligence, these reports included news about changes in the cabinet, initiatives taken by different parties in congress, the popularity of various leaders, signs of social unrest, and the activities of the military. In March 1933 Walter Van Deusen reported about political conditions in Peru. The situation was quite unstable. The confrontational politics of Luis Miguel Sánchez Cerro had brought the country closer to a "revolution."[31] The president's "civilista" supporters were spreading anti-Americanism and trying to stir up public support for a war with Colombia. The report touched also on government corruption, the new constitution, Sanchez Cerro's arbitrary arrests of opposition leaders, and the situation of the army and the navy. In addition, Van Deusen informed the CFR about the growing strength of the Aprista opposition, very popular among government employees.[32]

In May that year, Haring received a report about the Chilean situation. Under martial law and with enhanced executive privileges, the Chilean government was facing increasing political and social unrest.[33] A center-left opposition had formed around the charismatic figure of Arturo Alessandri. The economic situation was critical: exchange controls had created a black market in foreign currency, oil companies were unable to obtain the needed pounds or dollars, and the state nitrate company had mounting debts. From Valparaíso, Enrique Chirgwin sent Haring a long report (twenty-seven pages) that went into considerable detail about the history and situation of the nitrate industry in Chile: the technological backwardness of the industry, the lack of adequate port facilities, the dissemination of the Guggenheim amalgamation process, and cost-cutting mergers.[34] The decline in nitrate prices since 1927 had produced increased state intervention in the industry, leading to the liquidation of the Compañía del Salitre de Chile.

Haring was satisfied with the work of these informants. "It is exactly the sort of thing we want for distribution among the members of the Council of Foreign Relations," he wrote Van Deusen on 29 April 1932.[35] He had reasons to be grateful, for Van Deusen had given him and the CFR precise information about the candidates in the recent Chilean presidential elections and about the explosive political climate. All of the news Haring collected was, he believed, of crucial importance to hemispheric peace and governability. Through these sources, Haring reinforced his own perception of growing anti-American sentiments, learned about conflicts between neighboring countries, and was informed about nationalistic policies that might harm U.S. interests. Much of the intelligence referred to ongoing political and economic conditions. For instance, Van Deusen sent a condemning report about the Sánchez Cerro administration. The new Peruvian president was unwilling to respect business contracts signed by the Leguía administration; he considered the foreign debt a "forgotten incident."

Why did a chaired professor at Harvard involve himself in gathering political and economic intelligence? Unexpected political and economic developments in the period 1929–1933 had upset Haring's vision about South America, introducing new questions to his research agenda, such as nationalism, anti-Americanism, and national debts. Contemporary news helped to correct earlier impressions about the region, resurfacing the legacies of the colonial regime: incapacity for self-government and state control over key economic resources. The informants' reports placed in doubt much of what Haring had written about North and South American historical convergence in the 1920s. The Great Depression had altered significantly the historical path of South America. In 1933, at a series of lectures delivered at the Lowell Institute in Boston, Haring tried to incorporate this new information into his grand historical picture of South America.

The Weak Promise of South American Progress

Haring tried to assess the social and political evolution of the "southern republics" since independence in *South American Progress* (1934).[36] This remarkable work was comprehensive, synthetic, and erudite. Haring addressed the history and current problems of eight countries, using key conflicts to define the nature of each nation's history. For Brazil, Haring chose to deal with the question of the empire; for Chile, he focused on the conflict between the executive and congress; for Colombia, he addressed the tension between state and church. By focusing on representative problems and on particular moments of change in each republic, he was able to produce an authoritative grand narrative of South America.

The book provided a synthesis of the political and social evolution of each country. Argentina went from the "political chaos" of the post-independence (1820–1852), to a period of political stability presided over by an oligarchic elite (1880–1916), to a middle-class government responsive to popular demands (1916–1930). Chile went from an "autocratic republic" under Diego Portales, to an aristocratic republic under a parliamentary system (1860–1890), to an incipient experiment with democracy under the forces of organized labor and a new middle class (since 1925). Brazil's peaceful and progressive constitutional monarchy (1822–1889) had allowed for sixty-seven years of political stability. Then the country transformed into an aristocratic republic riddled with sectionalism and financial troubles (1890–1920). More recently, protests by young military officers (the *tenentes*) brought to the surface latent pressures for democratization. Only two of the countries examined had reached the level of a rudimentary democracy typical of "the Jacksonian era": Argentina since 1916 and Chile since 1926. The other republics showed demands for democratization, but were still far from reaching democratic governance.

Only Argentina appeared as a country with a level of political maturity comparable to the United States. Here was a country whose parallels with the United States Haring found "very striking." To begin with, Argentina's geography was "exactly analogous" to that of the United States, only in the Southern Hemisphere. Like the United States, Argentina possessed all types of climates, an abundance of natural resources, and comparable agricultural regions ("their pampas," "our prairies"). More important, Argentina was—like the United States—a country of immigrants. Masses of European immigrants had populated the country, turning its population "nearly all white." This whitening of the population "made for political steadiness" and facilitated "public order and sobriety."

In international relations, Brazil stood closer to the United States. Haring dealt with the process of abolition of slavery in Brazil as a reflection or learning effect of abolition in the United States. During the First World War, Brazil had decided to ally with the United States and had maintained this position ever since. In other regards, it offered few points of comparison. Brazilian economic development had been tied to Great Britain's, and its government had been monarchical for most of the nineteenth century. Still, the history of Brazil invited contrasts with the Hispanic American nations. The nation had gained its independence as a concession from the royal family, without the need for prolonged wars. The monarchy provided stability and peace and avoided the intense civil conflicts that characterized Hispanic American neighbors. Yet imperial Brazil left important problems unsolved. Here was a nation sparsely settled, with no reliable means of transportation. Though now a republic, the nation remained dominated by a political oligarchy.[37]

The march toward republican maturity took distinct roads. Argentina was a country that had run the whole gamut of political regimes: anarchy, caudillo despotism, constitutional order, aristocratic republic, and middle-class democratic government. Haring paid special attention to the conflict between unitarians and federalists. The Argentine civil wars provided a clear example of federalism turned into "feudalism." General Juan M. de Rosas was a shrewd caudillo, an authoritarian who had preserved Argentina's independence in the midst of blockades by imperial powers (1838–1840, 1845–1848), but at the cost of delaying the country's constitutional arrangement. Another caudillo, General Urquiza, acted as an organizer, calling for the constitutional convention that drafted the 1853 constitution. Then the republic divided into two states (Buenos Aires and the Confederation), a separation that reminded Haring of the U.S. Civil War. General Julio A. Roca received praise for solving the difficult problem of federalizing Buenos Aires and organizing a government coalition that minimized intra-elite conflicts.[38]

During the period 1880–1915, Argentina achieved order and progress, but not democracy. A national party (the Partido Autonomista Nacional) dominated politics and administration. The elite controlled elections to the exclusion of the majority of the population. Only in 1912 was the secret ballot enacted, and with it emerged the possibility for a middle-class party to win the elections. Haring depicted the Radical governments (1916–1930) as a "crude democracy" in which men without experience came to exercise government. With Hipólito Yrigoyen came greater doses of personalist rule, corruption, and machine politics, until finally, in September 1930, the aging caudillo was ousted by a military coup.

Chile exemplified an established constitutional order under the control of the landed class. From the time of Portales, there had been shifts between conservative and liberal elites, between congress and executive dominance, but by and large, political conditions were controlled by a closely knit aristocracy. In fact, what seemed like a modern political conflict—the constitutional crisis of 1890–1891—ended up with the victory of the landed aristocracy. This class supported the party of congress, which, with the aid of the navy, defeated the popular president José Manuel Balmaceda. The protracted conflict about two types of government (executive control versus parliamentarianism) could not obscure the oligarchic nature of the Chilean political order.

Brazil was a peculiar case in which an enlightened emperor, Dom Pedro II, had generated political stability and social order and granted individual liberties. But the regime moved only sluggishly on the problem of slavery, while abolition forces nurtured a movement for republican government; so a year after slavery was ended in 1888, the monarchy, too, was abolished. The old republic was basically an aristocratic regime, dominated by the political machines of the three major states (Rio Grande do Sul, Minas Gerais, and São Paulo), which formed the Mineiro-Paulista governing alliance. The ruling class was concerned more with economic and financial problems than with enhancing political participation. Starting in the mid-1920s, military revolts called for enhanced political participation.[39] The 1930 revolution, from which Getúlio Vargas emerged, was in fact a challenge to the monopoly of power of the Mineiro-Paulista alliance.

In comparison with the small republics of the Caribbean and Central America, the South American republics had experimented with republican government for over a century. Yet, starting in 1930, military coups and social revolts had suspended this trajectory (Haring 1931). Haring tried to minimize the effects of these revolutions, presenting them as part of the long march toward democracy. He considered coups and dictatorships in Chile to be temporary deviations from the country's long-term political trajectory.[40] The 1930 conservative revolution in Argentina took Haring by surprise. He thought Argentina had attained "an ordered and reasoned democracy" since the rise to power of the Radical Party and speculated that perhaps the 1930 coup was just a temporary setback in a long-term progressive evolution (Haring 1936).

The political disturbances of the early 1930s reshaped Haring's research agenda on the ground but did not affect his grand picture of South America. The region had inherited from its colonial masters problematic traits that were difficult to overcome. Emancipation from Spain and Portugal had opened up momentous changes that gradually transformed politics. The southern republics subscribed to new ideals—freedom, equality before the law, and popular sovereignty—difficult to carry into practice. As Haring conceded, "It had taken a century to eradicate the shortcomings of three centuries of colonial rule" (Haring 1934, 12). Military caudillos came to power and the republics soon developed landed aristocracies. In part, Haring thought, this development was inevitable, given post-independence conditions: mass illiteracy, lack of communications, and the absence of a national consciousness. Rather than launching the nations forward, the caudillos took them backward. While the capital cities showed some reforms, the interior provinces lapsed into "feudalism" (ibid., 17).

Geography and race helped explain the nineteenth-century setback in political evolution. Geographical features—mountains, rivers, and forests—divided nations into scattered settlements. Lack of effective communication across these divisions prevented the development of national economies and national sentiments. The exceptions to this trend were the ABC nations, where a better physical environment made possible the construction of railroads and the creation of a national economy. In the Andean nations, Spanish colonialism had left racially divided societies, in which whites had rights but Indians had none. This continued to be the case in the post-independence period.

In spite of great obstacles, Haring believed, South American nations as a whole had made significant political progress in the century following independence. Militarism in its more barbaric form had almost disappeared. So had violent revolutions, now displaced by bloodless coups d'état. Under the challenge of the middle classes, older aristocracies were everywhere losing their hold on the destinies of the republics. It was still true that, in the Andean region, where colonialism had a long-lasting effect, the republics had failed to elevate the standard of living and education of indigenous peoples, keeping them outside of politics. In contrast, the larger, most stable republics (Argentina, Chile, Uruguay, Colombia) were "developing a genuine democracy." Ballots were replacing bullets as means of resolving political conflicts. Sustained economic growth and long-term political stability had created the conditions for "greater moderation" of character and a new "sense of social responsibility."

Comparative and Comprehensive History

In 1944, at a lecture delivered at the Loomis School, Haring addressed the persistence of dictatorships or personalistic rule in Hispanic America.[41] He explained why, 120 years after independence, the republics were still unable to achieve democratic government: due to Spanish absolutism, the southern republics had not acquired sufficient experience in self-government. In particular, they had failed to learn notions of altruism and public service.[42] Thus, it was the colonial legacy that solved the paradox of how two lands, emerging from a common experience, ended up with different systems of government. The United States was democratic because its colonial experience prepared it for self-government. Latin America was undemocratic because its colonial experience had denied them that training. To an extent, Haring was extending the Black Legend of Spanish cruelty and misdeeds from historiography to the terrain of politics. Here, the Spanish empire had denied the peoples of South America the possibility of learning the public virtues and the sociability necessary for a working democracy. This was U.S. exceptionalism à la Tocqueville.

Searching in the remote past for explanations of the problems of the present showed the *practical utility of history*. History was a sack full of objective lessons from which one could take whatever best explained the present condition of Latin America. Conversely, the present could damage existing narratives of the past. If the colonial legacy was useful to explain contemporary dictatorial trends, then the whole post-independent period had been a failed experiment. Anticipating by more than twenty years the Stanley and Barbara Stein thesis of the persistence of the "colonial heritage," Haring refashioned the post-independence era as a continuity of the colonial period.[43] The revolutions of independence had overthrown the Spanish colonial government but not the old social system. A small ruling class made up of landowning aristocrats continued to dominate great masses of peasants and workers.

It is curious that a New Dealer and admirer of the Good Neighbor Policy (Haring) and a pair of *dependentistas* (the Steins) resorted to the same thesis of continuity, extracting from the colonial era the code to decipher the present. In both metanarratives Hispanic America carried the burden of an unshakable past in its present underdevelopment and dictatorial governments. As Haring was prompt to explain to his students and audiences, the independence leadership had built republics in paper, not in practice. Latin American constitutions were emptied of real content. Democratic governance could not have flourished in lands where illiteracy, exploitation, and servile labor were prevalent.[44] Like the land of the antipodes, South American republics generated the opposite of what they proclaimed. Seeking social equality, they perpetuated privilege; seeking popular government, they enthroned landed oligarchies; seeking federations, they created regionally fragmented nations.

In his courses as well as in his writings, Haring always returned to colonial history, for this was the nexus that united and gave meaning to present differences between Anglo-America and Latin America. However distant the one appeared to the other, the two Americas were marked by a common historical experience. Both Anglo-America and South America had developed into political adulthood by shaking off the chains of European colonialism. And both had experimented—with different degrees of success—with republican government. Because of this historical commonality, their destinies were united. To Haring, parallel historical experience was the basis for envisioning a peaceful and cooperative system of inter-American relations (Haring 1934, 216–17).

But historical experience also produced difference, and this difference justified U.S. tutelage over the most backward nations of South America. The post-independence period in South America had led to anarchy, political fragmentation, and civil wars, not to apprenticeship in self-government.[45] This apprenticeship could be attained only by transforming the mentality of South Americans through economic and institutional modernization. During the Second World War, U.S. technological and economic superiority over the southern republics became quite evident. To be modern and able to speak as an equal, South America needed to mimic the United States in matters of economic, social, and technological progress.

Had they managed to build industry, commerce, and middle class, perhaps the southern republics could have attained U.S. political modernity. But they had not, and the reasons for this failure lay deep in history, in the errors of Spanish monarchical absolutism and the failure of post-independence governments. Specifically, Haring blamed post-independence governments for not choosing the right policies: economic autonomy, industrialization, universal education, liberal government, and so on. *History* thus appears as an overdetermined system, a full circle of explanations. Starting from a contemporary difference, the historian could work his way into the past to recuperate traces that explained, reproduced, and consolidated such difference. The Hispanic American history that Haring practiced was such an exercise. It was "useful" in the sense of making "evident" the gulf that separated Anglo-America from Latin America. If the "great divergence" between the two Americas could be displaced to the colonial past, then the U.S. empire could relax its responsibilities for Latin American development and political democracy while, at the same time, insisting on the necessity for them.

Conclusion

From Harvard, Clarence Haring helped build the edifice of Hispanic American history. His stylized historical syntheses of the Spanish empire and of the social and political evolution of the South American republics were influential in the formation of the subdiscipline. He promoted the production of scholarly work on areas of colonial and national regional history and strove to sustain, within the AHA, a scholarly community dedicated to the history of Latin America. Haring's works translated the complex and elusive realities of Latin America to U.S. American educated audiences. Though simplified to the extreme, his historical narrative of the development of Hispanic American nations presented the advantage of locating the region's history within the grand scenery of comparative imperial history, something few other writers were able to accomplish.

His most important historical undertaking—the institutional and economic history of the Spanish empire—contained an inventory of errors to avoid: outdated economic policies, the introduction of premodern social relations, and the promotion of racial miscegenation. This rosary of mistakes had brought about the economic decline of the Spanish empire in the seventeenth century and shaped the social, economic, and political conditions of the independent Hispanic American republics. These nations inherited racially divided societies, political systems dominated by powerful landed elites, and populations with little experience in self-government and free markets.

This gloomy picture of Latin America was somewhat modified by Haring's visit to the region in the mid-1920s. His observations served to reveal the contemporary realities of South American progress and anti-American feelings. In the late nineteenth century, a group of progressive nations in the south—the ABC powers—had started to separate themselves from the rest, exhibiting by the second decade of the twentieth century political stability and economic progress. These nations, Haring thought, were particularly endowed to successfully adopt U.S. models of economic growth, social equality, and democratic politics. The discovery of South American "distrust"—that is, that members of the South American intelligentsia were criticizing the interventionist policies of the United States in the Circum-Caribbean—refocused Haring's attention on the question of local intellectuals, leading him to imagine cooperation among historians of the continent.

Haring's most important legacy was to posit the existence of a common and parallel history between Hispanic America and the United States. Earlier than Herbert Bolton, he envisioned the possibility of a comparative hemispheric history, one organized by race, the environment, political ideals, and institutional trajectories. It was, to be sure, an exemplary history rooted in the presupposition of U.S. technological, economic, and institutional superiority. In his stylized narrative the South American nations were undoing a legacy of colonialism, step by step. Mirrored in the achievements of the northern colossus, the new republics had still much to learn. Yet Haring's history contained a moment of optimism: the possibility of convergence of the ABC powers toward U.S. forms of modernity.

The Harvard historian was able to put the histories of the "two Americas" on the same plane at the cost of great simplification: reducing differences to the most basic fundamentals (race, environment, and national experience in terms of ideals and institutions); abstracting away important aspects of the geography and history of Latin American countries; and artfully creating forced analogies. It was this reductionist and simplified version of history that served to sustain the belief in the perfectibility of the region's democracy and welfare, and, therefore, in the possibility of peaceful interaction with the southern neighbors.

Like other scholars discussed in this book, Haring distinguished the progressive nations of the Southern Cone from the rest of the subcontinent, seeing in their trajectories the past history of the United States. The anomaly of the ABC powers complicated the simplistic version of the great divide (north vs. south of the Panama Canal) and served to reinforce the validity of the politics of U.S. Pan-Americanism. For at the basis of the U.S. desire for mutual co-operation and friendship among the American republics was a historical trajectory that, despite temporary setbacks and deviations, marched in the long term toward the same ideals.

Haring's grand narratives—of the Spanish empire and of the post-independence South American republics—made it possible to produce generalizations of hemispheric scope. Contemporary events, particularly developments related to the Pan-American movement, influenced Haring's ideas, research proposals, and historical narrative. Because of interconnections between economics and history, between the region's political evolution and the possibilities of Pan-American cooperation, between the history of the Spanish empire and the potentialities of the U.S. empire, I have presented Haring's history as useful knowledge at the service of empire.

One could read Haring's two most important interventions in the foreign-policy debate as side-steps in the career of a colonial historian. Yet, examined in the long-term trajectory of Haring's intellectual project, these works appear to be integral to his search for a comparative history of the Americas. His understanding of the decline of the Spanish empire informed and served as the background for evaluating and criticizing U.S. policies toward Latin America in the twentieth century. Indeed, most of his historical works show an enduring concern for empires and imperialism. Haring's more challenging historical arguments cannot be understood outside of the framework of a comparative history of empires.

Networks of scholars consolidate academic credentials and defend institutional positions within the academy. Deployed in the context of an expanding empire, these networks can also facilitate the gathering of information necessary for imperial visibility. Haring used networks of informants to help the U.S. foreign-policy community understand Latin American politics. The mobilization of evidence about South American peripheries through networks of local informants was crucial for "correcting" earlier predictions about the subcontinent's future. A regional history committed to the service of foreign policy needed to be constantly updated about contemporary developments. In this, Haring's commitment to empiricism served to check his otherwise unbounded generalizations about South America. Haring's predictions about the improvement and perfectibility of the southern republics changed as he made a constant effort to accommodate new facts to his grand historical narrative. His lectures at Lowell (1933) and at Loomis (1944) show this process of adjustment clearly.

Harvard and a host of connected institutions vested Haring's historical narrative and political analysis with scholarly prestige and authority. Haring's business informants and scholarly connections in Latin America provided fresh information and interpretation that he could recirculate in a variety of forums in the United States. Comparativity and intelligence (being updated on current events) gave Haring's history a practical and useful value that was appreciated by policy makers and scholars. Through him, Harvard was closely connected to the region.

The prestige associated with the enunciatory location—Harvard—cannot be overemphasized. It was at Harvard where Haring produced his grand historical synthesis of Hispanic America. From Harvard, he coordinated efforts to enhance Latin American studies, in the U.S. northeast as well as in the country as a whole. He promoted the idea of a great bibliographic catalog for researchers in the region. He fostered the formation of Pan-American societies, involving students in their organization. His lectures and public addresses provided students and audiences with an erudite and synthetic grand narrative of the long-term evolution of the southern republics. His research designs represent an attempt to combine economics with history in the search for a multidisciplinary science at the service of foreign policy. This project produced a comprehensive report on the causes of anti-Americanism in South America.

A Harvard professor could build a network of local informants and be in contact with foreign-policy makers and businessmen; Harvard expanded the resonance of Haring's ideas and predicaments. In the round tables at the University of Virginia, he discussed with businessmen, foreign-policy makers, and other scholars the "problems" of Latin America. The State Department and northeastern audiences alike expected the Harvard historian to keep them abreast of new political and economic developments in the southern republics.

One of my primary arguments concerns the relationship between Harvard's privileged location and the mobilization of useful knowledge through networks of scholars and businessmen. Harvard granted Haring the authority to articulate a grand historiographical narrative of Hispanic America and, from this enunciatory position, to influence U.S. foreign policy. Harvard concentrated knowledge and enthusiasm about Latin America, and this generated arguments about U.S. policy toward the region. Networks of relationships built around Haring and Harvard—networks that included businessmen, government officials, publicists, foreign-relations experts, and international lawyers—served to circulate those arguments within the sphere of imperial power and policy.

Haring's simplified narratives, forced analogies, and optimistic projections were sympathetic to a certain vision of empire: the benevolent imperialism of the Good Neighbor Policy. His vision of a common and parallel history of the Americas sustained the politics of Pan-Americanism. A benevolent empire, granting to the hemisphere peace, commerce, technological change, and cooperation in solving "common problems," appeared to be an improvement over the mistakes of Spanish colonialism and the following blunders of the post-independence "paper republics."

At Harvard, Haring gave reasons for integrating Hispanic American history into the formation of an educated gentleman. In his lectures, publications, and public speeches we find a set of quite articulate reasons for imperial visibility and engagement. His task was to interest students in Latin America, and to do so, he invoked imperial reasons: the contemporary crisis of governability in the American Mediterranean made it necessary to study the experience of the Spanish empire—in particular, the institutional architecture and cultural legacies it bestowed on South Americans. In this way, looking at the long trajectory of the Spanish empire and pointing out its major mistakes ceased to be an esoteric exercise. It became an urgent task of a regional knowledge committed to the politics of Pan-American unity.

SIX

Intellectual Cooperation: Leo S. Rowe, Democratic Government, and the Politics of Scholarly Brotherhood

———

If Pan-Americanism has any real meaning it must lead us to co-operate with our neighbors, not only in repelling aggression, but in assisting them wherever our experience can be of value. The service will be reciprocal; for there is much of Latin-American civilization by which we can profit. We have entered upon the era of good feeling with South America. —LEO S. ROWE, "The Awakening of Bolivia" (1907)

The political scientist Leo S. Rowe was undoubtedly a primary architect of the system of inter-American cooperation.[1] In addition to being among the first Latin American experts hired by the State Department (1919–1920), Rowe was in 1920 appointed director of the Pan-American Union (PAU), a Washington-based agency that gathered information and formulated policies for Latin America, where he remained for twenty-six years. During this period, he participated in the transformation of U.S. foreign relations from Dollar Diplomacy to the Good Neighbor Policy. In this chapter I investigate the interconnectedness between academic knowledge and foreign-policy principles in his writings. In particular, I am interested in the construction and transformation of Rowe's foreign-policy principles in relation to changes in his perception and thought on Latin America generated by the displacement from formal to informal empire.

Before coming to the State Department and the PAU, Rowe had pursued graduate studies in Europe, then built a reputation as expert in international law and theory of municipal government. He was appointed professor at the University of Pennsylvania in 1894.[2] In 1900 President William McKinley appointed him as member of the commission entrusted with the revision of the laws of Puerto Rico, and in 1913 he served on the Land Claims Commission in Panama. From 1902 to 1930, he presided over the American Academy of Political and Social Science. He was thus in a privileged position to observe the unfolding of the U.S. empire.

Rowe's intellectual trajectory can be summarized as follows. In his graduate studies in Germany, France, and Britain (1890–1894), he developed an interest in municipal government and finance. His book *Problems of City Government* (1908) addressed the great gap separating inherited political ideas from the conditions of life in modern U.S. and European cities. By 1900–1903, his experience in colonial administration led him to question U.S. governance in the Spanish Caribbean. He condensed these reflections in his book *The United States and Porto Rico* (1904). Then, circa 1906–1909, Rowe interacted with intellectuals of the Southern Cone, an experience that changed his view of inter-American relations. In a series of articles about "South American progress," he communicated the news of the southern republics' economic bonanza and political stability. After the First World War, he promoted "intellectual cooperation" as the most effective way to build U.S. hegemony in Latin America. From its inception, the idea of intellectual cooperation was related to the spectacle of progress in the Southern Cone. It was rapid economic growth and institutional stability that made the region comparable to the United States and sustained the hope of a hemispheric brotherhood of scholars.

By 1914, he was challenging President Wilson's doctrine of nonrecognition, taking a multilateral view of the Monroe Doctrine, and promoting the cause of "neutral rights" in South America. In his 1914 lectures at the University of La Plata, Rowe attempted to communicate the problems of modern society and government in the United States to the Argentine intelligentsia.[3] His observations on Argentina's government institutions were later condensed in *The Federal System of the Argentine Republic* (1921), where he criticized "presidentialism," the domination of the executive over the other branches of government, and Porteño centralism, the domination of the capital city over the interior provinces. After this, he used foreign-policy papers and addresses to convey the ideas and policies central to what he called "constructive Pan-Americanism," an approach to hemispheric integration that privileged mutual understanding through intellectual and cultural cooperation over economic and defense objectives.[4]

Along Rowe's intellectual trajectory we find the construction of two guiding principles: the principle of "education in self-rule" to be applied to the Circum-Caribbean protectorates; and the principle of "intellectual cooperation" to be used in relation to South America. While the former principle emerged from Rowe's experience as a colonial administrator in Puerto Rico, the latter was a by-product of his immersion in the academic circles of South America during 1906–1914. Rowe's reflections on the Caribbean dependencies influenced his views about the ABC countries (Argentina, Brazil, and Chile), leaving him with a comprehensive and differentiated view of Latin America. Thus, foreign-policy principles appear as the sedimentation of a long intellectual and policy trajectories. I call this composite result or synthesis "situated regional knowledge," a term that encapsulates the combination of certainties and passions that orient the scholar-administrator's views and policies to a given area of influence. Situated regional knowledge emerges out of the interaction of personal experience, geopolitical conjunctures, and academic concerns. This synthesis partakes of the attributes of "imperial knowledge," including comprehensive visibility and extranational sovereignty.[5]

Rowe's discussions of "insular" government and sovereignty in Puerto Rico and the Philippines spoke to a more general issue in U.S. government: the "elasticity" and adaptability of democratic ideas and institutions in colonial situations. When Rowe dealt with the question of Puerto Rico, he derived consequences for the whole set of U.S. interventions in the Caribbean and the Pacific. Similarly, his study of Argentine federalism contributed to a more general debate about the institutional parallels between the United States and the southern republics. This study took as given the national sovereignty, economic progress, and political stability attained by Argentina by 1914; the country did not seem to require education in self-rule. In the Southern Cone, Rowe discovered an illustrious elite willing to entertain a debate about European vs. U.S. models of progress and modernity.

Rowe's program of intellectual cooperation was his major contribution to the field of inter-American relations. His insights in this matter show a process of selection that corresponds with knowledge production in imperial contexts: out of a set of intellectual concerns, a scholar-statesman selects a subset of hardcore beliefs and principles that define the interests and ideals of his nation-state. Rowe's belief in the politics of scholarly brotherhood had a long-lasting influence in inter-American relations—more so than his contributions to understanding Argentine federalism, the problems of city government, or the transfer of colonial government.

Lessons in Imperial Governance

Rowe first engaged with Latin American institutions and culture in the context of formal empire, while participating in U.S. colonial administration in Puerto Rico and Panama. He considered the annexations and protectorates an opportunity to study the transfer of U.S. government overseas. He was particularly interested in the constitutional implications of the transition from military to civil rule in the new possessions. Most of his writings between 1900 and 1904 aimed to show that the U.S. empire was sustained by a legal-constitutional structure and that, in the end, the U.S. occupations could bring the dependencies closer to U.S. ideals of government.[6] His book *The United States and Porto Rico* (1904), together with a group of articles published during the years 1900–1903, could be read as a treatise on colonial governance. In these writings Rowe asserted that U.S. military occupations always gave way to provisional civil governments, which in turn could lead to self-government. To this extent, the U.S. empire was different from other imperial ventures, for U.S. protectorates enjoyed U.S. constitutional guarantees.

The political process of intervention, annexation, and ordering of the new territories followed a predictable path. At first, military rulers seemed to operate with absolute power. Then the president, with the support of Congress, appointed civil governors and gave them instructions to manage the affairs of the colony. In a third moment, a local government, commonly composed of a bicameral congress, a judicial system, and municipal authorities, was established. After this, the protectorate could administer its own affairs, under the limitations contained in the annexation treaty.[7] In Rowe's view, at each step of this transition there were constitutional provisions and jurisprudence that limited the authority of colonial administrators.

Rowe was a progressive imperialist who believed in the superiority of U.S. institutions of government. For him, it was self-evident that the U.S. constitutional government was a perfected political system, one that should be transferred to the newly acquired territories. Rowe presented the U.S. empire as a progressive force in the Caribbean. Given the proper instruction and enough time, the inhabitants of the new protectorates would learn to enjoy the advantages of U.S. constitutional government. Though he expressed concerns about the "preparedness" of Caribbean peoples to embrace U.S. institutions, he expected that the transfer of U.S. law and government would be beneficial to Puerto Ricans, Cubans, and Filipinos.

To him the U.S. constitutional government was a flexible, adaptable system that could incorporate within itself other modalities of rule and political traditions. In a way, the legal empire he imagined was a malleable system of rules of governance designed to bring order and civility to Caribbean and Pacific peripheries.[8] The bastion of imperial governance was the U.S. Constitution, a system of ideas embodied in institutions believed to be "perfect" for the attainment of "universal goods." Like other constitutional experts, Rowe seemed unaware of the provincialism of this position or of the historical and cultural embeddedness of "American government."

His experience in Puerto Rico in 1900–1901 influenced his views on empire. President McKinley gave him the unique opportunity of revising the laws of a recently acquired colony. While the other members of the commission charged with revising the laws of Puerto Rico dealt with criminal and civil laws, Rowe was entrusted with ordering existing legislation concerning urban affairs. Later he was given the task of writing the island's political code, designing the basic instruments of government: the limitations of the executive, the composition of the chambers, and the attributions of different judicial authorities. In addition, he helped to organize the electoral regime and the municipal system.

The legal transition from military to civil rule was a clear, unambiguous process. First, the occupation government acted under a state of war, its actions justified under the principle of "exigency." As soon as war ceased, military authorities had to protect the basic rights of local inhabitants, including personal, property, and religious rights. But during the transfer of government to local authorities, it was not clear what laws regulated the transition or whether the new authorities were bounded by U.S. constitutional principles. When Puerto Rico became a legal possession of the United States, the issue of constitutional supremacy came into question.

During Rowe's service in Puerto Rico, the Supreme Court issued new decisions affecting the status of the island (known as the "insular cases"). Rowe examined these decisions to reflect on the constitutional and legal status of the new U.S. empire.[9] The decisions contained a great deal of confusion and ambiguity.[10] The *Downes v. Bidwells* decision, in particular, brought about a problematic "in-betweenness" eroding all constitutional certainties. According to the Downes ruling, Puerto Rico was "domestic in an international sense" and "foreign in a domestic sense."[11] On only one point were all judges in agreement: they rejected the automatic incorporation of new possessions into the union. Congress retained the prerogative to accept or reject a new state. If this was so, the president had a free hand in dealing with the colonies during the transition. No constitutional restrictions prevented U.S. colonial authorities from establishing governments that temporarily departed from the "American system of government." Rowe justified the "free hand" to experiment with hybrid forms of governments by pointing to the cultural differences between Hispanic America and the United States (in race, customs, religion, and modes of thought).

In a subsequent article, Rowe argued that the transfer of Puerto Rico's sovereignty from Spain to the United States had imposed limitations on government and extended the protection of civil and individual rights. After the transfer of sovereignty was ratified by Congress, the "provisional civil authority" had to establish order, provide public health, and administer the internal affairs of the territory. Though freed from congressional oversight, the provisional government had to respect existing laws regulating property rights and could not innovate in matters of freedom of the press (Leo S. Rowe 1902c). Hence, Rowe argued, imperial expansionism was compatible with the reestablishment of the rule of law.

To Rowe, the Philippines case added a new dimension to the problem of insular government: an insurrectionary movement that prolonged military rule (Leo S. Rowe 1902a). But this altered neither the process of transition, nor the idea of a government bounded by constitutional provisions. The Philippines also underwent the three-stage process described by Rowe. To prevent the concentration of power in the hands of a military governor, President McKinley appointed a commission entrusted with legislative powers and with the mandate to reorganize the judiciary.[12] The commission enacted new laws that reorganized provincial and municipal governments and placed "natives" in charge of those positions (Leo S. Rowe 1902a). Soon after, the principle of separation of powers was restored.

From his experience in Puerto Rico, Rowe derived a few basic lessons about governance and culture (Leo S. Rowe 1904). First, the Spanish legal system was adaptable to the new conditions of U.S. rule. Second, the localism inherited from Spanish rule (under which city councils enjoyed considerable autonomy) provided a good basis for the establishment of a modern municipal government. Granting elections at the local level entailed little political risk, as long as U.S. authorities controlled the central government. But Hispanic political culture—and this was the third lesson—presented an important hurdle in the transition to self-government. Local politicians took politics too seriously, turning party disputes into family feuds and occasionally generating outbursts of political violence. From this, Rowe concluded that "Spanish-American values" were not particularly suited to democratic, republican government.[13]

The adaptability of "American government" was also successfully tested in the Philippine experiment. Rowe associated the success of municipal and provincial reform in the islands to the commission's decision to retain some features of the Spanish colonial administration.[14] The U.S. intervention government preserved control of the municipality of Manila as well as the power of police and sanitation in the islands. After the census was taken, Filipinos were allowed to hold elections for the national assembly, while the commission itself nominated the Philippine senate. The experience of Puerto Rico helped Rowe understand the Philippine transition. In both cases the Spanish colonial legacy presented an important "cultural" obstacle in the transfer of U.S. models of government. In the Philippines "paternal ideas about government" prevailed among local politicians. Rather than being devoted to the common good and the progress of the community, governments were captive to private passions and interests (Leo S. Rowe 1902d, 322). The establishment of civil government had to bring the new territories closer to "American standards of liberty" (Leo S. Rowe 1902c, 472). The U.S. interventions in the Caribbean had highlighted the difficulties of governing overseas territories and, at the same time, delineated more clearly the mission of the benevolent empire. The U.S. empire had to teach "natives" the basic notions of constitutional government so that they could achieve self-rule (Leo S. Rowe 1902b, 261). This peculiar notion of empire burdened the United States with a pedagogic responsibility.

In Rowe's view nothing short of full Americanization in the art and theory of government should satisfy U.S. colonial governors, experts, and statesmen. U.S. interventions had to "make Americans of the Porto Ricans." This meant two things: the transfer of laws governing the states of the union; and the introduction of "American standards of political liberty and self-government" (Leo S. Rowe 1902b, 261). The flexibility of the U.S. constitutional system could facilitate the legal transfer. The Constitution allowed transition governments to function on the basis of legal hybrids. But the empire's pedagogical imperative required more: it demanded a transformation of local political culture. Puerto Ricans, for instance, adhered to quite different notions of family relations, state authority, and religious liberty. Their "cultural foreignness" represented a monumental obstacle to overcome.

U.S. interventions in the Caribbean had tested the adaptability of U.S. government and had created new knowledge about how to administer foreign possessions. Rowe's experience in Puerto Rico had given him some important lessons, including "the necessity of a greater elasticity of ideas, a broader sympathy, and a readiness, or at least the willingness to understand the point of view of a people whose training, traditions and system of law are essentially different from our own" (ibid., 262). Rowe's empathy toward local cultures prefigured his future position on inter-American relations. The resolution of the problem of self-government required a better understanding of Hispanic American history and culture—a form of Latin American studies.

Imperial governance, in short, demanded new attitudes from U.S. statesmen, experts, and officials, specifically "the ability to appreciate the value of alien institutions which fulfill the same ends of justice as our own" and the determination to educate the peoples of the new dependencies into "the free and willing acceptance of our system of law and government" (ibid.). The full "Americanization" of the political culture of colonial peoples presented new challenges to knowledge-producers. Scholars had to better understand the history, culture, and institutions of insular possessions. To manage a modern empire, the adaptability of policy to local conditions and legal cultures was crucial. Consequently, it was desirable that insular governments retain the discretionary power to transfer U.S. ideas and institutions (Leo S. Rowe 1902a, 323).

South American Progress

Rowe was one of the pioneers in reporting South America's progress. The impression produced by the region's modern cities, ambitious educational projects, and progressive governments led him to reconsider the place of "South America" in the hemisphere and subsequently to imagine a different mode of imperial engagement. The novelties he "discovered" (political stability, economic progress, and urban renovation) were the bases on which he later grounded his argument about intellectual cooperation.

Rowe first traveled to Argentina in 1906, after the Rio Pan-American conference came to an end. Before reaching the cities of Buenos Aires and La Plata, he visited Entre Ríos and Santa Fe, areas of farmers' colonies, small-scale property, and active community engagement in municipal government. He spoke with provincial authorities, saw the city councils at work, visited local newspapers, and attended a producer's exhibit at Concordia. Avidly, he sought information on municipal government and finance, roads and railroads, agrarian production, public health, and other subjects relating to the region's recent progress. He was pleasantly surprised by what he heard. The littoral colonies showed both wealth and good administration.[15]

In La Plata Rowe entered into contact with the outstanding talents of the conservative-liberal elite, among them Joaquín V. González, the recently appointed rector of the university, and Rodolfo Rivarola, the dean of the law school. He took residence in the university college ("*internado*"), where he mingled with students of veterinary medicine and law. Accepting an honorary doctorate, Rowe spoke of the great similarity between the United States and Argentina and of the irony of the rediscovery: "How is it possible," he asked the audience, "that our countries had remained unknown to each other for so many years and that we have now to make *a second travel of discovery of America*?"[16] Next he praised the new scientific spirit he found at the University of La Plata, an institution that cultivated research for practical ends. Encouraged by the similarity in progress between the United States and Argentina, he made a remarkable proposition. University men in the Americas could unite in the solution of common problems. In our universities, he said, is the basis for the construction of the "*true unity of American culture*."

From June 1907 to February 1909, Rowe traveled through the main capitals of South America (Lima, Santiago, Rio de Janeiro, and Buenos Aires), carrying good news about U.S. willingness to intensify commercial and cultural relations with its southern neighbors. In an article published in the *North American Review*, Rowe (1907c) acknowledged that the southern republics had made great progress in terms of political stability. The impressive growth of its cities was the proof of its economic potential and progressive spirit. The region offered great market opportunities not yet fully exploited by U.S. manufacturers and merchants.

His speeches at the universities of Santiago and Lima in 1907 dealt with a novel and controversial issue: university reform. At the University of San Marcos (Lima), Rowe spoke of traditional universities as mere producers of academic degrees for the benefit of self-interested elites. It was time to prepare men willing to work for national progress and social welfare.[17] At the National University of Chile (Santiago), Rowe spoke of the common ideals of "American" universities and of the need of university men to study democratic governance. The Americas were a great experimental field for democratic governance. Hence, its universities should pay special attention to democracy. Modern universities had to be practical and useful, adapting to the changing circumstances of economic and social life. Rowe advocated closer relations between students and professors, emphasis on practical and business education, and a campus atmosphere propitious to community solidarity.[18]

This trip gave him the opportunity to observe closely the progress in urban renewal, municipal government, and education in Argentina, Brazil, Bolivia, and Chile. In 1908 he pondered the sanitary and educational improvement of São Paulo and other cities in southern Brazil (Leo S. Rowe 1908a). The coffee capital had recently improved its water supply and drainage systems, built new hospitals, and established sanitary controls. These reforms made São Paulo "one of the healthiest cities on the American continent" (ibid., 509). Supported by export taxes on coffee, the state had developed and impressive educational system, with model normal and technical schools. Rio de Janeiro also had undergone extensive renovation. A progressive mayor had built a broad avenue along the coast and great public buildings were being erected (ibid.).

In the rapidly growing cities of southern Brazil, Rowe found confirmation of his views about democracy and urbanization. Strong urban improvement movements showed that democracy and civility had taken root at the local level. U.S. investors were collaborating with city governments in the creation of basic infrastructure and transportation services. By all appearances, "American ideals" had been planted in fertile ground. Even in Bolivia, there was a "new spirit of progress." A U.S. syndicate was building a rail connection with Argentina, U.S. investments in mining were pouring in, and education was progressing at rapid pace. The Bolivian government's interest in education provided an opening for inter-American cooperation (Leo S. Rowe 1907a).

The U.S. experience in teaching colonial peoples could be extended to Bolivia, a new frontier for U.S. capital, knowledge, and influence. Rowe drew on bodily metaphors to present the idea of benevolent empire from a different angle: the double impulse of U.S. capital and local leadership was awakening the energies of progress, dormant for centuries, in the South American periphery. If this progress had local roots—if Paulistas, Porteños, or Limeños demanded U.S. expertise and capital for engineering projects—then U.S. interventions appeared as responses to South American requests. From the "Bolivian awakening," Rowe derived a notion of Pan-Americanism based on the exportation of U.S. advice. U.S. Americans could teach Bolivians all they had learned about modern education.[19]

Rowe's tour was highly successful. Everywhere he went, he was feted as a celebrity and showered with honors. Various universities of the region granted him honorary degrees. He was received with banquets, his addresses were printed in the local newspapers, and local learned societies treated him as a guest of honor. Rowe was quite excited about the results of his trip. After a banquet offered by President José Pardo in Lima (September 1908), he told the press that he "felt as if under a delightful spell" and that the whole trip had been "like an entertainment of the Arabian Nights."[20] Because he spoke in a familiar idiom of economic growth, social and moral improvement, and educational progress, South American elites treated Rowe as a friend.

Intellectual Cooperation

Back in the United States, Rowe reported to President Theodore Roosevelt and disseminated the "good news" in addresses to universities, business associations, and scientific societies.[21] The press interviewed him and printed his arguments under flashy headlines. He told the *Public Ledger* that South America was eager to imitate the U.S. educational system; to the *Enquirer* he reported that sentiments in South America were turning favorable to the United States; to the *New York Sun* he emphasized that U.S. Americans should "awaken" to the reality of the "marvelous social progress and economic development" attained by the southern republics.[22] His unbounded optimism paralleled that of John Barrett, who at the time was advertising South America as "the land of opportunity."

His second South American tour reinforced the impression he had reached earlier at Rio de Janeiro and Buenos Aires: Latin American statesmen and scholars would willingly form an inter-American "brotherhood of intellectuals." As Roosevelt now wrote to Rowe, personal ties among elite, university men could generate the goodwill needed for inter-American cooperation. A continental community of scholars, united in the resolution of common problems, could achieve more than an army of diplomats.[23] Implicit in this definition was a conception of scholarly research as instrumental to foreign policy. Rowe's idea of a brotherhood of scholars appealed to South American scholars and politicians, for it seemed that, as *Americanos*, they were invited to the banquet of inter-American science. At stake was the possibility of lessening their intellectual dependence on Europe.

Intellectual Cooperation: A Manual

In April 1909, immediately after his return from his South American tour, Rowe published an essay in the *North American Review* that can be considered his first manifesto of inter-American cultural and intellectual cooperation.[24] A response to European fear of the growing influence of U.S.-sponsored Pan-Americanism, the essay set the foundation of an enduring foreign-policy approach. The article called for a different approach to U.S.-South American relations, one centered on closer "moral and intellectual ties." The basis of his notion of "constructive Pan-Americanism," Rowe's manifesto articulated three arguments: one about the dissonance between U.S. power and U.S. consciousness; another about the need to acknowledge "South American progress," and a third about the ways to build an enduring inter-American system.

Its economic and military strength had elevated the United States to the condition of world power, yet its citizens continued to think in isolationist terms, ignorant of the world around and unaware of their nation's international responsibilities.[25] U.S. provincialism was especially problematic with regard to South America, a region whose recent progress was remarkable—not only in material wealth but also in matters of education, sanitation, and municipal government. The region seemed animated by a progressive spirit. The "striking similarity" of political institutions and historical trajectories made cooperation between the United States and South America a natural outcome (Leo S. Rowe 1919).

At a time when John Barrett was promoting "practical Pan-Americanism," Rowe argued for "intellectual cooperation" as the main modality of hemispheric hegemony.[26] Efforts on the commercial front should be complemented with a sustained policy of intellectual and cultural exchange. To illustrate his point, Rowe contrasted the imperial policies of Great Britain and Germany. While Britain dealt with Latin America mainly as a territory for commercial and financial transactions, Germany saw the region as a field of study and influence by expertise.[27] Germany presented a positive model to imitate, a deeper mode of engagement that invested in regional knowledge. By contrast, the U.S. failure to gain a prominent position in South American markets appeared as a failure of knowledge. The inability to understand recent "South American progress" placed the U.S. business community at a disadvantage in relation to German merchants, for Germany had paved the road to business with knowledge.

The United States, Rowe suggested, should follow the German path. It should become an empire of knowledge and influence. Intellectual cooperation should be at the center of its inter-American policy. If the United States wanted to replace Britain as the main supplier of capital and goods of South America, it had to become also the region's mecca of knowledge. It should bring Latin American students to her universities and send U.S. experts to the region. The responsibility for hemispheric unity rested on the shoulders of researchers, teachers, and university administrators. They had to teach students "a clearer appreciation of the significance and content of the Spanish American civilization" (Leo S. Rowe 1909, 593).

Rowe presented intellectual cooperation as crucial to the growth of Pan-Americanism. A more intense flow of culture and ideas could elevate the unity of the Americas to a higher plane. The United States should give priority to the study of economic conditions, political organization, and literary achievements of the people of Latin America. A clear appreciation of Spanish-American cultural differences was essential to the formulation of an informed and effective foreign policy.

Overcoming Latin American "distrust"—which Rowe considered a histori-cally specific manifestation of anti-Americanism—was the key to hemispheric integration. What had caused this particular form of anti-Americanism? First, the United States had acted under the erroneous idea that South America was like Central America and the Caribbean: a land of revolutions and "turbulent conditions." This misunderstanding short-circuited all efforts to establish en-during commercial relations with South America. Second was the question-able morality of U.S. merchants and manufacturers in South America; they did not respond to consumers' complaints, disregarded contract conditions, and were dishonest in their catalog descriptions (Leo S. Rowe 1907c).

Latin American "distrust" was a problem both of business culture and of foreign policy. Dismantling it required greater efforts in communication and education. The U.S. public and the business community needed to be aware of the new realities of South America, where political stability, modern industry, and urban lifestyles were increasingly the norm. Latin Americans in turn had to be persuaded of the good intentions of the United States. Conceived as a problem of communication, the solution consisted in the United States un-derstanding the "Latin American mind" and then choosing the proper speech. Rowe believed that scholarly cooperation and a more sensitive foreign pol-icy could mitigate South Americans' distrust. Deep-rooted prejudices and self-perceptions hindered understanding between North and South Amer-ica: U.S. Americans' sense of superiority regarding their political, social, and educational institutions, and their belief in the innate incapacity of "Latins" to build republican government (Leo S. Rowe 1907c). "South American prog-ress" confronted U.S. Americans with the need to revise their sense of superi-ority and mission.

Rowe presented his formulation of intellectual cooperation at the Second Pan-American Scientific Congress in Washington (1915–1916). His program included the exchange of university students and professors, the dissemination of basic knowledge about Latin America among U.S. teachers, and the training of Latin American technical-school graduates in U.S. factories (Leo S. Rowe 1917b). In an earlier version, Rowe had presented this policy as a derivative of the old belief in "commerce doux," according to which trade sweetens relations among trading partners, promotes knowledge among peoples, and contrib-utes to international peace.[28] The "unity of sentiments" among the Americas had to be based on "closer commercial and industrial relations" (Leo S. Rowe 1907c, 519). Later, Rowe revised this formulation, arguing that commercial and industrial integration was not enough. A deliberate policy of intellectual and cultural exchange was needed (Leo S. Rowe 1917b). Intellectual cooperation was the mode of operation of modern empires. Through the training of foreign students and the exporting of expertise, modern empires could accumulate the prestige and knowledge crucial for peaceful interactions with their hinterlands.

"American Problems": The Novelty of U.S. Democracy

In August 1914, as European countries were declaring war, Rowe delivered a series of lectures at the University of La Plata.[29] Two of them, devoted to the state of democracy in the United States, were outstanding for their practicality and boldness. They presented a new perspective on democratic government and a narrative of U.S. institutional history informed by social struggles and the transformation of the public sphere. These talks addressed the contemporary problems of state regulation and governance in a mass democracy.

Rowe started his first lecture affirming that democracy was not just a form of government, but a whole system of social organization. The U.S. system of government had gradually evolved, adapting itself to new demands from society. The U.S. Founding Fathers had designed a quite restrictive form of government, limiting abusive government and protecting property and liberty. After the Civil War, public opinion became more pressing, shifting political ideas on the role of government. From the 1890s, the people pushed government to control the growing power of monopolies. Central to this revision was the need to redress the unequal distribution of income with active policies (progressive income and inheritance taxes, and labor protection laws) in order to perfect democracy.

As the transition from proprietary to corporate capitalism had put individual liberties in jeopardy, people demanded greater government intervention to level the field. Rowe's argument sounded persuasive. He was saying that in the last two decades U.S. public opinion had changed the nature of U.S. government and put limits to business enterprise. A new force, "organized public opinion," had made both capitalism and government move in the direction of greater regulation and social equality. As a result, contemporary U.S. democracy was quite different from that imagined by the Founding Fathers. This was a view of the United States that the Argentine audience did not expect: a different perspective on things, *una verdadera novedad Americana*.

In the second lecture, Rowe redefined the meaning of democracy. He told the audience that the expansion of the role of government was a direct result of demands that stemmed from modern life: economic regulation, conservation of natural resources, protection of female and child labor, control of big business, and so forth. Government itself was changing, with greater centralization of decisions and stronger executives, both at the federal and municipal levels. These changes had radically altered the way people thought about "democracy." U.S. democracy was now a system based on the rule of organized public opinion (Leo S. Rowe 1915, 30–32).

The Argentine audience must have been surprised. Here was a professor of a prestigious U.S. university saying that the U.S. political system was not what its constitution stated, that it was centralized and strongly interventionist. A true democratic government, said Rowe, was one that facilitated social and economic equality, not one that just protected individual rights to life and property. Here was a U.S. scholar unsuspected of socialist leanings telling his audience that modern democracies necessitated economic regulation, labor protection laws, and urban controls. Otherwise, the citizens would fall prey to "industrial tyranny."

Rowe's assessment of the state of U.S. democracy came at a decisive moment in Argentine political and social life. At the very beginning of the European War, Latin American "men of letters" were looking for other signposts, reconsidering with anxiety the problems created by "progress."[30] The Argentine centennial had built enthusiasm for economic progress, but also generated disappointment and frustration about mass immigration, the absence of national sentiment, and the strength of the anarchist movement.[31] The electoral reform of 1912 foretold the end of oligarchic rule. Tensions in Europe had nearly stopped the flow of immigrants and had created economic uncertainty. Labor conflicts were on the rise, as inflation began to erode workers' incomes.

Rowe's eloquence added interest to the speech. He spoke a language the audience knew well: of history, of evolution, of ideas that readjusted to the economic and social environment. Rowe gave the "*nuevos rumbos*" (new paths or transformations) of U.S. democracy the certainty of an evolutionary law. Among his audience were positivists, socialists, and social Darwinists who could empathize with his preoccupations and predictions. The subject matter of the talk contained a supplementary attraction. Unlike other ambassadors of empire, Rowe spoke of the United States: of its problems of government, of its social and economic evolution, of the adaptation of its ideas. Though delivered in an assertive tone, the speech must have sounded like a confession, intimate and revealing.

The Pennsylvania professor presented a new perspective on democratic governance. Free elections were no longer the basis of democracies; now the press and the organizations of civic society were the true checks and balances that guaranteed freedom and equal opportunities. Neither functionaries' virtue nor good administration emerged automatically from constitutions. Norms of government conduct had to be imposed by public opinion. Mature democracies had to tolerate the concentration of political power in the hands of the executive. This enabled governments to challenge economic combines and established bureaucracies. As long as public opinion watched over the administration, the democratic principle was preserved (Leo S. Rowe 1915, 34).

The government of public opinion represented the demands of the educated reading public. The new sovereign was a community articulated by the media; the political nation could no longer be defined outside of "print-capitalism."[32] Common literacy was no longer sufficient. Modern democracies engendered good government only when their societies were organized and active, when collective actions sent messages to governments. This required citizens to gain experiential training in social-democratic interaction in a variety of associations and clubs. This "Tocquevillian turn" must have taken the audience by surprise. The Argentine intelligentsia still referred to Domingo F. Sarmiento's educational vision (to educate people for citizenship) with respect, but had abandoned all pretense of a democracy built from the bottom up.[33] Many believed that the preservation of republican government was the responsibility of the educated elite.[34]

Rowe presented the problems of U.S. government as a common concern of all Americans. He insisted that these were the problems of "our American democracies." The pronoun *our* was an invitation to consider the political evolution of the United States as a valid prediction of the South American republics' future. But the audience must have read this in terms of the cultural divide between Europe and America, which was to them problematic. His lecture had already raised alarm among conservative listeners, particularly when he spoke in favor of economic regulation. But then he went further, telling the audience that in a true democracy the working classes had to be free from "economic dependence." To perfect democracy, the state had to intervene to ensure workers' due share in the distribution of wealth.

To understand these lectures, we must locate Rowe in the Progressive Era.[35] Rowe belonged to a generation that, having experienced tremendous change during their lifetime, had reconsidered the notion of democracy.[36] Judging by his participation in public debates and other public appearances, Rowe was a "progressive liberal." He supported the cause of the education of African Americans, favored the growing participation of women in public and social life, and was sympathetic to the cause of industrial labor (he participated in public forums with Samuel Gompers).[37] Under his presidency, the American Academy of Political and Social Sciences discussed almost all issues in the progressive agenda. In 1914 the conservative trustees of the University of Pennsylvania threatened thirteen "progressive professors" with reprisals for their public positions in matters of social and industrial policy. Among them was Leo S. Rowe.

In his understanding, a modern democratic society required the elevation of the standard of living of workers, even at the cost of increased government regulation. He strove for equal opportunities in education at a time in which the U.S. South was clearly falling behind. He advocated that city administrators should be appointed on the basis of merits and results. His position on urban improvement was close to that of a Fabian socialist: cities should provide sanitation works, public transportation, and electric and gas facilities. As a member of the National Civic Federation, he promoted the involvement of experts in the redefinition of government policies.[38]

While in the early 1900s he had supported an imperialist position with regard to the Caribbean region, by 1914 he had significantly changed his views. The institutional stability and economic progress of the southern republics called for a shift toward a policy of cultural and intellectual cooperation. And he took a strong position against Woodrow Wilson's policy of intervention in Mexico. He thought that the defense of U.S. Americans in Mexico was not sufficient reason to involve the United States in the domestic affairs of Mexico (Leo S. Rowe 1914c). Now he was instructing Argentine audiences about the problems of industrial capitalism and how democratic government should adapt to new social demands. Had he suddenly become progressive? No, Rowe's conviction about the need of a welfare-regulated capitalism had developed in the 1890s (Leo S. Rowe 1892). What had changed was the geographic location of the problem of governance. In the Circum-Caribbean he had asked whether U.S. constitutional government could be exported to colonial peoples. In South America the relevant question was quite different: how could countries that had long experience with U.S. government institutions be assisted in confronting the problems of modern corporate capitalism?

Understanding Argentine Government

What does it mean to understand a country? Basically, it means to grasp the essential or constitutive elements of its character, history, and present condition. This ability to identify the fundamentals gives the knowledge-producer the authority to issue opinions. To a political scientist, these fundamentals are the country's political and administrative system. Rowe's book *The Federal System of the Argentine Republic* (1921) constitutes a systematic attempt to comprehend the Argentine system of government: its constitutional bases and its practice. In this book Rowe undertook a comparison of constitutional law and practice in the United States and Argentina, called attention to the most dangerous aspects of a presidentialist political regime, and presented federalism as the system most attuned to Argentine political traditions. He connected local concerns about the excessive powers of the executive and the centralized nature of Argentine federalism with transnational preoccupations about industrialization, municipal government, and social problems.[39]

To dissect "Argentine government," he drew on direct witness, reports from local informants, and a vocation for comparative history. The book was the result of observations he made during three periods of residence in Argentina, totaling fifteen months.[40] His full immersion in the academic life of the University of La Plata, his contacts with key members of the intelligentsia at Buenos Aires and La Plata, and his direct observation of relevant political developments made the book a treasure of knowledge. He recuperated popular criticism of the judicial system, uncovered the difficulties of the recently implemented secret ballot, and took notice of immigrants' apathy toward political affairs. The book provided also a detailed account of federal interventions in the provinces during 1906–1908: the central government had the power to intercede to address interior strife or external threat, but in practice the president took action to "fix" unfavorable electoral outcomes or to displace opposition governors.[41]

During the process of nation-building, Argentina had borrowed constitutional principles and statutes from the United States.[42] This "legal transfer" had taken place well before the country's age of progress (1880–1914). In the 1860s Argentine scholars had translated the *Federalist Papers*, Joseph Story's *Commentaries* (1833), and a compendium of important decisions by the U.S. Supreme Court (Leo S. Rowe 1921b, v–vii). In the 1880s and 1890s, in reaction against the worship of U.S. legal institutions, local experts proposed that the laws of the country should adapt to Argentine traditions and environment. But federalism survived as the organizing principle of Argentine government.

By the time of the Argentine centenary of independence (1910), the increasing complexity of the Argentine economy had added new industrial and social problems, which enhanced the powers of the central government. Provincial governments, lacking the necessary resources, had to yield powers to the central government if they wanted to expand railroads, build more schools, or provide sanitation to their cities. But centralization went too far, Rowe said: the provinces had become financially dependent on the central government. So a tension emerged between centralized government and popular preferences for the federalist system. Argentines' deep-rooted provincial separatism made it unlikely that this tension would be resolved in the short run.

Intellectual Cooperation

Judgments are one of the most synthetic by-products of knowledge. Rowe examined Argentine history, constitutional law, and political practice to pass judgment on fundamental aspects of the Argentine system of government. His overall verdict was very positive. Argentine constitutional guarantees to person and property were ample and effective. Argentina, having experienced the trauma of despotism and tyranny, had established clearly specified individual guarantees. Equality before the law and protection against unlawful arrest were already part of Argentine judicial traditions. There was the "widest possible" exercise of the freedom of the press (Leo S. Rowe 1921b, 126). Other personal liberties (of commerce, work, correspondence, etc.) were often observed. This favorable opinion extended also to the judiciary, which Rowe thought needed only minimal improvements.

While acknowledging the modernity of Argentine legal and political institutions, Rowe's book raised concerns about the way Argentines had translated U.S. constitutional theory and law into practice. Argentine government, despite its constitutional analogies with the United States, diverged in practice from true republican, democratic government. Despite clear guarantees of liberty, suspensions of basic liberties actually had been frequent (ibid., 121–23). At the center of Rowe's criticism was the tension between the ideal of republican federalism and the reality of an over-centralized government. The executive dominated over the legislative and the judiciary (presidentialism), and the capital dominated over the provinces (centralism). The most salient deviation was the ability of the central executive to manipulate provincial politics. Federal interference in the provinces represented the crudest manifestation of this unbalanced regime.

At the root of presidentialism, Rowe said, was the absence of organized public opinion (ibid., 106). Argentina lacked intermediary organizations that could translate people's demands into political initiatives. His notion of organized public opinion involved common people actively influencing the public-policy agenda. It required a rapid reduction of illiteracy, an improvement in the administration of justice, and an integration of immigrants into the nation's political life. Once these three changes were implemented, organized public opinion would emerge by itself, balancing the excesses of "presidentialism" and Porteño centralism. While acknowledging that Argentina had made great progress since the electoral reform of 1912, Rowe was nonetheless critical about the incompleteness of Argentine democracy. The electoral reform, he thought, had brought new forces into the political arena, established a legislative chamber more autonomous from the executive, and could in time enhance popular confidence in congress (ibid., 98). Argentine government was not yet controlled by "organized public opinion."

Rowe's book borrowed its problematic from local constitutionalist historians, most notably Rodolfo Rivarola and José Nicolás Matienzo. Argentine scholars had already established the contours of a debate about the true nature and implications of Argentine federalism (ibid., 36–37).[43] But Rowe valorized nineteenth-century federalism in a way that neither Matienzo nor Rivarola did. To Rowe federalism was a system of government in tune with the political ideas and traditions of the people. In the post-independence era, efforts to impose a centralist system of government failed utterly, chiefly because of autonomous political traditions. The 1860 constitutional compromise reflected the adaptation of political ideals to the country's reality. Similarly, Rowe departed from traditional interpretations of the Rosas period (1829–1852). Rosas's orderly government and his containment of provincial caudillos prepared the way for a future constitutional agreement. Rosas's undoing of the aristocratic bias of post-independence governments had put Argentine society back on the track of "real democratic government."[44]

What passes as knowledge—radical simplifications that make a country's "problems" transparent—are often solutions that rest on untestable generalizations. Rowe tended to attribute the practical failures of Argentine government to Hispanic ideas and traditions. To this extent, his view of "South America" did not depart much from his early observations about Puerto Rico. The Spanish legacy "explained" the absence of court challenges to the constitutionality of presidential decisions. If Argentines did not challenge presidential authority, were too critical of federal judges and deputies, and rejected unitarian constitutions, they were simply enacting political traditions inherited from Spain.

At the root of Rowe's explanation—the distance between legal statute and reality, the persistence of Hispanic traditions and mentality—was a basic dichotomy between Anglo-American and Spanish legal traditions. In one legal tradition the courts defended liberty and property; in the other the courts continued to defend royal absolutism. The Argentine federal system partook of the Spanish legacy. It was a political arrangement that, in spite of its apparent modernity, was rooted in colonial practices and ideas. Its localism, the people's disposition to follow caudillos, and the persistence of centralism all worked against the easy seeding of "American democracy" in Argentine soil.

Argentina was not Puerto Rico. Hence, Rowe could not use the innate incapacity for self-rule as the main explanation of the problem. Instead, Rowe argued, it was a socially and historically rooted localism that prevented the ideal U.S. system from generating, in practice, a fully democratic government. A skillful replication of the U.S. Constitution did not guarantee a similar form of government. The Spanish legacy had transformed federalism into "caudillismo" first and into presidentialism later. The dichotomy between Anglo-American constitutionalism and Spanish absolutism governed the architecture of Rowe's diagnosis about "Argentine government." If this is so, one must question the role of local data in the constitution of "situated regional knowledge." Were not the "facts" Rowe collected mere confirmations of a metanarrative already prefigured?

In addition, Rowe argued that economic progress presented the possibility of an institutional convergence between Argentina and the United States. Argentina's observable and tangible material progress had created the social problems typical of industrial society and, at the same time, engendered the forces that led to electoral reform and improvements in sanitation and urban facilities. Starting from completely different political traditions and popular ideas, the political development of the two countries could in the future converge. Viewed from an imperial perspective, this prediction appears as an optimistic gesture. In the most progressive of the ABC nations, the discourse on "South American progress" opened up the possibility of fully replicating the U.S. model. To this extent, Rowe was ready to abandon the rhetoric about the impossibility of self-government in order to embrace the future possibility of "full democracy" in Argentina. This possibility was part of the novelty of the ABC countries and made Rowe a welcome interlocutor among South American intellectuals.

Indirect Government: The Pan-American Union

The discovery of South American progress and, in particular, of a great developmental gap separating the ABC nations from the rest of Latin America, influenced Rowe's conception of Pan-Americanism and U.S. foreign policy. While others argued for abandoning the Monroe Doctrine altogether, Rowe defended the need to transform it into a multilateral policy, making the defense of the hemisphere and its political ideas the common endeavor of all American nations (Leo S. Rowe 1914b). In short, he believed in a concerted or multilateral Pan-Americanism, a community of nations cooperating for the resolution of common problems. Consistent with this belief, Rowe called on Washington to define a different set of policies for each region. Revolts and social upheavals in Central America and the Caribbean affected U.S. national security; consequently, the United States should retain the right to intervene.

South America, on the other hand, could be left to manage its own problems (Leo S. Rowe 1914a).

After becoming director of the PAU, Rowe devoted most of his energy to building the architecture of inter-American intellectual and cultural cooperation. He was instrumental in launching "Pan-American Day" (14 April) in U.S. government institutions and schools in 1931, helped commemorate Columbus's discovery of America with the building of the Columbus Lighthouse in the Dominican Republic, promoted the translation of Spanish-American authors for U.S. readers, and organized music concerts in Washington featuring a selection of Latin American music. With the support of Under Secretary of State Sumner Welles and President Franklin D. Roosevelt, he built the infrastructure of what later became the cultural division of the PAU.[45] Rowe's "constructive Pan-Americanism" put a premium on social connections: U.S. diplomats, scholars, and businessmen needed to cultivate personal links with statesmen, politicians, and professionals all across Latin America.[46]

From 1920 to his death in 1946, Rowe published extensively about U.S. foreign policy in journals, magazines, and newspapers. These essays and speeches sustained and reactualized the policy principles he had developed prior to the First World War.[47] Rowe was persuaded that hemispheric solidarity should be devoted to solving common problems, especially the resolution of boundary disputes and other conflicts among Latin American states. Rowe had facilitated the mediation of the ABC powers in the 1914 "Mexican imbroglio," when a tangle of events, including President Wilson's policy of nonrecognition of Mexico's President Victoriano Huerta, led to the U.S. invasion and occupation of Veracruz. Later he participated in important boundary arbitrations, the most notable being the Tacna-Arica dispute in 1925–1926.[48] Also important were activities that could improve the material well-being of Latin Americans, including Pan-American conferences that collectively addressed hemispheric problems.[49]

Two years after becoming director of the PAU, Rowe (1922) took an inventory of the achievements of the Pan-American movement. The South American republics, having already achieved political stability, now faced the challenge of bringing "their social organization into closer harmony with their political institutions" (ibid., 3). This required improving the welfare of large segments of the population living in "abject economic dependence," ending the control of oligarchies over political institutions, and disseminating the benefits of mass education. To prepare societies for democratic government, Rowe suggested progressive policies: comprehensive social legislation, minimum wages, better housing and sanitation, and agrarian reform. To correct wide social inequalities and foster greater political participation would require even greater government centralism. Further progress toward democracy demanded a long process of experience in building democratic sociability, something that "could not be imposed from without." To this extent, the United States should concentrate on administering hemispheric peace, again chiefly through the resolution of boundary disputes.

In 1942 Rowe summarized the contributions of the Pan-American system to continental democracy and world peace. To the future world order, the United States could contribute more than the lofty ideals of Wilsonian internationalism. Inter-American cooperation had produced tangible results: forty years of continental peace. The Pax Americana had kept Latin America isolated from European rivalries and wars. Since the Montevideo agreement (1933), the nations of the hemisphere had remained committed to peace, internal security, and mutual defense. In a recent meeting at Rio de Janeiro (January 1942), ten nations had declared war on the Axis powers, while another nine nations had severed diplomatic relations. What better evidence of the success of hemispheric solidarity and collective action? Moreover, in the midst of total war, it was time to think about postwar reconstruction. In this regard, the experience of Pan-Americanism could be especially helpful: "The example of this hemisphere will be a great practical value in the task of postwar reconstruction" (Leo S. Rowe 1942, 77).

An era of imperialism and white supremacy was coming to a close, wrote Rowe, claiming that "the period of white trusteeship for the less advanced peoples is a thing of the past, never to return" and that "imperialism can have no place" in this contemporary world (ibid., 78). Any postwar agreement should adopt the principles of national sovereignty and nonintervention, yet insist on cooperative solutions to maintain international peace (ibid.). In other words, the PAU could serve as a model for the future United Nations.

Conclusion

The process of knowing a region entails a constant displacement of the researcher's focus of interest. The arguments that connect and make a region a comprehensive totality tend to shift with changes in geopolitical conjunctures, disciplinary concerns, and insights from local informants. Knowledge previously acquired in a given periphery of empire becomes a privileged point of reference and reflection for examining the situation of a newer hinterland. Rowe's intellectual trajectory shows a clear shift in his perception of empire. After having legitimized U.S. interventions in the Caribbean based on the higher mission of educating "Hispanic peoples" in self-government, he conceived the idea of a hemispheric intellectual brotherhood that could unite the Americas in pursuit of common goals. A double "discovery"—that of "South American progress" and the possibility of "intellectual cooperation"—made this reconceptualization possible.

Rowe formulated his idea of "intellectual cooperation" in relation to his experience with colonial administration and to the novelties of progress and stability he found in the ABC countries. Perhaps his recommendations for more Spanish courses at high school, more Latin American students in U.S. universities, and more expert missions to the region sound too prosaic and inconsequential to be a new basis for U.S. hemispheric hegemony. But one should not underestimate the power of regional knowledge. Implicit in these proposals was the idea that Latin American studies could end the isolation and ignorance of U.S. culture while invigorating hemispheric commerce and investment. This pragmatic policy principle became part of the governmental machinery of informal empire. During the Good Neighbor era numerous institutions contributed to make the exchange of professors and students between U.S. and Latin American universities a reality.[50] Intellectual cooperation became an integral part of U.S. cultural diplomacy.[51]

Earlier studies in the United States and Europe helped Rowe observe the municipal and educational progress of Brazil and Argentina from a political-science perspective. The progressive achievements of the ABC republics caused Rowe to reconceptualize his problematic as one of institutional reform within an ongoing civilizing-developmental process. This conception in turn triggered a comparison (United States vs. southern republics) that informed a prior debate about the exportation and adaptability of U.S. government. In a way, the problematic came back to the center of empire—the United States—which had uniquely adapted democratic government to the needs of urban, modern, industrialized society.

Out of the comparative framework provided by enhanced visibility emerged two organizing foreign-policy principles. The first, "education in self-rule," a model rooted in Circum-Caribbean politics, endorsed a policy of recurrent colonial interventions in the region as part of the U.S. civilizing mission. The second, "intellectual cooperation," a model geared to the more mature polities of the southern republics, sanctioned a mode of indirect intervention via the collaboration of Latin American elites. This policy was thinkable only for countries that had already attained a certain degree of civility, institutional stability, and social order. In the Good Neighbor era this foreign policy principle was extended to the whole field of inter-American relations. Cultural differences between the Circum-Caribbean and the A B C powers persisted as key underlying reasons for U.S. foreign policy toward Latin America. In *The Federal System of the Argentine Republic*, Rowe simply reaffirmed the difference he had already established: the new peripheries of the U.S. informal empire, having replicated U.S. institutions, had much to learn to perfect this system.

The production of synthetic, regional knowledge involves a necessary simplification. The nuances that informed Rowe's early works disappeared in time, giving way to simpler arguments aimed at persuading policy makers and public opinion. The synthetic knowledge packaged in the principle of intellectual cooperation did not win Rowe enduring academic prestige. The causality ran in the other direction. It was Rowe's academic prestige before 1906 that facilitated his journeys to South America, and it was this cultural capital that placed him in contact with the South American intelligentsia.

The difference between the Caribbean and South America fit right into the general model of U.S. foreign policy. In the case of Puerto Rico, the political scientist had noted the tendency to family feuds and passionate politics as the main obstacle of "Hispanic culture" on the road to self-government. In the case of Argentina, the Hispanic legacy had survived in the forms of intrusive centralism and traditional localism. These were the most important lines of an argument about the adaptability of "American government" to Latin America, a project of knowledge in the field of comparative politics that emerged out of Rowe's colonial experience. Rowe transformed this argument into the principle of intellectual cooperation when he began to interact with the "progressive Southern republics." At a time of expanding commercial and investment flows, Rowe "discovered" that a network of "native intellectuals" could be productively integrated into the veins circulating ideas and policy of empire.

Rowe's writings on imperial governance (1900–1905) show the unbounded nature of national theories when enunciated from a location and a country with worldly ambitions. A particularistic set of principles about "American government" appeared endowed with universal validity. Colonial situations (Puerto Rico, the Philippines, Cuba) became experimental grounds where the flexibility and adaptability of this system of ideas and institutions were to be tested. Rowe's findings served to reassure metropolitan knowledge-producers of their own importance in the making of empire. In the disjuncture between theory and practice, the expert found a natural territory where he could act on his nation's behalf, seeking more knowledge about the region and suggesting policies that contemplated regional adaptations to the theory of "American government."

For the Circum-Caribbean, Rowe had shown, greater adaptability to local institutions and a greater understanding of local culture could improve the governance of protectorates. In South America other principles were at stake. These countries had already experienced the transfer of U.S. institutions in the second part of the nineteenth century. Hence, the question to pose was one of "democracy," rather than one of "self-government." South America appeared to offer good experimental grounds for examining economic and social progress in relation to "American government" in the Progressive Era.

SEVEN

Geographic Conquest: Isaiah Bowman's View of South America

The great epic of America is the conquest of the land. From the outset geography has participated in this conquest, leading the way at some junctures, profiting greatly from following leadership at others. Geographical science thus has had at its disposal *a laboratory of continental dimensions*. Out of it have come our techniques, our methods of analysis and synthesis, and our great contributions to geographic science and philosophy. There never was a time, however, when that laboratory invited our scientific attention more than it does today. Contemporary society, in trying to plan for the future, is taking stock of its human and its natural resources. In this stock-taking and in certain aspects of the planning, geography has a part. —ISAIAH BOWMAN, quoted in Charles C. Colby, "Changing Currents of Geographic Thought in America" (emphasis added)

In his 1935 presidential address to the Society of American Geographers, Charles C. Colby acknowledged the mutual interaction between building the field of geography and the expansion of the U.S. nation. He presented the U.S. West and, by extension, the American continent as a great laboratory for geographic research. A practical science, geography had participated in the "conquest of the land," contributing a continental inventory of resources for economic growth. In the mid-nineteenth century, through surveys and reconnaissance work, geographers had assisted the construction of the transcontinental railroad, mediated disputes around the U.S.-Mexico border, and facilitated the settlement of the Mississippi basin. Between 1900 and 1930, U.S. geographic inquiry extended to the whole hemisphere. U.S. geographers pioneered expeditions to the polar regions, explored the Amazon basin and the central Andes, and took inventory of the morphology, flora, fauna, and climate of South America.

In his address Colby paid tribute to pioneer geographer Isaiah Bowman, pointing to his interest in "the conquest of the land" as a critical topic of collaborative research (Colby 1936). The tribute was appropriate. Bowman was, without doubt, the pioneer U.S. geographer in South America.[1] He contributed three books and numerous articles to the understanding of the region's geographic problems.[2] Generations of geographers took as a model for regional geography his reconnaissance work in the Central Andes (1907–1913). Later on, his professional career exploded, as he became director of the American Geographic Society (AGS), president of Johns Hopkins University, science advisor for President Franklin D. Roosevelt, president of the National Research Council, and international expert in frontier settlements and land planning. By 1935, Bowman had become a geographer of international renown who transformed "American geography" into an almost indispensable resource for U.S. foreign policy. Initially a promoter of "regional geography," with a strong emphasis on geology and morphology, he turned in the 1920s toward "political geography" as the appropriate platform for disciplinary interventions in the field of international affairs.[3]

Bowman's participation in the 1919 peace negotiations at Versailles and in the remapping of postwar Europe made him the most influential U.S. geographer of his period. The historian Neil Smith (2003) has underscored the centrality of Bowman's ideas and undertakings to the shaping of U.S. hegemony in the modern world. My aim here is more modest. I concentrate on Bowman's travels and investigations on South America in order to recuperate his chief discoveries about the region: namely, regional fragmentation, failure of nationhood, racial and social oppression, and arrested development. I try to understand how geography was able to apprehend and better represent the regional diversity of South America. As director of the AGS, Bowman carried out the single most important cartographic effort of the whole subcontinent: the Millionth Map of Hispanic America (1922–1945).[4] This contribution enhanced the U.S. visibility of Spanish America.

As Smith has convincingly argued, Bowman's participation in the inquiry and the peace negotiations in Paris (1918–1919) transformed his view from a deterministic environmentalism to political geography. Bowman's book *The*

New World (1921) claimed that the era of territorial empires was ending—the world had been completely "parceled out" and hence could not support political territorial expansionism—and envisioned a world dominated by economic and technological supremacy. Earlier than Henry Luce, Bowman anticipated the American Century as one dominated by U.S. industrial production reaching all corners of the global economy. In the "new world" Bowman envisioned for the postwar era, geography had to engage with the problems raised by international politics. Bowman thought that the United States had to assume greater responsibility in the managing of world affairs and that geography could be of great help in this endeavor (Martin 1986).

In this chapter I critically read Bowman's works to test this notion of "geographic conquest," that is, the proposition that geographic science helped incorporate South America into the sphere of scientific visibility and knowledge of the emerging U.S. empire. By framing a multiplicity of observations in homogeneous spatial constructs called regions, geographers were able to provide simplified vistas of the subcontinent and to point out the obstacles facing further economic colonization in each region. Geography's regionalization made possible a more nuanced absorption of the subcontinent into the U.S. imperial imagination. By "regionalizing," the geographer sought to delimit the problems posed by each particular region and to evaluate the possibilities for the development of natural resources. Bowman's pioneer work presented South America as a mosaic of natural-economic regions, some of them quite impervious to the penetration of U.S. modernity and capital.

Geographic simplifications can be instrumental in rendering a region more understandable to outsiders. By marking blanks spots on a map (deserts, unconnected areas, dispersed settlements), geographers can pinpoint the weakness of a peripheral nation-state, question its actual sovereignty over natural resources, and imagine alternative policies geared toward frontier settlement. In this way, geographers contribute to the incorporation of peripheral frontiers into the scheme of capital accumulation and market integration designed by the core economy. As Bowman's works show, more integral and environmentally rooted geographic vistas could correct preexisting views of the subcontinent as a collection of nations. His regional perspective on human settlements cast doubt not only on the existence of well-integrated nations in Andean South America, but also on U.S. Americans' belief that the region's elites cherished U.S. ideals of democratic governance, social equality, and common welfare. In Bowman's view, environmental constraints and population patterns produced political effects.

Chapter 7

Geography provided U.S. Americans a harvest of knowledge about a region until recently relatively unknown: South America. The crafting of maps at detailed scale, the reports of explorations, and the comparative study of agrarian settlements, high plateaus, and river basins composed an informed assessment of the regions' resources and its possibilities for development. Regionalization helped U.S. scholars, diplomats, and businessmen understand the great diversity of South American landscapes and populations in ways that were instrumental to the formulation of U.S. policies. Geographic simplifications underscored the challenges of natural accidents—big rivers, high mountains, large deserts—posed for economic and political hemispheric integration. To an extent, the close reading of topographies and population settlements facilitated the political work of empire, granting scientific validity to prior indictments about the region's incapacity for economic and social change.

True knowledge of a region requires a full understanding of its problems and limitations, its social actors, and the way those actors relate to the natural environment. Bowman's generalizations and words of caution probably influenced contemporary U.S. discussions about the incorporation of different areas of South America into U.S. mass-consumer modernity. His geographic discourse was particularly pessimistic about neocolonial conquest. He thought the Andes, the Atacama Desert, and the Amazon would resist the transformations envisioned by representatives of U.S. economic and technological power. Bowman was among the first to caution U.S. policy makers against extravagant expectations about economic opportunities in South America.[5] He pointed out the true geographic barriers that confronted further economic progress through foreign investment. By emphasizing the efficiency of self-contained economic subregions, he dismissed the possibility of further economic penetration in the Andes. In the Atacama Desert, in particular, he found a delicate equilibrium between populations and the environment, crafted over centuries, that was unwise to tinker with. A cultural relativist and environmental determinist, Bowman predicted that after the end of commodity-export booms, each region would return to its previous way of life.

Bowman was also one of the first U.S. scholars to observe and denounce contemporary labor and racial oppression in South America.[6] Against the grain of conventional wisdom, he wrote about Indian oppression in the Andes, about rubber-tappers who reduced Amazonian peoples into slavery, and about the racism of Peruvian planters. In the 1930s, as U.S. geography sought to incorporate South America as a reservoir of natural resources and as a potential frontier for the settlement of white men, Bowman became a key voice in support of geography as a "science of settlement" concerned with new agricultural frontiers in the global landscape. While optimistic about new fringes in Siberia, Manchuria, and western Canada, Bowman remained pessimistic about transforming and incorporating key regions of South America. The Andean highlands, the Atacama Desert, and the Amazon basin would remain in the margins of global markets and modernity for the foreseeable future.

Comprehensive Visibility

In 1915 Bowman published *South America: A Geography Reader,* a textbook intended for geography courses on world regions. The book was a compendium of available geographical knowledge on the subcontinent addressed to public school teachers. Written in direct style and plain language, this manual presented readers with the most salient features of the relationship between humans and the environment in South America. Clearly, the compendium sought comprehensive visibility. The text was illustrated with 179 photographs and twelve maps. As if looking from above, the geography reader promised a synthetic description of the subcontinent, organized by natural regions: Patagonia, the central valley of Chile, the Gran Chaco, the highlands of Bolivia and Peru, Amazonia, and so on.

Organized in the form of a travel narrative, *South America* did not follow the usual travel routes. The description started in the "southernmost part" of the continent—the Strait of Magellan and the port of Punta Arenas—and moved north, first to Patagonia, then to the Argentine Pampas and to the central valley of Chile. From there, the reader was taken to the deserts of northern Chile and southern Peru, to the highlands of Peru and Bolivia, then east to the plains of the Gran Chaco, and from there to Uruguay and Brazil. Next came discussions of Amazonia, Ecuador, Colombia, the Venezuelan *llanos,* and the Guyanas. Bowman dealt with the whole continent, leaving no region unexamined. His south-to-north arrangement of regions produced a leveling effect: in principle all regions were equally interesting. Yet the book informed readers which regions were more accessible or presented greater economic potential. Regional divisions themselves were governed by natural accidents related in turn to geological formations. Within the descriptions of these natural regions, the geographer inserted important questions about human settlements and economic activities. The South American territory appeared as fragmented by great mountain ranges, salt lakes, deserts, and great rivers.

The book inventoried existing productive activities and potential areas of colonization. In Brazil, the largest country in South America, a multiplicity of climates and production provided the bases for a diverse political union.[7] In the northeast Bowman encountered extremely dry lands with little productive potential, where droughts caused people to migrate to other states. In southern Brazil, near São Paulo and Santos, there were excellent lands for coffee cultivation located near the sea. In Minas Gerais rich mines produced gold, silver, copper, and iron. In the Mato Grosso there were vast unexploited timber resources and grasslands for cattle-raising. This was not the case with the Amazon basin, where economic exploitation of forests seemed unviable. Conditionally, Brazil might even develop into an industrial power:

> If large quantities of coal are ever found in Brazil, or if electric smelting becomes effective, there is no reason why Brazil should not have a great iron and steel manufacturing industry and make its own steel rails, locomotives, bridges, steel buildings, sewing machines, and ships as well as those of the Argentine and other parts of South America. (Bowman 1915, 226)

This was a compliment that no other country of the region received.[8] Each nation had already established a comparative advantage in one or several export staples, also producing various commodities for internal markets. Paraguay had vast *yerbales*, abundant orange groves, good tobacco, and plenty of cattle. Uruguay exported meat, ox hides, and wool. In the Bolivian Chaco there was an active trade in rubber, sent to the Atlantic through the Mamoré River. In northern Patagonia European settlers owned large sheep herds that produced wool for global markets. Argentina was already on the road to becoming one of the primary granaries of the world, together with Russia, the United States, and India. Central Chile produced an assortment of foodstuffs (wheat, meat, and wine) to supply the mining districts of the north. Two U.S. mining conglomerates exploited the country's large deposits of copper. In the northern desert there was nitrate and borax.[9]

Despite the success of export economies, the possibilities of further colonization and settlement in South America appeared limited. While identifying a few territories that farmers and settlers could incorporate into production through investments in transportation and irrigation (among them, the grasslands of Paraguay and Bolivia near the upper Pilcomayo River), Bowman noted that most of the economically viable land was already under exploitation. South America was not that land of unlimited opportunities that promoters of Pan-Americanism had imagined (Salvatore 2005c).

The theme of "settlement" dominated Bowman's geographic compendium. Different types of settlers had populated the subcontinent, including both indigenous peoples and Europeans. Bowman asserted that native farmers and herdsmen were the "true conquerors of South America." By this he meant that pre-Columbian indigenous farmers and shepherds—not the Spanish conquerors—had effected the real colonization of the subcontinent.[10] Nonetheless, the presence of European settlers created favorable expectations of further colonization and production for export. The destructive effect of white settlements on indigenous cultures was barely mentioned.[11] In southern Chile, English and Scottish shepherds were imprinting the environment with the character typical of pioneer ranchers in Wyoming and Texas.[12] Bowman found a similar situation in southern Argentina. In Chubut Province, Scottish, Welsh, and German settlers had carried their trade skills and energy into an inhospitable environment (Bowman 1915, 28). Though the land was barren, foreign settlers had established a successful set of colonies.[13] Again and again, the U.S. geographer compared the successful U.S. westward movement with the movements of European immigrants in South America. But the comparison held only for a limited number of cases: the Central Valley of Chile, the Argentine Pampas, and the southern lowlands of Brazil. In the rest of the subcontinent indigenous and mestizo settlers had incorporated "fringe areas" into production following different patterns of settlement than Europeans.[14]

In the Bolivian highlands the lives of indigenous peoples were shaped by the extreme scarcity of resources. In an environment almost devoid of trees, it was difficult to find firewood or lumber. Indigenous peoples used cactus wood for their door frames, and burned *tola* brushes and llama dung for cooking. Unable to afford imported coal or kerosene, peasants spent the winter without heating. Bowman praised indigenous highlanders for their efficient farming and irrigation techniques. In conditions of scarcity, they had transformed barren lands into orchard gardens and green fields. Ingenuity and poverty constituted the two sides of the native economy. Due to the harsh climate, altitude, and vegetation, people lived with the bare minimum. For building, fuel, and irrigation, they made the most of what nature offered them.

To Bowman, there was probably no farmer more efficient and economical than the Bolivian highlander. The U.S. geographer pioneered the "efficient but poor" argument later associated with the work of anthropologist Sol Tax and economist Theodore Schultz.[15] Here was a limit to the expansion of U.S. commercial hegemony. Limited in their income and wants, indigenous Bolivians could not possibly adopt U.S. modernity. Hydroelectric power—and even electricity—was out of their reach. Highland markets, abundant in homemade blankets, shawls and ponchos, fruits and potatoes, lacked imported goods: to Bolivian peasants these commodities were unaffordable.

Yet the geography reader did more than identify regions with unexploited natural resources and locate the process of settlement in its historical and spatial context; it supplied readers with an explanation of political underdevelopment in the Andean nations. Some countries were so regionally fragmented as to resist all projects of national unity. Peru was not a nation but a composite of different regions, each one with its own dominant production and way of life. In refusing to look at the continent as a loose union of nations, Bowman presented an alternative to official U.S. Pan-Americanism. South America was still a mosaic of economic and human settlements that did not coincide with national borders. So U.S. policy makers could engage directly with the representatives of regions, rather than interact with national governments. Also, the incompleteness of nationhood in many South American countries presented U.S. policy makers with the challenge to intervene and support the development of Andean nations.

In chapter 8 of the reader Bowman discusses Inca civilization, drawing useful insights for modern empires. His praise for the Incas as paternalistic civilizers reminds us of the Inca Garcilaso's *Comentarios Reales*. The Inca rulers taught their people to build canals and to choose the appropriate crops for each altitude. They stimulated interregional trade and wisely collected taxes in kind, providing food security to the governed (Bowman 1915, 164–65). Bowman imagined the Twantinsuyo as a network of communities working for the common good.[16] The Incas' greatest wisdom was their capacity to adapt their way of life to the environment. Their civilization developed in the intermediate highlands, where they encountered spacious fields, wide pastures, and dense populations (ibid., 163). The Incas established a sort of transactional empire, similar to the hegemony Bowman imagined for the United States in South America, a benevolent empire committed to the provision of public goods. Indigenous peoples obeyed Inca rulers because they received from them good roads, wise laws, irrigation canals, food security, low taxes, and relative peace (ibid., 174).

Fragmented Territory, Limited Revolutions

Bowman's book *The Andes of Southern Peru* (1916) explored some key connections between physical geography and politics. Fragmented national territories led to dispersed, isolated settlements, and these in turn affirmed sentiments of localism that ran against nation-building. In this context, local "revolutions," though frequent, had limited impact on national politics. They themselves, argued Bowman, were the product of the environment.

To Bowman, Peru was a nation divided into four regions—the forests, the highlands, the eastern valleys, and the coastal desert—each one inhabited by a distinctive population. The book started with a fiction in which four informants summarized each region's problems: a former missionary with experience in a rubber establishment; a mestizo muleteer from Cotahuasi who described "plateau Indians"; the owner of a sugar plantation in the eastern valleys; and a great cotton planter in the coastal desert. The presumption that Peru was not a unified nation but a mosaic of quite different regions, each presenting peculiar problems, was the organizing principle of the book.

In the lowland forests Bowman encountered something unexpected: stories about the enslavement of forest Indians by rubber tappers. In the highlands the U.S. geographer found shepherds and farmers who lived in ways little different from colonial times (Bowman 1916a).[17] The highlands exhibited wide climatic and soil variation and high population density. Bowman pondered the adaptation of "plateau Indians" to the natural environment: they took advantage of green pastures at high elevations, used ancient irrigation canals, and planted different crops according to altitude. The dry eastern valleys presented the geographer with the problem of scattered settlements: the population was so dispersed that it was difficult to imagine the region's integration to coastal markets. People lived "walled in" their own geography. Indians inhabited the piedmont or the mountains, while mestizo and white sugar planters lived in the valleys. The system of "peonage" was the basic social relationship connecting the two groups. With promises of money and food, planters recruited "plateau Indians" as laborers, then kept them tied to plantations by bonds of debt and alcohol dependence.

In the coastal deserts a few permanent settlements and nomadic shepherds defied harsh weather conditions. Though energetic and hospitable, these desert peoples had exploited water and land resources to their limits, and could not extend the area of cultivation further. Coastal deserts presented enough humidity to allow nomadic shepherds to survive. In this relatively unknown region, every piece of information on climate, soil, and human settlements was valuable. So Bowman described in detail this peculiar environment, with its garden oases and its nomadic shepherds. Here, in the least inhabited of territories, Bowman encountered the most beautiful landscapes and the most romantic changes of light and color. To the south, in the nitrate districts, foreign firms fought a quotidian battle against nature.

Isolation and territorial fragmentation presented obstacles to national and social integration. Because the country was "broken" by mountain spurs, the population lived in settlements scattered in valleys distant from each other

(Bowman 1916a, 44). In addition, great climatic differences kept forest Indians separated from plateau Indians. They differed in clothing, eating habits, dwellings, and economic activities (ibid., 45). Altitude added another dimension to racial territorial fragmentation: on the elevated plateaus, he said, lived communities of "pure Indians," whereas in the valleys resided the mixed-race population. Geographic fragmentation created political factionalism, another hindrance to nation-building. The villages of the plateau lived isolated from each other and separated from the people of the coast (ibid., 69). In Peru great geographical features impeded the formation of a national market and a national political community. To this extent, railways connecting the plateau, the middle valleys, and the coast were crucial to the political development of the republic.

Through physiographic work, or the systematic classification and description of physical patterns of the Earth, the U.S. geographer was able to understand Peru's political underdevelopment.[18] Though apparently a united republic, Peru was only a mosaic of regions, made up of distinct populations, imbued with local traditions and sentiments. The country had failed to replicate the experience of the United States, a successful political federation united by modern transportation. Bowman's view of fragmented settlements laid the foundation for what would become a theme of development literature in the 1960s: the lack of national market integration perpetuated underdevelopment.[19] A nation fragmented by geography offered little prospects for economic development and, to this extent, resisted neocolonial engagement. Even a strong investment in railways would not suffice to defeat geographic fragmentation and scattered settlements. Populations that lived isolated from each other tended to generate enduring "regional social types" that conspired against the formation of national belonging.

Like many of his contemporaries, Bowman was intrigued with recurrent "revolutions" in South America. A small incident in a provincial town, the 1911 revolt of Abancay, confronted the geographer with a typical "South American revolution" (Bowman 1916a, 89). A group of elite young men had taken control of the city of Andahuayllas, capturing the police quarters. The rebels complained about excessive taxes, government abuse, and limited economic opportunities. The next day, the subprefect recruited a force made up of Indians and mestizos, stormed the police station, and arrested the rebels. Men of Abancay's best families were killed. This "revolution," Bowman concluded, was the work of idle and bored young men looking for adventure (ibid., 91).

Bowman searched in geography for the reasons for this failed "revolution." The deep canyons near the town afforded refuge to rebels and bandits. Once fugitives reached the eastern slope of the canyon, they had the whole Cordillera of

Vilcapampa to hide. The police would not bother to pursue them. Geographic isolation, Bowman concluded, created incentives for local "revolutions" (ibid., 92–93). From this particular observation, he generalized. Revolutions in the Andes were small, local events, usually involving just a few armed men. These local revolts were facilitated by geography: mountains and forests offered rebels easy refuge from the police.

Why Humboldt Was Wrong:
Limits to Colonization in the Amazon

Bowman kept mapping the possibilities of further economic colonization in the southern Andes in his writing. *The Andes of Southern Peru* (1916) warned U.S. readers against holding too optimistic expectations for development in the region. Geographic determinants—soil, climate, water availability, elevation, plant life, and human settlements—imposed severe limits on the expansion of the agricultural frontier. In addition, social and racial stratification prevented the introduction of modern transportation and farming methods. These views were complemented with an "efficient-but-poor" argument. Native inhabitants used the available resources efficiently, but they remained poor because the enormous dispersal of population limited the development of national markets.

Bowman used the term *conditional conquest* to name the limited changes that outside forces of progress could bring to these areas. In part, it was the natural environment that limited human life, transportation, and communications by fragmenting territories and dispersing settlements. It was difficult to foresee how modern transportation technologies and export booms could radically transform Andean peoples' way of life.

> For, even if railroads are run across the mountains, the desert reclaimed by scientific methods of irrigation, and rubber in enormous quantities gathered on all the highways and byways of a once impenetrable forest, all these are done by such methods and at such expense of human energy and capital, even of life, as to make them examples *not of sheer human conquest, but of a conditional conquest.* (Bowman 1916a, 144; emphasis added)

Conditional conquest was thus a form of progress imposed from the outside that could only proceed at a very high price in human energy and capital investment. Its continuity depended on the extraordinary profits derived from copper, nitrates, or rubber, activities in which local inhabitants were only tangentially involved. Anticipating a proposition central to dependency theory,

Bowman saw mining in the desert as an unsustainable activity that would not disseminate welfare among the local population. In spite of the "stir" produced by the mining boom, the farming and pastoral communities of Atacama would continue to live in their ancestral ways (ibid., 208).

In the early 1800s Alexander von Humboldt had predicted that hundreds of cities could emerge in the Amazon during the following century, but by 1913 no cities had materialized.

> It was the dream of Humboldt that great cities should arise in the midst of the tropical forests of the Amazon and that the whole lowland plain of that river basin should become the home of happy millions. Humboldt's vision may have been correct, though a hundred years have brought us but little nearer its realization. Now, as in the past four centuries, man finds his hands too feeble to control the great elemental forces which have shaped history. The most he can hope for in the next hundred years at least is the ability to dodge Nature a little more successfully. (ibid., 33)

Even with the help of tropical medicine and railroads, white men seemed incapable of conquering the tropics, much less of transforming the Amazon into a network of cities and burgeoning markets. Bowman's discussion of the utopian nature of Humboldt's prediction constitutes a salient assertion of "conditional conquest," if not of the failure of conquest. The apparent failure of the Madeira-Mamoré Railroad, which at first created great expectations for progress, presented Bowman with a pessimistic conclusion: U.S. Americans could not replicate in the Amazonian jungles the engineering marvels and managerial organization they had displayed in Panama (Bowman 1913b).

Labor scarcity constituted a most severe restriction. Even if white colonization would multiply by twenty, argued Bowman, it would be still impossible to transform the Amazon into a productive region connected to world markets. Like Francisco López de Gómara in the sixteenth century, the U.S. geographer could not foresee civilization taking root in this inhospitable environment.

> Where Humboldt saw thriving cities, the population is still less than one to the square mile in an area as large as fifteen of our Mississippi Valley states. We hear much about a rich soil and little about intolerable insects; the climate favors a good growth of vegetation, but a man can starve in a tropical forest as easily as in a desert; certain tributaries of the Negro are bordered by rich rubber forests, yet not a single Indian hut may be found along their banks. (Bowman 1916a, 34)

Geographic Conquest

When examined closely, the Amazon region presented great challenges to colonists. Apparently abundant resources (soil, rain, and forest) proved deceptive. Even local inhabitants could not settle permanently in a given area.

The coastal desert presented a situation similar to that of the Amazon basin: a natural environment too challenging for U.S. technology and knowledge. From the Chilean border to northwest Peru, the desert extended for hundreds of miles, broken up by deep transverse valleys and canyons of changing altitude and diverse vegetation. In these "dry valleys" irregular rainfall dominated the life of inhabitants. According to altitude, people cultivated alfalfa, barley, potatoes, or fruit trees, even vineyards (ibid., 114–16). Planters with enough capital could clear the land, open new canals, and cultivate cotton or sugar. But these were exceptions. Extending irrigation required large investments and transportation along desert trails was exceedingly expensive (ibid., 117). In the coastal valleys of eastern Peru, enclosed by canyons and deserts, population settlements had rather limited possibilities for travel and commercial exchange. Each valley produced the few crops allowed by its water resources, altitude, and basin size; but transporting their surplus produce to other regions was extremely costly.[20]

In the highlands of Peru and Bolivia, where most of the Indian population concentrated, the land was efficiently utilized. Highland Indians made a remarkable use of the different ecological levels.[21] They cultivated potatoes above the frost line (about ten thousand feet); below that limit, they planted barley and corn. If irrigation permitted, they cultivated sugarcane in the lower alluvial basins. Residing in middle altitudes, "plateau Indians" took their flocks of sheep and llamas to heights above twelve thousand to fourteen thousand feet (Bowman 1916a, 61–62). The vertical integration of production showed a successful adaptation of Andean peasants to their environment.[22] The wisdom of highland cultivators and shepherds was hard to match. Indigenous terrace cultivation and irrigation channels carved on stone were traces of an agricultural knowledge transmitted over generations (ibid., 59). Altitude had established an enduring racial stratification, one of Bowman's central concerns. White or mestizo planters lived in the valley while Indians occupied the plateaus or the mountain slopes (ibid., 55–56). Harsh climate and high altitude protected these indigenous peasants from contact with white planters, as Peruvian hacendados rarely ventured into high altitudes. Bowman projected onto the highland peasants visions of contentment, good health, and autonomy.[23]

Eastern Peru had numerous valleys with specialized production, yet they were too distant and isolated from each other to promote an active interregional trade. Eastern valley planters, unable to take their sugarcane to the coast due to prohibitive transportation costs, produced brandy (*aguardiente*) and shipped it on mule trains. Hacendados used aguardiente to "hook" Indian peons into dependence. Planters' recruiters (*enganchadores*) went to the highlands to get peons, and then, back on the plantation, retained them by means of alcohol and debt. Under conditions of labor shortage and scattered settlements, railroads seemed incapable of reproducing in Peru the nineteenth-century "transportation revolution" of the United States. The creation of free-labor markets required more than economic connectivity; it necessitated a reshaping of social relations, and this demanded a new "practical morality" from Peruvian planters. The state needed to outlaw debt peonage and combat peons' alcohol dependency by taxing the brandy trade out of existence (ibid., 76–77).

Here Bowman's "conditional conquest" found a social-racial boundary, one located beyond the geography of fragmented territories. Peruvian climatic and soil conditions limited production possibilities, yet local inhabitants made the best possible use of the natural resources at their disposal. To this extent, foreign capital was superfluous. People moved goods in mule trains or llama packs, catering to nearby towns or highland villages. These were small markets, limited by high transport costs, scarce rainfall, and the scattered nature of settlements. As in the Amazon, Bowman could not imagine a network of cities, animated by trade and new population settlements, rising in the arid lands of Peru.

Subalterns in Highlands and Forests

Bowman's interactions with indigenous subalterns are key to understanding his ideas about the relationships between humans and the environment in the Andes. In his writings the presence of indigenous peoples appears related to problems of labor scarcity, exploitation, and racial oppression. Bowman's Indian excursus reveals his ambivalence about indigenous subalterns' relations to economic progress, national fragmentation, and environmental management. That is, despite his denunciation of debt peonage and slavery, Bowman's own interactions with highland peoples were clearly coercive, and his scholarship did not treat them as fully civilized humans.

In *The Andes of Southern Peru* we can find at least five episodes in which the U.S. geographer dealt with "plateau Indians" on a personal basis. In the first episode Bowman was near Antabamba, preparing a trip to the mountains. Through a mestizo *teniente-governor*, he hired four "plateau Indians" as guides. But, as he feared the Indian peons would try to escape and steal his mules, he considered the possibility of chaining them to poles. The peons, probably aware of this possibility, ran away that night (Bowman 1916a, 97). In a subsequent episode Bowman confronted a difficult situation. On a cold winter night, he was left without porters to carry his equipment and supplies. So he stopped two Indian travelers (father and son) and, at gunpoint, forced them to work for him. When he least expected it, father and son ran away (ibid., 99).

In the third episode the U.S. geographer got more violent. Desperate and alone, unable to persuade anyone to carry his stuff, Bowman whipped an Indian porter into submission. Midway, he repeated the whipping to keep his porter going. When they reached the camp, Bowman rewarded the Indian with double pay. The native porter, who had not expected to get paid, then thanked and embraced Bowman (ibid., 100). In a fourth episode, while descending the cordillera toward Cotahuasi, the geographer decided to leave his equipment in the care of two Indians in a peasant's hut. At first they refused to help Bowman, taking him for a railroad engineer. The local peasants did not want railways to cross their lands, because railways tended to make people emigrate, depopulating the land (ibid., 101–2). In the fifth and final episode two Indian girls were riding a donkey and carrying potatoes; as soon as they saw the U.S. geographer, they abandoned the donkey, dropped the potatoes, and ran away. Bowman concluded: the girls were terrified of the white man (ibid., 102).

All of these episodes speak of Indians' fear of white men and of their reluctance to work for them. Paradoxically, Bowman's violent interactions with "plateau Indians" led him to write a strong textual indictment against racial oppression. He denounced the discriminatory and repressive actions of Peruvian elites as systemic: "The policy of the whites has been to suppress and exploit the natives, to abuse them, and to break their spirit" (ibid., 102). Indian fear of white men was its overt effect. Apparently unaware of his own role as an exploitative white foreigner, he proudly affirmed the "American" principle that every laborer, if paid accordingly, would work willingly and diligently.

His relationship with "forest Indians" was less ambivalent. The transnational rubber business had brought to the surface an old evil: Indian slavery. Bowman first heard about it in an encounter with Machiganga Indians in 1912. At first glance, his report on the exploration of the Urubamba basin appears to be a typical exploration tale (Bowman 1912). With the help of indigenous guides and a few canoes, Bowman was able to overcome the dangerous rapids of the Urubamba River and reach the lower tropical forest. Yet, at midpoint, the exploration narrative is disrupted by a story of fear, brutality, and enslavement.

When Bowman tried to persuade the Machigangas to contribute carriers and rowers to his expedition, they refused. They seemed paralyzed by the fear of encountering white "rubber hunters."

> Only after repeated assurances of our friendship could we learn the real reason of their refusal. Some of them were escaped rubber pickers that had been captured by white raiders several years before, and a return to the rubber country meant enslavement, heavy floggings, and separation from their numerous wives. Their recollection of their hardships, their final escape, the cruelty of the rubber men, and the difficult passage of the rapids below were a set of circumstances that nothing in our list of gifts could overcome. (ibid., 889)

When Machigangas revealed to him the hidden history of enslavement in the rubber country, Bowman understood better the problem of labor shortage. It was clear to him that "rubber hunters" had continued the predatory activities of Spanish conquerors. Gathering raw materials to produce mass commodities in the United States (automobile tires) entailed increased exploitation of, disease among, and enslavement of indigenous forest peoples.[24] Implicit in the Machigangas' tale was an indictment of the workings of neocolonial exploitation. Bowman tried to distance himself from the brutal coloniality implicit in the transnational rubber business, then subject to increased public criticism. (The first Yale Peruvian Expedition, in 1911–1912, coincided with the exposure of rubber men's atrocities in Putumayo, made by Irish humanist Roger Casement.)[25]

At the time of Bowman's second visit, some Machigangas had gotten caught by the trap of plantation labor. They had accepted work for short periods of time in exchange for brandy, machetes, and ammunition. Rubber companies, realizing that enslavement provided no permanent solution to the labor problem, had started to recruit Indians with such material incentives.[26] This contact with white people, Bowman thought, had broken the spirit of these Machigangas, turning them into a submissive, exploited group. Rubber tappers had used alcohol to produce this degradation (Bowman 1916a, 31–32). Other Machigangas had become fugitives. To escape entrapment and slavery, they had turned into a nomadic people, difficult to trace and hostile to white men. Now they lived in small scattered settlements on the banks of rivers, under the cover of palm-leaf huts that were easy to dismantle. To avoid discovery, they cultivated cassava fields during the night. They had developed the "consciousness of a fugitive," and some had turned hostile.[27]

Geographic Conquest

To place racial exploitation in context, Bowman underscored the transnational nature of the rubber business. The sad condition of Machigangas revealed the intricate connection between consumers in the United States and producers in the Amazon forests. The Indians gathered the raw material for rubber in the forest, then formed it into balls and rolled them down to the river to be loaded onto ships bound for U.S. ports. If one of those rubber balls could talk, Bowman speculated, all the brutality of the rubber business would come into the open.

> For this is one of the cases where *a direct road connects the civilized consumer and the barbarous producer*. What a story it could tell if a ball of smoke-cured rubber on a New York dock were endowed with speech—of the wet jungle path, of enslaved peons, of vile abuses by immoral agents, of all the toil and sickness that make the tropical lowland a, reproach! (ibid., 24; emphasis added)

Bowman compared the condition of indigenous peoples in the Amazon forests to that of black slaves in the U.S. South and in Brazil. In his view Amazonian "peonage" was a system of exploitation as egregious as slavery: "In South America there has lingered from the old slave-holding days down to the present, a labor system more insidious than slavery, yet no less revolting in its details, and infinitely more difficult to stamp out. It is called peonage; it should be called slavery" (ibid., 25). Indian peons remained captive to their masters, who flogged them at the slightest sign of resistance. Foreign businessmen and local state authorities shared responsibility in perpetuating this cruel condition. The rubber tappers flogged the forest Indian into submission chiefly because local authorities permitted them to do so. The lawless nature of the Peruvian borderlands perpetuated the rule of the rubber barons.[28]

Bowman's interactions with forest subalterns had rendered visible a terrible truth: the Peruvian Amazon was an enclave of white barbarism and terror. This is perhaps the moment of greatest moral condemnation in the whole book. Touched by the stories of Machigangas, the U.S. geographer launched a severe indictment against the rubber business as colonialist oppression. But he then returned to the middle ground of objectivity and disciplinary authority. Having understood the geographic basis of the problem, he considered the capitalists' point of view. The activities of rubber entrepreneurs reflected the perennial problem of labor scarcity. Forest peoples, unwilling to work for white and mestizo entrepreneurs, stood as a hindrance to progress.[29]

Contacts with indigenous peoples clarified Bowman's understanding of the economic and human geography of Peru. Machiganga Indians confirmed what had already been denounced in international forums: the revival of Indian en-slavement in the Amazon forests.[30] Bowman's violent interactions with plateau Ketchua peoples made explicit the relation between labor scarcity and peon-age. Indian labor could be recruited only by entrapment into debt and alcohol dependency. Indians' fear of white men signaled the persistence of unresolved racial and social conflicts in modern Peru. Bowman's challenge was to inter-pret these tensions within the field of geography: that is, as a problem of inad-equate transportation, fragmented settlements, and insurmountable physical hurdles.

A Desert Full of Life

How could U.S. capital and consumer culture incorporate the vast desertic areas of South America? Only an in-depth knowledge of life in the desert could answer this crucial question. Deserts, Bowman argued, contained valuable natu-ral resources, whose exploitation depended on local labor and supplies. If ob-served closely, deserts presented themselves as places full of life, indicating the presence of human communities that were much older than foreign companies (*salitreras* and copper mines).

Bowman's third book on South America, *Desert Trails of Atacama* (1924), communicated this new understanding about settlements in the desert. Ata-cama was a "true desert," a place with scarce rainfall, almost no vegetation, and very low population density. The traveler could ride for miles seeing nothing but "naked rocks and sand." At the same time, Atacama was full of activity and life. Here, in the most arid place in South America, were human settlements and trade. Surviving in this harsh environment demanded much ingenuity and effort. Desert peoples had to "mine" their wood. Over time the sand had bur-ied older *algarrobo* forests, so woodcutters had to dig into the sand for wood. Desert people used scarce water with utmost economy. Long water galleries cut in sandstone carried precious water to cave-like ponds and from there to orchards, vegetable patches, and homes. This ingenious water-recovery system matched the most sophisticated methods of Persia, India, Pakistan, and Cali-fornia (Bowman 1924, 20).

Villages were interconnected by a complex system of trade that extended into northern Argentina and Chile. If one stood long enough at one of these villages, one could watch the passage of the "llama caravans" that descended from the Bolivian highlands carrying needed supplies. Indian traders car-ried wool, firewood, blankets, and cloth and exchanged these items for local bread, candles, and barley. The northern Chilean desert was the territory of nitrate fields. Bowman visited an English salitrera near Lagunas. Instead of concentrating on the foreign enclave, he described the surrounding environment and its population. Small and sparse settlements were characteristic of the "nitrate country." Bowman passed by an abandoned copper mine at Victoria, where he found few inhabitants living meagerly; after the copper mines were exhausted, people had migrated to the nitrate districts for work (ibid., 38). The other central feature of the northern Chilean desert was the irregularity of rainfall. Sudden precipitation and snowfall in the cordillera could produce floods in the valleys that destroyed crops, houses, and roads.[31] Although infrequent and rare, floods could interrupt the railway service to the salitreras and paralyze export production.

Traveling along the desert trails from southern Peru to northern Chile, Bowman found great changes in vegetation. A landscape of bare rocks gave way to *pajonales* made up of bunch grass and shrubs, where sheep and llamas could graze. Looking at this changing landscape, he spotted the migratory shepherds of the desert (ibid., 45). People moved from place to place according to variations in rainfall. In wet years, green pastures abounded and the number of sheep and llamas multiplied. In the dry years, shepherds were forced to sell their stock (ibid., 58). Irregular rains caused shepherds to seek pasture on higher terrains or in the valleys bellow.

The term *desert*, Bowman explained, was confusing, for desert areas generally contained vegetation whose life was nurtured by underground water from drainage. In the United States people used to call the Great Plains a desert, but in time it proved to have a dependable water supply, a large acreage of irrigated land, and even forests. Most of the Atacama Desert was a "true desert," a zone of meager vegetation, scarce rainfall, and great daily variation in temperature. Between four thousand to eight thousand feet were some shrubs, but aside from that, there was little to sustain permanent human settlement (ibid., 61–62).

The nitrate district in northern Chile was also a desert in the strict sense. Nitrate deposits depend on the lack of rainfall. When, on rare occasions, streams of water reached these Chilean deposits, the alluvial material buried the nitrates. Capitalists foreign to the region had built towns, railroads, and nitrate establishments. These enclaves were surrounded by migratory shepherds who moved their cattle from place to place, responding to the vagaries of the weather. The desert itself was crisscrossed by trails that connected isolated villages. Each of these villages was a "self-contained community" formed prior to the nitrate boom, their existence inscribed in a long temporality (ibid., 65). Since the time of the Incas, the desert trails of Atacama had served to connect a larger economic space extending from central Chile to southern Peru. Recent economic colonizers (the British, the U.S. Americans, and the Chileans) operated on the surface of this older economic space.

The nitrate export economy was also part of the "conditional conquest," a costly economic penetration not deep enough to transform the way of life of local inhabitants (ibid.). *Desert Trails of Atacama* addressed the question of neocolonialism from a pessimistic perspective. Interconnected valleys generated a volume of trade that was negligible to U.S. exporters. The miserable condition of indigenous peoples placed them outside the calculations of U.S. export promoters and advertisers (ibid., 68). These communities lived under what Marx defined as "simple commodity exchange."

Available transportation technology (railroads) could only unite mine with port, leaving most human settlements in the region untouched. South American physiography presented great obstacles to the expansion of the U.S. informal empire. If indigenous peasants could not enter mass consumer markets, it was unlikely that railroads or engineering works could reconfigure life and culture in Atacama. Bowman's railroad pessimism was in this regard extreme. Railroads could complement the traditional "pack trains" over desert trails, but in no way affect the way of life of "desert people." Once the nitrate boom was over, these towns would go back to their daily routines and activities, to a way of life unchanged since colonial times. "The remote, isolated, self-dependent, desert village is therefore a permanent feature. The traveler of a century hence will still find certain groups unaffected, in the main, by the industrial development of the mines and the nitrate deposits of the desert of Tarapacá" (ibid., 71). Indeed, export-commodity booms were a transient, weak force in the long-term history of the region. The nitrate boom had multiplied the population of Iquique, mobilizing the surrounding areas to provide laborers, food, building materials, and services.[32] Yet the nitrate bonanza did not last. The First World War brought about the closing of many nitrate *oficinas*, forcing migratory workers to return to their towns.[33] In the early 1920s a new export staple, copper, shifted the center of economic activity toward the southern limits of the Atacama region. Copiapó, the center of the new copper bonanza, represented a new form of progress and civility. It was a city of clean streets, well-repaired buildings, and excellent administration, as well as the site of a famous school of mines. The signs of Euro-American modernity—railroads, telephones, telegraphs, gas works, and even an opera house—were everywhere (ibid., 100–101). In addition, Copiapó had developed complex regulations for the use of water, systematically and communally enforcing them. The communal distribution of water and the upkeep of canals facilitated the consolidation of "primitive democratic organisms" (ibid., 111, 118–19, 130).

Towns in the desert were highly dependent on scarce water resources. A flood or the deviation of a stream could affect livelihoods, more than could a fall in the price of copper or nitrates. Depending for their survival on the surrounding hinterland, desert towns were rooted in geography. This environmental dependence gave these communities social and political stability. Villages seemed immune to occasional "revolutions" and resilient to the shocks of the export economy. Coastal desert towns were isolated, provincial, and self-governing, not easy to transform by external forces.[34]

In Chile, during the first decade of the twentieth century, two U.S. mining conglomerates, Braden and Chuquicamata, had established the technical and financial bases for profits. These companies mobilized U.S. large-scale capital and modern technology to exploit low-grade ore.[35] Their corporate enclaves depended for supplies on native trade connections with the Chilean north, the Argentine northwest, and the Chilean central valley. But the reverse was not true. The economic life of a town in the Puna de Atacama did not depend on mining enclaves.

Geographers had much to contribute to the understanding of the role of great deserts in the hinterlands of the U.S. informal empire. The Atacama Desert and Puna were critical regions in the long-term history of empires in South America. Despite centuries of imperial incursions, the region had maintained its distinctive economy and way of life. Though apparently tied to world markets and empires, its towns and valleys were actually self-sufficient and inward oriented. It was this resistance to change that Bowman found most striking about the Atacama region (ibid., 344). At the end of *Desert Trails of Atacama*, Bowman turns the region into a synecdoche for the "whole history of Hispanic America." To Bowman, Atacama belonged to "a class of natural regions" in which the environment had produced a pattern of isolated settlements living outside the reach of great empires. Through natural impediments and great distances, physical geography had nurtured political regionalism and fragmented republics. Strong environmental factors had prevented the continental unification of former Spanish colonies—and also the fall of Andean South America into the grip of modern empires (ibid., 344–45). The Atacama Desert had delayed the absorption of this large territory within the sphere of economic and cultural influence of the United States.

Chapter 7

In the 1930s, with growing tensions in Europe and the sharp decline in multi-lateral trade, the search for raw materials and foodstuffs turned crucial to U.S. statesmen and policy makers. It was at this conjuncture that the distribution of natural resources and their potential use by industrialized nations became important geopolitical issues. U.S. geographers contributed to this debate, signaling South America as a new frontier for the development of natural resources. Mapping agricultural frontiers thus turned into a geopolitical priority.

At this time, Bowman launched the initiative of studying the "fringe areas" of the world. In 1931 he published *The Pioneer Fringe*, a study of areas of recent agricultural colonization: western Canada, Siberia, Mongolia, Manchuria, tropical Australia, South Africa, and South America. The book called attention to a new type of agricultural pioneer. The classic era of mass migration was gone, as was the figure of the western "pioneer settler." The pioneers were no longer Europeans but "natives" who were on the lookout for cheaper land, lower taxes, and less labor regulation. Now, national immigration quotas, the exhaustion of land in areas of high productivity, and the decline of world markets imposed new restrictions on settlement. Against Frederic J. Turner's prediction that the frontier had disappeared, Bowman found that U.S. farmers continued to move to new lands. New settlers demanded modern conditions and comforts: schooling, transportation, electricity, technical advice, and bank credit. Because of this, to facilitate the effective occupation of marginal lands, governmental planning was required.

People were moving from cities or overpopulated areas to new lands of low productivity. It was the role of geography to identify these settlement frontiers and study their characteristics. Bowman called for a new "science of settlement," an interdisciplinary initiative that would establish principles for new world agricultural frontiers.[36] No longer a hemispheric or regional exercise, this was a research effort of global scope. In a report published in 1937 Bowman identified and located on a map the different areas of South America where there was potential for further colonization. In Argentina the humid Pampas seemed already settled and, consequently, had no room for a new wave of immigrants. In the subtropical northern region (Chaco, Misiones, and Santiago del Estero), there was still space for migrants willing to cultivate cotton and yerba mate. But these were fragile lands that would support only a limited number of settlers. In Patagonia further colonization and settlement was not expected. Though two-thirds of the territory remained sparsely settled, the land was already "overpopulated" by sheep.[37] In southern Chile Bowman found energetic German farmers transforming the land: this was a true "laboratory of development."

The Brazilian interior could still support new settlers, at a very low standard of living. Most tropical lands remained unattractive to new settlers. Only Mato Grosso, a region with excellent grasslands, offered "greater promises" to new colonists. Yet the transportation problem had proven intractable, and Bowman predicted that the Brazilian interior would remain a "permanent experimental frontier."[38] In the southern plateau coffee cultivation was already suffering from overproduction. The Amazon basin remained as inhospitable to settlers as it had been in the first decade of the century. A little rubber, Brazil nuts, and palm fibers were insufficient incentives to attract great numbers of new colonists.

In the late 1930s Bowman moved toward political geography. Yet his developmental pessimism remained strong. The success of agriculture in Andean South America still depended crucially on the capacity of creoles to continue to exploit indigenous labor, an alternative that was morally reproachable.[39] In Peru and Bolivia limited immigration experiments—Mennonites in the Gran Chaco, Bavarians in eastern Peru—had ended in failure. The transportation revolution had failed to transform agricultural methods or ways of life in the Andes. And still, survival in the inhospitable highlands depended on the high productivity and ingenuity of local peasants. Further development in the Andes was possible, but only at the expense of additional burdens on the back of natives. "Conquest" was still "conditional."

Conclusion

Bowman's writings problematized U.S. expectations of the economic conquest of South America. He coined the term *conditional conquest* to highlight the great hurdles imposed by the natural environment to the introduction of modern technology and capital in the region. The southern Peruvian Andes was a region in which man had conquered the physical environment only partially and in an incomplete fashion. In the Atacama Desert, in the eastern lowland forests, and in the small valleys of coastal Peru, foreign economic colonization was unsustainable. Geographical accidents had established a pattern of dispersed settlements that was inimical to U.S. notions of economic progress.

Peru was the quintessential exemplar of a nation in which the forces of progress had failed to transform preexisting patterns of land use. Native peoples used efficiently the natural resources of highlands, lowlands, deserts, and forests. Yet, given the high cost of transportation, isolated settlements generated infrequent and small-scale economic exchanges. Feeble markets based on petty-commodity production did not constitute enticing markets for U.S. mass-manufactured products. Hence, for the time being, U.S. capital would continue to exploit a few mineral resources, leaving traditional ways of life almost unaffected.

Bowman's geographic determinism extended a pessimistic outlook to Peru's political development. Burdened by an excessive regional fragmentation, and the consequent cultural provincialism, Peru had been unable to build a successful national community. The highlands, the coast, the desert, and the forests constituted four different ecological regions with distinct sensibilities and quite provincial viewpoints. In addition, Peru had proven unable to overcome the racial and social divisions created by the colonial experience.

Bowman's notion of conditional conquest contradicted enlightened visions of progress. Neither the Atacama Desert nor the Amazon was ready for white-settler colonization and U.S. modernity. With regard to the Amazon basin, Bowman argued against Humboldt's predictions. Even with modern transportation technologies and tropical medicine, the region would not become a site of bourgeoning cities and growing commerce in the foreseeable future. Mining enclaves, too, were exploiting natural resources near the border of production possibilities. Why enter into diplomatic and economic conflicts with Britain when the resource itself (nitrates) could be washed away by rains?

Implicit in Bowman's arguments was a precautionary tale about development and about the potential conquest of Andean South America by U.S. capital and commodities. A large part of the eastern coast of South America, over which many speakers and statesmen had projected ambitious expectations of economic progress, was in actuality a desert, a territory inhospitable for human settlement due to insufficient rainfall and the lack of modern transportation. At great expense, railroads and roads could connect the west coast with the mining districts, but this would not confer any significant benefits on the local population.[40] U.S. geography thus carried a warning to U.S. businessmen. South America was not the "land of opportunity" publicized by the promoters of the Pan-Americanism. There were many obstacles to overcome before U.S. firms could sell typewriters, refrigerators, toothpaste, and breakfast cereal to Andean peasants.

Bowman's human and economic geography of South America had illuminated important social preconditions for modernity. The question of development could not be extricated from issues of labor and racial oppression and from the prejudiced outlook of local proprietary classes. Through his travels and research, Bowman discovered old and new forms of racial oppression and exploitation in the Peruvian Andes. His moral condemnation was directed against white Peruvian planters and hacendados who subjected their indigenous peons to crude forms of exploitation. In the forest lowlands Bowman found the worst form of human oppression, slavery, reactivated by the international rubber trade.

The intersection of race and environment contributed to racial oppression in Peru. In the low and warmer valleys soil fertility and abundant water made the land apt for the cultivation of valuable crops. This attracted white planters and merchants who, for the sake of profits, degraded the lives of indigenous peoples (Bowman 1916a, 43). On the cotton and sugar plantations, the geographer learned about the disdain and brutality with which white planters and mestizo officials treated their Indian laborers.[41] Here were traces of "feudal" personal dependence and colonialism. But it was rubber tappers who committed the worst forms of abuse, enslaving forest Indians.

Taken together, these denunciations (against peonage, slavery, and racial hierarchies) could be read as a counterdiscourse about Americanization and neocolonial conquest. They raised doubts about the impact of the "forces of progress" (railroads, highways, industry, and foreign trade) on the lives of native peoples. Bowman's "Indian exploitation" excursus constituted a departure or anomaly in the narrative of "geographic conquest." His discourse conveyed a genuine indignation about outdated forms of labor exploitation and racism. Repeated encounters with Indian subalterns helped him understand better Spanish colonialism. "Plateau Indians" were frightened at the sight of white men.

What lessons then could geography offer to U.S. policy makers and businessmen? An environmental—almost geological—view of the subcontinent brought to the surface long-term continuities in the relationship of humans to the environment. Andean native shepherds and farmers had resisted the successive waves of colonialism. Their poverty and efficiency carried a clear anticolonial message. Geography, on the other hand, promised further conquests. Scientific inquiry could establish the features and regularities in human settlement and illuminate the true problems in the expansion of agricultural frontiers. Bowman's regional geography offered policy makers and businessmen the possibility of understanding "development" from the perspective of environmental barriers and the longue durèe of coloniality.

At the end of a long discussion about the relationship between human settlements and the environment in the Atacama Desert, Bowman wonders what might be the role of these isolated villages in the middle of the South American desert. Seen from the perspective of "progressive men" in the industrialized nations, these villages were "inviting gardens" offering comfort and rest to the Western traveler. As links of communication, these old towns could still play a strategic role in the unfolding of the U.S. informal empire (Bowman 1916a, 204). These villages were sites of transit and also living memory of people's long-term efforts to adapt to the natural environment. Oasis settlements were also enticing to the foreign geographer, for there he could discover the great organizing principles of human settlements.

Perhaps geography could complete the "conquest" that U.S. capital had begun and only conditionally achieved. This conquest, of course, would not be based on the expanded reproduction of profits, but on the promises of comprehensive knowledge. Regional science could provide the basis for understanding societies and natural resources in South America. Based on that knowledge, Washington could design better policies in relation to their southern neighbors. By fitting South America's problems of population and agriculture into particular theories about "frontier settlement," geography could help U.S. policy makers understand the strategic and economic importance of key regions: the central Andes, the Atacama Desert, Patagonia, the prairies of southern Brazil and Argentina, and the fertile valleys of central Chile. More important, geographic science held the key to understanding regional politics and thus could help foster better interaction with local elites.

In *Desert Trails of Atacama* Bowman revealed the secret about the political history of South America. Physical geography could explain why the region had failed to create integrated national economies and self-conscious national communities. Here was dependency theory *avant la lettre*. Since colonial times, settlers had accommodated into particular locations and lived without much communication or trade with other regions. Unable to overcome great natural barriers, each area developed a provincial spirit inimical to nation-building. In the early twentieth century Andean nations remained a mosaic of self-sufficient regions where local revolts were a recurrent possibility.

Bowman read in South America's geography the reason for the region's political incompleteness and lack of modernity. Fragmented territories translated into forms of regionalism that resisted U.S. visions of progress predicated on transportation improvements. In the Atacama Desert Bowman found instances of the successful adaptation of native populations to their harsh physical environment. Their ways of life predated the arrival of foreign corporations and, Bowman predicted, would outlive their presence. If this were so—that is, if market development and technological progress were only conditional conquest— policy makers could derive interesting corollaries. South American economic and political elites did not truly represent the majority of the population. The region not only confronted the problem of underdevelopment but also suffered from incomplete nationhood and regionalism. Elites, attached to outdated forms of labor control, were unlikely to share "American ideals" of political democracy, legal equality, and minimum welfare. Consequently, there was little point in conversing with Andean elites. Only in certain regions—in the humid Pampas of Argentina, in southern Chile, and southern Brazil—U.S. Americans faced equal interlocutors. It was with them that U.S. policy makers had to discuss issues of hemispheric scope.

EIGHT

Worldly Sociology: Edward A. Ross
and the Societies "South of Panama"

———

South America is the victim of a bad start. It was never settled by whites in the way that they settled the United States. . . . The masterful whites simply climbed upon the backs of the natives and exploited them. Thus, pride, contempt for labor, caste, social parasitism, and authoritativeness in Church and State fastened upon South American society and characterized it still. It will be yet long ere it is transformed by such modern forces as Industry, Democracy, and Science. —EDWARD A. ROSS, *South of Panama* (1915)

In this chapter I present sociologist Edward A. Ross's *South of Panama* (1915) as a significant contribution of the emerging U.S. sociology to the "rediscovery" of South America. The race factor, labor, and sociability constituted the axes organizing Ross's particular vision of South America. His "discovery" of racial oppression, labor servitude, and medievalism in the Andes was related to his progressive ideological agenda. Ross disseminated the information he had collected in South America in his sociological tracts and college textbooks. In his textbook *The Outlines of Sociology* (1923), he turned South American nations into examples of greater sociological generalizations about the condition of Euro-American modernity.

Ross was a leading sociologist of the progressive era. A disciple of Lester Ward, he contributed greatly to the consolidation of the discipline in the

United States, together with other pioneers such as William Sumner, John Gillin, Albion Small, Franklin Giddings, and Charles Cooley.[1] In 1891, after a year of study at Berlin, he took a doctorate at Johns Hopkins, and later taught at Stanford and Chicago before settling at the University of Wisconsin (1906). There, he taught sociology for thirty-one years, becoming chairman of the newly created Department of Sociology and Anthropology in 1929. He was a leading figure in the American Sociological Association and one of the founders of and major contributors to its journal, the *American Journal of Sociology*.

Among scholars, Ross is remembered for having defied the corporate university in defense of academic freedom. Opposed to the railroad company practice of hiring cheap Chinese labor, Ross entered into a dispute with the Stanford family that cost him his job (Downing 2005). This triggered one of the first scandals around academic freedom in the nation's history. He is also known for his public advocacy of restrictions to mass immigration. Ross warned his contemporaries that unchecked Chinese immigration endangered the standard of living of "American" workers, and he wrote about the cultural primitivism and racial inferiority of Southern and Eastern European immigrants. Though controversial, his works dealing with immigration—*Changing America* (1909), *The Old World in the New* (1911), and his 1911 Report to the Congressional Immigration Commission—were influential in the U.S. adoption of immigration quotas in 1921 and 1924.[2] His unhappy coinage of the term *race suicide*—used also by President Theodore Roosevelt—continues to be the object of critical attention.

According to the sociologist J. O. Hertzler (1951), Ross was one of the last "system-builders" of American sociology. Ross's theorizing concentrated on social phenomena and social processes.[3] Influenced by contemporary currents of thought in Germany and France (Georg Simmel, Émile Durkheim, and Gustave Le Bon), Ross tried to build the edifice of U.S. sociology as a composite of many elementary parts. He thought sociologists should gather data on "cases" in order to produce generalizations or "regularities" that substituted for unassailable "social laws." To him, society was composed not of individuals or groups, but of "social types" constantly under the pressure of "social forces."

Ross's works on foreign societies are less known, yet in my view they constitute the bedrock of his sociological theories. His "sociological portraits" of China, Mexico, Russia, South America, and Africa helped acquaint U.S. Americans with areas later known as the Third World.[4] His travels across half the globe supplied him with a wealth of observations and insights about foreign lands. Processed in the sociologist's comparativist lab, these "social facts" created the basis for contrasting hypotheses about "social forces" and "social processes" in modern society. In addition to being a pioneer social theorist, Ross was a "sociological interpreter to Americans of foreign peoples and cultures" (Hertzler 1951, 598).

As one of the first transnationally informed sociologists, Ross contributed to the enterprise of rendering South America visible to U.S. Americans. In 1914 he took leave from the University of Wisconsin to travel along the western coast of South America. He visited Colombia, Ecuador, Peru, Bolivia, and Chile, then crossed to Argentina. His sociological portraits of these nations are condensed in *South of Panama* (1915), a book that combines features of travel writing, sociological observation, and political commentary. In the Andean countries Ross found nations corroded by landlord despotism, labor servitude, and racial exploitation. In Ecuador, Peru, and Bolivia, indigenous peoples were living in conditions so primitive they resembled medieval Europe. Chile, a mixed-raced country, was making some progress, while Argentina, a white settler colony, had already advanced along the road to progress and civilization. *South of Panama* underscores the legacy of Spanish colonialism as constitutive of Andean backwardness.

While other disciplines produced regional knowledge—for example, history and geography developed the subfields of Hispanic American history and South American geography, respectively—sociology did not. Yet the study of South America contributed to the formation of a comparative international sociology. *South of Panama* was part of a broader study of world problems and trends that included China, Mexico, and Russia. Ross's sociological portraits of world regions constituted the elementary parts of a project of "international sociology," a project for a science of society based on "cases" construed through direct observation in different areas of the world.

Before Direct Observation, Race Generalization

Before traveling to the region, Ross used the term "South America" to evoke a population made up of Catholics, uninstructed in self-government, and endowed with traits characteristic of "Latin peoples": indolence, inability to save, and a preference for feasting. A racial polarity between whites and nonwhites marked Ross's sociological comments about Latin Americans. To this extent, "South America" was not different from Mexico, Central America, or the Caribbean. Their populations lived under quite primitive conditions, without incentives to work harder and with no vision of the future (Edward A. Ross 1901a, 76).

In contrast, white U.S. Americans possessed the "energy" that was proper to regions receiving free European immigration. In 1901 Ross wrote an influential essay, "The Causes of Race Superiority," wherein he examined this superiority of white U.S. Americans over other races. U.S. Americans were blessed with a competitive and egalitarian culture that praised individual success over inherited social status. The conquest and settlement of the West had rewarded the industrious, the self-reliant, and the entrepreneurial. In addition, U.S. Americans were highly successful in mastering industrial technology

Energy, self-reliance, foresight, and stability of character formed the basic character traits of "superior races." The Anglo-Saxons, possessing all the attributes of the mercantile races, also had the strength, the determination, and the foresight to settle new territories and control their natural resources. While the Britons had built a large overseas empire, white U.S. Americans had conquered the West and then successfully embraced the Industrial Revolution. Spanish Americans, on the other hand, lacked the crucial attributes of self-control and reflection needed to master industrial technology: Mexicans, Colombians, Venezuelans, and Brazilians all shared the traits of the "mañana culture."[5]

In the era of empire, Ross argued, determination, productivity, and energy put "superior races" in command, while the absence of these traits made other races dependent and subservient: "Latin sociability is the fountain of many of the graces that make life worth living, but it is certainly a handicap in just this critical epoch, when the apportionment of the earth among the races depends so much on a readiness to fight, trade, prospect or colonize thousands of miles from home" (Edward A. Ross 1901a, 84–85). To preserve their superiority, imperial nations needed to restrain interracial marriages to prevent miscegenation. Spanish and Portuguese civilizations had promoted racial mixing, and, as a consequence of this mistaken policy, their empires declined and fell apart. In the United States, by contrast, racial separation resulted in "the highest type of civilization" (ibid., 85). Through miscegenation, unwanted immigrants (Italians, Spaniards, and the Chinese) could steal away the energy of the industrial (white) U.S. America. If, for the sake of maintaining a certain standard of living, a nation reduced its birth rate and allowed "inferior races" to enter the country, the future of the mainstream population was at risk. Ross called this policy "racial suicide" (ibid., 88).

Progressive U.S. America

Ross's progressive credentials are well established. Despite his support of selective immigration, his views on workers' conditions, the situation of women, child labor, monopolies, and higher education projected the agenda of a more egalitarian society.[6] He looked at South America through a progressive lens and found it saturated with aristocratic government, racial oppression, and forced labor. Thus, his eugenicist progressivism rendered a pessimistic yet compassionate view of indigenous Andeans while projecting an optimistic portrait of "white" Argentina and Chile.

Before traveling to South America, Ross wrote an influential book about the challenges posed to contemporary U.S. society by internationalization and capitalist development. *Changing America* (1909) presented the agenda of the U.S. progressive movement to ordinary "Americans" so that they could better evaluate world contemporary tendencies. While deploying a broad-ranging agenda on race, gender, labor, and democracy on the world scene, Ross grounded his perspective on a narrow, parochial center: the rural communities of the U.S. Midwest. The book identified several world trends that were bound to affect the way of life, the social interactions, and the political rights of ordinary U.S. Americans, among them the influence of big business in politics; the great social inequalities created by mass-production capitalism; the gradual emancipation of women; new protective labor legislation; and the government's new interest in social welfare.

In the first trend Ross saw democracy expanding worldwide. Populations long ruled by monarchs and despots (particularly in Asia and the Middle East) were now demanding responsible popular government (Edward A. Ross 1914 [1912], 21). In this terrain, progressive U.S. scholars had much to teach the world. Democracy was not just a matter of popularly elected government, but of the rule of "mature public opinion." Indeed, only an enlightened public opinion, guided by progressive intellectuals, professionals, and bureaucrats, could check business power.[7]

The strengthening of secular government was a second important world trend. Everywhere in the West he observed an increasing separation between church and state, which was good news for the spread of democratic values. In particular, U.S. missionary societies promoted the expansion of democracy worldwide, liberating people from the grip of state-sponsored churches. This was an important indicator of social modernization. The significant fall in birth rates was the third worldwide tendency, and was the result of changes in family aspirations and gender roles that were themselves the product of modern life. Common folks had chosen to free up money for consumer goods or savings by having fewer children. In the United States, France, the United Kingdom, and other industrialized nations, increasing opportunities for women in labor markets tended to delay marriages and thus reduce birth rates.

Ross warned that this demographic trend would trigger a dangerous racial dynamic. The rapid demographic growth of Asia, Russia, and Spanish

America could well displace whites from the center of the civilizing process (Edward A. Ross 1914 [1912], 37–39). In the United States, massive immigration from Southern Europe and Asia threatened to undermine centuries of progress. Race deteriorates a population, wrote Ross, "if the successful withhold their quota while the stupid multiply like rabbits" (ibid., 45). Italians, in particular, showed high fertility rates. To counteract these demographic tendencies, Ross proposed that the United States restrain mass immigration.

A fourth important dimension of Western modernity, connected to the decline of fertility, was the emancipation of women. At the time that Ross wrote, five million women were gainfully employed in the United States. While he found this a welcome development, he worried that the massive inflow of women into labor markets could jeopardize the rights of male workers and undercut their wages. Young women were disorganized, weak, and uninformed, unable to fight against factory work speed-up demands, the extension of the workday, or deteriorating work conditions (ibid., chap. 5).

Fifth, *Changing America* alerted readers to the dangers of "rampant commercialism." The book indicted U.S. business for its mentality, ethics, and practices. Ross accused corporations of accelerating the work process, introducing cheap labor from non-Western nations, carelessly exploiting nonrenewable natural resources, and causing millions of work-related accidents per year.[8] Moreover, he pointed out that business influence had reached the citadel of knowledge; its representatives sat on the boards of the most important research universities. Yet the greatest danger to democratic society was the erosion of free expression. The newspapers, increasingly funded by advertising revenues, were actually suppressing important news.

To mitigate or even reverse all these trends, Ross supported a wide-ranging social-reform agenda that provided "for the legal protection of the weak in industry, workingmen's compensation, legal standards of housing, the regulation of public utilities, the supervision of insurance, perhaps the guaranty of bank deposits, and the taxation of site values" (ibid., 83). And in the egalitarian, farming communities of the U.S. Midwest he found the forces that could rejuvenate "American democracy." Midwesterners had opposed the advance of Eastern capital and its corrupting influence on government. At the end of the book, however, Ross described how enterprising young men were leaving Midwest communities to migrate to the cities. "Folk depletion" was the name Ross gave to this phenomenon, raising the possibility of moral decline in the very cradle of democratic sociability.

In 1915 Ross traveled to South America himself, visiting Ecuador, Peru, Bolivia, Chile, and Argentina. South of Panama, he found societies that lacked the key elements for replicating U.S. democracy. Three main topics dominate his interpretation: (1) the race factor; (2) the existence of servile labor and great landed estates; and (3) the lack of democratic sociability. While the first two topics related directly to the Spanish colonial experience, the third factor underlined the backwardness of South America in relation to U.S. sociopolitical modernity. In the Andean region Ross encountered countries that suffered from "landlordism" (the excessive power of landlords over tenants and laborers) and premodern labor arrangements. Only in Argentina did he find modern social relations (free wage labor) and a prosperous farming middle class.

While on occasion Ross steps back from the racial explanation to analyze culture, sociability, and government, the whole book is permeated by racial pessimism. Race served to explain the progressive or stagnant state of the different countries Ross visited. To Ross, Andean nations still retained "feudal" features inherited from colonial times. Big landed estates, peons trapped into debt, and various forms of personal servitude were defining characteristics of Andean South America.[9] Ross also paid attention to democratic sociability, the conditions that made people cooperate for the common good. In this regard, too, he found the societies of South America undeveloped. They lacked a universal system of elementary public education, a competitive free press, modern political parties, and universities that fostered the "collegiate spirit."

THE RACE FACTOR

Traveling south along the Andes, Ross also encountered an incredible confusion of social landscapes. All of South America seemed saturated by miscegenation.[10] Diverse types of "mixed breeds" held social progress in check. Racial mixture was the crucial difference separating Spanish America from Anglo-America. And unlike in the United States, in Spanish America the many gradations of skin color prevented the development of a clear "color line." Ross tried to bring some order to this confusion by arranging his commentary and description by color, from black to Indian-mestizo to white. Then, on the basis of these racial gradations, the U.S. American sociologist divided South America: Andean countries remained trapped into the colonial past, while Southern Chile and the Argentine Pampas seemed to live in contemporary modernity.

In these multicolored societies blackness was the marker of uncivilized autonomy. Remaining separate from white and creole society, African South

Americans remained premodern in their customs and sociability. In the jungles of Choco, not far from the Panama Canal, lived a population of former slaves, in conditions that combined primitivism with independence from other groups. Men and women wore few clothes, built their houses with bamboo canes, and produced what they consumed. The Choco blacks lived a life of abandonment and indolence, enjoying freedom (Edward A. Ross 1915, 4). Having been slaves, they refused to engage in wage labor. Even where blacks lived among whites or Creoles, they maintained a level of autonomy and pride. To the south, in other Colombian towns, residents considered blacks to be good laborers. In Cali, in the Cauca Valley, the close proximity of people from different races attracted Ross's attention. Almost nude men and women, black and white, bathed in the same river. Black laborers, imbued with a sense of egalitarianism, did not tolerate rough language from their bosses (ibid., 8–11).

In contrast, in Ecuador the mestizo stood for disorder and violence. To underscore their innate violence, Ross recounted the Alfaro uprising of 1912 at Quito. Middle-class rebels staged a coup against the government, but were unsuccessful and went to jail instead. Then the *cholos* (mestizos) killed the jailed revolutionists, engaging in a blood orgy. Heads were cut off, bodies were dismembered (ibid., 31–32). Locals and scholars alike sought to understand what could have generated this type of violence in an otherwise tranquil town. The mestizos' innate violence and vengefulness emerged as a possible explanation, as did a history of political instability during the nineteenth century.

Ross sought a racial form for understanding the subcontinent, but could not find easy associations between race and social, economic, and political problems. In Peru he found that new waves of immigration had complicated the readability of race. Besides the fourfold division of white, cholo, Indian, and black, now there were Asian immigrants. Sugar plantations had brought Chinese coolies to Peru, and this had added another layer of racialized subalternity to the already multicolored Peruvian nation. "Coolies" mixed with native women, giving birth to a new caste, the "*chino-cholo*" (ibid., 39–40). The presence of hyphenated subjects revealed Peru's continued tradition of mixing races.

This increased racial diversity led Ross to proclaim, "*There is no color line* [in Peru]" (emphasis added). In Andean societies, he found, mestizos contributed diversity, violence, and disorder to the social landscape, yet they constituted only the middle ground in a larger and deeper conflict between two races: the whites and the Indians. White and "near-white" ruling classes kept the Indian majorities subordinated and marginalized. Ross blamed white elites for holding back the Indian masses in education, political participation, and associative life.

Religiosity marked the endurance of the Spanish colonial legacy on the lives of indigenous communities. At Chincheros, a town in the Peruvian highlands, the author was so impressed by the sight of an Indian procession that he detailed it in his narrative: "The eyes of the kneeling worshipers followed the chanting procession as it wound its way about the church, and at the supreme instant of the mass they lifted their hands, pressed palm to palm, and yearned toward the altar in a mute, but passionate, adoration" (ibid., 72–73). The scene conveyed deep religiosity and devotion, similar to that of Tibetan monks. The Indians' colorful dresses, the simplicity of their houses, and the piety of their ceremonies confronted the author with a perpetual and unchanging time.[11] Everyday life in the Peruvian highlands still evoked the Spanish colonial past.

From his observations, Ross inferred certain features of the "Indian character": religiosity, passive tolerance, and a subservient attitude. Over time, Peruvian Indians had learned to fear the presence of white masters. When a white man passed, they got off the road; if a strange white man spoke to them, they kneeled on the floor and begged not to be hurt. Their submissive attitude caused Indians to accept whatever payment was offered them in lieu of wages. Three centuries of colonialism and exploitation had eroded their capacity for resistance and nullified their expectations. The Indian had learned to behave submissively, something also observed by Isaiah Bowman.

In Ecuador Ross encountered Indian peasants degraded to the condition of "beasts of burden." They differed little from draft animals, both in their workloads and in their passive endurance of pain.

> Slavery and ill treatment have sunk the native population into the depths of degradation and hopelessness. Perhaps nowhere on the globe do human beings *so much resemble passive beasts of burden*. In fact, the Indians used to be designated in documents as "smaller beast of burden" to distinguish them from pack-animals. Loaded, they clamber up the steep streets as stolid as little gray burros. One sees many an urchin of seven years bearing on his back a load of bricks as heavy as he is. . . . Here is a file of barefoot women bent under loads of earth or bricks, escorted by a man with a whip! (ibid., 24–25, emphasis added)

However archetypical, the image of an Indian bent by a huge load on his or her back marks the presence of a historical process; a centuries-old system of exploitation had reduced indigenous peoples to an infrahuman condition.

Ross described the Mapuches of southern Chile as people living in quite primitive conditions, given to theft, and naturally indolent. He considered the "pure Mapuche" a vanishing race. Famous for their resistance to colonialism, they had been decimated by alcoholism, disease, and miscegenation. Their influence on the common mestizo laborer of Chile had been negative. Ross blamed the "Mapuche blood" for the alcoholism that kept the working classes in perpetual poverty, for the excessive sexual appetite of lower-class males, for the spread of prostitution and venereal disease in the mining districts, and for the repeated pilfering of Chilean custom houses (ibid., 220–24). He noted also that Mapuche lands were now occupied by enterprising German farmers and British missionaries.[12]

But his mourning for the vanishing race was overshadowed by his optimistic comparisons of Chile with U.S. western expansion in the previous century. In southern Chile, as in the U.S. Midwest, European immigrants had settled after the displacement of Indian tribes, giving rise to egalitarian and industrious rural communities. Thus, the old "dark and bloody ground" of the continent—Araucania—was gradually turning into a "rough frontier of democracy," just like Montana and Wyoming after the suppression of the Sioux (ibid., 101–2). For Ross, whitening stood here for civilization, free labor, and individual initiative. Ross repeats an anecdote from a German rancher, mocking the innocence of Mapuches for selling their lands in exchange for liquor, in order to inform the reader that Mapuches' degeneration and demise were preordained and inevitable.

LANDLORDISM AND LABOR SERVITUDE

In all western South America Ross found no traces of an independent farmer class (ibid., 139–41). In the Cauca Valley, in the Ecuadorian sierra, and in the highlands of Peru and Bolivia, he instead encountered large estates under the control of absentee landowners.[13] He attributed this situation to Spaniards' residential habits since colonial times. Finding no appropriate social life in the countryside, Spaniards preferred to reside in urban areas, managing their estates through mestizo superintendents or *mayordomos*. By exploiting the semi-servile peasant-laborers, absentee landlords accumulated rents that enabled them to live in the cities with style. As a result of this, the countryside showed few agricultural improvements and also few social interactions.

In addition to absentee ownership, Ross found debt peonage to be a pervasive feature of social relations in Andean nations. He first discovered it in Colombia. In the Pasto region, peons worked for five to ten cents per day in exchange for the use of a plot of land. "Of course, such pitiful earnings do not suffice for the needs of his family, so he is obliged to run into debt to his 'amo' or master for money and supplies," Ross wrote (ibid., 149). He encountered similar conditions in Ecuador, Bolivia, Peru, and Chile. In Ecuador there were traces of corvée labor: agricultural laborers worked four days a week for the landowner, receiving only twenty to forty cents. Having to purchase all their supplies from the landowner, they remained trapped in debt. In Bolivia, the pongo laborer worked for the landlord three to four days a week without pay, receiving only coca leaves, aguardiente (alcohol), and food. Landowners maintained work discipline with whips (ibid., 157).

In the Peruvian highlands Indian peasants earned fifty cents a month tending alpacas, llamas, and sheep, having to purchase from landlords their provisions of wheat, maize, and coca leaves. In addition, peasants had to pay a tribute in kind to the landlord: a quintal of alpaca wool, one sheep, plus the labor required during sheep-shearing (ibid., 150–52). In central Chile the inquilinos were wholly dependent on landlords. The were allowed to plow two to six acres of the landlord's land for their own crops; in exchange, they had to work three hundred days a year for ten to eighteen cents a day. With such low wages, the inquilinos had no hope of acquiring land (ibid., 158–59).

Andean peasants were a dependent, servile class. Low agricultural wages and debt peonage were part of an exploitative system with roots in the colonial era. Large estates, absentee proprietors, and semi-servile Indian peasants had all been features of Spanish land and labor policies since the sixteenth century. Customary practices, such as tribute and corvée labor, had pushed the price of labor below subsistence level. Low wages forced peasants to ask their landlords for credit until, trapped into unpayable debts, they were unable to abandon the estate.

Corvée labor and debt peonage turned the rural districts of west coast South America into "feudal" lands. That is, the contemporary situation of peasants and laborers reminded Ross not only of sixteenth-century Spain, but of conditions in Europe in the Middle Ages.[14] Visiting the Andean countryside was like traveling to the European past. Johannes Fabian (1983) calls this type of confusion between space and time the "refusal of coevalness." At one point, Ross reached even further back than the Middle Ages: under Spanish colonialism, he said, agriculture had regressed to a biblical past. The Ecuadorian peasants that Ross encountered were threshing wheat in the same way as Egyptian peasants did in the time of the pharaohs (Edward A. Ross 1915, 21–22).

Spanish colonialism had left a spatially differentiated pattern of "servility." As the visitor traveled from north to south along the Andes, the degree of "feudality" declined: "Broadly speaking, light and freedom wax as you go south from

Panama" (ibid., 148). At the end of the journey was Argentina, a country where the agricultural laborer was completely free. Looking at Argentina's contractual labor arrangements, the relatively high standard of living of its workers, and the general prosperity of the population, Ross concluded that here was the only country in South America that had shaken off the legacy of colonialism (ibid., 134).

Ross pointed to two historical moments as the origin of landlordism and servile labor: the early colonial period and the post-independence assertion of national sovereignty. In the sixteenth century ruthless conquistadors had distributed among themselves large tracts of land and the labor and tribute of indigenous peoples. In Peru the colonizers had gone even further, destroying the Inca irrigation system and thereby damaging the livelihood of many Indian communities. The "*mita*," a system of coerced labor in the Potosí mining complex in colonial Upper Peru, greatly reduced the number of cultivators, leading to the shrinking of tillage (ibid., 47). In the post-independence period national states pushed back the Indian frontier, while rapacious land-seekers robbed indigenous peoples of their lands.

Ross's sympathy clearly lay with the colonized Indian. Life was hard in the Bolivian highlands. At fourteen thousand feet, peasants had to endure extremely cold temperatures without fuel, living almost in isolation. Dire poverty rendered Bolivian peasants unable to understand American notions of material comfort.

> Surely it is a cheerless existence that the Indians lead on this lofty table-land. Home is a thatched adobe hut in the corner of a farmyard fenced with sod or loose stones, in which are folded at night the merinos and the llamas. Lonely and insignificant, the little hut stands in the vast cloud-shadowed, wind-swept spaces. No trees, no shrubbery or flowers, no birds, no color, no roads, no neighbors or town to visit— nothing but the dreary moor, the lowering clouds and the moan of the chill wind. . . . Never once in their lives have these people been comfortably warm, nor do they even know that there is warmth in the world. (ibid., 62)

In the central valley of Chile living conditions were less severe. Here, the beauty of the cultivated landscape projected the image of abundance: green wheat fields, exuberant alfalfa patches, and luxuriant vineyards. Yet one detail of the panorama startled the U.S. American observer: there were no substantial dwellings. "From end to end of this agricultural paradise one never sees what we would call 'a good farm residence.'" Again, instead of investing in estate houses, the rents from the fields went to sustain luxurious houses in provincial capitals or in Santiago (ibid., 100).

In many regards, Argentina was the exception. Here was a country projecting hope, in which welfare was rising, not only for the landowners but also for tenants and agricultural laborers.[15] Laborers could become tenants; tenants in turn could acquire some land. The welfare of urban workers was rapidly improving. The possibility of social ascent was quite visible: Ross observed that workers at Buenos Aires were moving into the suburbs, taking advantage of installment plans and relatively high wages.[16] In a few years, an immigrant worker could aspire to build a modest house. True, Argentina was also marked by the problem of latifundia. Yet the "peon class" was improving its condition, under the favorable influence of common schools, military service, and sanitary campaigns.

DEMOCRATIC SOCIABILITY

Nothing concerned the Wisconsin sociologist more than the way South American societies were structured. He knew that manners, customs, and common understandings—sociability—kept societies together. In countries where colonial dynamics persisted, he found traces of colonial sociability: aristocratic mentality, dismissive treatment of servants, no sense of social equality, and unwillingness to cooperate. Conversely, in modernizing societies, people had a "democratic sensibility," a sense of personal worth that affirmed social equality (ibid., 208–9). In particular, Ross was interested in evaluating the degree of democratic sociability that different countries had achieved. To do so, he looked for the presence or absence of certain U.S. institutions: a public opinion mobilized by a competitive free press, youths trained in the discursive practices of a democratic society, men organized around common purposes, and universities that trained young men in high ideals. In all these dimensions he found that South America still lagged far behind the United States.

South American elites, in particular, failed Ross's test of democratic sociability. Though modern in appearance, they remained aristocratic in spirit. Their attitudes and behavior betrayed their embrace of an aristocratic type of modernity. Foreigners were often impressed by the affection South American men showed to family members and friends. But this affection was restricted to the inner circle of relatives and friends; it did not extend to the community as a whole. Generous within the family, South Americans were egotistical in the social terrain. They did not bequeath their personal fortunes to hospitals or educational institutions. They let the church administer most charities. Each looked after his own welfare and failed to cooperate for the common good.[17]

Disinterested help was not easily extended to strangers. Although Argentine gauchos were famously generous, U.S. machine experts were unable to procure drinking water from them (ibid., 212).

In the United States multiple associations and institutions had contributed to create a "cooperative feeling." In South America, race, class, family life, and ill-conceived educational institutions conspired to prevent this development. Ross found the South American family to be disorganized and unable to transmit "character" to boys and girls. The avoidance of marriage favored impermanent relations between men and women. As a result, many children grew up without a father figure. South American men were unable to cooperate, chiefly because of their inherited sense of pride. Their associations, whether a literary club or a political party, tended to fall apart due to internal disputes, driven by jealousy, distrust, or sheer intolerance. Local political parties were unlike those of the United States. Groups of men followed a caudillo in order to appropriate the spoils of government. To the South American, politics was a competition for state jobs and kickbacks. Their "predatory politics" limited the prospects of building democratic sociability.

South America's lack of democratic sociability was rooted in premodern social relations. The great landed estates, labor servitude, and elites' infatuation with urban life prevented the formation of a rural middle class, the true foundation of U.S. democracy (ibid., 144). Having vacated the countryside, the elites had robbed South America of its only chance to replicate U.S. political development (ibid., 141). The two exceptions to this rule—southern Chile and littoral Argentina—tended to confirm this socially grounded theory of democracy. In southern Chile, German landlords had displaced Mapuche occupants and were teaching Chilean farmers industriousness and perseverance. In Argentina the impact of mass European immigration had created the conditions for moral uplift in towns and countryside.

A sociologist needed to distinguish between two types of sensibilities: the politeness of equality and the politeness of hierarchy. Peru showed upper-class politeness, but not democratic manners. Argentina, by contrast, presented a greater sense of social equality and cooperation. Again, only in Argentina did Ross find a society that had laid the groundwork for building a modern sociability. He found the Argentine elite "open-minded" and unafraid of change. To them, progress was not only material prosperity, but also the adoption of new institutions and new forms of associative life. Argentines were, in this regard, the only "postcolonial" elite in South America. For they had actually rejected the foundations of the old colonial order: disdain for labor, contempt for business, personal pride, social exclusiveness, clericalism, and patriarchal customs.

Its policy of lay education, its democratic school system, its reliance upon the woman elementary teacher, its cultivation of athletic sports, its boy scouts, its public libraries, its bacteriological laboratories, its experiment stations, its boards of health, its National Department of Agriculture, which spends half as much as the United States Department of Agriculture—all these innovations witness to the willingness of Argentina to risk change of soul. (ibid., 136–37)

Ross's high expectations for Argentina's future were shared by many eminent foreign visitors during this time.[18] These expectations led Ross to pronounce that Argentina would converge toward U.S. modernity in the future. "The Argentines are the one South American people likely to have enough in common with us to found a genuine friendship. Our people ought to feel a sisterly sympathy with this new motley people, engaged in subduing the wilderness and making it the seat of civilization" (ibid., 137–38).

In contrast to Leo S. Rowe, who argued that any intellectual or elite member in South America could be a good friend, Ross was sure that it was similarity in culture that made for good neighbors. This situation suggested that the United States should take a different policy approach with Argentina than it did with other Latin American countries. Convergent paths of progress and democracy enabled a sympathetic understanding between the two countries, running in both directions. "Americans" should show sympathy to the Argentines and understand some of their shortcuts and detours in the road to progress and civility. Argentines, in turn, should study U.S. history in order to learn about how their northern neighbor had handled similar problems in the past (ibid., 138). This is the only moment in which the U.S. sociologist presents the possibility of a two-directional exchange between the United States and a South American republic.

The expectation of sociopolitical convergence and inter-American friendship was clearly grounded on race: the fact that Argentina was the whitest country in the region. The overwhelming presence of European immigrants made intelligible Argentina's institutional development, public sociability, even its moments of agrarian protest. In the Southern Cone, due to the magic of whiteness, the "South American character" could engender a democratic society. In Andean South America, by contrast, social relations remained "feudal," a type of backwardness not easy to undo.

Ross devoted a whole chapter to the role of women in the region (ibid., chap. 7). As a progressive, Ross expected to see progress like that made by women in the United States. He was disappointed. He found South American societies incorrigibly male-dominated and patriarchal. Divided spheres dominated norms in sexuality, family relations, and the law. Women lived in the domestic, familial sphere, while men controlled most of the space devoted to public life. And he found South American males to be sexual predators. In the street and the house, all women were fair game; incest and rape abounded in the southern republics.

Coloniality and the South American Character

On the bases of miscegenation, colonial land policies, and the persistence of servile labor, the U.S. sociologist was able to assemble the typical "South American character." The social and political man of the region—the Andean South American in particular—revealed four major deficiencies in character: indolence, want of persistence, mutual distrust, and excess of pride.

The reluctance to exert physical effort was an important failure of the South American character. A person of high status would never carry his own luggage or work alongside his employees. South American elites enjoyed being served; the number of servants constituted a marker of relative social standing. Though characteristic of elites, this trait pervaded the whole society. Because of mutual distrust and excessive pride, the "South American" was unable to cooperate. Clubs and associations wasted energy in internal disputes and personal antagonism. Too sensitive to criticism, the South American scholar did not return to seminars or groups where he had been criticized. Good at starting a project, elite men were unable to carry it to completion. Universities in the region lacked the basic facilities and institutions that made young men in the United States cooperate. They had no athletic club, no gymnasium, no tennis court, no debating society, and no poetry recitation sessions on campus. Students did not interact much with their professors or with other students. This precluded the cultivation of the "collegiate spirit."[19]

As a progressive, Ross assumed that educated men were responsible for making societies and governments. In Latin America colonialism had created an enormous social distance between elites and masses, yet elite men had failed to establish themselves as models worthy of imitation, and it was now clear why. Elite men (the scientist, the functionary, the literati, the professional) displayed aristocratic sensibilities, showed disdain for manual labor, and rejected social equality. Their institutions and way of life, while modern and European in appearance, betrayed the influence of centuries of Spanish rule. Consequently, educated elites would not effect the institutional reforms demanded by a democratic society: a professional bureaucracy, equal opportunities for women, an honest and disinterested press, the regulation of monopolies, modern labor laws, and municipal reform.

The author projected images of progressive "America" on the lands south of Panama and found them lacking. All the traits of coloniality marked a lack of sociopolitical modernity relative to the U.S. model of government in the Progressive Era, not relative to models of popular sovereignty from the French Revolution or from British constitutional government. It was in relation to this ideal that the elites and the masses of the southern republics appeared lacking in character and seemed incapable of building democratic sociability.

Here, we confront a double subalternity. The failings of the Indian and mestizo subalterns were, in the last instance, the responsibility of South American elites, men who had shown themselves unable to teach virtue and civility to the masses. In fact, we are full circle back into the "American model."

> Many of the faults of contemporary South American character can easily be duplicated in the *history of our own people*. To-day we succeed in making certain virtues fairly general among ourselves because gradually our society has equipped itself with the *home training, the education, the religion, the ideals of life, the standards of conduct, and the public opinion* competent to produce these virtues. Societies that lack the right soul molds will of course fail to obtain those virtues. But there is no reason why they may not borrow such molds from the more experienced societies, just as we ourselves have sometimes done. (Edward A. Ross 1915, 249–50; emphasis added)

This is an interesting twist to the idea of empire. The benevolent empire needs to conduct its civilizing mission by example. Like a blueprint ready for reproduction, it must export its standards of conduct, its social and cultural institutions, its religious and educational values, its instruments for shaping public opinion, and its architecture of local government. In other words, the United States needed to become a teacher to the South American republics.

Key features of South American sociability—the aristocratic mentality, the subsistence of feudal obligations, and the lack of cooperative spirit—were attributed to the persistence of colonial heritage. The racial miscegenation prevailing in the subcontinent was directly associated with the permissive Spanish policies regarding marriage and reproduction. Similarly, colonial land policies generated a land-owning class with aristocratic pretentions. Transplanted "feudal" relations had persisted in the twentieth century under the form of debt peonage and corvée labor. More important, Spanish absolutism had prevented the development of self-government in the colonies. To overcome coloniality,

Ross suggested institutional and social reform that presupposed a modern way of life, characteristic of the United States. The transplantation of the U.S. progressive agenda informed the failings of the "South American character." The "race factor" complemented this view, facilitating or hindering social democratic change.

Between Medieval China and Modern Social Revolutions

When the sociologist turns world traveler, he becomes a comparativist. Observations made in one region serve as models for inquiries in other regions. Ross's visit to China in 1910 served to confirm his prior conceptions about the influence of race on socioeconomic and political development. In addition, China presented him with a vision of a remote past that later helped him interpret South American societies. Ross considered Chinese cities to be contemporary remnants of medieval Europe: "China is the European Middle Ages made visible," he wrote (Edward A. Ross 1911b, 721). Walled cities, people littering the streets, confusion in traffic, no sanitary provisions, and crowds struggling to survive struck him as utterly "medieval." Ross associated "medievalism" with the lack of concern for public spaces and for the common good. Living in the past, in a condition close to subsistence, the Chinese could not fathom modern ideas of public welfare and democratic interaction (ibid.).

Ross inflected the sociological portraits of Andean South America with the image of medievalism, a term that came straight from his book on China. The same could be said in connection with sociability. The "medieval cities" of China produced societies in which clan, family, and private interest dominated over the public good. The enterprising Chinese polluted the cities, deforested the woods, and contributed nothing to the upkeep of public roads. The societies south of Panama were in this regard similar to Chinese cities, lacking any notion of the public good. Yet *South of Panama* (1915) constituted a watershed in Ross's conceptions of the social, due to the interaction of race and colonialism. Ross presented an empathetic, though condescending, view of Aymaras and Kechuas, indigenous peoples defeated by the force of three hundred years of colonialism.

Similarly, Ross's "discovery" of land concentration and labor servitude in South America proved a lightning rod for future observations in Mexico and Russia. Three years after his return from Buenos Aires, Ross spent a semester in revolutionary Russia (July–December 1917), where he examined the social changes and conflicts that led to the October Revolution.[20] Ross visited Mexico in 1922, after the revolution had come to a halt and agrarian reform was in progress. *South of Panama*—it is my contention—served as a crucial point of reference for examining these two all-important revolutions of the twentieth century.

In *Russia in Upheaval* (1918), Ross attempted to explain the roots of the revolution. The sociologist underscored the oppression of workers and peasants under the tsar, and the unbounded cruelty and violence of the police. He compared the tsar's police violence to the cruelty of Spaniards during the Conquest. The Russian peasantry had been kept in a situation of poverty, ignorance, and superstition for three hundred years. The revolution had fostered great expectations. The Bolsheviks were able to impose order by creating a workers' army. Ross admired the organization of Russian workers and praised the land policies of the Soviets.[21]

Similarly, in *The Social Revolution in Mexico* (1923), Ross applauded the efforts of the Mexican revolutionary government to restitute land to Indian communities. Yet he condemned the "Indianization" produced by the revolution. After the fall of the Díaz regime, white and mestizo elites took control of government, and in the countryside the revolution empowered the Indian masses to an extent previously unimaginable. As a result, the previous "color line" (white-Indian) was rapidly blurring.[22] Mexican peasants were people without future, less alert and with less mental edge than the "bucolic Chinese." Ross also compared the innate racial inferiority of Mexicans with that of U.S. blacks, bringing to the discussion "evidence" of the inferior IQs of Mexican children in schools of the U.S. Southwest.

South America within the Textbook

In 1923 Ross published *The Outlines of Sociology*, a textbook intended for college undergraduates.[23] In this book knowledge he had gained through extensive foreign travel (in China, Russia, South America, Mexico, and Japan) appears as supporting evidence of universal sociological principles. Impressions are transformed into "facts," and facts are accommodated into the procrustean bed of "social theory." This textbook constitutes an important landmark in U.S. strategies for understanding South America. Reading this book, sociology students could see "South America" as an exemplar region of failed paths of social organization and political culture.

To homogenize South America, Ross compressed distinct temporalities into three categories: "ancient," "modern," and "advanced." To explain the persistence of colonial institutions and social practices in contemporary South America, he referred to historical works about the European Middle Ages.

Thirteenth-century Europe illuminated the reading of a process extending from the sixteenth century to the eighteenth—Spanish colonialism—that in turn served to explain contemporary social-racial inequalities and aristocratic government. Spanish America appears as the realm of a transplanted feudality, a subcontinent locked in a double temporality, combining the European Middle Ages and twentieth-century Euro-American modernity.

The term "South America" works generally as a negativity that confirms the reader's presumptions about progress, civilization, democratic sociability, and race adaptation. Specific South American examples serve to validate notions of social domination, class government, clericalism, and social control. Chile appears at least three times in the book: as an example of government corruption; as a place where "hacendados" constitute the "governing class"; and as a country where elites expressed disdain for manual labor (Edward A. Ross 1923a, 101, 189, 250, respectively). Peru is mentioned as a place where Indian peasants are "hooked" into debt peonage by unscrupulous labor contractors (111), and as a country of enduring traditions, where servants accompany local ladies to church to protect familial honor (250, 253). Colombians are noted by their "politeness" (174). Bolivia and Ecuador evoke images of exploited and drunken Indians, living in fear of white men (41, 113). Argentina, a country praised for its successful immigration policies, appears also as a land of great landed estates (239).

These cases functioned for Ross as examples of general theories about social organization. The factual content of the information is the same as in his earlier work, but he reaches a greater level of generalization. South America was to Ross a "land of exploitation," a territory where the conquistadors' unmatched cruelty and heartless exploitation still persisted. Masses of landless peasants and laborers lived in complete dependence on great landowners and subordinated to their will. The ubiquitous presence of "debt peonage" had prevented the emergence of "free labor" in agriculture, a key sign of social modernity.[24] In addition, the region suffered from the lack of religious plurality and from limited political participation.[25]

This was the "South America" that transpired from Ross's sociological tracts. The elites dominated the sphere of politics, keeping the masses ignorant and uninformed (ibid., 218–19). Deprived of education, the masses could not aspire to positions of public responsibility or get their grievances heard by government.[26] The "governing class" monopolized state revenues and employment, maintaining the control of elections through fraud and intimidation.[27] Excessive pride made South Americans politicians unwilling to reach compromises with political adversaries. To resolve political disputes, elites often resorted to violence.[28] South American societies remained segmented into strata and factions as in colonial times. Instead of following common values and norms, each ethnic component adhered to its own standards of conduct.[29] Hence, there was no cross-class civilizing influence and no common social purpose. The region's vast experiment in race-crossing had not facilitated the social bonding required to build a democratic and industrial society.

These faults of the "South American character" became integral to the lessons imparted to sociology students. The student who completed Ross's sociology class learned that South America was a land of elite-controlled government, widespread corruption, great inequalities in wealth, debt peonage, aristocratic sensibilities, and premodern social interactions. Andean South America, in particular, represented the opposite of U.S. economic, social, and political modernity. The U.S. Midwest and the industrialized Northeast embodied all the features that South America had failed to attain: a strong rural middle class, an egalitarian ethos, and a free and skilled workforce.

In the history of land policies the U.S. sociologist encountered a fundamental difference between the two Americas: the existence in the United States, but not in South America, of a farming middle class. Though presenting an excess of "commercialism," the United States stood as an advanced capitalist society that had successfully experimented with constitutional popular government (ibid., 455). There was internal division, however: the backward U.S. South was the site of aristocratic pretension, economic backwardness, and racism, and to this extent, resembled Andean South America. The planter class of both societies exhibited the same refinement of conversation and manners, the same disdain for manual labor, and a similar degree of male domination in the household (ibid., 89, 250, 256). The Chinese, the Russian, the Mexican, the Hindu, the Portuguese in Africa, and the South American all now formed part of Ross's stylized theory about the functioning of society, in which modernity and tradition were arranged in time and space. "South America" fed a system of comparative sociology. The Incas appear as a civilizing empire comparable with other ancient empires, such as the Gauls and the Romans (ibid., 177). Chilean landlords' control of politics was assimilated to that of Junkers in Prussia and to the eighteenth-century English gentry (ibid., 189). When Ross blamed the ignorance of the masses for the low life expectancy in the less-developed world, he provided as examples Brazil, Ceylon, and Cuba (ibid., 9).

In *The Outlines of Sociology* we see the emergence of an internationally comparative or transnational sociology, a comparative sociology of cultures grounded in fairly homogeneous geocultural regions. Propositions about organization, professionalism, schooling, class exploitation, and so on are presented as universal because they are supported by evidence from different world regions. Long before area studies consolidated itself in the U.S. academy, Ross talked of the Far East, the "Mohammedan world," Russia, and China as world regions, each with peculiar but comparable institutions, social organization, and customs.

At the end of the book, Ross deals with social "balances" and "excesses" (ibid., 461). Societies lacking social balance presented excesses labeled "militarism," "clericalism," "commercialism," and "the rule of the death." Each of these social maladies was associated with the excessive influence of a different social actor: the military, the clergy, businessmen, and ancestors. China was typical of societies where excessive respect for tradition and ancestor worship prevented the development of new ideas. Mexico, Peru, and Colombia presented examples of "clericalism," places where the Catholic Church had given society its moral imprint. The United States suffered from "commercialism," a social imbalance due to the exaggerated influence of big business.

From this textbook U.S. college students learned what Ross had argued in his more scholarly texts: that South America was a land of exploitation and servile labor, where the Catholic Church had excessive influence on the populace and dominant elites had little concern for the poor. These negative features were associated with the colonial heritage. A great social, economic, and cultural distance separating the haves from the have-nots made it difficult to envision the introduction of democratic sociability. Two systems of comparison were at work in this textbook: hemispheric, contrasting Andean South America to the most advanced aspects of the United States; and transnational, naming South America as another world region, comparable to Russia, China, Muslim nations, the Far East, Africa, and Oceania.

Conclusion

I have shown the importance of Ross's "sociological portrait" of South America to his discovery of a land-labor problematic associated with coloniality. *South of Panama* (1915) underscores the long-term impact of Spanish colonialism on Andean societies. At first glance, the book appears as a racial heterology, the forced imposition of a racial viewpoint on quite diverse societies and cultures. Yet a closer reading produces a quite different impression. *South of Panama* is perhaps the first devastating criticism of landlord domination and exploitation of indigenous peoples written by a U.S. sociologist.[30] At the beginning of the First World War, Ross "discovered" that South America still carried the imprint of its colonial heritage.[31] The west coast countries, in particular, were still trapped into the evils of landlordism, elitist government, widespread corruption, state-sponsored religion, and the exploitation of indigenous peoples. There was little chance that these republics would join the rank of modern civilized nations in the near future.

Ross projected onto his social panoramas of South America a full-fledged progressive agenda. He brought into the discussion about the societies south of Panama questions of public opinion, university culture, and democratic sociability that were at the very core of progressive ideology. Yet his progressive impulses clashed against a wall of medievalism, and he could not integrate the two visions (progressive America and premodern Andean South America). In the end his solution consisted in allocating countries into two separate groups: the progressive and the nonprogressive.

Ross's sociological panoramas divided the region into two types of societies. Modern democratic sociability was more likely to emerge in places such as southern Chile or the Argentine littoral, where the presence of European immigrants, widespread education, and associative life created favorable conditions for the development of a democratic society. In most of Andean South America, by contrast, Spanish colonial institutions preempted the possibility of following the path of U.S. progress. As a consequence, Andean America was unable to acquire and enjoy the blessings of U.S. modernity: industry, democracy, and science. While at first, Ross had tried to look at South America through the lens of racial difference, in the end it was the colonial heritage that he blamed for the premodern condition of Andean America.

The work of Edward A. Ross followed in scope the passage of the United States from isolated nation to Caribbean empire to hemispheric hegemon. His later writings, to an extent, betrayed sociology's ambition for universal scope. Just as the United States imagined itself, during the Wilson years and beyond, poised to become a powerful actor on the world scene, Ross's sociology went from parochial to international. His early works on social control and immigration were informed by the "American" national experience. In contrast, his book *The Outlines of Sociology* was supported by a system of references relating to the world at large. Firsthand observations in Asia, South America, Russia, Central Europe, and Africa enabled the Wisconsin sociologist to gain a comprehensible view of "world trends" that allowed wide-ranging international comparativity.

Ross's exposure to foreign nations and cultures helped him envision a transnational scholarship. His "sociological portraits" of China, South America, Mexico, and Russia contained the foundations of a "worldly sociology," a comparative ethnography of regional cultures and sociopolitical organizations. This was a sociology that sought to find regularities of international validity. This "worldly sociology" was an antecedent to the fragmentation of the world into "areas of study," an approach that consolidated and prospered during the Cold War period.

Many of Ross's observations about South American societies were inflected by the forces of race, landlordism, and the lack of democratic sociability. Ross's great "discovery" was to confirm that many of these features remained dominant in the second decade of the twentieth century—except in Mexico and Argentina. In Mexico a social revolution put an end to Spanish medievalism; Argentina had done the same through mass European immigration. Nowhere in his works did Ross deal with the Circum-Caribbean, where the United States set up temporary colonial administrations.[32]

After Ross, U.S. sociology became an abstract and highly structured science of society, whose principles were purportedly universal in scope and validity. Under Robert K. Merton and C. Wright Mills, the science distanced itself from its earlier dependence on "sociological portraits" of regions, silencing in this way all traces of its own imperiality. In 1947 the sociologist W. Rex Crawford argued for universalizing the discipline: sociology should be a science for understanding world societies, not just a set of principles applicable to the United States. If U.S. sociology was to reclaim its role in the making of a more peaceful world under U.S. guidance, it was necessary to return to the understanding of "cultural areas," as Ross had done. Crawford called attention to the fact that sociology majors were graduating without any knowledge of Latin America. The discipline's neglect of the region was also noticeable in books on rural sociology, population and family studies, criminology, and social problems. Crawford (1948) called sociologists to rediscover the lost interest in regional specificity to better promote sociology as a transnational science in the service of international relations.

NINE

U.S. Scholars and the Question of Empire

U.S. scholars working on problems of Latin America from distinct disciplinary perspectives had to deal at some point with the question of empire. This was a multifaceted problem that included various interconnected questions: should the United States preserve its dependencies in the Caribbean and the Pacific? When and under what conditions would it be convenient to withdraw from occupied territories? Was education in self-government essential to the divestiture of power and the beginning of self-rule? Was the Monroe Doctrine obsolete with regard to the South American republics? Could the South American republics be trusted as allies in the preservation of regional peace and in the pursuit of common international goals? How could the distrust expressed toward the United States be dismantled? Would a policy of intellectual cooperation and cultural enticement pay off in the long run? Would the United States be able to attain hegemony without dominance?

These were the main questions that scholars, businessman, and policy makers in the United States asked about the empire. It was clear to contemporaries that the United States had colonial possessions in the Caribbean and the Pacific. Through loans and the marines, the United States dominated the political and economic destinies of small countries in Central America. Yet it was also clear, particularly after 1906–1914, that south of Panama there were republics with a long tradition in self-government, with economies already integrated in the world economy, and with standards of living that made them potential consumers of U.S. products. Scholarly engagements with South America after 1906 underscored the importance of these nations, particularly the so-called ABC powers (Argentina, Brazil, and Chile). In them U.S. observers saw the possibility of gaining market shares from European traders, bankers, and industrialists. During the First World War, the United States had gained new markets in South America. To maintain them, greater economic, institutional, and cultural engagement with South Americans was required. Pan-Americanism was the ideological and institutional solution to this problem.

The question of empire referred to both formal dependencies and informal areas of influence. It included the question of whether it was better and simpler that independent countries emulate U.S. institutions and cultural modernity—and, to some extent, acquiesce to its international policies—rather than to maintain costly colonial dependencies, with added responsibilities for policing, sanitation, education, and financial control. This type of calculation was implicit in discussions of U.S. hegemony and imperialism. While at moments it seems that commentators suppressed formal colonies when dealing with the question of informal empire in South America, the relationship between the two forms of hegemony was always present. In fact, it is my contention that it was the "rediscovery" of South America that confronted U.S. policy makers with the need to rethink its imperial, hegemonic engagement in the hemisphere. Scholars were alerted to the tensions between the formal and informal areas of U.S. influence and were eager to intervene in the debate, either to reinforce the belief in the hemispheric great divide or to extend toward Central America and the Caribbean the blessings of a more benevolent and less imperialistic hegemony.

In this chapter I deal with the ways in which new knowledge about South America influenced the U.S. scholarly perspectives on the question of empire. In general, five prominent scholars—Hiram Bingham, Clarence H. Haring, Leo S. Rowe, Isaiah Bowman, and Edward A. Ross—found arguments and reasons for rejecting U.S. colonial interventions and for expanding the forces of cultural engagement and scientific cooperation. The "novelty" of South America pointed in two opposite directions. On the one hand was the discovery that South Americans were enthusiastically acquiring the instruments of Euro-American modernity. This authorized the continuity and intensification of U.S. expert assistance in institution-building and sustained the illusion of developmental convergence between the United States and the white settler nations of the Southern Cone. On the other hand, scholars discovered in South America the enduring legacy of Spanish colonialism, manifested in servile labor, the exclusion of indigenous peoples, and an outdated aristocratic culture. Therefore they repeatedly placed the question of U.S. hegemony in comparison with the experience of Spanish colonialism. The colonial legacy pointed toward the need to reform social structures, to correct the distribution of property rights, and to abolish outdated forms of social and racial discrimination.

Rejecting the Monroe Doctrine

The relevance of the Monroe Doctrine to twentieth-century inter-American relations was on the minds of U.S. Latin American experts. In 1913 the historian and archaeologist Hiram Bingham published a scathing condemnation titled *The Monroe Doctrine: An Obsolete Shibboleth*. The 1823 proclamation, Bingham argued, was no longer applicable to most Latin American nations. Certainly, it was obsolete in relation to the ABC countries. With time, the doctrine had come to stand as a justification for various forms of U.S. intervention in Latin America, generating widespread resentment across the subcontinent. To remedy this situation, Bingham proposed to abandon the ninety-year-old doctrine and to start building a more reasonable and productive U.S. foreign policy toward Latin America.

In rejecting the applicability of the doctrine, Bingham challenged every one of the arguments raised by its supporters. The Monroe Doctrine, he argued, was not a legal principle agreed on by a group of nations; it was a unilateral declaration by the United States that carried no international legal force. By making the defense of a group of countries the responsibility of the strongest nation, the doctrine contradicted the common and accepted principle that every nation had the right to defend itself. The argument that there was a "natural sympathy" between the United States and the Latin American republics was simply not true. As South American intellectuals were arguing, a great cultural gulf divided Hispanic America from Anglo-America. Any recent traveler, said Bingham, knew that South American intellectuals were writing about the important differences that separated the two Americas: Catholicism versus Protestantism, Yankee individualism versus Spanish state-centric life, and materialism versus spiritualism. The region's elites felt more affinity with Europe than with the United States; their intelligentsias were fascinated with French ideas and culture (Hiram Bingham 1913c).

Bingham acknowledged that in the 1820s the Monroe Doctrine had served to protect the independence of the Spanish-American republics from the threat of Spanish recolonization. This protection was no longer needed. Others saw the doctrine as a protective shield that gave the South American republics the time it needed to catch up in economic, political, and cultural development.

Yet this progress had failed to materialize: the Western countries of South America were still trapped in the past, suffering from outmoded transportation systems and exploitative labor relations. If anything, the gap separating the United States from South America had widened.[1]

The United States, Bingham argued, had maintained a rhetorical commitment to the doctrine without enforcing it.[2] In fact, the United States had committed acts of aggression against Latin American nations in the name of the Monroe Doctrine. Theodore Roosevelt in particular had established with the Roosevelt Corollary a new de facto Monroe Doctrine that implied U.S. sovereignty on the American continent. Bingham criticized the United States for taking an aggressive stand in the Venezuelan affair (1895), risking war. As intensely, he criticized the negative diplomatic consequences of the Spanish-American War. The war brought "fear and apprehension" among "our South American neighbors." While New York newspapers praised the courage of U.S. soldiers for "saving" the Cubans from "Spanish tyranny," he pointed out, newspapers in Buenos Aires were filled with caustic criticism of U.S. imperialism.

In practice, the United States had taken colonial possessions, contradicting the letter of the original Monroe Doctrine. Diplomatic incidents in the region had increased since 1898. Bingham denounced U.S. imperialist aggression in Panama in 1903. To control the Canal Zone, the United States had literally taken a province from a sovereign nation (Colombia) and made it into an independent state (Panama). The Panama affair sparked bitterness among South Americans. Secretary Elihu Root's goodwill tour to South America (1906) was intended to mend relations. But Root's speeches proved to be only empty rhetoric, for a mere two years later the United States sent warships to settle a dispute in Honduras. Meanwhile, in 1904, European creditors had attempted to seize the customs house of the Dominican Republic to cash in unpaid debts. The United States then instituted a receivership, unduly disposing of the revenues of a previously independent state.

In the face of all these actions, said Bingham, South Americans concluded that the Monroe Doctrine was synonymous with "interference and intervention" (1913c, 42). It was natural that less-developed nations would borrow to build infrastructure and public improvements, running occasionally into arrears in their payments. Yet there was no reason why the United States had to act as collector of unpaid debts. First, it was the Dominican Republic, then Honduras, then Mexico. The implications were ominous: under the Roosevelt Corollary, the United States had become responsible for the good financial behavior of small American nations. This was unacceptable to Bingham. The Roosevelt Corollary also caused great alarm in South America. This conception ran counter to an established principle of international law: the independence of sovereign states.

Bingham's criticism of the Monroe Doctrine was explicitly anti-interventionist, based on the observed resentment these policies caused among South American intellectuals.[3] After examining his 1913–1914 confrontation with Peruvian *indigenistas* and cultural nationalists, we are in a better position to understand his "obsolete shibboleth" publication. U.S. interventions in the Caribbean since the Venezuelan affair (1895) had caused such resentment among South American intellectuals that they were ready to boycott the work of U.S. scientists in the region.

Transforming the Monroe Doctrine

Rather than abandoning the Monroe Doctrine, the promoters of Pan-Americanism wanted to transform it into a multilateral policy of continental self-defense. Among them, nobody was as influential as political scientist Leo S. Rowe. In 1914 the American Society of International Law invited Rowe to discuss his position on the Monroe Doctrine (Leo S. Rowe 1914a). He argued then that the doctrine, as a principle of national self-determination, was still vital. Europe no longer entertained projects of colonization in Latin America, but its politics and ideologies (from left and right) continued to influence the American continent. So it was crucial to prevent the Latin American nations from being dragged into European rivalries. Yet Rowe considered that, instead of a unilateral policy statement of the United States, the doctrine should be sustained by all the nations in the Americas and collectively enforced. He stressed the need to make the Monroe Doctrine Pan-American, that is, a cooperative enterprise of mutual protection of national sovereignty.

He noted that not all countries in the hemisphere were equal. Mexico, Central America, and the Caribbean were bound to the national interest of the United States, as their raw materials and foodstuffs were crucial for the well-being of U.S. workers. The United States should be able to intervene in areas where disorder and instability threatened the region's security. In South America, by contrast, nations with sufficient political stability and economic assets shared the same interests and ideals as the United States. The ABC countries in particular posed no threat to the economic or political welfare of the United States: they could be instrumental for the peaceful settlement of regional disputes. In his lecture Rowe affirmed the diplomatic great divide. Due to reasons of "national security," there were areas where the United States had a legitimate right to intervene.

We are interested in the welfare of Mexico, of Central America, and the West Indies primarily because their stability and their progress ultimately affect the well-being of our own people, and we are interested in their attitude toward us because that attitude has a distinct bearing on our national safety. (Leo S. Rowe 1914b, 24)

But there were other places of relative peace and stability, governed by progressive men, where the United States should never intervene directly (South America). Consequently, he thought the United States should establish principles of "American foreign policy" differentiated by region.

The Monroe Doctrine could be accepted as a foreign-policy principle, he argued, only if it was not applied as an undifferentiated mantle of protection over the whole continent. Rowe envisioned an "American concert" with the South American nations, able to bring peace to the region by disarming long-standing rivalries. Argentina, Chile, and Brazil could play an important part in the making of this regional peace. Rowe agreed with Bingham on three points. First, political international conditions had changed dramatically since 1823. Now that Europe had moved toward republican forms of government, America and Europe were no longer so different in their political ideals. Second, Washington policy makers had twisted the original meaning of the doctrine so that now it stood for U.S. dominance. In addition, the doctrine had sparked much criticism and opposition in Central and South America. With regard to U.S. responsibility for the financial mismanagement of small nations, Rowe was unequivocal: it was not the role of the United States to attempt to keep European bankers out of Central America and the Caribbean. In this regard, Rowe's talk challenged President Woodrow Wilson's call to emancipate Central and South America from the grip of European capital (the so-called Mobile Address). To him, Wilson's call sounded like Dollar Diplomacy.

As to the nature of U.S. hegemony, Rowe was in favor of "soft power." Gunboat diplomacy or threats based on sheer economic or financial supremacy should be abandoned and replaced by a policy of "influence through example." South Americans would appreciate the United States leading the region in the resolution of conflicts through arbitration and in the improvement of education and living standards. That is, in addition to promoting the ABC as a leading force of peace in the region, he advocated U.S. involvement and responsibility in economic and social development. He viewed the Pan-American system as an empire by consent, as a commonwealth in which Latin American nations voluntarily agreed on principles designed by U.S. policy makers. Crucial to this entente was the agreement among the intelligentsias of the American republics on common principles and ideas ("intellectual cooperation"). Later, during the Wilson presidency, Rowe presented the Pan-American system as a sanctuary of peace in a world at war and thus a model to be imitated by the League of Nations.

Hemispherical Racial Cooperation?

In *South of Panama* (1915) the sociologist Edward A. Ross mentioned the Monroe Doctrine only in connection with the question of Asiatic immigration. Peru, in particular, and South America, in general, seemed to be receiving increasing numbers of Chinese immigrants. The Chinese constituted cheap labor and as such, threatened the existing wage level in the region. Furthermore, Ross considered Chinese immigration to threaten indigenous cultures. He predicted that by the end of the century, twenty to thirty million "Orientals" would find their home in South America, erasing all possibility of "Indian improvement." Ross called for U.S.-South American cooperation in limiting the Asian immigration wave. Thus, in a curious way, he invoked the Monroe Doctrine to defend the Americas from the "teeming Orient" (Edward A. Ross 1915, 93).

But Ross's use of the Monroe Doctrine held little appeal for Latin Americans. U.S. Americans and South Americans were not ready to cooperate on racial issues. Elite South Americans, for the most part—the indigenistas excluded—were not particularly worried about the disappearance of indigenous cultures. In the countries most transformed by European immigration, indigenous peoples were excluded from the discourse of progress. Argentines and Uruguayans were ready to point out to foreign visitors that "Indians" had long before disappeared. Ross had extrapolated to South America a problem that was politically decisive in the United States.

Race was an overriding concern for the U.S. sociologist. In this terrain he found a possible parallel between the U.S. Indian frontier and the Chilean frontier south of the Bío Bío River. In the new territory recently conquered by the Chilean army from the Mapuche peoples, Ross found the energy of a rough and egalitarian democracy, like that of the United States after the Indian Removal Act (Edward A. Ross 1915, 101–2) In this sense, Ross seemed to uphold the Western movement as a civilizational conquest productive of a democratic culture. Fortunately, his proposal for a racial Pax Americana found few supporters.

Obstacles to Commercial and Capital Penetration

What did U.S. scholars think about the economic conquest of South America? While generally in agreement with commercial and financial expansionism, they raised doubts about the transformative power of U.S. technology and mass consumer culture. In addition, U.S. scholars showed concern about the ethical dimension of U.S. enterprise abroad.

The archaeologist Hiram Bingham was not enthusiastic about the opening of the Panama Canal. In a 1914 article he estimated that the economic benefits that would derive from this technological marvel would be ephemeral. Though he acknowledged that the interoceanic canal was already generating great expectations among Ecuadorians, Peruvians, and Chileans, he thought this reflected a temporary wave of economic optimism, a passing collective delusion. Any long-term profitability of such investments would depend on adequate geographical knowledge. Bingham's own geographical inquiries convinced him that the Andean cordillera was like a "Chinese wall" that rendered much of the inland territories of the region inaccessible. The lack of navigable rivers made the introduction of mass consumer products quite problematic. For the moment, the building of railroads across the Andes was an enormously costly proposition. The markets of South America offered few real opportunities for the immediate future.

Ross and the geographer Isaiah Bowman also found the U.S. economic penetration of South America problematic. To Bowman, the natural environment of Andean nations presented great obstacles that even U.S. advanced technology and large capital could not easily overcome. To Ross, race, social inequalities, and local custom imposed severe limitations on the development of mass consumption on the western coast of South America. Their pessimism about the possibility of progress in the Andean nations underscored the exceptionality of the ABC nations, whose economies, societies, and cultures were much influenced by Europe and not yet in the economic orbit of the United States. The "modernity" they observed in Argentina, southern Brazil, and Chile was more European than "American."

In *The Andes of Southern Peru* (1915) Bowman addressed the question of economic penetrability in detail. Here was a region that, due to the diversity of its climate and environments, presented vast natural resources to be developed. But the very conditions of the natural environment—high plateaus, large deserts, isolated settlements, harsh climate—limited the feasibility of an easy deployment of U.S. capital and modern technologies in the Andes. True, there were already U.S. mining companies extracting copper and silver in Peru and Chile, U.S. firms participating in the extraction and processing of nitrates in northern Chile, and U.S. engineers building impressive railroads in the region. But none of these enterprises had been able to transform the traditional landscape of poverty and petty-commodity production in Andean valleys and deserts.

Bowman's term *conditional conquest* underscored these severe limitations to economic development. The conquest of the region by modern technology and mass consumer goods was reserved for a distant future. For the time being, the "true conquerors" of the environment were the Andean shepherds and farmers who, through the centuries, had adapted their lifestyles to the harsh conditions of highlands, deserts, and dry valleys. By contrast, foreign mining enclaves had failed to conquer the environment. Their company towns lived in closed spaces wholly dependent on outside supplies produced by the peasant economies of the highlands. Nitrate firms, however financially sound, depended on the vagaries of climatic changes. A year of unusual rains could wash away the nitrates and, consequently, the companies' profits.

Regarding the question of "commercial conquest," Ross was pessimistic about the power of U.S. companies to transform the consumer habits of South Americans. Deeply rooted social habits, great social inequalities, and the lack of "energetic races" conspired against the development of mass markets in the region. In Colombia traditional habits and customs limited the purchasing capacity of local markets (Edward A. Ross 1915, 12). He reported the story of an U.S. entrepreneur who opened a shoe factory in Cali, only to discover that upper-class Colombians preferred imported shoes and lower-class Colombians wore no shoes at all. Ross depicted the Cauca Valley as "an indoor patio," shut off from the Pacific by the jungle and the cordillera. Isolated, people lived "uneventful lives" and spent the day visiting each other and gossiping about trivialities (ibid., 10). The opening of the Panama Canal had begun to awaken the dormant energies of Colombians. Enterprising Antioqueños had introduced the U.S. spirit of progress to Colombia, if not what he called a "Hebraic" energy.

> It is a striking fact that not only do the Antioquians often show the Semitic countenance and Hebraic traits, while their province abounds in Biblical place names, but they regard themselves, and are regarded by others, as Hebrews. It is supposed that long ago numerous converted Spanish and Portuguese Jews settled in this province, and became the seed of this pushful race. (ibid., 14)

Yet outside of this region, people's energies were dormant, the way of life quite provincial. In Quito and Cajamarca he saw traces of Moorish influence that

Scholars and the Question of Empire

dated back to Spanish colonial times. In Lima poverty, disease, and overcrowding reinforced his belief in the social and cultural backwardness of the region. The city of kings had birth and mortality rates typical of Oriental countries (ibid., 42–44). Hence, it was difficult to think of Peru, Ecuador, and Colombia as thriving markets eager to import U.S. goods.

In the Central Valley of Chile, Ross found green, cultivated fields and well-kept towns. Yet large social inequalities limited the development of markets. The miserable huts of rural *inquilinos* contrasted with the marble mansions of absentee landowners in Santiago (ibid., 100). The low standard of living of tenants and laborers in rural Chile anticipated reduced markets for modern imported commodities. Only in southern Chile, where German immigrants had settled after the defeat of the Araucanos, did Ross find an emerging "rough frontier democracy" with traces of social egalitarianism: maids and farmers' daughters were difficult to distinguish by their clothes (ibid., 101–2). Argentina, by contrast, had accepted the improvements of U.S. modern technology. It was the "most metallic country" of South America; its countryside displayed many "metal fences, posts, gates, railway ties, windmill towers, and telephone poles" (ibid., 117). Here was a "country of hope" where general prosperity was spilling over to the average worker.[4]

Enclave Economies Absolved

These U.S. scholars were perhaps too lenient toward U.S. corporations operating in South America: banana, copper, nitrate, and petroleum companies in particular. Ross's judgments about U.S. enclave economies in Peru and Mexico were especially empathetic and favorable. The real enemies of social equality and progress were local landowners and local elites, not U.S. companies.[5] This was a departure from his previous work, *Changing America* (1914), where Ross had launched a striking condemnation of U.S. business culture.[6] Now Ross failed to extend this criticism to U.S. investment in Latin America. The sociologist found no fault with the labor policies of Cerro de Pasco Mining, the largest firm in Peru owned by U.S. Americans. The company, producing two thousand tons of pig copper a month, employed over twelve thousand local workers, most of them Indians from the highlands. Work conditions were hard, due to the thin air of high altitude and the prevalence of pulmonary disease, but the company provided local workers with medical checkups and good housing. Indian miners had good appearance: "red cheeks, magnificent chests, and strong back muscles, but their arms and legs are poorly developed" (Edward A. Ross 1915, 48–51).

Nevertheless, U.S. mining corporations used an indentured labor system called the *enganche*. Recruiters called "hookers" (*enganchadores*) made drunken Indian peasants sign labor contracts, advancing them loans for fiestas. After sobering up, the Indian found himself sent to a distant mining camp, to toil in a freezing mine gallery. Asked why they did not use the regular wage system to attract miners, the manager of the firm said that it was impossible to get Indian laborers to work underground unless compelled by debt (ibid., 153–54). To Ross, this outdated recruitment system was but a small stain in the modernizing and humane record of U.S. mining companies in the Andes. Similarly, in his book about the aftermath of the Mexican Revolution, Ross portrayed U.S. managers of mining and industrial conglomerates as reasonable businessmen who had accepted the transformations brought about by social upheaval. They silently accepted the new labor rights established in the 1917 constitution, learned to negotiate with the unions, and were grateful that "Bolshevism" had not produced greater expropriations and state controls. Some of them, he said, were happy to see their workers well paid, well fed, well housed, and enjoying the new hospitals and schools (Edward A. Ross 1923c). It was not U.S. capitalists but local landowners who longed for a return to their lost privileges and the restitution of their confiscated lands.

For all his condemnation of corporate culture in the United States, then, the sociologist failed to see major faults in the conduct of U.S. business enterprise in South America. He exculpated Cerro de Pasco Mining with regard to its exploitative recruitment system. He praised the pragmatism of U.S. firms in Mexico for adapting to the postrevolutionary social environment. Ross saw nothing disconcerting about the U.S. informal empire in the region. Other scholars thought otherwise. Rowe was one of the earliest to condemn U.S. business practices, Washington's unilateral Pan-Americanism, and U.S. armed interventions in the Caribbean. As early as 1911, he blamed U.S. corporations for the bad reputation of the United States in South America: early U.S. entrepreneurs in Latin America who resorted to fraud to close business deals, and the "lawlessness" of U.S. corporations, which on occasion financed revolutions in the Caribbean. In addition, Rowe argued, the U.S. "missionary spirit" had created ill will among South Americans.[7]

South American Attitudes and Economic Imperialism

Whether or not U.S. scholars viewed the activities of U.S. corporations abroad with suspicion, they agreed that South Americans had developed negative attitudes toward U.S. economic expansionism and U.S. military interventions.

The historian Clarence H. Haring purposefully studied U.S. business practices and South American reactions to these practices. In *South America Looks at the United States* (1928) Haring framed the issue within the contours of "economic penetration," a term that stood for what we now call economic imperialism, neo-colonialism, or, simply, dependency. Countries endowed with natural resources could become the object of ambition of more powerful nations.

> But regions so favored, unless they have also a responsible government, a numerous population and a vigorous industry, may become the theatre of the economic ambitions and rivalries of more powerful countries, or at least the scene of intensive foreign capitalist enterprise which may undermine their economic if not their political independence. (Haring 1928, 80)

In Haring's view the First World War presented an exceptional opportunity for U.S. business firms to capture markets previously dominated by European traders and industrialists. Trade to the region increased 300 percent between 1910–1914 and 1926. As a result, specializations based on comparative advantage developed. The United States sold manufactures and some commodities to South America (machinery, motor cars, iron and steel, cotton goods, lumber, and grain), while South America exported to the United States raw materials and foodstuffs (coffee, nitrates, copper, wool, hides, rubber, and cacao). At this point in time, this specialization was not an issue of contention (ibid., 82).

U.S. foreign direct investment, though modest in comparison with European investment, was already quite large by 1910, particularly in mining. This was superseded by U.S. private loans to South American governments.[8] While these loans may have exerted some economic leverage in the southern republics (favoring U.S. firms in government contracts), it was not evident that they served as instruments of political intrusion.[9] After the end of the war, the extension of U.S. banking facilities in South America, in conjunction with a series of technological advances, transformed the United States into something more than a commercial competitor to Europe. It was at this time that the United States became synonymous with economic exploitation and political intervention. To Haring, much of this negative image was the artful creation of foreign and local publicists engaged in anti-American propaganda. By itself, economic supremacy in areas of trade and finance were not sufficient to explain the degree of anti-Americanism Haring found in South America.

Haring considered the problem of "economic imperialism" to be another name for intensified competition, from 1900 to 1930, between European and U.S.

manufacturers for South American markets. In reaction to this economic struggle, the local press and radical agitators disseminated an increasing volume of anti-American propaganda in the subcontinent. The arguments they used to generate anti-American feelings were deceitful and, in some cases, outrageous. To Haring, the opening of South American markets during the First World War had caught U.S. business firms unprepared. As a result, their early business practices were sloppy and impolite, and this gave U.S. firms a bad reputation (Haring 1928, 82–83). After the war, the extension of U.S. communication, banking, and shipping gave U.S. companies a firmer base on which to compete for South American markets.[10] The crisis of 1920–1921, in particular, forced U.S. corporations to improve their methods to meet the challenge of European competition.

Haring noted that German and British traders responded to the invasion of U.S. goods, trademarks, and technologies with "sharp commercial practices" such as price-cutting, secret discounts, gifts to customers, and outright bribery of government officials. In addition, European traders, with the help of friendly newspapers or viva voce, disseminated anti-American propaganda. Haring accepted these practices as normal in situations of intensified competition. The traditional press in the ABC countries, hitherto friendly to the United States, had begun in the early 1920s to disseminate anti-American propaganda. Newspapers leveled charges of "economic imperialism" against U.S. big business and U.S. banks. An economic weekly in Buenos Aires blamed U.S. banks for the depreciation of the Argentine currency. The main Brazilian newspaper characterized the "coffee loan" as an entry door to U.S. financial domination. Even as traditional and reasonable a newspaper as *La Razón* (Buenos Aires) claimed that the United States had used the settlement of Tacna-Arica to gain important concessions for U.S. firms in Peru. In addition, South American papers claimed that U.S. investors had turned Cuba into an "economic colony" of the United States.

To anyone who picked up and read a newspaper in Rio de Janeiro, Buenos Aires, or Santiago in the mid-1920s, the idea that the U.S. firms were building an economic empire in Latin America was evident. Understandably, radical propaganda—particularly after the Russian Revolution—contributed ammunition to the increasing rejection of U.S. "economic imperialism." Socialist unions saw any U.S. intervention in Mexico or Central America as a cause that justified important political mobilizations.[11] But, in Haring's view, if the traditional press and radical labor communities coincided in the prognosis of "Yankee imperialism," this was something more than mere anti-American propaganda.

Scholars and the Question of Empire

Haring took the threat of South American anti-Americanism seriously. He attributed it to past U.S. interventions in Central America and the Caribbean and to the continued use of Dollar Diplomacy. U.S. high-tariff policies produced further animosity. Past U.S. interventions in Panama, Haiti, Santo Domingo, and Central America had predisposed South Americans to think that the United States, despite claims to the contrary, was gaining political control in smaller nations. Haring saw the politics of Dollar Diplomacy dangerously extending to poor and small states in the Andes.

> As the Monroe Doctrine operates today, American loans, at least when made to small and weaker states, tend to political control and the people become increasingly suspicious of the American hand in their affairs. This is not only true of the tiny Caribbean states, but as has already been intimated, may easily become the situation in some parts of South America, as Bolivia today. (Haring 1928, 97)

To counter charges of economic imperialism and political interference, Haring called for a complete separation between U.S. business and U.S. foreign policy. The U.S. government should not support or give any protection to U.S. loans in the region.[12] By calling on the State Department to adopt a Gladstonian attitude toward business imperialism, Haring was extending the great divide to the terrain of Dollar Diplomacy. If in small Caribbean states, some intersection between finances and government were tolerable for the sake of "national security," in South America that intermixing of finance and foreign policy was unacceptable. In addition, Haring demanded that the State Department implement guidelines for proper business conduct for U.S. corporations in the region.[13] Furthermore, U.S. diplomats should seek "open doors" in South America, without engaging in local politics or being in any way connected to particular business interests (ibid., 100–101).

In short, the Harvard historian rerouted the charges of "economic imperialism" toward the territory of foreign policy. U.S. corporations and products were in fact engaged in a fair competition with European traders and manufacturers. The charges of "economic imperialism" were a reflection of South Americans' disgust concerning U.S. past interventions in the Circum-Caribbean and the current practices of Dollar Diplomacy. A policy of hemispheric cooperation based on the principles of Pan-Americanism should pay adequate attention to these charges. If the United States were to persuade the South American elites of its benevolent intentions, important changes in U.S. foreign policy were required.[14] Just befriending South American intellectuals was not enough. The United States needed to put an end to military interventions in the Circum-Caribbean and to restrain U.S. corporations from meddling in Latin American politics.

Toward a Theory of Informal Empire

Bowman was the first to enunciate a defense of informal empire, as a reassurance against the impending demise of territorial empires. Bowman returned from the Paris Conference (1919) with a Wilsonian global vision.[15] The new world order would require a remapping of political boundaries. Wilson's principle of national self-determination required that negotiators allocate ethnic groups within fixed geographic boundaries, in ways that would prevent future wars. Old balance-of-power diplomacy needed to be abandoned. National representation in the League of Nations would facilitate the peaceful resolution of international disputes. The economic position of global powers would no longer be dictated by the possession of colonies.[16]

This new "global vision" was clearly advantageous to the United States. The nation with the strongest economy—the best technology, the most appealing consumer products, and the most advanced methods of mass production—would prevail without the need for military interventions or the acquisition of colonies. Wilsonian liberal internationalism masterfully represented the expansive tendencies of the U.S. corporate world. A world with no barriers to the expansion of trade, investment, and technology would favor the most competitive economy and society. This world vision was consistent with a critique of European colonialism.[17] In 1919 the world had been completely parceled so that no expansion of national territories seemed feasible. Soon, territorial colonialism would give way to economic expansionism (Neil Smith 2003, 184). After the war, U.S. policy makers expected that U.S. capital, technology, and ways of life would expand across Latin America and Asia. This expansion would necessitate no territorial acquisition. U.S. economic and technological preponderance would safely restore U.S. exceptionalism. For, unlike European colonialism, U.S. economic supremacy was predicated on superior technology, mass production, and modern advertising.

To the extent that Bowman shared this view he was an anti-imperialist. The historian Neil Smith writes,

> Bowman's attitude toward empire captures the new mix of geography and politics that defined these formative years of the American Century. Imperialism to Bowman was a system of direct political coercion

and control over a people and had no place in the modern world. Its rationale was economic exploitation—of labor, raw materials, crops, and commodities—and political and cultural domination. (ibid., 187–88)

U.S. economic supremacy over Latin America was, in this sense, a non-imperialistic type of hegemony. To Bowman, the principle of national self-determination was absolute. But he also deeply believed that some populations lacked enough civility and practice in government to determine their own affairs. He was prepared to admit that a collective organization of strong nations should be granted a mandate over more primitive and disorderly nations. In this way, the new League of Nations could legitimate prior U.S. interventions in Central America and the Caribbean. Interestingly, this idea of a soft imperialism, exercised for the protection of the weak, was the basis of the British policy of "colonial trusteeship."[18]

Bowman used a similar argument—the tutorship over inferior peoples—to justify U.S. colonial possessions in the Caribbean and the Philippines. In addition, he argued that the U.S. monitoring of the finances and politics of weaker nations in Central America and the Caribbean was preferable to direct U.S. rule (Bowman 1921). The expansion of U.S. influence in South America, moreover, was not a form of imperialism; it was a development that followed naturally from the expansion of U.S. capital and technology. Increased U.S. needs for tropical foodstuffs, the existence of undeveloped natural resources in the region, and the superiority of U.S. institutions had fueled U.S. economic expansionism in Latin America. This type of supremacy was the inevitable outcome of unregulated market forces.

In a 1948 article Bowman tried to adjust his previous views of Latin America to the conditions of post–Second World War trade and the communist menace. The United States had embraced a responsibility in world affairs that it was determined to keep, he stated. The policy of isolationism was consigned to the past. Further industrial development, given its limited natural resources, required U.S. companies to look outside to "world pioneer lands." It was imperative for the United States to have free access to mineral resources, food, fibers, and oil produced by the dependent and colonial world. Accessibility to trade and investment were now the key to international development (Bowman 1948).

In the new world opened to U.S. investment and trade, Latin America would continue to play a role, but one smaller than those of other world regions. During the war, the United States had maintained a mutually beneficial trade in raw materials and foodstuffs with the region. Yet the region was unprepared for

postwar development. Bowman based his prognosis on geographic and historical reasons. In spite of its connections to world markets, Latin America had not
overcome the isolation, separateness, and lack of transportation that he had
observed in 1913–1915. Geographic isolation continued to reproduce intense
regionalism and internal political fragmentation. In the concert of backward
nations Latin American countries faced an additional difficulty: the coexis-
tence of dependence on foreign capital and "primitive" peasant economies.[19]
To these two features Bowman added the other legacies of Spanish colonialism: political elitism, disdain for work, continuity of great landed estates, and
disregard for legal norms. In this, his prescriptions were different from those
of dependency theory. U.S. capital, aware of all these obstacles to development,
would be reluctant to invest in the region. Moreover, as most good land was already occupied and cultivated, there was little room for additional agricultural
development. And the region had not successfully dealt with its monumental
"Indian problem." Countries with a majority population of Indians would simply bypass the opportunity for rapid development: "It is idle to talk of universal
suffrage and democratic majority *procederes* to an Indian group ignorant of
political theory, incapable of choice, and walled off by centuries of deep-seated
hostility toward whites" (Bowman 1948, 138).

Latin American countries had changed substantially, he acknowledged. They
all had signed the Act of Chapultepec (1945), favoring a regional defensive
union over the great experiment of a new world order, the United Nations.
But they were hesitant about the new ideological divide of the day. If in the
1930s the region had been the target of Nazi propaganda, now it was a "soil
prepared for the Communist sowing." After so many efforts to push Latin
America in the direction of liberal capitalism and republican democracy,
the United States could not trust the support of Latin America in this new
ideological conflict (ibid., 136). Apparently, the cultural policies of Pan-
Americanism first and Good Neighbor-hood later had failed to produce a
convergence in political and social ideas. By 1948, Bowman was disillusioned
with the whole hemispheric idea. The informal empire had produced neither
domination nor hegemony.

Some Empires Are Better than Others

In the interwar period U.S. scholars were clearly redefining the nature of empire. Modern empires had to provide public goods to their extraterritorial subjects, and in order to exert technological and cultural influence, they had to
engage more closely with the life and history of their hinterlands. This entailed

moving the question of imperial influence or hegemony to the territory of culture and knowledge.

Haring was an expert on the comparative history of empires. He considered European expansion overseas since the sixteenth century to be a "stupendous achievement" of Western civilization. In 1921 he offered his Yale students a course on the "Expansion of Europe" (History 169), which focused on the question of empires.[20] In this course, he presented as the central dynamic of history the evolution from "old" to "modern" empires. At the beginning, it was discovery that gave some nations (Spain and Portugal) the right to colonial possessions. With time, however, naval power became the decisive force in inter-imperial competition. At that point, France, England, and Holland displaced the older Iberian empires. During the nineteenth century, the British empire achieved the largest expansion of sovereignty ever known. Over time, Great Britain shifted from an "old empire" built on naval supremacy and commerce to one based on the emigration and colonization of new lands. The settler colonies in Australia, South Africa, New Zealand, and Canada were part of Britain's "new empire," which reflected a less aggressive type of imperialism.

In these classes Haring defended the U.S. empire in the Caribbean and the Pacific as a provider of public goods. The British had given India political unity, internal peace, and a stable justice system. In similar ways, U.S. rule in the Caribbean and the Philippines had built social infrastructure and promoted a series of institutional reforms that were equally civilizational in nature.[21] In Haring's view the "American Empire" was a composite blueprint for doing things: government, architecture, roads, education, agriculture, public health, and so on.

Empires were to Haring laboratories of learning. Through the acquisition of the Indian subcontinent, Britain had come to administer an extraordinary diversity of races, religions, and grades of civilization. India was "the greatest living museum of races and languages."[22] Since early on, the British colonial administration had understood the necessity to study Indian languages, traditions, and forms of thought as a means to better govern this diversity. Later, experience demonstrated the fragility of such territorial empires. The British failed to understand that in order to survive, modern empires had to give in to colonial demands for self-rule. U.S. rule in Puerto Rico and the Philippines constituted a notable improvement in this direction. As colonial peoples would struggle for independence, it was the task of the modern colonizer to prepare them for self-government.[23]

Modern empires, argued Haring, were no longer territorial dominions or systems of trade protected by gunboats. They were cultural extensions of the metropolis. The ascent of former colonies on the world scene was sufficient proof of the good services of empire. The British Commonwealth was, in this regard, exemplary: Canada, Australia, New Zealand, and South Africa had become prosperous self-governing nations, tied to England by "bonds of race and sympathy," whose voices were taken into account in the formulation of dominion policy. A similar reasoning could be applied to the Latin American republics. After emancipating from Spain, they had constituted republican governments and gained experience in self-government. From the U.S. perspective, the relevant question was how to make these nations embrace Anglo-American traditions in economic, political, social, and cultural spheres.

Modern imperial hegemony was based on the dissemination of metropolitan culture over its hinterlands. Haring argued that the United States should try to spread intellectual and cultural influence in its Latin American hinterland, as the British had done in its dominions. Rather than a territorial empire, the modern U.S. empire should be a loose confederation of self-governing nations, guided by a Big Brother. Without mentioning it, Haring was describing the Pan-American Union (PAU), as it was conceived in the 1920s. We know that Haring enthusiastically embraced Pan-Americanism. The leaders of this movement had envisioned a new type of empire: one based on the persuasion of ideas and culture.

But there was a problem. In the 1920s members of the South American intelligentsia began to question the good intentions of the northern colossus, due to its repeated military interventions in the Caribbean and Central America. It became harder to explain to them that U.S. dominion in Cuba, Puerto Rico, the Dominican Republic, Haiti, and Nicaragua was different from the old Spanish empire. In a way, the residual presence of "old empire" was undermining the project of a "modern empire" of culture and expert knowledge. In the late 1920s Haring grew impatient with U.S. policy in Central America and the Caribbean. In an interview given to the *Harvard Crimson* in 1927, he criticized Washington's policy in Nicaragua.[24] Recurrent military interventions in Central America and the Caribbean made it quite difficult to promote Pan-Americanism. Although the United States should maintain its long-term strategy of defending canal rights and political order in the region, there was no need to intervene in the affairs of Nicaragua every time an election result was not acknowledged by the losing party.[25]

In the 1930s Haring came to see South America as the future frontier of ideological persuasion. In part, this reformulation was related to the new political climate: military coups, Nazi sympathizers, and autarchic economic policies. Now spreading the gospel of democracy, economic progress, and social equality became crucial for extending U.S. hegemony. The Spaniards had created hierarchical societies based on racial oppression and labor servitude and had restricted education to elites. To overcome these obstacles, the only open avenue was a new wave of colonizers—experts, entrepreneurs, and social reformers—who would put South America's natural resources in motion, under conditions of greater social equality. In this way the region might return to the path of progress and civility pioneered by the United States.[26]

Postcolonial Pan-Americanism

Rowe was among those who argued for a more benevolent and cooperative U.S. empire. On the issue of Washington's control of the agenda of inter-American relations, he favored a policy of multilateral hemispheric cooperation. He coined the term *constructive Pan-Americanism* to refer to the reforms he expected to see implemented in the inter-American system. Four principles were the basis of his reform agenda: (1) the countries of the Americas should banish forever the fear of mutual or external aggression; (2) they should avoid falling into the trap of the European balance of power; (3) within the region, it was necessary to prevent the hegemony of one group of countries over another; and (4) American nations should help each other solve their common financial, social, and industrial problems.[27]

The first two principles called for the construction of a defensive system, based on a concerted effort to keep the continent isolated from European conflicts. Within the PAU, peace could be sustained through the arbitration of regional disputes. During the 1920s, Rowe thought the inter-American system could be the model for the League of Nations. The fourth principle entailed an extension of cooperation to areas under the sovereignty of national states: social, industrial, and financial policies. Underneath his notion of hemispheric cooperation was the conception of the United States as the grand arbiter of Latin American disputes. Since the expertise in policy problems resided in the United States, inter-American cooperation would consolidate U.S. prestige in areas of government, sanitation, policing, education, finance, and technology. In short, Rowe's vision of U.S. continental hegemony relied on U.S. expert knowledge.

Rowe's "constructive Pan-Americanism" required a 180-degree turn in U.S. policies as they were conceived in the 1920s.[28] Rowe was among the first to demand a multilateral or cooperative approach to hemispheric defense. His most resonant diplomatic success was the recruitment of Argentina, Brazil, and Chile as brokers in the resolution of the 1914 Mexican imbroglio. After the fiasco of the Vera Cruz naval assault, President Wilson took Rowe's advice and called the ABC powers to mediate in the U.S. conflict with Mexico.[29] Challenging Wilson's nonrecognition policy, Rowe argued that the United States should not place itself in the position of judge of constitutional government for Mexico. His promotion of the ABC powers as arbiters in inter-American affairs was greatly appreciated in South American diplomatic circles.

Rowe (1917a) called for greater efforts in inter-American cooperation for the solution of common problems. The United States, he thought, should become a partner in the promotion of "democracy." It should help Latin America to raise its standards of living, eliminate peonage, enact protective labor legislation, produce agrarian reform, and generate educational opportunities for all. The cooperation he had in mind would work chiefly through the educational system. Financial and commercial cooperation was not enough; a true better understanding should be attained at the intellectual and cultural level (ibid.).

At first glance, Rowe's progressive stand—his promotion of a multilateral and constructive Pan-Americanism, concerned with solving social problems and with monitoring the development of democracy—seems to contrast with his early positions on "insular government." Rowe had previously supported U.S. colonial ventures in the Caribbean and the Pacific, presenting U.S. interventions as legal, constitutional, and progressive. To an extent, Rowe's changing views about U.S. policies toward Latin America were the product of his spatial displacement—and the greater knowledge gained—from the formal to the informal dependencies of the U.S. empire. His extensive travels across South America presented him with a new imperative: here were well-consolidated nation-states, republics with sufficient political stability and fiscal prudence to avoid situations favorable to European gunboat diplomacy.[30] Temporal displacement also mattered. It was one thing to speak of Latin America at a time dominated by Theodore Roosevelt's vision of the right of the United States to exert tutelage over the poor and unstable small Caribbean republics. It was quite another to speak about the inter-American order during the interwar period. Secretary Root's visit to South America in 1906 had opened the discussion of national autonomy, peaceful resolution of disputes, and the benefits of mutual knowledge. This was later complemented by Wilson's principle of national self-determination and the participation of South American representatives in the League of Nations (ibid.)

Rather than representing a break in Rowe's thinking about empire, then, "constructive Pan-Americanism" constituted an adaptation of his conception of U.S. superiority and "helpfulness" to the South American situation. The opening of the Panama Canal, in his opinion, was more than a U.S. engineering feat. It provided a practical lesson in governance. In the Canal Zone, U.S.

Scholars and the Question of Empire

Americans had demonstrated that modern sanitation methods could control endemic diseases and that clear and enforceable rules could bring order to the most disorderly of populations. Rowe's enthusiasm about the persuasive power of U.S. expert knowledge and the superiority of U.S. government institutions remained strong after the outbreak of the First World War. During this period, he shifted his focus from constitutional government to democracy. Whereas Caribbean nations were not ready for constitutional government, the ABC nations could entertain the idea of experimenting with political, industrial, and social democracy. During his visit to Buenos Aires and La Plata, Rowe realized that Argentines and U.S. Americans had much in common. If this were so, a policy of cultural enticement and intellectual cooperation would do the trick.

Rowe (1902c) came to prefer economic supremacy over formal empire, and, with time, he came to see cultural and intellectual engagement as the best assurance for economic and political hemispheric unity. In South America indirect influence through economic supremacy could only go so far. Rowe was aware that in order to coopt South Americans, a great effort should be made in undoing previous misconceptions. The cooperation from South American governments and peoples would not come as the spillover of more intense economic interactions. Rowe came to envision the PAU as a sort of U.S. commonwealth, guided by common interest and ideals. Clearly, he attributed the greatest responsibility to the United States in steering the ship of Pan-Americanism toward peace, prosperity, and mutual understanding.

But he repeatedly insisted that, in order to gain sufficient consensus about policies and ideals, the PAU should conduct a well-planned and sustained effort in cultural and intellectual cooperation. This was Rowe's idea of informal empire. In his view, U.S. hegemony would be the end result of a long, laborious effort in cultural diplomacy. To a certain extent, he projected a progressive theory of empire. The inter-American system would serve as a political mechanism for the cooperative solution to "common problems," a label that included issues such as child welfare, common education, labor legislation, a robust public opinion, and so on.

A Continent for Democracy

In an article published in 1922 Rowe addressed the question of the state of democracy on the continent. The republican form of government, he said, was well established across the Americas. What was now at stake was the future of democracy. In his view Latin American nations were striving to "bring their social organization into closer harmony with their political institutions" (Rowe *land reform?*

1922, 3). The problem of democracy was that small landed elites controlled the political destinies of Latin America. The majority of the population, on the other hand, lived in poverty and in "abject economic dependence." In South America the workforce remained unorganized and with relatively low standard of living. Efforts to raise the well-being of workers through popular education were failing. Bad nutrition, inadequate housing, and unhealthy cities conspired against social leveling. Latin America, proposed Rowe, had to push harder for social equality. The spread of democracy in the American continent required a "comprehensive plan of social legislation." The great landed estates should be divided up and sold to landless tenants in order to create a class of small-farmers, the true basis of a democracy (Leo S. Rowe 1922).

In political terms the Latin American nations needed to bridge the gap between their constitutions and their actual government. Though the federalist system had been established by constitutions, most governments were centralized. Mexico and Argentina were examples of this divide between constitutional forms and governmental reality. The greatest challenge facing the southern republics was to create governments responsive to the wills of the majorities. Latin Americans had yet to learn political self-control, true respect for the law, and the art of reaching consensus through public discussion. This required a long process of education, which Rowe now said the United States could not provide. Departing from his own earlier recommendations, he said that the Latin American republics themselves had to learn these lessons.

Twenty years later, in the midst of the Second World War, Rowe revisited the question of democracy in the Americas. He recounted the story of Pan-Americanism as a successful building of hemispheric solidarity. The Good Neighbor Policy had radically changed the spirit of cooperation between the United States and Latin America. After the Montevideo (1933) and the Buenos Aires (1936) conferences, the American republics had united in the defense of hemispheric peace and had agreed on the principle of nonintervention. After Pearl Harbor, the nations of the hemisphere were ready to defend democracy. Despite minor deviations, the Latin American nations had sided with U.S. democracy and rejected European totalitarianism. At the end of the Rio de Janeiro meeting (1941), ten nations declared war against the Axis powers, and nine more severed diplomatic relations with them (Leo S. Rowe 1942).

Faced with an attack on democracy, the Latin American nations had joined the United States in the greatest struggle in history. More diligently and more resolutely than the British Commonwealth, the countries of the PAU had responded to the call of the hour. Rowe was enthusiastic about this response. Latin American nations were united for the defense of democracy against Nazi aggression and against the lack of respect for international treaties and the rule of brute force. And Rowe imagined—as he had done before with reference to the League of Nations—that the hemispheric union would continue to serve as an example for the world (ibid., 77).

Conclusion

In several ways, U.S. scholars dealt critically with the question of empire. They questioned the contemporary validity of the Monroe Doctrine, pondered the transformative power of U.S. enterprise in the Andes, suggested a shift toward the provision of technical assistance to growth and welfare, tried to build a multilateral system of hemispheric cooperation, and emphasized the need to promote a better understanding of "American democracy." These views contributed to project new responsibilities for the United States in South America: those of promoting hemispheric peace, increased economic integration, and better understanding between the two Americas. While at first scholars criticized U.S. interventions in the Caribbean and the principle of the Monroe Doctrine, it is clear that by the mid-1920s and early 1930s, the center of the debate had shifted toward issues of culture and knowledge.

Criticism of the Monroe Doctrine extended to the question of U.S. interventions in the Circum-Caribbean. Scholarly positions varied substantially in this regard. Some thought the U.S. colonial experience in the Caribbean could help the United States understand the new diplomatic scenario in South America. Others flatly rejected outmoded forms of interaction in favor of cooperative diplomacy, international law, and the arbitration of international disputes. For instance, there were important differences between Bingham and Rowe. Bingham favored the application of the Drago Doctrine to inter-American relations, rejecting the role of the United States as an "international policeman" for European creditors. Rowe, though condemning the methodology of Dollar Diplomacy, tended to view the Circum-Caribbean as an area of political instability and fiscal disorder that demanded occasional U.S. interventions. With regard to South America instead, he recommended building a spirit of cooperation and trust geared to the solution of common problems.

In the scholarly discussions of Rowe and Haring, we can discern a clear preference for "modern" forms of imperial engagement, that is, for empires that provided public goods and general welfare to their subject populations, and for an imperial bureaucracy ready to engage with the question of culture in the peripheries. In a way, these scholars anticipated the shift in U.S. foreign policy toward Pan-Americanism first, and Good Neighbor Policy later. A wiser and more enduring hegemon would consider the ways of life of originary inhabitants of the land, would more closely monitor the behavior of U.S. corporations in South America, and would take inventory of the growing dissent among the southern intelligentsias about the perils of foreign economic intrusion and dominance.

The "rediscovery" of South America opened the way for scholars to project U.S. progressive and reformist impulses on the social and cultural landscape of the subcontinent. For example, Ross and Bowman introduced the question of social and racial inequality in the dialogue between the two Americas. The benevolent empire not only carried the banner of regional peace and national self-determination, but also presented itself as a moral force for the reduction of such inequalities in the region. While the U.S. colonial experience in the Caribbean and Central America had imposed on the United States the roles of law-giver, instructor of self-government, and financial, sanitary, and police advisor, South American nations presented to U.S. experts the opportunity for studying the different dimensions of "development," a magical fountain from which unending words of expert advice could flow.

CONCLUSION

Between 1906 and 1930, five notable U.S. scholars in the fields of archaeology, geography, history, political science, and sociology traveled to South America to evaluate and appraise anew the realities of the region. At the time, U.S. diplomacy, capital, and technology were attempting to incorporate South America as an area of influence. After Secretary Elihu Root's visit in 1906, Washington opened up the possibility of diplomatic and cultural rapprochement with the southern republics. The works of Hiram Bingham, Isaiah Bowman, Clarence H. Haring, Leo S. Rowe, and Edward A. Ross enhanced U.S. knowledge of the region, making South America more easily apprehensible and legible to students and the general public. Their findings constituted a "rediscovery" of South America: new characterizations, based on disciplinary concerns, observations, and theories, about the present and potential of the subcontinent. These disciplinary interventions brought some order to the apparently chaotic and heterogeneous reality of the region. By simplifying the geography, history, government, antiquity, and societies of South America, U.S. scholars produced a more comprehensive and nuanced understanding of the different countries and subregions. Their work highlighted problems in comparative development, particularly in the region's potential for adopting U.S. modernity and democracy.

U.S. scholars "rediscovered" South America in a double sense: they presented novel panoramic vistas of the region, based on closer scrutiny and observation, from a range of disciplinary viewpoints; and they contrasted their findings with the achievements and failings of the Spanish colonial system. References to the Spanish conquest underscored the novelty of the discoveries and the vast research opportunities they opened up. Whether the object of study was Inca ruins, the Spanish commercial monopoly, life in the Andean desert, South American attitudes toward the United States, or the question of South American revolutions, the new knowledge adumbrated a new understanding of the subcontinent that, in turn, provided a new platform to rethink U.S. policies toward the region.

The U.S. scholars who visited South America in the first two decades of the twentieth century themselves viewed their experiences as a second discovery, making explicit references to the sixteenth-century Iberian colonization. Bingham thought of himself as the "second Pizarro," while Bowman talked of the desert of Atacama as his own "El Dorado." Haring found in Spanish colonial history a well of unending comparisons with the British colonies in North America. Similarly, Rowe went back to study Spanish *cabildos* in order to understand Puerto Rico's political culture. Ross discovered the persistence of "colonial traits" in the contemporary societies of the Andes, presenting highland communities in Peru and Bolivia as living in the middle ages.

While drawing a connection between the Spanish colonial past and South America's present, U.S. scholars also made clear that their conquest differed because it was scientific: a set of findings made possible by the application of modern research methods. Their discoveries were meaningful only within the boundaries of disciplinary knowledge. Their enunciatory authority stemmed from the prestige of emerging U.S. research universities and learned societies, not from papal bulls, *capitulaciones*, or royal charters. As the first "scientific observers" of the subcontinent, these scholars felt empowered by a sense of mission: to uncover deep-rooted structures and regularities in its history, societies, environment, and culture.

When Bingham returned to the United States after his discovery of Machu Picchu, he informed reporters that he was the "first white man" to see the ruins that provided refuge to the Incas escaping from the Spanish conquerors. The Yale explorer, a historian and archaeologist, was able to correct a huge Spanish oversight. In their quest for gold and glory, the Spanish colonizers had failed to see major Inca ruins near the Urubamba Valley. Though Spanish chronicles

Conclusion

provided clues to the puzzle of Inca fortresses and citadels, imperfect maps and a deep forest had kept Inca sites hidden from view. Bingham's discovery made clear that modern archaeology, properly equipped, could generate new knowledge of ancient civilizations in the Andes and thus complete and correct the unfinished narrative of the Spanish conquest. Equipped with modern survey methods, the Yale Peruvian Expedition (1912–1915) was able to locate the sites where crucial events of the conquest of Peru took place (Hiram Bingham 1922, 127). Bingham's attempt to retrace the escape route of Inca warriors chased by Pizarro's forces was not metaphorical. Based on William H. Prescott's account and Spanish chronicles, Bingham knew that the Incas had intended to make their last stand at Urubamba and, defeated by a superior army, had escaped over snowy passes into the "fastnesses of Uilcapampa" (Bingham, *Inca Land*, 1922, 108).[1]

In 1947 Isaiah Bowman told the reporter of a New York newspaper that in the Atacama Desert, back in 1907, he had discovered his "El Dorado." One moonless night, the sand of the desert seemed to flow like a river of gold; it turned out to be a subterranean water current glowing in the dark (Martin 1980, 37). The underground water was the true gold of the desert, though the evidence of it was not easy for the casual observer to detect. That was his discovery. Water was everything in Atacama, and the scholar who understood this could begin to grasp the life and thought of the peoples of the desert. Apparently poor and empty, the desert was actually full of life; its inhabitants were the "true conquerors" of this harsh environment.

U.S. scholars were the new "discoverers" of the realities of South America, the door-openers of new research opportunities, the utterers of generalizations that could serve as basis for a disciplinary understanding of the region. Their new findings began to come together at a time when U.S.-centered modernity expanded its reach to the southern half of the continent. U.S. scholars saw themselves as pioneers in the knowledge of a subcontinent until recently considered "terra incognita." Their suggestion that U.S. men of science were replacing the Spanish conquistadors was more than metaphorical. They thought that Spanish colonizers had failed to understand Hispanic American peoples, especially the indigenous inhabitants of the land.

In his work on Andean societies, Ross, a sociologist, underscored the persistent legacy of Spanish colonialism. Under the facade of European modernity lay an infrastructure of premodern social norms, interactions, and prejudices. Indian servile labor, racial oppression, great landed estates, and aristocratic presumption were the marks left by Spanish colonialism in the contemporary societies of Peru, Ecuador, and Bolivia. These signs of coloniality hindered

Conclusion

the march of modernity and social reform in the twentieth century. Due to Spanish colonialism, Andean indigenous peoples had been degraded to the condition of "passive beasts of burden." Living in fear, they shunned the presence of whites and accepted with resignation their subordinate and miserable condition in life. Ross's observations reignited U.S. interest in the question of colonial persistence, now called "coloniality."[2]

Contemporary Andean societies exhibited racial divisions and tensions not so different from those of the Spanish colonial period. Despite previous discourse among scholars about racial miscegenation and the role of mestizos in South American politics, Ross discovered that the polarity between whites and Indians still dominated social relations. Deeply divided by race, Andean nations were not prepared to achieve modern nationhood. Only Argentina had broken away from the colonial legacy. Transformed by mass European immigration, the country exhibited all the transformative powers of free labor, small property holdings, and modernizing elites. Here, Ross found the only dominant class in South America that had rejected the foundations of the colonial order.

Haring's studies on Spanish colonial institutions raised fundamental questions about their effectiveness, durability, and strength. He launched a devastating critique of the Spanish commercial monopoly, showing the extent to which other European powers had benefited from this apparently exclusive regime. The impressive bureaucratic structure of the Casa de Contratación ended up suffocating the development of Spanish mercantile capital while stimulating widespread corruption and smuggling. Colonial inhabitants were subject to the tyranny of irregular supplies and exorbitant prices. The Spaniards deluded themselves trying to control the gold and silver produced by the American colonies. European "price inflation" was hard evidence that bullion flew out of Spain to pay for manufactures that Spain could not produce.[3]

Haring located the fiscal and commercial predicaments of the Spanish empire in the geopolitics of competing empires. He argued that Spanish policies were out of tune with the mercantilist policies of its rivals, France and England. Spaniards had failed to understand that in order to maximize revenue, kingdoms had to charter commercial companies, build a solid navy, and promote local manufactures. At a time in which new ideas about government blossomed throughout the Atlantic, Spaniards created an old-fashioned landed aristocracy in America. The sale of public office put in motion a system of power that undermined all possibility of responsible government. These erroneous policies prevented the development of self-reliance, the work ethic, and social equality in Hispanic America.

Conclusion

The early twentieth century presented Hispanic America with a second opportunity to realign itself with the geopolitics of the time. Latin America's production of raw materials and foodstuffs became important to the core economies of the North Atlantic. Haring presented this as a "second hemispheric beginning" coincidental with the Pax Americana (1941, 12). The European War (1914–1918) had given the Latin American republics a new awareness of their position in the world economy. In addition, the United States opened to them opportunities to participate in international forums: the League of Nations, the Hague International Court, and the Pan-American Union.

Ordering through Disciplines

The new disciplinary panoramic vistas of South America promised accuracy, simplification, and greater insight. The disciplines themselves, with scientific methods of inquiry and verification, aimed to make truth claims that could overcome centuries of prejudicial enunciations and crude generalizations. By providing more accurate visions and narratives, disciplinary interventions sought to order the U.S. debate about what constituted "South America." Simplification, the reduction of existing diversity and complexity for the sake of rational comprehension of the whole, was perhaps the greatest contribution of disciplinary interventions.[4] New information about ancient civilizations, historical processes, natural environments, human settlements, political institutions, and social norms, now organized under disciplinary concerns and rules, could account for intraregional differences and for the region's backwardness vis-à-vis the United States. With the help of simplifying devices such as maps, charts, tables, concepts, and theories, the data gathered through direct observation could be accommodated into larger explanatory schemes within disciplinary domains.

Different scholars negotiated the relationship between micro-observations and macro-generalizations differently. Ross imagined his "social portraits" as pieces of a bigger jigsaw puzzle of "world regions" in social transition toward modernity. Mexico, Russia, and China provided materials for a transnational comparative exercise about "great social upheavals." In the same fashion, Andean indigenous religiosity could be compared with that of Tibetan peoples, and the farming communities in the Argentine Pampas could find parallels in the U.S. Midwest. To Ross, regional evidence served to illuminate international "social trends" that supported his own sociological theories. Others, like Bowman, sought to detect differences in physiography, natural resources, and patterns of settlement in order to identify and delimit subregions. These great areas of purported homogeneity (the forest, the highlands, the coastal desert, and the inland valleys of Peru) could serve as points of comparison with other subregions (the Argentine Pampas, the Brazilian Mato Grosso, or the Argentina northwest) and thus illuminate discussions about the "potentiality" of South America.

Simplified panoramic vistas (geographic, social, and political) rendered more easily readable the ways of life of local inhabitants in South America. Bowman's diagrams and sketches exemplify well what James C. Scott (1998) calls "simplification." Bowman used the term *geographic control* to refer to the limitations the natural environment imposed on human activities. His geographical surveys of South America were applications of this rather deterministic concept; they could divide a vast territory into homogeneous subregions on the basis of shared features of soil, rain, temperature, or vegetation.[5] Simplified sketches and diagrams could help bring attention to the distribution of land type and use, underscoring the dominant role of the environment.

Bowman connected human settlements, production, commerce, transportation costs, and economic motivations to a single explanatory framework. His various arguments revolved around a single pivotal point: the environment. Physiography, in particular, was at the root of Bowman's generalizations about economic, social, and political interactions in the Andes. Rivers, mountains, and valleys determined the patterns of settlement and greatly influenced local ways of life. A generalization about the effect of "isolated settlements" in the political development of a country (Peru) could easily be transported to others (Bolivia, Ecuador) to replicate the diagnosis.

Though dominated by physiography and land use, Bowman's concept of region included a concern for economic connectivity. During his 1913 trip to South America, Bowman followed the 73rd meridian, carefully annotating variations in vegetation, rainfall, temperature, and soil so as to delimit subregions. Though he was initially interested in the Atacama Desert, existing commercial connections made him extend his observations to the grasslands of northeastern Argentina and Bolivia. In the preface of *Desert Trails of Atacama* (1924) he wrote, "I have not limited the story to the desert country alone but have included a brief account of the Chaco or grasslands of northeastern Argentina and adjacent Bolivia, because the currents of business flow naturally from these border settlements across the Atacama country and deeply affect its life." He found that centuries before, to overcome the limitations of their local environment, plateau and desert inhabitants had established trade routes connecting Peru, Bolivia, and northern Argentina. These commercial connections remained unaffected by the recent intrusion of foreign corporate capital.

Map-making is a form of ordering the multiplicity of observable phenomena in a given space. The American Geographical Society, under Bowman's leadership, extended the project of mapping and regionalizing Peru to the whole of Hispanic America. The Millionth Map of Hispanic America, Bowman thought, had brought order to both complexity on the ground and the existing cartographic chaos: "The Millionth Map of Hispanic America has taken a continent and a half out of a state of cartographic disorder into one of order, and thus it has so far advanced the world map that the urge to complete it is now higher than ever" (1946, 321). Now researchers could experiment with various regionalizations, speculate on the reasons behind the concentration of population in certain areas, and think about the possibility of extending the agricultural frontier.

Ross's "sociological portraits" of South American nations were also exercises in simplification, this time aimed at classifying nations by level of modernity. He followed certain organizing principles in compiling these portraits, looking for social organization, in particular paying attention to race, servile labor, landed property, and democratic sociability. Manners, customs, and shared understandings were important indicators of modernity and backwardness. Ross examined the "rule of courtesy" in South America. Countries that exhibited the "politeness of hierarchy" were still premodern, while those showing the "politeness of equality" were further along the road to modernity. In the latter type of societies Ross expected to see institutions of self-government: transparent voting systems, a competitive free press, youths trained in debating societies, and men pursuing civic goals through association.

Comparative hemispheric history was a productive disciplinary grid tailored to the understanding of the region's past. Haring tried to bring order to Hispanic American history, emphasizing the need to filter out unnecessary details to concentrate on the parallels in the long-term trajectories of Anglo-America and Hispanic America. By comparing great moments in the history of the two Americas (discovery and colonization, colonial life, emancipation, nation-building), he would bring to light the true differences between the two civilizations. Concepts such as "race," "environment," "frontier conditions," "policy restrictions," and "independent spirit" helped in articulating the comparison. But it was the disposition to write a comparative history of the two Americas that provided the simplified historical perspective needed to grasp the subcontinent's developmental state.

Similarly, Rowe's studies of Caribbean and Argentine government opened a road to understanding comparative politics. He endeavored to distinguish between societies prepared for "republican government" from those already

Conclusion

on the path to "democracy." In Caribbean dependencies the United States still had the burden of teaching self-government; in the Southern Cone, by contrast, the central question was whether each progressive nation had the means to develop a democratic political culture. Exploring urban reform, federalism, municipal finance, university education, and constitutional government, Rowe posed new questions about political life in South America in relation to Hispanic political culture.

Modern conceptions of institutional and economic history, as well as the use of the best available documentation, characterized Haring's history of the Spanish colonial empire. Facts and processes were demonstrated with the aid of archival documents, tables, and figures. Statistics supported his statements about the Spanish colonial exchequer. His analysis of the Casa de Contratación was based on the best available archival evidence. His colonial history was organized around certain key questions: why did the largest empire the world had known, in possession of rich mines of gold and silver, go financially and economically bankrupt in the seventeenth century? Why did attempts to reform the colonial system in the late eighteenth century fail? Answering each question with documentary and statistical evidence—and in relation to a model trajectory (the British empire in North America)—kept the historical narrative within clear bounds.

Harvest of Useful Knowledge

U.S. scholars brought a harvest of new knowledge about the nations of South America back to their universities and learned societies. This harvest was doubly useful: for the consolidation of regional disciplinary knowledge and for the formulation of U.S. foreign policies toward the region. It included better maps of land use and physiology, comparative histories, bones and artifacts from Inca ruins, lessons in colonial government, and sociological panoramas, to mention only the most relevant. This knowledge production helped scholars and policy makers understand the role of the United States in the hemisphere. From these disciplinary interventions, policy makers could better comprehend the mission of U.S. capital, enterprise, and culture in South America.

Bingham tried to make the work of the Yale Peruvian Expedition (YPE) useful to various departments of the U.S. government. He thought Inca roads, irrigation methods, and terrace cultivation should interest the Department of Agriculture and other divisions of government. He was right. These government agencies paid attention to the discoveries coming from the Urubamba Valley, not only those relating to roads and agriculture, but also those relating to metallurgy, taxation, and geology. Some of the materials gathered by the YPE—boxes of bones, textiles, and ceramics—were not immediately useful. These boxes remained stored in the halls of a college at Yale University for decades. But other materials—crania, insects, plants, bronzes, and soil samples—engendered a bounty of research activity at labs, museums, and departments across the United States. Bingham liked to boast about the impressive array of scientific publications produced by the members of the YPE.

Bowman conceived of geography as a science for government. Hence, many of his endeavors were oriented toward practical applications. His project for a comprehensive map of Hispanic America, his work at the inquiry and at the Paris Conference, his "risk maps" during the Great Depression, and his vision of the role of a research university all underscored his commitment to useful, practical knowledge. The Millionth Map of Hispanic America turned into a compelling reference for scholars, business, and government. Geographers used this collection of maps as a basic instrument for identifying types of human activity by region. Merchants, industrialists, and investors resorted to these maps to locate future investments, plan distribution channels, and target consumer markets (Bowman 1946). In addition, the maps proved advantageous in the settlement of boundary disputes between Guatemala and Honduras (1919), Chile and Peru (1925), Bolivia and Paraguay (1929), Colombia and Peru (1932), Colombia and Venezuela (1933), and Peru and Ecuador (1941) (Martin 1980, 95). Bowman was proud that the Millionth Map, a major undertaking of expert knowledge, was employed for the amicable resolution of conflicts (ibid., 73).

An inquiry assembled by President Woodrow Wilson to anticipate the challenges of the postwar settlement is another example of useful knowledge. Dividing the task into six areas of study—government and politics, geography, social science and history, economics and business, international law, and strategy—the inquiry asked experts to compile information about all countries that could present territorial claims at the peace conference. Most of the 126 members employed by the inquiry came from only five institutions: Harvard, Yale, Columbia, Princeton, and the American Geographical Society. Though geographers, cartographers, and historians predominated in the inquiry, there were also economists, psychologists, lawyers, and classicists. They produced 2,000 reports and 1,200 maps, which were later used to consider the division of Europe and its hinterlands. At the Paris Conference, expert advice acquired poignant political significance. The U.S. delegation headed by Bowman was tasked with translating Wilson's principles and the demands presented by former belligerents into "reasonable lines" on maps. The proposals Bowman presented to the Big Four—Wilson, Clemenceau, Orlando, and Lloyd George—were extremely useful for setting the new boundaries of Poland, Hungary, Yugoslavia, Romania, and various other countries that emerged from the Paris settlement (Neil Smith 2003, chaps. 5 and 6).

As president of Johns Hopkins University, Bowman promoted the development of science in the service of the state. This was especially transparent during the First World War. Johns Hopkins cooperated with a hundred war-related research projects, training college students for jobs in industries producing war materiel, and contributing technological innovations to modern warfare. One of these research teams produced a "proximity fuse" that increased the efficiency of anti-aircraft artillery threefold. The involvement of the premier research university in war-related programs interconnected science and state in unprecedented ways (ibid., 252–56).

Hispanic American history also presented itself as a useful discipline at the service of enhanced visibility and informal empire. Haring's parallel history of the hemisphere was designed to produce similarities and differences between the two Americas in support of Pan-Americanism. Haring discovered what he considered the fundamental similarities between the British and the Spanish colonial experience in the New World. Making explicit the problem of parallel but divergent trajectories, Haring anticipated the 1960s and 1970s debates on economic backwardness and dependent development. Out of these forced parallels, Haring derived the thesis of convergent trajectories that reinforced the Pan-American movement. The United States and the ABC nations appeared to be moving toward a similar modernity.

In the mid-1920s, Haring proposed a research program to study the reactions of South Americans to the U.S. presence in the region. The results proved quite useful, alerting the foreign-policy community to widespread anti-Americanism among Latin American intellectuals and the media. In the following decade Haring gathered intelligence about the recent military coups in the Southern Cone for the Council on Foreign Relations. In the late 1930s his reports about the Nazi activities in Brazil and how they were neutralized by President Getúlio Vargas served to assess the true dimension of this problem. In the midst of the Great Depression, through a series of round tables held at the University of Virginia, Haring helped businessmen, bureaucrats, and other scholars understand Latin America's contemporary problems.

Rowe's studies of colonial governance in the Philippines and Puerto Rico showed that the transition from military to civil rule could proceed in orderly fashion, under U.S. constitutional guarantees. Occupation governments prepared the way for self-rule, organizing the judiciary and the police, training teachers, carrying out sanitary reforms, and gradually introducing elections and political parties. Rowe's disciplinary intervention granted legitimacy to these acts of colonialism, at least from the point of view of constitutional theory. By contrast, Rowe's study on Argentine government showed that under the mask of federalism hid a centralized form of government that differed substantially from the U.S. model. Argentine centralized federalism was a reflection of Argentine popular traditions and history. South of Panama, one could find working variants of "American government" that supported less democratic interactions between citizens and elected officials.

In addition, the extension of disciplinary knowledge over South America generated useful assessments of U.S.-South American economic relations. Based on their direct observation of transportation and human settlements, Bingham and Bowman evaluated South America as a field for U.S. investment and as a market for U.S. goods. Bingham thought that the opening of the Panama Canal would not by itself mobilize the dormant energies of west coast nations. Bowman presented an even more pessimistic assessment, arguing that foreign investment in mining, oil, and transportation could do little to transform the way of life of inhabitants of the Central Andes. Their insights acted as cautionary tales against the too optimistic predictions of Pan-American ideologues.

Visions of Economic and Cultural Hegemony

The question of empire encompassed the discussion of how to treat the areas north and south of the great divide. U.S. policy toward formal colonies and dependencies in the Caribbean and Central America required little adjustment. But South America presented new challenges that needed to be addressed. The region's political and economic modernity confronted U.S. scholars with the need to rethink U.S. policies with regard to its Caribbean dependencies. Conversely, the experience of teaching self-rule to Cubans, Puerto Ricans, and Filipinos informed the ways in which U.S. scholars interpreted South American societies, politics, and cultures. While contributing to the construction of a discourse about the hemisphere, scholarly interventions tended to reinforce, rather than dissolve, the borderline dividing the two areas of U.S. influence and power.

As a result of the rediscovery of South America, the idea of a continent reserved for Americans and free from European interference came under attack. South American elites' distrust of the northern colossus brought about further scholarly criticism of the Monroe Doctrine. By 1910–1915, it was clear that U.S. adventures in the "American Mediterranean" had become an embarrassment to the United States in its dealings with the southern republics. Some scholars rejected the Monroe Doctrine as an obsolete principle ill-adapted to the realities of contemporary international relations. Others endeavored to transform the doctrine into a multilateral principle of hemispheric defense. Most agreed that in the early twentieth century the Monroe Doctrine had turned into a crude justification for imperialism, no longer acceptable.

On the question of "economic conquest," both Bowman and Ross contributed pessimistic assessments about the continued growth of U.S. capital and technology in the region. Geographic fragmentation and high transport costs imposed insurmountable obstacles to the penetration of U.S. mass consumer capitalism. To Bowman, the natural environment constituted the greatest hurdle. U.S. corporations were, in comparison to native inhabitants, only temporary settlers, their activities dependent on provisions and labor forces from local valleys and highlands. To Ross, great social inequalities and local custom limited the further expansion of markets for U.S. products. It was only in Argentina, a country of free labor and with a growing class of rural proprietors, that the expansion of the domestic market looked promising.

Criticisms of the activities of U.S. corporations in South America were few and rather mild.[6] While critical of corporate culture in the United States, Ross absolved U.S. enclave economies in Peru from any wrongdoing. He found U.S. managers in Mexico pragmatically adapting to the changes introduced by the revolution. Early in the 1910s, both Bingham and Rowe criticized the sloppy and deceptive methods employed by U.S. firms operating in the region. Haring, who studied the issue in the mid-1920s, concluded that since the economic depression of 1920–1921, U.S. corporations had entered into a phase of economic consolidation, as a result of which their dealings had improved in fairness and transparency.

The anti-Americanism that Haring found in his 1925–1926 visit to South America was not a reaction to U.S. direct investment in the region. The charges of "economic imperialism" leveled against the United States referred rather to the fear of being at the mercy of Wall Street and U.S. banks. The criticism of local publishers and radical thinkers had nurtured anti-American feelings. To alleviate these fears, Haring proposed that the Secretary of State distance itself from private business interests, suggested a code of business ethics for U.S. firms operating in the region, and recommended greater cultural cooperation with the southern republics.

On the question of the expansion of U.S. influence toward South America, Rowe and Bowman provided the clearest formulations. Bowman developed a vision of the Pax Americana as an economic and technological form of hegemony. In 1919–1920 he anticipated the decline of old empires and predicted that in the future, economic and technological superiority would be the true measures of a nation's international power. Due to its advantage in mass production, modern distribution, and advertising techniques, the United States would become a contender for world power. Yet, faithful to the imperative of the great divide, Bowman admitted the need for the continued U.S. tutelage of the weak Central American and Caribbean states—adding that now these dependencies should come under the oversight of the League of Nations.

Rowe believed in "influence through example." His recommendations entailed applying the experience acquired in the "American Mediterranean" to the terrain of informal empire. The United States should present itself as a leading force in technology, sanitation, education, social welfare, and international law. By way of example, cooperation, and advice, the United States could guide its South American sister republics into a future of regional peace and prosperity. South America would become a privileged site for the deployment of the U.S. progressive and benevolent agenda. Rowe projected onto the Pan-American commonwealth the vision of a benevolent empire committed to improving the living standards of its inhabitants. Cultural engagement and intellectual cooperation were the chief policies designed to attract the South American intelligentsia to a common hemispheric agenda.

In Haring's view the chief contribution of the United States to the Caribbean dependencies had been the provision of public goods: police, sanitation, fiscal administration, and legal reform. In relation to the whole hemisphere, he thought the United States had contributed more, for Pan-Americanism had provided the institutional infrastructure of a lasting peace, secluded from European balance-of-power politics and imperialist wars. Pan-American conferences had built effective institutions for the resolution of disputes among nations, imposing norms of consultation, arbitration, and resort to international courts. Haring believed that Pan-Americanism had acted as an important deterrent force among nations historically prone to initiate hostilities against one another.[7]

Both Haring and Rowe conceived of informal empires as commonwealths of culture. Haring distinguished "old empires" whose hegemony was based on naval supremacy and territorial control from "new empires" (settler colonies) that spread cultural influences through the exportation of human capital. In the twentieth century, he argued, only by exerting cultural influence could empires maintain strong bonds with their former colonies. In this regard, he supported policies that promoted the continued transfer of "American" notions of government, economic growth, and social organization to South America. Supporting a cultural conception of the U.S. mission in the Americas, Haring came close to Rowe's arguments about hemispheric cultural and intellectual cooperation. It was better to pursue U.S. hegemony in the terrain of culture than to insist on the outmoded forms of financial dependency and military might.

Rowe was the Macaulay of the Pax Americana. He wanted the intelligentsia in South America to voluntarily cooperate in making the flows of commerce, investment, ideas, and culture with the Americas more fluid and extensive. In the end, he expected that South American intellectuals would understand and share the core ideas of U.S. modernity and democracy. Ross basically shared most of Rowe's progressive principles. He wanted to uplift the condition of the Andean indigenous peasant by abolishing racial oppression, improving wages, redistributing land, and providing better access to common education. He greatly resented Chilean landlords who believed that Mapuche peoples did not deserve access to elementary education.

Repeatedly, U.S. scholars contrasted the twentieth-century U.S. expansion in South America against the backdrop of the Spanish colonial legacy. Bowman considered that modern technology and foreign capital would be unable to undo the effects of Spanish colonialism in Andean nations. There, the territory remained fragmented, separated by large distances and high transportation costs, the population so scattered as to prevent the development of a national economy. To Ross, the Spanish legacy was quite visible in contemporary Andean societies. Peru was a nation of landlordism, indigenous oppression, and premodern attitudes toward work and industry. The U.S. sociologist doubted that U.S. modernity could effectively penetrate lands so marked by premodern attitudes, values, and social relations.

Encounters with Native Informants

More often than not, the writings of U.S. scholars tended to obscure the presence of native informants. The visitors interacted with two types of native informants: upper-class intellectuals and indigenous peoples. Their scholarly panoramas of South America gave greater visibility to indigenous subalterns than to local intellectuals. Through their condemnation of Spanish colonialism, U.S. scholars underscored the suffering of Andean indigenous peoples. Before the spread of *indigenismo*, Bowman and Ross took to heart the question of the racial oppression of indigenous peasants in Peru. Haring's colonial history presented the exploitation of indigenous peoples as the enduring mark of Spanish colonialism. In their treatment of the "Indian question," U.S. scholars took, by and large, a progressive position.

Engaging with the Spanish colonial past to highlight the current exploitation and oppression of indigenous peoples was a common feature in the writings of U.S. scholars. They empathized decidedly with the Indian side of the racial divide. As a geographer, Bowman provided extensive commentary to his encounters with native subalterns, chiefly plateau and forest indigenous peoples. Machigangas brought to his attention the existence of slavery in the Peruvian Amazon. From this ensued a sharp criticism of the rubber business as a return to premodern forms of exploitation and brutality. He considered Machigangas to be a degraded ethnic group that had fallen into the trap of white plantation labor. With "plateau" or highland Indians, Bowman established a contradictory relationship. On the one hand, he tried to forcefully impose on them the disciplinary authority of the white man, forcing Indian carriers to work at gunpoint or whipping them into submission. On the other hand, he recognized the indelible marks of colonialism in the Indian psyche. From this followed a progressive indictment against contemporary Peruvian planters' brutality and racial oppression. His condemnations of Indian slavery in the rubber country and of Indian peonage on the coastal plantations were undoubtedly progressive, a sort of indigenismo *avant la lettre*.

As a sociologist, Ross came to the Andean nations persuaded that the Spaniards had failed to protect indigenous peoples from brutality and exploitation, something he confirmed with local informants. Yet his greatest condemnation was directed against contemporary Andean hacendados and office-holders, who kept Indian laborers and tenants in a servile dependence and without education. His moral indignation was loud and clear when writing about Chilean landlords who saw no point in educating the Indian or about Ecuadorian elites who compared Indians to monkeys. In Peru he detected that Indians were afraid of the white man and thus avoided contact with him. Here was a racially divided society, still working under the hierarchies built by Spanish colonialism. He admired the solemn and deep religiosity of Indian towns, yet he thought that Andean peasants were a race degraded by the effects of alcohol and coca, unable to escape from the traps of labor peonage. He attributed the laziness and sexually predatory nature of Andean Creoles to their Indian ancestry. Racist presuppositions short-circuited the sociologist's empathy with the plight of indigenous peoples.

Though Haring probably never interacted with living Indians, his colonial history included an unambiguous criticism of Spaniards' brutal treatment of indigenous peoples. He recounted how in the early *encomiendas* of New Spain, Indians were taken from their homes, forced to travel for long distances, made to sleep on the ground, and subjected to frequent floggings. Decrees to alleviate their suffering were not really enforced. The policy of relocation and concentration of indigenous peoples into *reducciones*, argued Haring, had disastrous consequences for Indian subjects. This was a "careless and stupid" policy that only led to corruption and injustice.[8] On the fringes of empire, the situation was even worse. Mapuches captured in the Araucanian wars were treated as chattel slaves. With time, in all the Spanish colonies, tribute in money and kind gradually replaced the original encomiendas, yet forced labor remained the rule until the mid-eighteenth century.

The presence of local intellectuals was less visible in the text. Relations varied—from confrontation to friendly partnership—according to individuals and particular circumstances, yet in the politics of citation U.S. scholars showed a dismissive attitude toward their southern colleagues. Of the five U.S. scholars, Bingham was the only one to have a direct confrontation with local intellectuals. The excavation work of the YPE gave local intellectuals a golden opportunity for asserting nationalistic claims over Peruvian patrimony. Tensions started when it became locally known that Bingham had complained about the "stench" of Cuzco. Animosity escalated when rumors spread that the YPE was searching for Inca gold. Later on, the Cuzco and Lima press implicated Bingham in trying to illegally export Inca artifacts through Bolivia. These skirmishes over cultural property left sour memories in Bingham's diary. Worn out by so much red tape, press opposition, and *indigenista* meddling in the YPE work, he abandoned field research in 1915 and did not return to South America until 1947. Though he continued to write about the archaeology of the southern Andes into the 1930s and 1940s, he failed to keep abreast of the new literature in the field. He did not acknowledge, for instance, the work of emerging Peruvian archaeologists such as Julio Tello or the new work of his U.S. colleagues, A. Kroeber and P. A. Means.

At the other extreme stood Rowe, who tried to interact with Argentine intellectuals on a fairly egalitarian basis. His 1914 lectures on "American democracy" and U.S. foreign policy constituted an attempt to build bridges with local intellectuals. He interested them in the problems facing U.S. democracy: the rise of big business and organized labor, the need for social legislation, the importance of a vigilant public opinion, and so on. Though agreeing with his fundamental ideas—hemispheric solidarity and partnership in the civilizing mission—the members of the local intelligentsia differentiated their circumstances from "American problems," making explicit their admiration for

Conclusion

European culture. Having recently experienced an extension of the electoral franchise, Argentine intellectuals were more concerned with the working of republican institutions than with problems of "democracy."

Rowe's positive assessment of the economic growth and political maturity of Argentina and his firsthand knowledge of the Argentine university system no doubt contributed to his favorable reception among local intellectual circles. He resided in the Internado of the University of La Plata for a semester, interacting with university students and scholars. He considered the University of La Plata a modern institution, training young men in practical sciences appropriate for an export-agrarian economy. During his repeated visits to Argentina, he cultivated enduring relations with leading scholars in law, constitutional history, and diplomacy. By contrast, Ross found Argentine universities backward in comparison to U.S. colleges. There was in them no spirit of collegiality, no debating societies, and little daily interaction between professors and students. In his view South American university men suffered from the same elitism as the landlord classes, being reluctant to do any manual work and depending heavily on the work of assistants.

U.S. scholars tended to be dismissive of the work of their South American colleagues. In his 1937 address to historians gathered at Buenos Aires, Haring described how, in each country, a bundle of scholars worked with limited library and archival resources to produce "national histories." Their efforts, however well-intentioned, lacked the scope, rigor, and structure of European or U.S. history. Though acknowledging the isolated efforts of some historians (such as Ricardo Levene in Argentina and Manuel Gamio in Mexico), Haring found most of the production of these national histories parochial. Only the United States, the nation endowed with rich library and archival resources and with a significant number of specialists, could pioneer the cause of hemispheric history. The parochial histories stemming from Central and South America could contribute only "facts" (documents, dates, heroes, and events). In Haring's *South of the United States* (1928) we can find elements of a disavowal of the local intelligentsia. The local intellectual was busily criticizing the colossus of the North for its imperialistic adventures in Central America and the Caribbean, but producing little original knowledge.

As U.S. experts considered the academic work of local scholars inferior, they tended to borrow from local publications without quoting the sources. Though Ross dedicated his book *South of Panama* to the Argentine sociologist Ernesto Quesada, he did little to emphasize Quesada's contributions to the understanding of Argentine society. From Ernesto Nelson, Ross learned about the failure of the Argentine school system to consider the psychology of the child. From Bolivian, Chilean, and Peruvian scholars, Ross received crucial information and observations about race and social relations. But he mentioned these local informants only in passing—naming Julio Tello (Lima), Manuel Ballivian (La Paz), and Valentín Letelier (Chile)—and as contributors of mere social commentary. Nowhere in the book did he cite any of their publications. Though Ross affirmed that he weighed the opinion of various sources before coming to conclusions, he clearly privileged the word of foreign residents over that of local intellectuals.[9]

The same could be said about Bowman and Haring. When collecting information for *Desert Trails of Atacama* (1928), Bowman took little notice of the work of local geographers or archaeologists.[10] In a narrative full of citations from European and U.S. sources, local sources received were rarely cited.[11] From his point of observation—the American Geographical Society Library in New York—European travel books superseded in number and quality local descriptive materials. In the writing of *Trade and Navigation* (1918), Haring relied mostly on archival sources and printed documents obtained in Spain. Yet he tended to dismiss the work produced by Spanish scholars as antiquated or of "small value." Works by other European scholars dominated his references in matters of history of navigation, silver mining, and commerce.[12] Although he acknowledged some of the production of colonial historians in Hispanic America, he thought their work contributed little to the understanding of economic history.[13]

With time, Haring became aware of the production of other historians of South America and duly acknowledged their value. In particular, he thought the Buenos Aires Instituto de Historia Americana, directed by Emilio Ravignani, was one of the few centers producing high-quality historical research.[14] In this rapprochement we can detect the workings of the new ideology of Pan-American cooperation. As a result, Haring's 1947 volume, *The Spanish Empire in America*, included a greater number of citations from Hispanic American authors.[15]

During his 1911–1915 stay in Peru, Bingham met with local intellectuals. The students at the University of Cuzco were trying to recover Inca culture, reenacting poetry and plays, and reproducing indigenous rituals. Local historians had discovered the importance of the *ayllu* as an elemental form of social organization in the Andes. *Huaqueros* and local collectors in turn tried to advise Bingham about other sites that indicated the existence of pre-Inca civilizations. Bingham discarded all these signals of local knowledge as irrelevant to his historical-geographical quest of Inca citadels and fortresses. With the help of Spanish chronicles and modern methods of survey and exploration, Bingham expected to uncover the secrets of Inca archaeology.

The New South American Difference

U.S. scholarly interventions presented the realities of early twentieth-century South America in a new light: its natural environment, its regional economies, its political development, its social life, and its historical legacies. New observations and interpretations led to further differentiations within the subcontinent in ways that business promoters had been anticipating since the late nineteenth century. One could no longer talk of "South America" without immediately qualifying that generalization with the acknowledgment that great differences separated the east from the west coast, the Andean nations from the ABC powers. The new panoramas, analyses, and generalizations tended to further discredit Andean elites, finding faults in their behavior, attitudes, and beliefs. Rediscovering the subcontinent produced a new array of enunciations that tried to locate South American nations within the developmental scale of U.S. modernity, progress, and democratic civility. The new vistas underscored the gulf separating the progressive nations of the Southern Cone from the backward Indian nations of the Andes.

In Ross's social panoramas we find a clear example of the subalternizing effect of the new knowledge. The Spanish colonial legacy translated into a new stereotype of the "South American character." This was a personality structure characterized by excessive pride, disdain for manual labor, want of persistence, distrust of others, and total incapacity to cooperate. Attributed to South American elites in general, these "failings" made evident these nations' unpreparedness for democratic sociability and modern economic progress. Ross's indictment against "feudal" relations in the Andes reproduced images of Andean indigenous peasants and laborers as passive and quiet victims, incapable of shaking off the burdens of the colonial legacy.

Bingham coincided in this characterization. South Americans had copied the U.S. constitution, yet they had failed to build a political culture that could sustain representative government. Lack of cohesion characterized the political life of the republics. Hispanic Americans were individualistic, not given to cooperation, attached to cities rather than to the nation. Their provinces constantly rebelled against central power. A "municipal spirit" inherited from Spain prevented the development of national feelings. Thus, when Hispanic Americans gained independence from Spain, they fragmented into multiple, disunited republics. The contrast between political disunion in South America and political cohesion in North America remained a crucial differential between the two Americas (Hiram Bingham 1910a).

Ross's sociological panoramas, Haring's historical generalizations, and Rowe's commentaries about political development provided nuanced distinctions with regard to the societies south of Panama. This view complicated the picture of U.S. foreign policy, reinforcing the need to cooperate with the nations of the Southern Cone while raising the possibility of U.S. tutelage and expert intervention in the Andean nations. Ross stretched the difference between Andean nations and Argentina along the medieval-modern axis: Ecuador, Peru, and Bolivia were clearly premodern and backward, incapable of rapid modernization, while Argentina was already a free-labor, small farming, and entrepreneurial country. Brazil, in turn, was the "land of tomorrow," still not ready to embrace U.S. modernity (except for its southern states and its principal cities, pondered by Rowe and Haring). Chile was in between, similar to Argentina in some regards, similar to Andean nations in others. The internal differentiation south of the great divide helped to support arguments for a differentiated foreign-policy approach to the region.

Rowe agreed with this assessment. In particular, he pointed out the need for a differentiation between countries that were economically progressive and politically stable and countries that were economically backward and politically unstable. The former were potential partners in the U.S. civilizing mission in the region; the latter were immature republics, similar in nature to those of Central America and the Caribbean. The progressive ABC nations deserved special consideration in U.S. diplomacy. As partners in civilization and progress, Argentina, Chile, Brazil, and Uruguay could help generate productive alliances leading toward the establishment of common Pan-American policies and principles.

The new "South America" that U.S. scholars construed was located midway between the old Spanish colonial regime and the modern United States. Scholars placed Andean nations closer to the colonial pole to underscore their economic backwardness, their failure in nation-building, and the innate incapacity of their aristocratic elites. By contrast, they located the nations of the Southern Cone closer to the United States, converging toward "American standards" of sociability, governance, and economic progress. The Andean nations still had much to learn from U.S. experience. Their elites exhibited an aristocratic spirit, disdain of labor, lack of cooperation, and refusal of social equality. This presented an opportunity for U.S. experts to inculcate lessons in modern sociability, republican governance, and free-market capitalism. Anticipating

Conclusion

the rhetoric of development, U.S. scholars discovered the advantages of backwardness for the continued deployment of hegemonic expertise.[16]

Curiously, this idealized image of the United States as teacher of South American republics replicated older conceptions of U.S. tutorship in the Caribbean and Central America. Yet, in South America, the call was for a complete social, cultural, and institutional renewal. The United States contained within its own society and culture the appropriate blueprints to export to South America. As Ross boasted, "[We have] the home training, the education, the religion, the ideals of life, the standards of conduct, and the public opinion competent to produce these virtues" (1915, 249). The transfer should include standards of conduct, social organizations, cultural institutions, religious and educational values, the gospel of social equality and democratic political participation, and the architecture of local government. Though some nations would prove more stubborn than others in the reception of these lessons, the region appeared in need of a persistent pedagogy in "American" values and institutions.

By subalternizing South Americans, U.S. scholars built "American civilization" as an exemplar prototype to be gradually replicated in the societies south of Panama. The United States could become the great crucible for the creation of modern, democratic virtues in South America. In an informal, benevolent, and civilizational empire, this model role was crucial for the dispensation of hegemony. Modern "America" was the mirror in which South American elites should look at themselves in order to understand better their own backwardness and incivility and, hence, to anticipate the challenges to confront in order to bring their countries into the modern era. To convince South American elites that this was the case, a persistent persuasion was needed, one that suggested a cultural diplomacy based on education through example.

By advancing the model role of "American experience," U.S. scholars contributed to pushing U.S. foreign policy into the terrain of culture: that is, intellectual cooperation, cultural missions, and the continued study of "Latin American civilization." This was, after all, the goal of the collective quest for knowledge: the conquest of the fortress of culture. The imperial question—that is, the question that interested Pan-Americanists in the 1920s and 1930s—was whether the region as a whole would be able to import and adapt "American modernity," for the economic penetration of U.S. capital, technology, and advertising in South America required a certain convergence and understanding at the level of culture. This may explain perhaps the continued relevance of culture in the agenda of Latin American studies, even after the emergence of the new social sciences. With the advent of Good Neighbor Policy, the State De-

Conclusion

partment had learned the lesson and started to promote cultural diplomacy on a greater scale. Additionally, it fostered the exploration into South America's folklore, music, dance, poetry, and literature as key factors for a more comprehensive understanding of the "South American character."

A Coda on Influence

Two propositions should by now be clear: (1) that the writings of these U.S. scholars was directly or indirectly connected with the great themes of international relations (the role of the United States in the hemisphere, the nature of future economic and commercial hegemony in South America, the ways to undermine South American anti-American sentiments, the proper conduct of U.S. business in the region, etc.); and (2) that all five scholars collaborated in one way or another with the State Department or other departments of the U.S. government in the conduct of inter-American relations. Bingham's attack on the imperialistic implications of the Monroe Doctrine, Haring's intelligence-gathering on coups and Nazi activities during the Great Depression, Rowe's promotion of ABC mediation during the Mexican imbroglio, Ross's suggestion that the United States should cooperate to prevent Asian immigration to Peru, Bowman's warning about environmental limits to foreign direct investment in Andean nations—all are forms of scholarship concerned with and activated by the preoccupations of U.S. policy.

To what extent did these scholars' interventions affect the direction of U.S. policy toward Latin America? In principle, it is almost impossible to calculate the influence of each scholar on a changing and controversial field (U.S. foreign policy toward Latin America). Nonetheless, if we narrow down the meaning of "influence" in relation to the proximity to power, we can give a partial and tentative answer to this question. Each scholar had a different connection with the U.S. government and, to this extent, could exert a quite different degree of influence.

In this regard, the top ranking goes to Bowman, not only for advising two presidents (Woodrow Wilson and Franklin D. Roosevelt), but also for intervening directly in affairs that changed the history of the world, namely, the Paris Peace Conference (1919) and the Dumbarton Oaks Conference (1944). His book *The New World* (1921) was compulsory reading for U.S. consuls abroad and was duly distributed among them. If we add to this his promotion of a "science of settlement" to monitor the expansion of the world's agricultural frontiers, his clash with German geographers over rescuing "political geography" from Nazi appropriation, and his efforts on the home front—as chairman of the National

Conclusion

Research Council and as president of Johns Hopkins University—to put geography at the service of government, it is difficult to find a scholar with greater influence.

Second place would go to Bingham, not only for creating the mythical figure of the "American explorer" who reveals archaeology's secrets while facing key political opponents, but also for promoting from elected positions issues that were crucial to the U.S. engagement in the colonial world—namely, his interventions in relation to the Philippines and the Samoa Islands while serving as chairman of the Senate Committee on Territories and Insular Possessions (1925–1927). Having gained credentials as a historian and archaeologist of South America, he launched a devastating criticism of the Monroe Doctrine. Later, he used his fame as a war hero to launch a quite successful political career. From his Senate seat, he spoke with authority about South America and U.S. Pacific possessions.

In close third place would be Rowe. As a leading figure of U.S. relations with Latin America over twenty-six years, he carried the message of inter-American friendship, intellectual cooperation, and open circulation of goods and investments. Putting into practice the policies of the U.S. State Department, Rowe was instrumental in building the architecture of ideas and institutions that sustained inter-American cooperation in the interwar period. Though not as directly influential as Bowman, Rowe also promoted the United Nations, to the extent that he presented the Pan-American Union as the blueprint for a world organization. Rowe worked closely with Sumner Welles and Cordell Hull to influence President Roosevelt's Good Neighbor Policy.

It is quite unfair that, due to the small dimensions of his domain (Harvard University), Haring qualifies only for fourth place. For it is clear that he did much to push U.S. policy toward Latin America in the definite direction of hemispheric cooperation and mutual understanding. Through his teachings, his promotion of Pan-American societies, and the creation of networks of businessmen, scholars, and functionaries devoted to the discussion of inter-American problems, he articulated a form of scholarship that combined academic prestige with activism in foreign relations. He exerted influence over foreign policy through his reports and meetings at the Council on Foreign Policy. His comparative long-term history of the Americas—a project he was unable to complete—offered knowledge that was functional to the intellectual, cultural, and political integration of the continent under U.S. leadership.

And finally, Ross. He was enormously influential in the formation of "American sociology" and in contemporary domestic debates about progressive reform, but less so in the politics of inter-American relations. (The closest he got to government power was to befriend the future secretary of state William Jennings Bryan when he lived in Lincoln, Nebraska, from 1901 to 1906.) Ross's social panoramas of South America served to connect the "current problems" of the two Americas. He projected onto the social landscape of South America the U.S. progressive view about land reform, social relations, and democratic culture. In the United States he is remembered for his advocacy of academic freedom and selective immigration, as well as for his influential essays on "world trends." His books on social revolutions in Mexico, Russia, and China brought into public discussion—much earlier than did the works of Samuel Huntington or Barrington Moore—the potential convulsions in Third World peasant societies. His transnationally comparative sociology anticipated the emergence of social sciences at the service of global knowledge-power.[17]

In their search for the "true nature" of the southern republics, U.S. scholars traveled across the region, gathered information, took photographs, made maps, and recorded their impressions of the societies and cultures they observed, leaving in print generalizations and simplifications that rendered visible the complex realities of the region. Their intellectual interventions, presented as a "second discovery," provided new knowledge that proved instrumental to rethinking the role of the United States in the hemisphere, moving the discussion about empire into the territory of culture. Perhaps it was the discovery of the complexities of transferring free-market capitalism, machine civilization, and political democracy to lands permeated by premodern sociability, Hispanic traditions, and colonial residues in culture that led these scholars to imagine the possibility of a different form of U.S. hegemony. They imagined the United States as an empire of educational, technological, and cultural influence, one that would renounce military occupations and devote its expert human capital to the solution of hemispheric problems. These disciplinary interventions tried to add another layer to existing claims of U.S. superiority: primacy in the terrain of specialized knowledge. By building the contours of Andean archaeology, South American geography, and Hispanic American history, U.S. scholars opened the gates to a more comprehensive and empirical knowledge of the region, something that local and national archaeologists, geographers, and historians have failed to do. In the disciplines of sociology and political science, U.S. scholars were not ready to establish regional fields of knowledge, yet they claimed to have attained crucial insights for understanding the political life and social relations in South America. By doing so, they contributed to building the bases of Latin American studies in the United States, an arrangement of disciplinary knowledges whose reason for being remained tied to the debates and questions of U.S. foreign policy.

Conclusion

Introduction

1 A strong defense of Latin American studies as an area-study program is made in Harvey L. Johnson 1961. On the strength acquired by Latin American studies in the 1960s, see Hanke 1967. For a Latin American perspective on Latin American studies, see Osorio Tejeda 2007. For a critical appraisal of Latin American literary studies, see de la Campa 1999.

2 On the history and significance of the Pan-Americanist movement, see Fagg 1982; Gilderhus 1986; Crapol 2000; and Sheinin 2000a.

3 In 1881, Blaine called the states of the hemisphere to attend a Pan-American conference. His ideas about U.S. hemispheric hegemony through peace and commercial reciprocity started to develop after the French occupation of Mexico in 1864 (Crapol 2000, 10–21, 73).

4 On the Good Neighbor Policy, see Wood 1967; Green 1971; Gellman 1979; Ninkovich 1981; and Haglund 1984. On the U.S. policy of disengaging from Caribbean dependencies, see Perkins 1981.

5 In the area of history, a more in-depth study of Brazil developed only in the 1950s and 1960s. See Shepherd 1933; and John J. Johnson 1985. Duke University had started collecting Brazilian materials early. See Manchester 1933.

6 John Barrett was the director of the International Bureau of the American Republics from 1907 to 1910, then the director of the Pan-American Union until 1920. He promoted U.S. economic expansionism in South America, and strove to transform the Monroe Doctrine into a multilateral policy. See Prisco 1973.

7 Vision is an element constitutive of "evidence" in Enlightenment and modern notions of science and legal processes. Enhanced visibility is the capacity "to see" beyond our own limited horizon of sight, by means of other instruments: telescopes, maps, treatises, inquiries, dictionaries, and catalogs. In actuality, I am not talking of the eye's capacity, but of the human intellect's ability to imagine larger regions and

worlds. Human sight has been constructed, says Foucault, as a mirror (inner reflection) and as a lamp (external extension) that illuminates certain areas. It is in this latter dimension that I evoke the figure of human sight, and often more metaphorically, as it could help us to understand the scope and problematic of a scientific discipline.

8 Though I do not present an extended argument about this topic, there is an indication that this particular form of power knowledge generated a "subalternity through knowledge," which needs to be investigated further.

9 Scholars agree that prior to 1918 there was little that could be considered professional discourse about Latin America and that, though the Second World War gave an unprecedented boost to the field, Latin American studies consolidated in relation to the emergence of Cold War politics. A commonsense view of the matter was that to specialize in Latin America before Fidel Castro was "a passport to obscurity." Ratliff 1989–1990, 61.

10 In practice, intellectual history often overlaps with the history of knowledge and the history of intellectual culture. See Collini 1985; Brett 2002; and Cowan 2006. See also Palti 2010.

11 See Joseph, LeGrand, and Salvatore 1998.

12 See, in particular, Latour and Woolgar 1986; Latour 1987; Latour 1990; and Latour 1999.

13 There were, however, inquiries into the social and political "thought" of Latin Americans. See Martz 1966; and Davis 1963.

14 For the rise and diffusion of "progressive" ideals, see McGerr 2003; Wiebe 1967; Kloppenberg 1986; Dorothy Ross 1992, chaps. 5–8; Rogers 1982. About the professionalization of the social disciplines and the emergence of expert knowledge, see Kuklick 1976; Haskell 1977; Sarfatti Larson 1977; Dorothy Ross 1978; Creutz 1979.

15 On the impact on culture of U.S. overseas expansion, see Cheyfitz 1991; Kaplan and Pease 1993; John Carlos Rowe 2000; Wexler 2000; and Kaplan 2002. For studies of cultural history relating to U.S.-Latin America relations, see, among others, Streeby 2002; Murphy 2005; Salvatore 2006a; and Pérez 2008. On connections between economic, cultural, and intellectual developments, see Livingston 1994.

16 Walter Mignolo and other representatives of the "coloniality school" have argued along these lines. See Mignolo 2000; Mignolo 2001; Mignolo 2005; and Moraña, Dussel, and Jáuregui 2008.

17 On the question of "situated knowledge," see Hunter 1999. For an anthropological interpretation of "local knowledge," see Geertz 1983. On the dynamic between local and global knowledge, see Salvatore 2007a.

18 On the notion of Occidentalism, see Coronil 1996.

19 See John J. Johnson 1990; Fifer 1991; Pike 1992; Peter H. Smith 1996.

20 See Latour 1987.

21 See Foucault 1980; and Burchell, Gordon, and Miller 1991.

22 See Messer-Davidow, Shumway, and Sylvan 1993.

23 Though Bordieu has coined the term *cultural capital*, other authors have actually extensively studied cultural accumulation in colonial and neocolonial conditions.

Notes

Useful works in this regard are Bennett and Silva 2011; Dubois 2011; and Prieur and Savage 2011, among others. Of the many works by Bourdieu, few represent this point of view as clearly as *La distinción* (1979), *Capital cultural, escuela y espacio social* (2003), and *Homo Academicus* (2008).

24 I do not deal in detail here with the forms of cultural accumulation that constituted the bases of Latin American studies. See, in this regard, Salvatore 2005b.

25 See Salvatore 2014.

26 William Louis George's many works contain a critical view of British imperial history, emphasizing the influence of Ronald Robinson and John Gallagher to disarm the previous consensus about the discipline. See also Hyam and Martin 1975. For a critique of "old imperial history," see Hopkins 1999; Ballantyne 2005; and Gosh 2012.

27 On the changing notion of Americanism, see Kazin and McCartin 2006. In a quite limited fashion, I have dealt elsewhere with the question of "Americanization." Salvatore 2005d.

28 See Pagden 1990, chap. 1.

29 Bibliographies, guides, and other reference works produced between 1900 and 1945 contain thousands of entries each. Only a laborious and time-consuming quantitative study of U.S. publications about the region would be able to produce an accurate figure.

30 The Germans "were ready to furnish South America with scientists for their universities, with teachers for their schools, with specialists in administrative, technical, and sanitary problems." Leo S. Rowe 1909, 592.

31 I have discussed different aspects of U.S. Pan-Americanism in "Early American Visions of a Hemispheric Market in South America" (2002), "Library Accumulation and the Emergence of Latin American Studies" (2005), "Imperial Mechanics" (2006), and "The Making of a Hemispheric Intellectual-Statesman" (2010).

32 See Guy 1998; Ehrick 1998; and Sheinin 2000b. For literary figures, see Faber 2003. For art production, see Fox 2013.

33 On anthropology's complicity with colonialism, see Asad 1979; Stocking 1991; Thomas 1994; and Cooper 2005.

34 The literature is ample with regard to the British empire. See, for instance, Edney 1990; Baber 1996; and Cohn 1996. Similar studies are available for France. See Paul 1985.

35 See Christopher Simpson 1998, in particular, the contributions by A. Needel on Project Troy and by E. Herman on Project Camelot. The latter project is examined in Horowitz 1967 and Solovey 2001. For a critical examination of the Rockefeller Foundation's activities with regard to public health in the region, see Zulawski 2007. A recent debate shows that the politics of academic knowledge is an important concern. See "Commentaries on 'Knowledge and Empire'" 2010.

36 See, in particular, Drake 1989; Cueto 1994; Anderson 2006; and Rosenberg 2003.

37 See, for instance, de la Campa 1999; and Moreiras 2001. On the current debates on area studies, see Mirsepassi, Basu, and Weaver 2003.

Notes

---

1   Iván Jaksic (2007) has suggested that these early Hispanists sought in old Spain the basis for constructing their own "American culture." In the history of the Spanish colonial empire, they saw interesting lessons for understanding the fragilities of the U.S. republic. See also Kagan 2002.

2   See Delpar 2008, 25–26; and Schoultz 1998, chap. 5.

3   See Salvatore 1995; and Fifer 1991.

4   This argument is developed in Kagan 2002.

5   Mark T. Berger (2005) locates the origins of professional study of Latin America in the early decades of the twentieth century. The first historians to teach Spanish-American history were Bernard Moses at Berkeley (1895) and William Shepherd at Columbia (1904). All other pioneers of the field, except Hiram Bingham, started to teach after 1910. See Delpar 2008, 33–39.

6   See Berger 1995; de la Campa 1999; and Delpar 2008.

7   Charles A. Thompson to Haring, 11 January 1941, Harvard University Archives, Clarence Haring Papers (CHP), HUG 4447.512, Special Files.

8   See Salvatore 2002; and Prisco 1973.

9   Recent commercial development in the Oriente region made it feasible to study Amazonian tribes hitherto unknown: the Zaparo, the Napo, the Murato, and the Iquito, among others.

10 Páramos are mountain ecosystems proper of the Andean region. They are flat-lands located at high altitude. Subjected to a tropical climate and dramatic variations in temperature from day to night, they tend to generate a scarce vegetation comprising primarily grass and shrub.

11 "A whole social structure has been growing wild on the coast of Ecuador since the days of the Conquest, which in our time has reached a state of highest interest for students of semi-primitive society." Long 1941, 17.

12 The leaders of the research-university movement promoted not only specialized research, but also interdisciplinary connections between different departments of knowledge. See Douglas 2007, chap. 1.

13 Among them were Hiram Bingham, Alexander Hamilton, Aleš Hrdlička, Isaiah Bowman, Mark Jefferson, and others.

14 See Cramer and Prutsch 2012. See also Reich 1996.

15 In 1911–1912 a group of U.S. bankers took control of the new Banco Nacional de Nicaragua and of the Ferrocarril del Pacífico, and loans were granted to the Nicaraguan government on the security of a customs receivership, making it clear that Nicaragua had become tied to the empire through "dollar diplomacy." Schoultz 1998, 216–19.

16 See Rosenberg 1975, 144–45; and Sloan 1978, 291–94.

17 Boaz Long was a privileged observer of labor resistance in the formative years of labor organization in Cuba. O'Brien 1993.

18 Over time, Ambassador Long learned to appreciate the doctrine of intellectual cooperation developed by the political scientist Leo S. Rowe.

Notes

19 According to M. P. Friedman, ambassador Long had to negotiate with the presidents of Ecuador, Nicaragua, and Guatemala the detention and deportment of Germans suspected of Nazi sympathies. Friedman 2003a, 115, 148, 154.

20 Galo Plaza was a U.S.-born president of Ecuador (1948–1952) who later served as secretary general of the Organization of American States (1968–1975). He had studied economics at the University of California, Berkeley, and diplomacy at Georgetown University. At the time of his friendship with Ambassador Long, Galo Plaza was Ecuador's minister of war. Later on, in 1944, he was appointed Ecuador's ambassador to the United States. The American College of Quito opened its doors in 1940, headed by the Radcliffe graduate Hazel Tucker.

21 The Good Neighbor Policy was predicated on economic cooperation, the respect of Latin American territorial sovereignty, and multilateral consultation in matters of hemispheric concern. For the importance of culture in American diplomacy, see Espinosa 1976; Ninkovich 1977; Ninkovich 1981; Fein 1994; Tota 2009; Sadlier 2012; and Fox 2013.

22 See Salvatore 2002.

23 See, for instance, "Commerce with South America" (1911).

24 The problem of Portuguese emerged later in the 1930s, as Brazil came to be recognized as the future economic giant of the region.

25 James W. Van Cleave, for instance, wrote, "But we need something more than a merchant marine to enable us to win new markets, or to hold those which we now have. We must learn the world's needs and tastes in merchandise, and set to work intelligently to supply them. This is particularly true of South America." Van Cleave 1907, 31.

26 Van Cleave wrote, "They go to the importing countries with a linguistic and technical knowledge incommensurably beyond that of the average American promoter, and they pursue their work with a skill, an energy, and a persistence which our representatives do not approach." Ibid., 32.

27 In addition to advertising and other marketing techniques, U.S. colleges and universities were teaching mostly technical subjects. Lord wrote, "There are courses in ocean transport, methods of shipping goods, in foreign tariffs, and foreign markets. All things are, of course, necessary. Some opportunity is given to the study of foreign languages, although here the courses are glaringly superficial." Lord 1921, 16.

28 Boston University was planning a second venture into China. There was also a plan to set up an International School at Panama for training North and South Americans in Pan-American trade. James E. Downey wrote, "One series [of lectures] given to the Seniors is made up of ten lectures on transportation in New England, six on salesmanship, and about twenty on commercial possibilities in South America." Downey 1913, 226.

29 Charles D. Warner was a well-known northeastern man of letters, a friend of Mark Twain, with whom he coauthored "The Gilded Age" (1873). He worked on the editorial staff of *Harper's Magazine*. He was president of important professional and academic institutions (such as the National Institute of Arts and

Notes

Letters and the American Social Science Association), as well as an active social reformer.

30 The biggest obstacle, however, was the lack of cheap and reliable sea transportation to South America. Warner (1896) reviewed the situation of ports in Peru, Uruguay, northeast Brazil, and Venezuela to conclude that these "splendid fields" for American enterprise were wasted by the lack of adequate transportation facilities.

31 See Werking 1981.

32 The institutions of higher education that offered training for the foreign service in 1915 were Harvard, Yale, Columbia, University of Pennsylvania, George Washington, Northwestern, University of California, University of Colorado, University of Illinois, University of Iowa, University of Miami, University of Minnesota, University of Nebraska, University of Missouri, Dartmouth, and Pennsylvania State. Duniway 1915, 157.

33 As Root recapitulated later, "It was a business trip, but the business was not only the promotion of American trade and commerce, but the promotion of intellectual ties and personal relationships, for all these are of the business of statesmanship." Jessup 1938, 477.

34 "The material resources of South America are in some important respects complementary to our own; that continent is weakest where North America is strongest as a field for manufacturers. . . . In many respects, the people of the two continents are complementary to each other; the South American is polite, refined, cultivated, fond of literature and of expression and of the graces and charms of life, while the North American is strenuous, intense, utilitarian. Where we accumulate, they spend." Ibid., 489.

35 See Berger 1995; de la Campa 1999; and Delpar 2008.

36 This proposition could be extended to the natural sciences. It is not by chance that Louis Agassiz chose Brazil to look for evidence to disprove Darwin's theory of natural selection. See Menand 2001, chap. 6.

37 Though there were several U.S. scientific exploring expeditions to South America during the nineteenth century, these findings failed to constitute new fields of study, nor did they give birth to new institutions for the study of the subcontinent. See Goodman 1972.

38 See Berger 1995; de la Campa 1999; and Delpar 2008.

39 Bingham did not brand this new field of knowledge Latin American history or Hispanic American history—he named it "South American History and Politics." This was the subject matter that Bernard Moses had introduced to him at Berkeley.

40 Over time, Bingham discovered, the "political" part of the course in actuality contained a discussion of U.S.-South American relations.

41 In fact, after his return from Peru, Bingham attempted to convince Yale to create a course that would combine the teaching of history, geography, and business in South America.

42 The series editor, Richard Elwood Dodge, assured readers that this textbook contained "a standard treatment of the world by regions, from the modern

Notes

standpoint that geography is a study of the earth in its relation to man and life." Bowman 1915, viii.

43 A few years later, I. Eric Thompson (1936) published another summary on the area's archaeological knowledge, focusing on the countries of the west coast.

44 Later, Alfred L. Kroeber's work on Peruvian textiles, Wendell C. Bennett's work on the Lambayeque Valley, Samuel K. Lothrop's work on Chavín ornaments, and John H. Rowe's chronology of Andean cultures brought about a more comprehensive panorama of the field.

45 "An Economic and Social Study of the Caribbean Area," 1932, CHP, HUG 4447.508.

46 In 1937 Haring, attempting to explain to his colleague historians from South America why Harvard University had to cover all areas of world history, attributed the expansion of Harvard's history department to the development of historical studies in general. He said, "We have also entered into the history of Europe and of nations of the Orient," considering it "natural" that Harvard's teaching and research efforts were in part devoted to "the Hispanic nations of the world." "II Congreso de Historia de América," 1937, CHP, HUG 4447.508.

47 See Shepherd 1933.

48 Though many scholars of Hispanic American history participated in these discussions, few left their positions in writing. Among those who did were Isaac Joslin Cox of Northwestern University, William R. Shepherd of Columbia University, and Charles Hackett of the University of Texas. See Hispanic American History Group 1927.

49 Luther Bernard, acknowledged as an expert in South American sociology, never recognized this as a field of study, speaking instead of South America's "social, economic, and political problems." His approach in this regard was similar to that of Frank Tannenbaum's, as evidenced in Tannenbaum's *Whither Latin America?* (1934).

50 See Leavitt 1941. A Center of Inter-American Studies was created at George Washington University in 1934. See "A New Inter-American Center" (1934).

51 In the 1930s, Carl Sauer tried to create an Institute of Latin American studies at the University of California, Berkeley. See Parsons 1996.

52 Anthropology, Julian Steward (1943) argued, needed to concentrate studies in the cultural contact between blacks, Indians and mestizos, for mestizaje was one of the most enduring features of Latin American culture. "Acculturation studies" needed to engage the historical process of "acculturation," that is, the four-hundred-year-old experience of European contact with other races.

53 See Naylor, Helguera, and McGann 1962.

54 See Vessey 1965; Jarausch 1983; Geiger 1986; Rothblatt 1997; Goldin and Katz 1999; and Newfield 2003.

55 Classical works on the progressive movement, such as Wiebe 1967, have been now superseded by Dawley 2003; McGerr 2003; and Stromquist 2006. On professional middle-class authority related to higher education, see Radway 2004.

56 William E. Leuchtenburg (1952) has argued that progressives, though domestically liberal, supported imperialist causes overseas. This does not seem to be the case with the scholars I studied.

Notes

57 Much work since the 1970s has dealt with the question of professionalization and the social sciences. See, among others, Furner 1975; Kuklick 1976; Dorothy Ross 1978; Creutz 1979; and Jarausch 1983.

58 Though other associations and institutes related to the work of our five scholars—such as the American Geographic Society (1851) and the Archaeological Institute of America (1879)—were founded earlier, they also became interested in South America in the early 1900s.

59 There is an abundant bibliography on U.S. investments and trade with South America during this period. See, among others, Rippy 1931; Phelps 1939; Wilkins 1970; Seidel 1973; O'Brien 1993; and Pletcher 1998.

60 The tension between universality and locality in the making of Western knowledge is addressed in different ways. For Mary Poovey (1998), the tension is between systematic and practical knowledge. Others have presented the tension as one between "indigenous" and "scientific" knowledge. See, for instance, Agrawal 2008; and Mato 2008. Other scholars, have criticized the universal pretentions of Western knowledge while affirming local specificities. See, among others, Chakrabarty 2000; and Buck-Morss 2009. Historians of science have claimed that all knowledge is local. See Turnbull 1993–1994.

61 See Delpar 2008, 49.

62 See Salvatore 2008a.

63 See Hanke 1947.

64 Clarence H. Haring, "Conocimiento y desconocimiento de la America Latina en los Estados Unidos," Round Table Conference, San Juan, Puerto Rico, 23–28 April 1956, CHP, HUG 4447.520 (Lectures and Addresses).

65 Of 2,000 colleges and universities, 821 were offering courses in Latin American studies, and 44 of them had specialized programs that granted degrees for graduate work.

66 See Harvey L. Johnson 1961.

67 See Salvatore 2006b.

68 As Ella Shohat (1991) has shown, the idea of "terra incognita" is a close relative to that of "dark continent" as applied to Africa.

2. Five Traveling Scholars

1 Abundant biographical information is provided in Alfred M. Bingham 1989 and Patterson 1957. See also Heaney 2010. Popular biographies, such as Cohen 1984, are also useful.

2 William Scheller (1994) places Bingham in the company of those "amazing archaeologists" who discovered the legends of Assyria, the walls of Troy, the temples of Angkor and Chichén Itzá, the tombs of Tutankhamen and Knosos, and the city of Jericho.

3 It was the cuzqueño José Gabriel Cosio who in 1912 called Bingham the *descubridor científico*, as opposed to the various persons—among them, local indigenous peasants—who had visited the place before, but were not scientists.

4　Later, other archaeologists discredited some of Bingham's interpretations. Phillip Ainsworth Means (1931) did not find it credible that Machu Picchu was, as Bingham insisted, the old "cradle" of the Incas, arguing that the citadel was simply one of the various fortifications built by Inca Pachacutec to protect his people. Alfred Kroeber showed the same skepticism. George Kubler thought that Machu Picchu was one of various frontier towns or settlements from where the Incas observed and controlled lowland jungle tribes. Kroeber reviewed Bingham's *Machu Picchu: A Citadel of the Incas* (1930) in *American Anthropologist* 34:1 (1932), 152–53; see also Kubler, "Machu Picchu," *Perspecta* (1960), 48–55.

5　Bingham was a curator of South American history and literature at Harvard Library between 1903 and 1915, and he held a similar position at Yale between 1908 and 1930. Patterson 1957.

6　See Cohen 1984, 59–60.

7　The first rendition of Bingham's 1907 adventure appeared in a geography journal. Bingham 1908a.

8　Secretary of State Elihu Root had asked Bingham to attend the First Pan-American Scientific Congress at Santiago as a U.S. delegate.

9　Bingham's biographer wrote, "Only then [after a visit to the ruins of Choqquequirau] did he begin to take interest in the Incas." Alfred M. Bingham 1989, 189.

10　When Bingham found Old Vilcabamba, he was already in the southern jungle near River Pampaconas, in a place Indians called "Espíritu Pampa." Ibid., 194–96.

11　The most authoritative biography of Bowman is Martin 1980. Neil Smith discusses in *American Empire* (2003) the intersection between geographic knowledge and the transition toward globalization in U.S. foreign policy, building his argument on Bowman's work.

12　The society's Special Publications series made available important geographical monographs on Hispanic America. These publications included, besides Bowman's monographs, the works of Mark Jefferson (Argentina), George M. McBride (Mexico), and Robert S. Platt (Hispanic American maps).

13　See Neil Smith 2003, 192–200.

14　See Martin 1980, chap. 7.

15　Among his students were Howard Cline, Lewis Hanke, and Arthur Whitaker.

16　On Bolton's influence, see Bannon 1978; and Hanke 1964.

17　Authors such as Daron Acemoglu, Simon Johnson, James A. Robinson, Stanley Engerman, Kenneth Sokoloff, Stephen Haber, and Francis Fukuyama have reopened the question of when and why Latin America "fell behind" vis-à-vis the United States.

18　Some scholars trace the origins of U.S.-Latin American scholarly exchanges to the 1908–1910 correspondence between Secretary Root and the philanthropist Andrew Carnegie.

1 In some territorial empires, the military participated in crucial scientific or humanistic inquiries. Peers 2005. In other cases, religious missionaries pioneered scientific inquiries. Maxwell 2008. On the formation of British knowledge about colonial India, see Edney 1990; Baber 1996; Cohn 1996; and Cooper 2005, chap. 2. On the census as a form of U.S. imperial, racial knowledge, see Rafael 2000; and Scarano 2009.

2 James C. Scott considers these "simplifications" crucial for statecraft. They are part of a project of "state legibility." Scott 1998, 76–77, 80–83.

3 Archaeology, for instance, demands the transportation of antiquities and artifacts from the ruins to the museum cabinet. See Podgorny 2008; and Latour 1990.

4 See de Certeau 1986; Ahearne 1995; and Barbieri 2002.

5 See Said 1979.

6 The civilian governments that followed entered into a more ambivalent legal terrain. Their acts, controlled by the laws that guided the transition, were no longer under the supervision of the U.S. Congress. Leo S. Rowe 1902c; and Leo S. Rowe 1905.

7 See Leo S. Rowe 1912.

8 Foote collected mostly insects and nonflowering plants. He collected three thousand specimens in this first stage. Other members of the expedition had no research work.

9 See Hiram Bingham 1912c.

10 With the ruins detected near the Urubamba basin (Machu Picchu, Choqque-quirau, and Palcay), Bingham was confident U.S. archaeologists would begin "to solve the mystery connected with Ancient Peoples of South America." Bingham to Grosvenor, 19 January 1914, Yale University Library, Yale Peruvian Expedition Papers (YPEP) no. 664.

11 In a report published that year, Bingham wrote, "It is our plan to make a geographical reconnaissance of a portion of Southern Peru, including the Cordillera Vilcabamba and portions of the Apurimac and Urubamba watersheds." Hiram Bingham 1914d, 677.

12 Bingham to Grosvenor, 19 January 1915, YPEP no. 664, National Geographic Society.

13 "Assuredly, the value of the source material will increase in time, and the Society will become, accordingly, a unique Western Hemisphere center for cartographic research." Bowman 1946, 320.

14 Bowman was one of the first U.S. intellectuals to criticize the idea of Lebensraum, from the geographic point of view.

15 Proposal found in Harvard University Archives, Clarence Haring Papers (CHP), HUG 4447.512, Special Files.

16 Correspondence 1925–1926, 1932–1933, Harvard University Archives, CHP, HUG 4447.509.

17 Correspondence 1925–1926, 1932–1933, Harvard University Archives, CHP, HUG 4447.509.

18 Correspondence 1925–1926, 1932–1933, Harvard University Archives, CHP, HUG 4447.509.

19 In 1931 the bureau published Frank Normano's *The Struggle for South America*, a study about the competition for South American markets between the United States and Europe. Haring wrote the foreword.

20 This was precisely the topic Haring addressed in his book *South America Looks at the United States* (1928).

21 See Rippy 1934; and Ferrell 1965. See also Langley 2005, 89–81; and Coerver and Hall 1999, 56–58.

22 See Schoultz 1998, chap. 10. For a typical assessment of Latin America as lands of revolution, see Crichfield 1908.

23 The exception was the U.S. South, which Ross probably considered a backward area wholly dependent on the industrialized Northeast and Midwest.

24 On the Hispanic American history group's interest in revising the history of the Spanish empire, see Salvatore 2013.

25 See Hanke 1964. For a discussion of the debate, see Barrenechea 2009.

26 "II Congreso de Historia de America, Buenos Aires, 1937," Harvard University Archives, CHP, HUG 4447.508.

27 "II Congreso de Historia de America, Buenos Aires, 1937," Harvard University Archives, CHP, HUG 4447.508.

28 Helen Delpar calls these historians of the 1930s the "second generation of pioneers." Delpar 2008, 45–48.

29 "Memorandum on the work of the Research Committee on Latin America," by Parker T. Moon, 2 January 1933, Special Files, Harvard University Archives, CHP, HUG 4447.512.

30 "Economic Internationalism in the Caribbean," 1925, Correspondence 1925–1926, Harvard University Archives, CHP, HUG 4447.509.

31 "An Economic and Social Study of the Caribbean Area with Special Reference to Its Relations to the United States," Research Proposal, ca. 1931–1932, Harvard University Archives, CHP, HUG 4447.508, Bureau of Economic Research on Latin America.

4. Yale at Machu Picchu

1 Max Uhle, the so-called father of Peruvian archaeology, had made important findings before Bingham's 1911 expedition. See Kaulicke 1998.

2 In Peru, the most salient representatives of this current of thought were Luis E. Valcárcel, José C. Mariátegui, José Uriel García, José G. Cosio, and Luis F. Aguilar. See Earle 2007, 185–92; de la Cadena 2000, 22–25, 63–68; and Miller 1999, 152–63.

3 Bingham to Hadley, New Haven, 10 March 1914, Yale University Library, Yale Peruvian Expedition Papers (YPEP), series 2, box 10.

4 Bingham to Morkill, Cuzco, 14 July 1912, Yale University Library, YPEP, series 2, box 7.

5 Hrdlička to Bingham, Smithsonian Institution, 14 May 1913, Yale University Library, YPEP, series 2, box 9. Emphasis added.

6 Bowman to Bingham, 23 January 1914, Yale University Library, YPEP, series 2, box 10.

Notes

7   Bingham to Pickering, 14 January 1914, Yale University Library, YPEP, series 2, box 10.

8   Bingham to Means, New Haven, 6 October 1914, Yale University Library, YPEP, series 2, box 11.

9   Braden to Bingham, 18 December 1914, Yale University Library, YPEP, series 2, box 11.

10 Cerro de Pasco Mining Co. to Bingham, Lima, 14 December 1914, Yale University Library, YPEP, series 2, box 11.

11 See Salvatore 1998b.

12 See Bowman 1916a.

13 Bingham to Eastman, 15 April 1912, Yale University Library, YPEP, series 2, box 14.

14 The agreement Bingham reached with Kodak in 1911 consisted of a simple exchange of images and experimentation for sponsorship. Bingham to Eastman, 16 May 1911, Yale University Library, YPEP, series 2, box 14.

15 Bingham to Eastman, 15 April 1913, Yale University Library, YPEP, series 2, box 14.

16 Griffin to Bingham, 11 July 1914, Yale University Library, YPEP, series 2, box 14.

17 A set of the pictures went to the National Geographic Society. Another set went to Bingham, who arranged the pictures in albums, ordered by theme and date. Later, a group of these photographs appeared in scientific journals, illustrating articles published by Bingham and other members of the expedition. The public at large only saw a small fraction of the photographic collection.

18 Contract between the National Geographic and Yale University, 25 February 1914, Yale University Library, YPEP, series 2, box 15. Emphasis added.

19 I am extending Benedict Anderson's notion of "print-capitalism" to the age of photography.

20 Bingham to Grosvenor, 8 March 1912, Yale University Library, YPEP, series 2, box 15.

21 Grosvenor to Bingham, 12 May 1912, Yale University Library, YPEP, series 2, box 15. Emphasis added.

22 Grosvenor to Bingham, 5 May 1913, Yale University Library, YPEP, series 2, box 15.

23 See Lutz and Collins 1993, chap. 3.

24 "De la Universidad de Yale: Exploración científica," El Comercio (Cuzco), 22 June 1911.

25 Two days later, the newspaper remarked on the altruism of the Yale men. "La Comisión Científica de la Universidad de Yale: Su arribo al Callao . . . ," El Comercio (Cuzco), 24 June 1911.

26 In July 1911 a group of cuzqueños grouped under the Sociedad Protectora de Monumentos Público questioned the minister of justice and education about the authorization granted to the YPE. El Comercio (Cuzco), 1 July 1911.

27 "La conferencia de anoche en la Sociedad Geográfica," La Prensa (Lima), 5 December 1911.

28 Valdivia to Bingham, Lima, 12 June 1912, Yale University Library, YPEP, series 2, box 7; Bingham to Hadley, Cuzco, July 1912, Yale University Library, YPEP, series 2, box 7.

29 Bingham to Hadley, July 1912, Yale University Library, YPEP, series 2, box 7.

Notes

---

30 See Alfred M. Bingham 1989, 275–89.

31 Reported by *El Sol* (Cuzco), 7 May 1912.

32 Curiously, the cuzqueñistas and indigenistas did not react to Bingham's ironic view of Inca culture. Hiram Bingham 1911a, 262–63.

33 Bingham to Hadley, Lima, 4 October 1912, Yale University Library, YPEP, series 2, box 7.

34 The Instituto Histórico de Cuzco's director, Larrabure, told Bingham he was opposed to any exportation of archaeological remains. Bingham to Hadley, Lima, 7 October 1912, Yale University Library, YPEP, series 2, box 7.

35 Bingham to Hadley, Lima, 14 October 1912, Yale University Library, YPEP, series 2, box 7.

36 José Gabriel Cosio was president of the University Association in 1909, and later the assistant and secretary of Albert Giesecke at the *Revista Universitaria*. Gabriel Cosio is the author of *El Cuzco prehispánico y colonial* (1918) and *Cuzco: The Historical and Monumental City of Peru* (1924).

37 During August, Bingham took about seven hundred photographs of Machu Picchu and the Apurinac Valley, while the rest of his team made topographical survey and excavated various archaeological sites.

38 Bingham to Hadley, Lima, 14 October 1912, Yale University Library, YPEP, series 2, box 7, General Correspondence.

39 Bingham to Hadley, Lima, 21 October 1912, Yale University Library, YPEP, series 2, box 7.

40 Bingham to Hadley, Lima, 26 October 1912, Yale University Library, YPEP, series 2, box 7. Emphasis added.

41 The agent from W. R. Grace, Mr. Ballent, convinced the new president of Peru that Bingham was a scientist and that his motivations were not commercial. Ballent to Bingham, Lima, 4 November 1912, Yale University Library, YPEP, series 2, box 7.

42 Bingham to Noel, 12 February 1913, Yale University Library, YPEP, series 2, box 8.

43 W. R. Grace and Company to Bingham, 8 January 1913, Yale University Library, YPEP, series 2, box 8.

44 Another nine cases had been shipped in July 1912, before the political turnaround, apparently without government permission.

45 It was in 1913 that Bingham published his articles criticizing the Monroe Doctrine in the *Atlantic Monthly*.

46 Bingham to Grosvenor, 21 September 1915, Yale University Library, YPEP, series 2, box 15.

47 Bingham to Grosvenor, Ollantaitambo, 19 May 1915, Yale University Library, YPEP, series 2, box 15.

48 "Only recently," commented Bingham in June 1915, "our enemies here in Cuzco have been trying to make life miserable for us by diligently circulating exaggerated rumors and malicious lies." Bingham to Grosvenor, Ollantaitambo, 19 May 1915, Yale University Library, YPEP, series 2, box 15.

49 Valcárcel was a collaborator of José Carlos Mariátegui in the journal *Amauta*. Mariátegui promoted the cultural elevation of the Indian and pioneered studies in

Notes

Inca culture and history. His book *Tempestad en los Andes* (1927) is considered a manifesto of the movement. Among other works, he authored *Del Ayllu al Imperio* (1925), *De la vida incaica* (1925), and *Mirador indio* (1937).

50 Bingham to Grosvenor, Cuzco, 29 June 1915, Yale University Library, YPEP, series 2, box 15.

51 Bingham to Morkill, Cuzco, 19 June 1915, Yale University Library, YPEP, series 2, box 11.

52 Bingham to McMillan, Cuzco, 19 June 1915, Yale University Library, YPEP, series 2, box 11.

53 Mariano Gibaja, "La expedición de Yale," *La Crónica* (Cuzco), 18 June 1915.

54 Bingham to Instituto Histórico de Cuzco, Cuzco, 18 June 1915, Yale University Library, YPEP, series 2, box 11.

55 Costa Laurent to Bingham, Cuzco, 26 June 1915, Yale University Library, YPEP, series 2, box 11.

56 They had continued excavating the ruins of Patallacta at Quente, as well as minor sites at Pampacahuana and Vilcabamba. Bingham to Harkness, 10 November 1915, Yale University Library, YPEP, series 2, box 12.

57 "Whatever exploration I do in South America in the near future will, I am afraid, have to be done in other countries, and probably not in southern Perú." Bingham to Harkness, 10 November 1915, Yale University Library, YPEP, series 2, box 12.

58 The resolution granting E. C. Erdis permission to export the seventy-four boxes was issued on 27 January 1916.

59 In January 1916 the government granted permission to export the boxes, but customs officials delayed the process for another five months. Grace to Bingham, Lima, 13 April 1916, Yale University Library, YPEP, series 2, box 13.

60 Peberdy to Bingham, New Haven, 17 August 1916, Yale University Library, YPEP, series 2, box 13.

61 See Alfred M. Bingham 1989, 310; and Heaney 2010.

62 Bingham to Director of *El Sol* (Cuzco), 25 June 1915, Yale University Library, YPEP, series 2, box 11.

63 Abraham Campana, a local foreman in charge of getting peons for the YPE, found staunch resistance from landowners in Ollantaitambo. Campana to Bingham, Ollantaitambo, 3 August 1912, Yale University Library, YPEP, series 2, box 7.

64 "La criminal excavación de Machupiccho," *El Sol* (Cuzco), 16 June 1915.

65 "La exportación de antigüedades peruanas," *El Comercio* (Cuzco), 14 August 1915.

66 "Día a día: La exportación de objetos arqueológicos," *La Prensa*, 8 January 1916.

67 "Let wise men come to the monuments and not the other way round," concluded the paper (ibid.).

68 "Por la Historia Nacional," *El Sol* (Cuzco), 14 August 1916.

69 In the Cuzco Rebellion of 1814 the Angulo brothers and the cacique Mateo Pumacahua organized a peasant army that besieged and then entered the city of La Paz.

70 "Investigaciones arqueológicas inconvenientes," *El Comercio* (Cuzco), 9 June 1915.

71 The year in which the Instituto Histórico inspected the YPE camp and Valcárcel presented his cultural preservation bill (1915), the Centro de Arte Incaico and the

Asociación Universitaria were presenting the first Inca drama in Cuzco: *Ollantay*. The flyer advertising the play is dated 28 July 1915.

72 Valcárcel published *Tempestad en los Andes* in 1927, Maríategui published *Siete ensayos sobre la realidad peruana* in 1928, and Haya de la Torre founded the American Popular Revolutionary Alliance (APRA), a party dedicated to creating an alliance of all "Indo-América" against U.S. imperialism, in 1924.

73 *La Crónica* said it explicitly: "[La comisión] explota escandalosamente *las minas que descubre* en excavaciones que no están permitidas exportando vía Bolivia cantidades de objetos." "La Comisión Bingham in Machu Picchu," *La Crónica*, 15 July 1915.

74 What was the content of this cargo? Chiefly, "trepanned and diseased skulls, one or two mummies, and various bones taken from large burial caves at Patallacta, Paucarcancha and Ollantaytambo, in the vicinity of Machu Picchu." Bingham to Walcott, New Haven, 28 July 1916, Yale University Library, YPEP, series 2, box 13.

75 Domingo Canepa, the owner of a *tienda de abarrotes* at Pisco, offered Bingham a collection of Inca artifacts. Domingo Canepa to Bingham, Pisco, 5 November 1912, Yale University Library, YPEP, series 2, box 7, General Correspondence. In 1915 P. Dieguez, a merchant from Guadalupe, offered Bingham one thousand huacos in sale. Dieguez y Co. to Bingham, Guadalupe, Peru, 7 June 1915, Yale University Library, YPEP, series 2, box 11.

76 See Riviale 2000; and Mould de Pease 2002. See also Mould de Pease 2008.

77 "All the graves we dug into had been previously disturbed, except that beneath the South Wall of the highest building." Eaton to Bingham, Cuzco, 24 October 1912, Yale University Library, YPEP, series 2, box 7.

78 Rosas to Bingham, Cerro de Pasco, 11 September 1912, Yale University Library, YPEP, series 2, box 7.

79 In 1915 Rosas wrote back to Bingham, offering his services as a practical archaeologist. Now he tried to interest Bingham in the stories of fabulous secret ruins. Rosas to Bingham, Lima, 27 April 1915, Yale University Library, YPEP, series 2, box 11.

80 Book collection was an integral part of the expedition's efforts. Bingham had been the curator of Latin American history during his appointment at Harvard (1906–1907). Alfred M. Bingham 1989, 60.

81 Contract between Bingham and Perez de Velazco, Lima, 25 October 1912, Yale University Library, YPEP, series 2, box 7.

82 Pérez de Velazco to Bingham, Lima, 22 January 1913, Yale University Library, YPEP, series 2, box 8.

83 Bingham to Pérez de Velazco, New Haven, 13 February 1913, Yale University Library, YPEP, series 2, box 8.

84 Ulloa described himself as a failed historian and a poor old man. In his own view, he suffered the inferiority of the location. Peru could not afford professional historians, so he had to devote his time to politics, a risky game that reduced him to poverty. Ulloa to Bingham, Lima, 5 January 1914, Yale University Library, YPEP, series 2, box 10.

Notes

85 Ferro to Bingham, Cuzco, 7 July 1912, Yale University Library, YPEP, series 2, box 7.

86 Belli to Bingham, Ica, 5 July 1915, Yale University Library, YPEP, series 2, box 12.

87 *Boston Record*, 1 January 1914; *New Haven Register*, 26 December 1913.

88 "It is our object to make a map of ancient Perú, showing the location of the early tribes, the growth of the Inca influence, the extent of the Inca empire, and the steps by which this extent was reached." Bingham to Harkness, New Haven, 12 March 1914, Yale University Library, YPEP, series 2, box 10.

89 Bingham to Hardy, New Haven, 24 September, 1914, Yale University Library, YPEP, series 2, box 10.

90 Bingham to Hardy, New Haven, 10 October 1914, Yale University Library, YPEP, series 2, box 11.

91 See Valcárcel 1938.

92 See Chatterjee 1993; and Chakrabarty 2000.

93 Curiously, the English "Orientalists" produced the same operation with regard to India. In the late eighteenth century, India became a land of "ancient glories and present ruins." See Adas 1989.

5. Hispanic American History at Harvard

1 I use the terms "Hispanic American history" and "Latin American history" as interchangeable because the practitioners of this period did so.

2 Wood Bliss had traveled widely in Latin America and, at the time of the First World War, had worked in the U.S. embassy of Paris delivering food provisions to the needy.

3 Haring had published his Oxford thesis, *The Buccaneers in the West Indies in the Seventeenth Century*, in 1910.

4 See Haring 1927a; and Haring 1927b.

5 See, among others, Haring 1931a; Haring 1931b; Haring 1932; and Haring 1936.

6 "Lecture Notes for Harvard Classes," Harvard University Archives, Clarence Haring Papers (CHP), HUG 447.616.

7 "Records of Courses Taught," Harvard University Archives, CHP, HUG 447.512.

8 Argentina, his class notes said, "should be especially interesting to us, because in geography, location, topography, products, climate, she presents many analogies with the United States. Since 1860 [she] has pursued somewhat parallel social and economic development; land of immigrants; has [a similar] political constitution; her popular culture now entirely European; has less of indigenous elements than that of any other Latin American country except Uruguay." History 176, "Lecture Notes for Harvard Classes," Harvard University Archives, CHP, HUG 447.616.

9 "The political conditions described are accounted for in these countries in part by ther colonial inheritance; but in part they were due to circumstances of geography and race." Haring 1934, 17.

10 "Lecture Notes of Courses Given at Bryn Mawr and Yale," Harvard University Archives, CHP, HUG 4447.515.

11   "Lecture Notes for Harvard Classes," Harvard University Archives, CHP, HUG 4447.516.

12   Haring's comparative perspective anticipated the comparative transnational histories now in fashion. See Elliott 2006; and Burbank and Cooper 2010.

13   The sociologist Edward Ross articulated the same type of criticism about the introduction of "feudality" in the Andes, a process that he attributed to Spanish colonialism. See chapter 8 in this volume.

14   Keeping a system of fixed ports, annual fleets, and a list of prohibited goods only to sustain the flow of American silver to the royal exchequer was a "stupendous blunder" based on an erroneous reading of the international system. Haring 1918, 153.

15   "Lecture Notes for Harvard Classes," Harvard University Archives, CHP, HUG 4447.516.

16   History 174, Course Notes, Spring 1934, Harvard University Archives, CHP, HUG 4447.516.

17   "Pan Americanism," address by Prof. Haring, delivered at the lecture hall of the Boston Public Library, 31 January 1928, Harvard University Archives, CHP, HUG 4447.520.

18   History 174, "Lecture Notes for Harvard Classes," Harvard University Archives, CHP, HUG 4447.516. Emphasis added.

19   See Sheinin 2000a.

20   Recent studies on "anti-Americanism" have tended to overlook this early concern with mapping anti-American reactions in South America. See McPherson 2003.

21   "Latin American Round Table," Harvard University Archives, CHP, HUG 4447.508.

22   "Latin American Round Table," Harvard University Archives, CHP, HUG 4447.508.

23   Turlington, author of *Mexico and Its Foreign Creditors* (1930), was an expert in claims made by U.S. creditors to Latin America. Alfaro was also a historian and an expert in international law, noted for his interventions in favor of Pan-Americanism.

24   See Scarfi 2009, 89–90.

25   These workshops were comparable to those Leo S. Rowe put together at Williamstown, Mass.

26   Frank's embrace of an idealized version of the "Hispanic mindset" could only bring confusion to discussions about the "real" economic, political, and foreign-policy issues. Haring to Charles Maphis, Cambridge, 5 March 1932, CHP, HUG 447.508.

27   Haring was the key advisor and the organizer of these round tables. The director of the institute, Charles Maphis, had the program checked by state institutions.

28   "Confidently," Haring answered Rivera, then the executive director of the review, "I may say that I believe the Academy to be the project of a small group of third-rate scholars who would use this way of assuring to themselves a position of importance in the fraternity and election to the board of the Review. . . . I feel confident that the proposal will be turned down in Philadelphia. Should it be accepted it will destroy the unity of the Latin American group." Haring to Rivera,

Cambridge, 13 December 1937, CHP, HUG 4447.508, Correspondence and Papers to 1940.

29 The CFR received other reports from Argentina, Brazil, and Uruguay. Scroggs to Haring, New York, 2 March 1932, Harvard University Archives, CHP, HUG 4447.509.

30 Haring to Van Deusen, Cambridge, 9 January 1933, Harvard University Archives, CHP, HUG 4447.509.

31 Van Deusen to Haring, 14 February 1933, Harvard University Archives, CHP, HUG 4447.509.

32 Van Deusen to Haring, Grace Liner "Santa Bárbara," 14 February 1933, Harvard University Archives, CHP, HUG 4447.509.

33 Van Deusen to Haring, Santiago, 7 May 1932, Harvard University Archives, CHP, HUG 4447.509.

34 Chirgwin to Haring, Valparaíso, 6 May 1933, Harvard University Archives, CHP, HUG 4447.509.

35 Haring to Van Deusen, Cambridge, 29 April 1932, Harvard University Archives, CHP, HUG 4447.509.

36 The book condenses the Lowell lectures Haring delivered at Boston the year before.

37 Notice the similarity with Bowman's characterization of Peru's fragmented political community.

38 Haring considered Roca's defeat and removal of southern Indian tribes (1879) as a precondition for the settlement of the Argentine prairies. Haring 1934, 47.

39 Haring mentioned the revolts of Rio de Janeiro in 1922 and São Paulo in 1924.

40 Haring talked of six years of dictatorships and recurrent revolutions. The 1932 elections seemed to mark a "return to normal political procedure." Haring 1933.

41 "Our Relations with Countries of South America," Loomis School Lecture, 25 February 1944, Harvard University Archives, CHP, HUG 4447.520, box L-W.

42 Curiously, this was the verdict passed by the sociologist Edward Ross.

43 See Stein and Stein 1970.

44 "So in actual practice of government, these new nations were soon torn apart by internal dissension, private ambition, intolerance, mutual jealousies." "Our Relations with Countries of South America," Loomis School Lecture, 25 February 1944, Harvard University Archives, CHP, HUG 4447.520, box L-W.

45 Haring 1934, 220–21. See also Haring 1944.

6. Intellectual Cooperation

1 There is no extensive biography of Leo S. Rowe. Eulogies by Sumner Welles (1947), E. M. Patterson (1947), and Roscoe Hill (1947) provide useful information about his career. For insights about his contributions to Pan-Americanism, see Castle 2000. Axel A. Schäfer (2000) places Rowe among progressives because of his early association with German social reform and for being a disciple of economist Simon N. Patten.

Notes

2   Having earned a doctorate at the University of Halle, Rowe returned to the United States as a lecturer at the Wharton School of the University of Pennsylvania (1894). He received a law degree and entered the bar in 1896.

3   The lectures were later translated and published in Spanish as *Problemas Americanos* (1915).

4   For the meaning of "Constructive Pan-Americanism," see Leo S. Rowe, "The Essentials of Pan Americanism," lecture ca. 1924, University of Pennsylvania, Leo S. Rowe Papers, box 1.

5   See chap. 2 in this volume.

6   Courtney Johnson (2009) refers to these studies as "imperial understanding."

7   See Leo S. Rowe 1902b; and Leo S. Rowe 1902c.

8   For the U.S. construction of a "legal imperialism," see Gardner 1980. See also Scarfi 2014.

9   Two questions appeared as most relevant in this regard. One was the fact that the modus operandi of empire preserved certain individual and civil rights. The other was the divergence of opinion within the Supreme Court, which put in doubt some basic constitutional principles "at home." Leo S. Rowe 1901.

10 The judges offered quite distinct interpretations of the conditions for incorporation into the union, of the difference between a state and a territory, and of the situations under which colonial authorities were bound by the U.S. Constitution.

11 Amy Kaplan has argued that this case constituted a pivotal moment in U.S. culture, for the "insular cases" forced the legal community to debate the very nature and limits of the nation. Kaplan 2002, 1–12. See also Burnett and Marshall 2001.

12 Judge Taft, chairman of the commission, fostered a rapid transition to civil rule and self-government.

13 Rowe also examined the racial following of each political party. While the Partido Federal appealed to the most conservative elements of the white elite, the Partido Republicano appealed to poor whites and blacks. See Meléndez 1993, 45.

14 As in the colonial *cabildos*, the mayor presided over the town meeting, his vote counting double in case of a tie.

15 "Mr. Rowe. sus impresiones," *La Nación*, 19 October 1906; "El Doctor Rowe en Santa Fé," *Nuevo Día*, 20 October 1906; and "La visita de Mr. Rowe," *La Tribuna*, 18 October 1906.

16 "En la Universidad de La Plata: La recepción del Dr. Rowe," *La Prensa* (Buenos Aires), 4 November 1906. Emphasis added.

17 "Rowe en Lima," *El Comercio* (Lima), 5 September 1907.

18 The modern university was, after all, a leveling instrument. "El Profesor Leo S. Rowe: Altamente honrado por la Universidad Nacional de Chile," *La Prensa* (Buenos Aires), 12 December 1907.

19 Rowe praised the improvements in education made by Argentina, but was disappointed to learn that the country's educational system was based on French models. Leo S. Rowe 1910b.

20 "Rowe Peru's Guest," *Press* (Philadelphia), 1 September 1908.

Notes

21 During his return to the United States, Rowe stopped in Panama for a week, to ponder the wonders of the Panama Canal, still under construction. "Impressed by Canal Progress," *North American*, 8 February 1909.

22 "Dr. Rowe Back in the U.S.," *Public Ledger* (New York), 27 September 1908; "South America Likes U.S.," *Enquirer* (Philadelphia), 19 February 1909; and "A View of Out Neighbors," *New York Sun*, 17 April 1909.

23 Theodore Roosevelt to Rowe, December 1907, Leo S. Rowe Papers, MS-1, box 8, press clippings.

24 A first text with these ideas, titled "An Educational Exchange between North and South America," was published in the *Outlook* on 18 July 1908.

25 Two years earlier Rowe had presented a similar argument, criticizing both U.S. isolationism and the U.S. superiority complex. Leo S. Rowe 1907b.

26 On Barrett's notion of Pan-Americanism, see Prisco 1973; and Salvatore 2002.

27 "With a broad and statesmanlike view, Germany has been ever ready to furnish South America with scientists for her universities, with teachers for her schools, with specialists in administrative, technical, and sanitary problems; and she is now reaping the benefit of his far-seeing plan. In a word, German culture has come into organic touch with the life of these nations." Leo S. Rowe 1909, 592.

28 See Hirschman 1997 [1977].

29 Leo S. Rowe, "Nuevos rumbos de la democracia," lectures delivered at the Universidad Nacional de La Plata, 1914, Leo S. Rowe Papers, box 23. Later published as *Problemas Americanos* (1915).

30 Oscar Terán (2000) examines the climate of ideas of this period, focusing on the tensions between a "scientific" and a "humanistic-aesthetic" culture.

31 The elite exhibited pride in the accomplishments of progress and concern for the urban and social problems associated with modernization. A powerful anarchist movement had taken control of important labor unions and threatened to disturb the social peace. Solberg 1969.

32 An "ignorant democracy," Rowe said, is a "falsified democracy." Here the Argentine audience must have nodded, associating Rowe's words with President Domingo F. Sarmiento's program of elementary education for good citizenship.

33 Clearly, some of Rowe's elite connections in Argentina—Rodolfo Rivarola, Estanislao Zeballos, Emilio Frers, and José N. Matienzo—were not ardent defenders of a democratic society; they defended instead an instrumental notion of republican government. See Salvatore 2007b.

34 Natalio Botana and Ezequiel Gallo (1997) call this conception, following Alberdi, "*la República Posible.*"

35 For a discussion of the progressive movement, see Filene 1970. The goals of this movement are discussed in De Witt 1968 [1915]. Historians have noted how the passage from populism to progressivism entailed a transition from farmers' mobilization politics to a politics of reform informed by experts. See Goodwying 1978.

36 Rowe was present when in 1896 Henry Carter Adams delivered his presidential speech to the American Economic Association challenging the notion of competitive capitalism. Livingston 1994, 173–74.

37 In 1914 Rowe did fundraising for the Tuskegee Institute, directed by Booker T. Washington.

38 The National Civic Federation united a diverse group of experts committed to changes in government. Cyphers 2002, 17–28.

39 The problem of a centralized government functioning under the mask of a federalist system had been already raised by Rodolfo Rivarola in *Del régimen federativo al unitario* (1908) and by José Nicolás Matienzo in *El gobierno representative federal en la República Argentina* (1917 [1910]). Rivarola and Matienzo were Rowe's key "native informants."

40 Rowe stayed six months in 1906–1907, four months in 1908, and five months in 1914.

41 As Rowe confided, he was a privileged witness to some of these interventions. Leo S. Rowe 1921b, 76.

42 The Argentine Constitution of 1853 was so similar to that of the United States that in the 1860 convention the delegates discussed whether a "perfect system" (the U.S. Constitution) could be improved.

43 For a good summary of Rivarola's and Matienzo's arguments about the nature of Argentine federalism, see Chiaramonte and Buchbinder 1992.

44 Rowe borrowed heavily from Ernesto Quesada's *La época de Rosas* (1898). On the importance of "cabildos" and on the people's preference for federalism, he relied on Francisco Ramos Mejía's *El federalismo argentino* (1889), reedited in 1915.

45 For a recent history of the cultural division during the Second World War, see Sadlier 2012.

46 Due to his extensive travels in the region, his personal relationships with influential men, and his commitment to Pan-American conferences, Rowe was the U.S. American with the greatest number of personal friends in Latin America. Welles 1947.

47 Among his most important interventions in the foreign-policy debate are his essays: "The Danger of National Isolation" (1907); "Our Interest in a United America" (1909); "The Need for a Constructive American Foreign Policy" (1914); "The Development of Cultural Ties between the Republics of America through the Interchange of Professors and Students" (1917); "The Development of a Democracy on the American Continent" (1922); and "The Mission of the Americas in World Affairs" (1942).

48 The Tacna-Arica dispute involved a territorial conflict between Chile and Peru resulting from the War of the Pacific.

49 For Rowe's lifetime commitment to the cause of inter-American cooperation, the governing board of the PAU granted him in 1947 the title "Citizen of America." Doyle 1945.

50 Most notable among them were the Carnegie Endowment for International Peace, the Social Science Research Council, the PAU, and the Office of the Coordinator of Inter-American Affairs.

51 On the history of cultural diplomacy, see Ninkovich 1981; Haines 1989; Fein 1998; Sadlier 2012; and Fox 2013.

Notes

7. Geographic Conquest

1 In addition to Bowman, other noted geographers worked in the region during this period, including Mark Jefferson, Robert S. Platt, Clarence F. Jones, Carl Sauer, and Preston James.

2 As chairman of the American Geographical Society, Bowman promoted geography as a useful science devoted to the study of the interaction between the physical environment and human societies. Bowman's ideas about the mission of geography were influenced by William Morris Davis, his teacher at Harvard.

3 Bowman's successful career is narrated in Geoffrey Martin's *The Life and Thought of Isaiah Bowman* (1980) and Neil Smith's *American Empire* (2003). See also Ogilvie 1950; Wrigley 1951; and Martin 1986.

4 See discussion in chap. 2 in this volume.

5 This discourse was articulated by John Barrett and other business prospectors between 1900 and 1915. See Salvatore 2002.

6 Bowman's first essay denouncing slavery in the Peruvian forests dates from 1912. A few years later, Edward A. Ross published similar conclusions in *South of Panama* (1915).

7 In Bowman's view Brazil was the "United States of South America." Bowman 1915, 200.

8 The Chileans were an "energetic race," the "Yankees of South America," but lacked crucial resources to become an industrial nation. The Argentines, though entrepreneurial, did not possess sufficient capital and cheap energy. And the Uruguayans had allocated most of their land to raising livestock.

9 Even the apparently barren lands of the Bolivian highlands were quite productive, contributing wool, textiles, potatoes, and forage to domestic markets.

10 Bowman extended this accomplishment to mestizo farmers and herdsmen working on the fringes of the Spanish empire. Bowman 1915, 3–4.

11 In Tierra del Fuego, white settlers displaced the Onas and hunted almost to extinction the *guanaco*, the Onas' main source of food and clothing.

12 Bowman wrote of the shepherds that they "[led] a careless, free, out-of-door life with much privation from winter storms, snows, and cold, with plain fare, rough speech, a cheerful hospitality, and a certain frankness not always found in the manners of people who dwell in cities." Bowman 1915, 20.

13 Bowman paid particular attention to the story of the settlement of Colonia 16 de Octubre, where a group of two hundred Welsh colonists had departed from Puerto Madryn, traveled west toward the Andes, and established a pioneer settlement where they raised cattle and sheep. Ibid., 34.

14 South American "pioneer fringes" were "stationary" rather than mobile.

15 See Tax 1953; Schultz 1964; and Schultz 1980. See also Ball and Pounder 1996.

16 Like U.S. presidents, Inca rulers traveled to the different corners of their empire to show their governed populations interest in their welfare. Bowman 1915, 170–72.

17 See also Bowman 1916b.

18 Physiography, also known as physical geography, is the study of the natural environment.

19 See, for instance, Demas 1965. The idea that foreign railroads had contributed to the disintegration of the national economies was prevalent in dependency theory. See Frank et al. 1969.

20 Because of this, populations in the highlands and along the coast had to import flour from the United States.

21 See also Bowman 1916b.

22 Bowman's observations on multiple-altitude production anticipated John Murra's thesis about the "vertical control" of different "ecological floors." On Murra's thesis, see Van Buren 1996.

23 Near Antabamba, walking along an Indian trail seventeen thousand feet high, Bowman found "rosy-cheeked and fat children" sharing their mountain refuge with sheep and alpacas. Bowman 1916a, 52.

24 Rubber was an indispensable material for making automobile tires, raincoats, shoes, conveyor belts, and sporting goods.

25 Yet Bowman's article failed to make any reference to these massacres. See Jordan Goodman 2009.

26 For fifty cents a day, the companies were able to secure labor for road-building and rubber-picking for a period of eight to ten months. Bowman 1916a, 32.

27 Their nomadic life had made them a "self-reliant, proud, and independent" people. Ibid., 29–31.

28 "When a man obtains a rubber concession from the government he buys a kingdom." Ibid., 25–26.

29 "The peonage system continues by reason of that extraordinary difficulty in the development of the tropical lowland of South America—the lack of a labor supply." Ibid., 26.

30 Denounced by Roger Casement, the case of the Putumayo atrocities attained notoriety between 1910 and 1913. See Jordan Goodman 2009.

31 In 1911, a flood had affected the whole region, interrupting all communications between Tacna and Arica. Bowman 1924, 42–44.

32 Over time, the area supplying the nitrate region extended into central Chile and Argentina. Ibid., 76–78.

33 The port of Antofagasta, shipping copper and silver, came to replace Iquique as the center of export growth. Ibid., 80–81.

34 Bowman wrote, "The frontier communities are immeasurably isolated and provincial, in-growing, self-governing, substantial, rooted to the soil, permanently related to natural conditions—in short, established." Ibid., 110.

35 U.S. corporations, Bowman predicted, would in time displace existing British and Chilean small mining companies. Ibid., 182.

36 See Bowman 1932a; and Bowman 1932b. Bowman presented this project on world "pioneer settlements" to the December 1931 meeting of the Association of American Geographers at Ypsilanti.

Notes

37 Though timber and hydroelectric resources existed, the dominance of wool production prevented the diversification of the economy.

38 Bowman wrote, "Here as in the Eastern valleys the long haul to market makes agricultural production unprofitable. Neither the railway nor the motor car has yet overcome the handicap of distance, nor does there appear to be real progress in this direction." Bowman 1937, 325.

39 Bowman wrote, "In most of Hispanic America more than three centuries of agricultural history can be written around the exploitation of native labor through the hacienda system." Ibid., 298.

40 "Railroads will never connect these towns except as they lie by chance upon the line of some future route between mine and seaport." Bowman 1916a, 209.

41 "The policy of the whites," he wrote, "has been to suppress and exploit the natives, to abuse them, and to break their spirit." Ibid., 102.

8. Worldly Sociology

1 While Lester Ward is the acknowledged "father" of sociology in the United States, Albion Small and Edward A. Ross are often presented as runners-up to the title. See Page 1969; and Hertzler 1951. On the contribution of sociologists to the progressive movement, see Weinberg 1972; and Bannister 1987. Recent work revalorizes Ross's contributions in relation to other great European sociologists. See, for instance, Gross 2003 on the connection between Ross and Simmel.

2 Thomas C. Leonard (2003) places Ross among the economists of the progressive era who contributed a eugenic perspective on social policy. Howard Horwitz (1998b) underscores the role of Ross as advisor to President Theodore Roosevelt in the shaping of racial social policies. Jess Gilbert (2001) groups Ross with Richard T. Ely and John R. Commons as agrarian economists of Wisconsin who prefigured the reformist policies of the New Deal.

3 Ross's best-known contributions to the field are *Social Control* (1901), *Foundations of Sociology* (1905), *Social Psychology* (1908), and *The Principles of Sociology* (1920).

4 Ross's books containing "sociological portraits" of great regions include *The Changing Chinese* (1911), *South of Panama* (1915), *Russia in Upheaval* (1918), *The Russian Bolshevik Revolution* (1921), *The Social Revolution in Mexico* (1923), and *Report on Employment of Native Labor in Portuguese Africa* (1925).

5 "Industrial evolution places a rising premium on reflection, and self-control, the foundations of character. More and more it penalizes the childishness and frivolousness of the cheaply-gotten-up, *mañana* races." Edward A. Ross 1901a, 83.

6 See Weinberg 1972, chap. 6; McMahon 1999, chap. 4; and Page 1969, chap. 7. To Howard Horwitz (1998a), Ross's works appeared to be an example of progressives' engagement with "moral engineering." Benjamin Kline Hunnicut (1988) places Ross among authors who favored the reduction of work time and the emergence of a leisure economy.

7   Specifically, a corps of factory inspectors, sanitary agents, forest rangers, and health officers, assisted by an honest and professional press and by intellectuals committed to the public good, could curb the excesses of mass-production capitalism.

8   Corporate "managerial mentality" disregarded important social costs, such as the spread of infectious diseases, the exploitation of women and children, and the corruption of city government. Edward A. Ross 1914 [1912], chap. 6.

9   Ross's discourse anticipated the rhetoric of leftists in the 1960s and 1970s who considered twentieth-century Latin America to be "feudal." See Laclau 1972; and Frank 1971. For a critical appraisal, see van Bath 1974.

10 The subject of miscegenation has been a common feature in U.S. travel writing since the nineteenth century. See Salvatore 1995.

11 After the procession, Ross met the town's Indian officials, all wearing their old-time dresses and holding their emblem of office—the *vara*—as if still living in the colonial past.

12 Near Temuco, in the southern frontier, Ross encountered a British mission teaching industrial habits to Mapuche children. Edward A. Ross 1915, 103.

13 "All the productive land of the Ecuador Sierra . . . is owned by absentees, who live in Riobamba, Ambato, or Quito—when they do not live in Paris—and leave their estates—sometimes of vast extent—to be managed by a '*mayordomo*' of mixed blood." Ibid., 140.

14 "For all its stucco front of modernism and liberalism, *Peru is feudal at the core.* One the great ranches in the plain north of Lake Titicaca *one gains a peephole into the thirteenth century.*" Ibid., 152; emphasis added.

15 "In Argentina agricultural labor is as free as it is with us. . . . This, indeed, is the one society in which I found a visible social capillarity, some laborers rising to be tenants and some tenants becoming land-owners." Ibid., 161–62.

16 This thesis was later sustained by James Scobie in *Revolution on the Pampas* (1967).

17 To assert this finding, Ross gave voice to local informants: a Quito minister, a Lima sociologist, and a German merchant in Bolivia. Edward A. Ross 1915, 211.

18 Among them George Clemenceau, once the prime minister of France and now a journalist; Pierre Denis, a French geographer who wrote a well-known treatise on Argentine regions; Adolfo Posada, a Spanish historian, international relations expert, and socialist, in the country on an official mission of intellectual cooperation; and Rafael Altamira, a famous legal historian, also sent by Spain to foster Pan-American relations.

19 Though leading Argentine, Peruvian, and Chilean scholars agreed on the necessity of university reform, few saw the importance of minor reforms that could build the "collegiate spirit": the students' dining hall, competitive sports, and debating societies. Edward A. Ross 1915, 236.

20 Having personally witnessed the October Revolution, Ross was asked to give many lectures (forty-two in five months) when he returned to the United States. Edward A. Ross 1977 [1934], 168.

Notes

21 The interest of publishers made Ross concentrate on the "Russian problem." After his successful *Russia in Upheaval* (1918), he wrote two additional books: *The Russian Bolshevik Revolution* (1921) and *The Russian Soviet Republic* (1923).

22 Ross replicated in Mexico the same pronouncement he had made about Peru eight years earlier: "There is no color line."

23 As Ross explains in the preface, the "Outlines" contain the materials of *The Principles of Sociology* (1920), significantly reduced, rearranged, and prepared for class use. Edward A. Ross 1923a.

24 "From Panama to Magellan, free agricultural labor as we know it does not exist, for peonage binds the rural masses to the owners of the haciendas." Ibid., 261.

25 Since the sixteenth century, the Roman Catholic Church had enjoyed the protection of the state. Members of other faiths had to practice their religion in private, subject to the disdain of the Catholic masses. Ibid., 165.

26 "For example, although the governments of South America are republican, the needs of the common people receive from them but scant consideration." Ibid., 100.

27 The Chilean Conservative Party controlled government through the purchase of votes. Ibid., 101.

28 "The ready resort to revolution in Latin America comes from the inability of the losers of a political contest to reconcile themselves to defeat." Ibid., 285.

29 For instance, while the *gente decente* (the white elites) took care to safeguard the chastity of their daughters, no such vigilance was noticed among the cholos or the Indians. Ibid., 382–84.

30 We find a similar and earlier criticism in Bowman's geographic panoramas of the southern Andes and the Amazon.

31 When the Steins published *The Colonial Heritage of Latin America* (1970), they referred to the failure of independence to transform the economic structures of dependency. For the multiple resonances of this view in Latin American historiography, see Adelman 1999.

32 Ross did comment on the Philippines, saying that the U.S. occupation had had a civilizing influence. Edward A. Ross 1923a, 279.

9. U.S. Scholars and the Question of Empire

1 Bingham mentioned in passing the recent Putumayo massacres to validate the view that in nations devoid of state controls, extreme human rights violations were possible. Hiram Bingham 1913c, 331.

2 When in 1866 Chile requested U.S. assistance in its conflict with Spain, the U.S. secretary of state refused to take a position. It was not until 1895 that an international conflict in Venezuela forced the United States to intervene.

3 Bingham's anti-imperialist essay was written in response to an invitation from the editors of the *Atlantic Monthly* after they read his book *Across South America* (1911).

4 Not everywhere in Argentina. In Tucumán, in the Argentine northwest, Ross found low wages and oppressive living conditions. The peons of sugarcane fields

reminded him of the wretched condition of "the Louisiana Nigger." Edward A. Ross 1915, 162.

5   As Diana Scifres argues, Ross's concerns about foreign policy were simple extrapolations of domestic issues. Scifres 1964.

6   See, in particular, Edward A. Ross 1914 [1912], chaps. 6 and 7.

7   Leo S. Rowe, "Attitude of Latin American Peoples towards the U.S.," lecture delivered 21 February 1911, University of Pennsylvania, Leo S. Rowe Papers, box 1.

8   Total U.S. investment in South America had increased from $170 million in 1912 to near $1,230 million in 1924. Haring 1928, 82.

9   As it emerges clearly from Drake 1989, the smaller countries were more responsive to the advice of the U.S. economist Edwin Kemmerer in matters of financial reform.

10 "With more than a dozen branches of American banks established in South America, American steamship lines to both coasts, and an efficient cable service, they are no longer at the mercy of their European rivals." Haring 1928, 87.

11 Haring wrote, "For every 'crisis' in the diplomatic relations between the latter country [Mexico] and the United States there are socialist meetings, protests and broadsides in Buenos Aires, Montevideo and Santiago." Ibid., 91.

12 Haring wrote, "Likewise in South America there should be no extension of governmental responsibility to private or public lands, or the sort of semi-political, semi-financial engagements we have been drawn into in some of the Caribbean states." Ibid., 98.

13 The guidelines had already been drafted by Arthur N. Young, a functionary of the State Department, in 1925.

14 Along with this new code for U.S. businesses in South America, some revisions of U.S. protectionist tariffs and a better effort to explain U.S. national interests in the Caribbean could begin to undo the widespread distrust and apprehension of South Americans.

15 For a discussion of Wilson's global vision, see Levin 1968. Its repercussions in the colonial world are examined in Manela 2007. The Wilsonian view of the hemisphere is examined in Gilderhus 1986.

16 Bowman spelled out this new vision in *The New World* (1921).

17 Emily S. Rosenberg calls this ideology "liberal developmentalism." Rosenberg 1982.

18 Even against demands for self-rule from its white settler minorities, Britain retained tutorship over its colonies in Africa and New Zealand. At the root of this stubborn tutorial role was a moral obligation to defend the rights and welfare of native Africans and Maoris from artful white settlers. Hyam 1999.

19 Here Bowman anticipated one of the key claims of dependency theory: "The pack mule, the trail, the simple exchange of goods at weekly, monthly or annual fairs, the dependence on foreign capital, foreign reduction-plants, and foreign demand and consumption of mineral and other raw materials, were the enduring marks of a primitive economy whose control lay outside Latin America." Bowman 1948, 137.

Notes

20 "Lecture Notes of Courses Given at Bryn Mawr and Yale," Harvard University Archives, Clarence Haring Papers (CHP), HUG 4447.575.

21 "British rule has also given India the material benefits that American rule has given to Porto Rico or Philippines: government roads, cheap postal services, well-planned railways, gigantic systems of irrigation to transform deserts into farmlands, beginning of a system of popular education . . . , etc." "Lecture Notes of Courses Given at Bryn Mawr and Yale," Harvard University Archives, CHP, HUG 4447.515.

22 "Lecture Notes of Courses Given at Bryn Mawr and Yale," Harvard University Archives, CHP, HUG 4447.515.

23 "Lecture Notes of Courses Given at Bryn Mawr and Yale," Harvard University Archives, CHP, HUG 4447.515.

24 This opinion was clearly part of the discussions on South American attitudes and the state of Pan-Americanism Haring included in *South America Looks at the United States* (1928), then in preparation.

25 "Haring Goes Over Nicaragua Policy," *Harvard Crimson*, 19 January 1927.

26 "First of Forums of Two Americas Attract 900," *Springfield Daily*, 29 January 1936.

27 Leo S. Rowe, "The Essentials of Pan Americanism," lecture ca. 1924, University of Pennsylvania, Leo S. Rowe Papers, box 1.

28 For a complete definition of Rowe's views on "constructive Pan-Americanism," see Leo S. Rowe 1914b.

29 Rowe's proposal for the mediation of Argentina, Brazil, and Chile is more clearly stated in his article "The Scope and Limits of Our Obligations toward Mexico" (1914).

30 Rowe never recanted his prior positions about the right of the United States to intervene in the Circum-Caribbean. He only thought that, in the effort to court the South American republics, these military interventions in the Caribbean and in Central America had become too costly in terms of inter-American reputation and goodwill.

Conclusion

1 The account of Manco's retreat is reproduced in Hiram Bingham 1922, chap. 9.

2 On the concept of "coloniality," see Moraña, Dussel, and Jáuregui 2008. See also my criticism of this approach, in Salvatore 2010b.

3 Haring condensed these arguments in *Trade and Navigation between Spain and the Indies in the Time of the Hapsburgs* (1918) and, much later, in *The Spanish Empire in America* (1947).

4 See Scott 1998.

5 See, in particular, Bowman 1916a; and Bowman 1924.

6 Other contemporary scholars were quite critical of U.S. direct investment in Latin America. See Rippy 1931; and Inman 1942, chap. 9 and 13.

7 See Haring 1941.

8 Going against the grain of contemporary revisionist attacks against the Black Legend, Haring insisted that Spanish colonialism had destructive effects on the life and culture of indigenous peoples. See Haring 1947, chap. 3, esp. 60–67.

9   For a more extensive discussion, see chapter 8 of this volume.

10 Bowman quoted J. B. Ambrosetti and Gunardo Lange from Argentina, as well as a report by the Chilean physician Ricardo Dávila.

11 Among others, Bowman cited Eric Boman, Walther Penck, Clements R. Markham, G. M. Wrigley, Kirtley F. Mather, George E. Church, Johann J. von Tshudi, Wilfred B. Grubb, and Rodolfo A. Phillippi Banados. In addition, he read Barros Arana's account of the War of the Pacific in its French version, as well as older travel narratives, including Allan R. Holmberg's narrative of travel to the Andes and Alejandro Bertrand's narrative of travel to the Atacama Desert.

12 Haring cited six major secondary works as important support to his research; four of them were published in Paris, two in New York.

13 Haring mentioned Diego Barros Arana's *Historia general de Chile*, José Milla et al.'s *Historia de América Central*, José Toribio Medina's *Historia de la Inquisición en Chile*, and Eduardo Madero's *Historia del puerto de Buenos Aires*. All were works of the mid- to late nineteenth century.

14 Haring also praised the work of the Argentine historians Ricardo Levene and Torre Revello.

15 Haring cited, among others, Silvio Zavala, Francisco Yanes, José Torre Revello, Rubén Vargas Ugarte, Ricardo Levene, Manuel Orozco y Berra, Gil Fortuol, Francisco Encina, and José Milla—that is, an assortment of the leading colonial historians of Peru, Argentina, Mexico, Venezuela, Chile, and Central America.

16 I am referring here to Alexander Gerschenkron's theory of the advantage of economic backwardness, in *Economic Backwardness in Historical Perspective* (1962).

17 Ross's book *South of Panama* was used in book-reading clubs and cited by economic geographers, sociologists, historians, and commentators of the west coast nations, but did not win the acclaim of his other popular books on social trends.

REFERENCES

Selected Works

HIRAM BINGHAM

Bingham, Hiram. 1908a. "On the Road of Bolivar's Great March." *Geographic Journal* 32.4: 329–47.

———. 1908b. "The Possibilities of South American History and Politics as a Field of Research." *Bulletin of the International Bureau of the American Republics* (Washington): 283–300.

———. 1909. *Journal of an Expedition across Venezuela and Colombia, 1906–1907.* New Haven: Yale Publishing Association.

———. 1910a. "Causes of the Lack of Political Cohesion in Spanish America." *American Political Science Review* 4.4: 508–15.

———. 1910b. "The Ruins of Choqquequirau." *American Anthropologist* 12.4: 505–25.

———. 1911a. *Across South America: An Account of a Journey from Buenos Aires to Lima by Way of Potosí; with Notes on Brazil, Argentina, Bolivia, Chile and Peru.* Boston: Houghton Mifflin.

———. 1911b. "Potosí." *Bulletin of the American Geographical Society* 43.1: 1–13.

———. 1912a. "The Ascent of Coropuna." *Harper's Magazine*, March, 489–502.

———. 1912b. "The Discovery of Prehistoric Human Remains Near Cuzco." In *Contributions from the Yale Peruvian Expedition*, 297–333. From *American Journal of Science* 33 (April 1912). New Haven: Yale University.

———. 1912c. "Preliminary Report of the Yale Peruvian Expedition." *Bulletin of the American Geographical Society* 44.1: 20–26.

———. 1913a. "The Discovery of Machu Picchu." *Harper's Magazine*, April, 709–19.

———. 1913b. *In the Wonderlands of Peru: The Work Accomplished by the Peruvian Expedition of 1912.* Washington: National Geographic Society.

———. 1913c. *The Monroe Doctrine: An Obsolete Shibboleth*. New Haven: Yale University Press / Oxford University Press.

———. 1914a. "The Probable Effect of the Opening of the Panama Canal on Our Economic Relations with the People of the West Coast of South America." *Journal of Race Development* 5.1: 49–67.

———. 1914b. "The Ruins of Espiritu Pampa, Peru." *American Anthropologist* 16.2: 185–99.

———. 1914c. "Should We Abandon the Monroe Doctrine?" *Journal of Race Development* 4.3: 334–58.

———. 1914d. "The Yale University and National Geographic Society Peruvian Expedition." *Geographic Journal* 43.6: 676–78.

———. 1915. *Exhibition of Photographs Taken by the Peruvian Expedition of the National Geographic Society and Yale University in 1911, 1912, 1914, and 1915*. Washington: National Geographic Society.

———. 1916. "Further Explorations in the Land of the Incas." *National Geographic Magazine* 29.5: 431–73.

———. 1922. *Inca Land: Explorations in the Highlands of Peru*. Boston: Houghton Mifflin. New edition, Washington: National Geographic Society, Adventure Classics, 2003.

———. 1927. "An American Empire or a Union of States?" Speech delivered in the United States Senate, 19–20 January 1927. Washington: State Papers.

———. 1930a. "Latin-American Immigration Quotas a Menace to Pan-American Comity." Speech delivered in the United States Senate, 10–11 April 1930. Washington: U.S. Government Printing Office.

———. 1930b. *Machu Picchu: A Citadel of the Incas*. New Haven: Yale University Press.

———. 1948. *Lost City of the Incas: The Story of Machu Picchu and Its Builders*. New York: Duell, Sloan and Pearse. New edition, London: Phoenix House, 2002.

ISAIAH BOWMAN

Bowman, Isaiah. 1909. "Regional Population Groups of Atacama." *Bulletin of the American Geographical Society* 41.3, part 1: 142–54; 41.4, part 2: 193–211.

———. 1912. "The Canon of the Urubamba." *Bulletin of the American Geographical Society* 44.12: 881–97.

———. 1913a. "First Report of Professor Bowman's Expedition." *Bulletin of the American Geographical Society* 45.10: 750–53.

———. 1913b. "Geographical Aspects of the New Madeira-Mamore Railroad." *Bulletin of the American Geographical Society* 45.4: 285–81.

———. 1914. "Results of an Expedition to the Central Andes." *Bulletin of the American Geographical Society* 46.3: 161–83.

———. 1915. *South America: A Geography Reader*. Chicago: Rand McNally.

———. 1916a. *The Andes of Southern Peru: Geographical Reconnaissance along the Seventy-Third Meridian*. New York: American Geographical Society.

———. 1916b. "The Country of Shepherds." *Geographical Review* 1.6: 419–42.

———. 1921. *The New World: Problems in Political Geography.* New York: World Book.

———. 1924. *Desert Trails of Atacama.* New York: American Geographic Society.

———. 1926. "The Scientific Study of Settlement." *Geographical Review* 16.4: 647–53.

———. 1931. *The Pioneer Fringe.* Freeport, N.Y.: Books for Libraries Press, 1971 reprint.

———. 1932a. "The Pioneering Process." *Science* 75.1951 (May): 521–28.

———. 1932b. "Planning in Pioneer Settlement." *Annals of the Association of American Geographers* 32.2: 93–107.

———. 1934. "Applied Geography." *Scientific Monthly* 38.2: 173–77.

———. 1937. *The Limits of Land Settlement: A Report on Present-day Possibilities.* New York: Council of Foreign Relations.

———. 1942a. "The Ecuador-Peru Boundary Dispute." *Foreign Affairs* 20.4: 757–61.

———. 1942b. "Geography vs. Geopolitics." *Geographical Review* 32.4: 646–58.

———. 1946. "The Millionth Map of Hispanic America." *Science* 103.2672: 319–23.

———. 1948. "The Geographical Situation of the United States in Relation to World Policies." *Geographical Journal* 112.4–6: 129–42.

CLARENCE H. HARING

Haring, Clarence H. 1910. *The Buccaneers in the West Indies in the Seventeenth Century.* New York: E. P. Dutton.

———. 1918. *Trade and Navigation between Spain and the Indies in the Time of the Hapsburgs.* Cambridge, Mass.: Harvard University Press.

———. 1927a. "South America and Our Policy in the Caribbean." *Annals of the American Academy of Political and Social Science* 132: 146–52.

———. 1927b. "The Two Americas." *Foreign Affairs* 5.3: 264–78.

———. 1928. *South America Looks at the United States.* New York: Macmillan.

———. 1931a. "Chilean Politics 1920–1928." *Hispanic American Historical Review* 11.1: 1–26.

———. 1931b. "Revolution in South America." *Foreign Affairs* 9.2: 277–96.

———. 1932. "Presidential Elections in South America." *Foreign Affairs* 10.2: 327–31.

———. 1934. *South American Progress.* Cambridge, Mass.: Harvard University Press.

———, ed. 1935. *The Economic Literature of Latin America: A Tentative Bibliography.* Cambridge, Mass.: Harvard University Press.

———. 1936. "Depression and Recovery in Argentina." *Foreign Affairs* 14.3: 506–19.

———. 1937. "Race and Environment in the New World." Paper presented to the Il Congreso de Historia de América, Buenos Aires, August 1937.

———. 1941. "Latin America Comes of Age." In *Latin America in World Affairs 1914–1940,* ed. Leo S. Rowe et al., 1–13. Philadelphia: University of Pennsylvania Press.

———. 1944. "The Setting for Dictatorship in Latin America." *Proceedings of the Massachusetts Historical Society,* third series, 67: 549–61.

———. 1947. *The Spanish Empire in America.* New York: Harcourt Brace Jovanovich.

———. 1958. *Empire in Brazil: A New World Experiment with Monarchy.* New York: W. W. Norton.

References

Ross, Edward A. 1901a. "The Causes of Race Superiority." *Annals of the American Academy of Political and Social Science* 18: 67–89.

———. 1901b. *Social Control: A Survey of the Foundations of Order*. New York: Macmillan.

———. 1905. *Foundations of Sociology*. New York: Macmillan.

———. 1906. "The Field of Modern Sociology." *American Journal of Theology* 10.2: 382–83.

———. 1908. *Social Psychology: An Outline and Sourcebook*. New York: Macmillan.

———. 1911a. *The Changing Chinese: The Conflict of Oriental and Western Culture in China*. New York: Century.

———. 1911b. "Sociological Observations in Inner China." *American Journal of Sociology* 16.6: 721–33.

———. 1914 [1912]. *Changing America: Studies in Contemporary Society*. New York: Century.

———. 1915. *South of Panama*. New York: Century.

———. 1918. *Russia in Upheaval*. New York: Century.

———. 1920. *The Principles of Sociology*. New York: Century.

———. 1921. *The Russian Bolshevik Revolution*. New York: Century.

———. 1922. *The Social Trend*. New York: Century.

———. 1923a. *The Outlines of Sociology*. New York: Century.

———. 1923b. *The Russian Soviet Republic*. New York: Century.

———. 1923c. *The Social Revolution in Mexico*. New York: Century.

———. (1924). *Roads to Social Peace*. Freeport, N.Y.: Books for Libraries Press, reprint 1970.

———. 1924. "The Greatest Research Chance in the World." *Journal of Social Forces* 2.4: 549–50.

———. 1925. *Report on Employment of Native Labor in Portuguese Africa*. New York: Abbott.

———. 1977 [1934]. *Seventy Years of It: An Autobiography*. New York: Arno Press.

Rowe, Leo S. 1892. "Conference of the Central Bureau for the Promotion of the Welfare of the Laboring Classes." *Annals of the American Academy of Political and Social Science* 3: 73–88.

———. 1901. "The Supreme Court and the Insular Cases." *Annals of the American Academy of Political and Social Science* 18: 226–50.

———. 1902a. "The Establishment of Civil Government in the Philippines." Reprint, *Annals of the American Academy of Political and Social Science* (September): 313–27.

———. 1902b. "The Extension of American Influence in the West Indies." *North American Review* 175.2: 254–62.

———. 1902c. "The Political and Legal Aspects of Change of Sovereignty." *American Law Register* 41.8: 466–76.

References

———. 1902d. "Political Parties in Porto Rico." *Annals of the American Academy of Political and Social Science* 19: 21–39.

———. 1904. *The United States and Porto Rico.* New York: Longmans, Green.

———. 1905. "The Reorganization of Local Government in Cuba." *Annals of the American Academy of Political and Social Science* 25: 109–19.

———. 1907a. "The Awakening of Bolivia." *Independent* (New York): 861–62.

———. 1907b. "The Danger of National Isolation." *North American Review* 185.4 (June): 422–25.

———. 1907c. "Our Trade Relations with South America." *North American Review* 184.5 (March): 513–19.

———. 1908. *Problems of City Government.* New York: D. Appleton.

———. 1908a. "Municipal Progress in Brazil: The Cities of the State of San Paulo." *American Journal of Sociology* 13.4 (January): 508–12.

———. 1908b. "The Transformation of Rio de Janeiro." *Independent* (New York): 249–52.

———. 1909. "Our Interest in a United America." *North American Review* (April): 587–93.

———. 1910a. "The National University of Mexico." *Outlook* (15 October), 341–42.

———. 1910b. "Progresos educacionales en la República Argentina." *Anales del Instituto de Enseñanza General* 1: 415–37.

———. 1911. "The Present Situation in Mexico." *Independent* (New York): 464–69.

———. 1912. "The Mexican Revolution: Its Causes and Consequences." *Political Science Quarterly* 27.2: 281–97.

———. 1914a. "Misconceptions and Limitations of the Monroe Doctrine." *Proceedings of the American Society of International Law* 8: 126–43.

———. 1914b. "The Need of a Constructive American Foreign Policy." *Political Quarterly* 4 (September): 17–37.

———. 1914c. "The Scope and Limits of Our Obligations toward Mexico." *Annals of the American Academy of Political and Social Science* 54: 219–35.

———. 1914d. "The Work of the Joint International Commission on Panama Claims." *American Journal of International Law* 8.4: 738–57.

———. 1915. *Problemas Americanos.* La Plata, Argentina: Talleres Gráficos Chistmann y Crespo.

———. 1916. "America as a Defender of Neutral Rights." Address delivered before the American Philosophical Society, 13–15 April 1916, Philadelphia.

———. 1917a. "Bringing the Americas Together." *Proceedings of the Academy of Political Science in the City of New York* 7.2: 272–78.

———. 1917b. "The Development of Cultural Ties between the Republics of America through the Interchange of Professors and Students." Paper delivered at the Second Pan-American Scientific Congress, 27 December 1915–8 January 1916. Washington: Government Printing Office.

———. 1921a. "Developing Trade between the Americas." *Office Appliance Exporter* (spring): 13–15.

———. 1921b. *The Federal System of the Argentine Republic,* publication no. 258. Washington: Carnegie Institution of Washington.

References

295

———. 1922. "The Development of Democracy on the American Continent." *American Political Science Review* 16.1 (February): 1–9.

———. 1927a. "Inter-American Problems." Paper delivered at the Latin American Seminar, School of Foreign Service, Georgetown University, Washington.

———. 1927b. "The Pan American Union: Constructive Pan-Americanism Extends Far beyond the Mere Field of Government Action." *National Republic* (June).

———. 1935. "Hands across Our Southern Borderlands." *Ship, Rail and Air* (New York), May 1935, 13–30.

———. 1942. "The Mission of the Americas in World Affairs." *Annals of the American Academy of Political and Social Science* (July): 74–79.

Secondary Sources

Adas, Michael. 1989. *Machines as the Measure of Men: Science, Technology, and Ideologies of Western Dominance*. Ithaca: Cornell University Press.

Adelman, Jeremy. 1999. *Colonial Legacies: The Problem of Persistence in Latin American History*. New York: Routledge.

Agrawal, Arun. 2008. "Dismantling the Divide between Indigenous and Scientific Knowledge." *Development and Change* 26.3: 413–39.

Ahearne, Jeremy. 1995. *Michel de Certeau: Interpretation and Its Other*. Stanford: Stanford University Press.

Aikman, Duncan. 1942. "The Machinery for Hemispheric Cooperation." *Public Opinion Quarterly* 6.4: 549–62.

Anderson, Warwick. 2006. *Colonial Pathologies: American Tropical Medicine, Race, and Hygiene in the Philippines*. Durham: Duke University Press.

Asad, Talal. 1979. "Anthropology and the Colonial Encounter." In *The Politics of Anthropology*, ed. Gerrit Huizer, 85–94. The Hague: Mouton.

Baber, Zaheer. 1996. *The Science of Empire: Scientific Knowledge, Civilization, and Colonial Rule in India*. Albany: State University of New York Press.

Baker, George W. 1964. "Ideals and Realities in the Wilson Administration's Relations with Honduras." *Americas* 21.1 (July): 3–19.

———. 1966. "The Wilson Administration and Nicaragua, 1913–1921." *Americas* 22.4 (April): 339–76.

Ball, Richard, and Laurie Pounder. 1996. "Efficient but Poor Revisited." *Economic Development and Cultural Change* 44.4: 735–60.

Ballantyne, Tony. 2005. "Religion, Difference, and the Limits of British Imperial History." *Victorian Studies* 47.3: 427–55.

Bannister, Robert C. 1987. *Sociology and Scientism: The American Quest for Objectivity, 1880–1940*. Chapel Hill: University of North Carolina Press.

Bannon, John Francis. 1978. *Herbert Eugene Bolton: The Historian and the Man*. Tucson: University of Arizona Press.

Barbieri, William A. 2002. "The Heterological Quest: Michel de Certeau's Travel Narratives and the 'Other' of Comparative Religious Ethics." *Journal of Religious Ethics* 30.1: 23–48.

References
———

Barrenechea, Antonio. 2009. "Good Neighbor/Bad Neighbor: Boltonian Americanism and Hemispheric Studies." *Comparative Literature* 61.3: 231–43.

Barrett, John. 1909. "South America: Our Manufacturers' Greatest Opportunity." *Annals of the American Academy of Political and Social Science* 34.3: 82–93.

———. 1914. "Pan-American Possibilities." *Journal of Race Development* 5.1: 19–29.

Bennett, Tony, and Elizabeth Silva. 2011. "Introduction: Cultural Capital—Histories, Limits, Prospects." *Poetics* 39.6 (December): 427–43.

Bennett, Wendell C. 1937. "Archaeological Work in South America, 1934 to 1936." *American Antiquity* 2.4: 248–59.

Berger, Mark T. 1993. "Civilizing the South: The U.S. Rise to Hegemony in the Americas and the Roots of Latin American Studies 1898–1945." *Bulletin of Latin American Research* 12.1: 1–48.

———. 1995. *Under Northern Eyes: Latin American Studies and U.S. Hegemony in the Americas, 1898–1990.* Bloomington: Indiana University Press.

———. 2007. "Keeping the World Safe for Primary Colors: Area Studies, Development Studies, International Studies, and the Vicissitudes of Nation-Building." *Globalizations* 4.4: 429–44.

Bingham, Alfred M. 1989. *Portrait of an Explorer: Hiram Bingham, Discoverer of Machu Picchu.* Ames: Iowa State University Press.

Blakemore, Harold. 1990. *From the Pacific to La Paz.* London: Lester Crook.

Botana, Natalio, and Ezequiel Gallo. 1997. *De la República Posible a la República Verdadera (1880–1910).* Buenos Aires: Ariel.

Bourdieu, Pierre. 1979. *La distinción: Criterios y bases sociales del gusto.* Madrid: Taurus.

———. 2003. *Capital cultural, escuela y espacio social.* Buenos Aires: Siglo XXI Editores.

———. 2008. *Homo Academicus.* Buenos Aires: Siglo XXI Editores.

Bowd, Gavin, and Daniel Clayton. 2005. "Tropicality, Orientalism, and French Colonialism in Indochina: The Work of Pierre Gourou, 1927–1982." *French Historical Studies* 28.2: 297–327.

Brands, Hal. 2010. *Latin America's Cold War.* Cambridge, Mass.: Harvard University Press.

Brett, Annabel. 2002. "What Is Intellectual History Now?" In *What Is History Now?*, ed. David Cannadine, 113–31. London: Palgrave Macmillan.

Buck-Morss, Susan. 2009. *Hegel, Haiti, and Universal History.* Pittsburgh: University of Pittsburgh Press.

Burbank, Jane, and Frederick Cooper. 2010. *Empires in World History: Power and the Politics of Difference.* Princeton: Princeton University Press.

Burchell, Graham, Colin Gordon, and Peter Miller, eds. 1991. *The Foucault Effect: Studies in Governmentality.* Chicago: University of Chicago Press.

Burgin, Miron. 1947. "Research in Latin American Economics and Economic History." *Inter-American Economic Affairs* 1: 3–22.

Burnett, Christina Duffy, and Burke Marshall, eds. 2001. *Foreign in a Domestic Sense: Puerto Rico, American Expansion, and the Constitution.* Durham: Duke University Press.

"Caracas Sheet of the Map of Hispanic America." 1945. *Geographical Review* 35.2: 25–27.

References
———

Carmin, Robert, Kenneth Grieb, and N. Merrill Rippy. 1975. "A Brief Outline History of the Midwest Association for Latin American Studies." *Latin American Research Review* 10.2: 173–80.

Castle, David Barton. 2000. "Leo Stanton Rowe and the Meaning of Pan Americanism." In *Beyond the Ideal: Pan Americanism in Inter-American Affairs*, ed. David Sheinin, 33–44. Westport, Conn.: Praeger.

Chakrabarty, Dipesh. 2000. *Provincializing Europe: Postcolonial Thought and Historical Difference*. Princeton: Princeton University Press.

Chapman, Charles E. 1918. "The Founding of the Review." *Hispanic American Historical Review* 1.1: 8–23.

Chatterjee, Partha. 1993. *Nationalist Thought and the Colonial World: A Derivative Discourse*. Minneapolis: University of Minnesota Press.

Cheyfitz, Eric. 1991. *The Poetics of Imperialism: Translation and Colonization from The Tempest to Tarzán*. New York: Oxford University Press.

Chiaramonte, Juan Carlos, and Pablo Buchbinder. 1992. "Provincias, caudillos, nación y la historiografía constitucionalista argentina, 1853–1930." *Anuario Instituo de Estudios Histórico Sociales* (Tandil) 7: 93–120.

Cline, Howard F. 1966. "The Latin American Studies Association: A Summary Survey with Appendix." *Latin American Research Review* 2.1: 57–79.

Coerver, Don M., and Linda B. Hall. 1999. *Tangled Destinies: Latin America and the United States*. Albuquerque: University of New Mexico Press.

Cohen, Daniel. 1984. *Hiram Bingham and the Dream of Gold*. New York: M. Evans.

Cohn, Bernard S. 1996. *Colonialism and Its Forms of Knowledge: The British in India*. Princeton: Princeton University Press.

Colby, Charles C. 1936. "Changing Currents of Geographic Thought in America." *Annals of the Association of American Geographers* 26.1: 1–37.

Collini, Stephan. 1985. "What Is Intellectual History?" *History Today* 35.10: 46–54.

"Commentaries on 'Knowledge and Empire: The Social Sciences and the United States Imperial Expansion.'" 2010. Special issue of *Identities* 17.1: 45–71.

"Commerce with South America." 1911. *Annals of the American Academy of Political and Social Science* 37.3 (May): 70–84.

Conn, Steven. 1998. *Museums and American Intellectual Life, 1876–1926*. Chicago: University of Chicago Press.

Cooper, Frederick. 2005. *Colonialism in Question: Theory, Knowledge, History*. Berkeley: University of California Press.

Coronado, Jorge. 2009. *The Andes Imagined: Indigenismo, Society and Modernity*. Pittsburgh: University of Pittsburgh Press.

Coronil, Fernando. 1996. "Beyond Occidentalism: Toward Nonimperial Geohistorical Categories." *Cultural Anthropology* 11.1: 51–87.

Cowan, Brian. 2006. "Ideas in Context: From the Social to the Cultural History of Ideas." In *Palgrave Advances in Intellectual History*, ed. Richard Whatmore and Brian Young, 171–88. London: Palgrave Macmillan.

Cramer, Gisela, and Ursula Prutsch, eds. 2012. *¡Americas Unidas!: Nelson A. Rockefeller's Office of Inter-American Affairs (1940–46)*. Madrid: Iberoamericana / Vervuert.

Crapol, Edward P. 2000. *James G. Blaine: Architect of Empire*. Washington, Del.: Scholarly Resources.

Crawford, W. Rex. 1948. "International Relations and Sociology." *American Sociological Review* 13.3: 263–68.

Creutz, Alan. 1979. "The Matrix of Professionalization: Three Recent Interpretations." *Michigan Law Review* 77.3: 641–54.

Crichfield, George W. 1908. *American Supremacy: The Rise and Progress of the Latin American Republics and Their Relations to the United States under the Monroe Doctrine*. New York: Brentano's.

Cueto, Marcos, ed. 1994. *Missionaries of Science: The Rockefeller Foundation and Latin America*. Bloomington: Indiana University Press.

Cyphers, Christopher J. 2002. *The National Civic Federation*. Westport, Conn.: Greenwood.

Davis, Harold E. 1963. *Latin American Social Thought*. Washington: University Press of Washington, D.C.

Dawley, Alan. 2003. *Changing the World: American Progressives in War and Revolution*. Princeton: Princeton University Press.

de Certeau, Michel. 1986. *Heterologies: Discourse on the Other*. Translated by Brian Massumi. Minneapolis: University of Minnesota Press.

de la Cadena, Marisol. 2000. *Indigenous Mestizos: The Politics of Race and Culture in Cuzco, Peru, 1919–1991*. Durham: Duke University Press.

de la Campa, Román. 1999. *Latin Americanism*. Minneapolis: University of Minnesota Press.

Delpar, Helen. 2000. "Inter-American Relations and Encounters: Recent Directions in the Literature." *Latin American Research Review* 35.3: 155–72.

———. 2008. *Looking South: The Evolution of Latin Americanist Scholarship in the United States, 1850–1975*. Tuscaloosa: University of Alabama Press.

Demas, William G. 1965. *The Economics of Development in Small Countries, with Special Reference to the Caribbean*. Montreal: McGill University Press.

De Vos, Paula. 2007. "Natural History and the Pursuit of Empire in Eighteenth-Century Spain." *Eighteenth-Century Studies* 40.2: 209–39.

De Witt, Benjamin P. 1968 [1915]. *The Progressive Movement: A Non-partisan, Comprehensive Discussion of Current Tendencies in American Politics*. Seattle: University of Washington Press.

Domosh, Mona. 2006. *American Commodities in an Age of Empire*. New York: Routledge.

Douglas, John Aubrey. 2007. *The Conditions for Admission: Access, Equity, and the Social Contract of Public Universities*. Stanford: Stanford University Press.

Downey, James E. 1913. "Education for Business: The Boston High School of Commerce." *Journal of Political Economy* 21.3: 221–42.

Downing, David B. 2005. "Academic Freedom as Intellectual Property: When Collegiality Confronts the Standardization Movement." *symploke* 13.1–2: 56–79.

Doyle, Henry Grattan. 1936. "The Work of the Harvard Council on Hispano-American Studies." *Modern Language Journal* 20.6: 367–70.

References

———. 1945. "The First Citizen of All the Americas." *Hispania* 28.4 (November): 555–56.

Drake, Paul W. 1989. *The Money Doctor in the Andes: The Kemmerer Missions, 1923–1933*. Durham: Duke University Press.

Dubois, Vincent. 2011. "Cultural Capital Theory vs. Cultural Policy Beliefs: How Pierre Bourdieu Could Have Become a Cultural Policy Advisor and Why He Did Not." *Poetics* 39.6 (December): 491–506

Duniway, C. A. 1915. "Training in Universities for Consular and Diplomatic Service." *American Journal of International Law* 9.1: 153–66.

Dussell, Enrique. 1995. *The Invention of the Americas: Eclipse of the "Other" and the Myth of Modernity*. New York: Continuum.

Eakin, Marshall C. 1998. "Latin American History in the United States: From Gentleman Scholars to Academic Specialists." *History Teacher* 31.4: 539–61.

Earle, Rebecca. 2007. *The Return of the Native: Indians and Myth-Making in Spanish America, 1810–1930*. Durham: Duke University Press.

Edney, Matthew H. 1990. *Mapping an Empire: The Geographical Construction of British India, 1765–1843*. Chicago: University of Chicago Press.

Ehrick, Christine. 1998. "Madrinas and Missionaries: Uruguay and the Pan American Women's Movement." *Gender and History* 10.3: 406–24.

Elliott, John H. 2006. *Empires of the Atlantic World: Britain and Spain in America, 1492–1830*. New Haven: Yale University Press.

Engerman, David C. 2007. "Bernath Lecture: American Knowledge and Global Power." *Diplomatic History* 31.4: 599–622.

Espinosa, J. Manuel. 1976. *Inter-American Beginnings of U.S. Cultural Diplomacy, 1936–1948*. Washington: U.S. Government Printing Office.

Faber, Sebastian. 2003. "Learning from the Latins: Waldo Frank's Progressive Pan Americanism." *CR: The New Centennial Review* 3.1: 257–95.

Fabian, Johannes. 1983. *Time and the Other: How Anthropology Makes Its Object*. New York: Columbia University Press.

Fagg, John E. 1982. *Pan Americanism*. Malabar, Fla.: R. E. Krieger.

Fein, Seth. 1994. "Hollywood, U.S.-Mexican Relations, and the Devolution of the 'Golden Age' of Mexican Cinema." *Film-Historia* 4.2: 103–35.

———. 1998. "Everyday Forms of Transnational Collaboration: U.S. Film Propaganda in Cold War Mexico." In *Close Encounters of Empire: Writing the History of U.S.-Latin American Cultural Relations*, ed. Gilbert M. Joseph, Catherine LeGrand, and Ricardo Salvatore, 400–450. Durham: Duke University Press, 1988.

Ferrell, Robert H. 1965. "Repudiation of a Repudiation." *Journal of American History* 51.4 (March): 669–73.

Fifer, Valerie J. 1991. *United States Perceptions of Latin America, 1850–1930: A "New West" South of Capricorn?* Manchester: Manchester University Press.

Filene, Peter G. 1970. "An Obituary for the 'Progressive Movement.'" *American Quarterly* 22.1 (spring): 20–34.

Foucault, Michel. 1980. *Power/Knowledge: Selected Interviews and Other Writings, 1972–1977*. Edited by Colin Gordon. New York: Pantheon.

References

Fox, Claire F. 2013. *Making Art Panamerican: Cultural Policy and the Cold War*. Minneapolis: University of Minnesota Press.

Frank, Andre Gunder. 1971. *Capitalism and Underdevelopment in Latin America*. New York: Monthly Review Press.

Frank, Andre Gunder, et al. 1969. *América Latina: Feudalismo o capitalismo?* Medellín, Colombia: Editorial La Oveja Negra.

Friedman, Max Paul. 2003a. *Nazis and Good Neighbors: The United States Campaign against the Germans of Latin America in World War 2*. Cambridge: Cambridge University Press.

———. 2003b. "Retiring the Puppets, Bringing Latin America Back In: Recent Scholarship on United States–Latin American Relations." *Diplomatic History* 27.5: 621–36.

Furner, Mary O. 1975. *Advocacy and Objectivity: A Crisis in the Professionalization of American Social Science, 1865–1905*. Lexington: University of Kentucky Press.

Gardner, James A. 1980. *Legal Imperialism: American Lawyers and Foreign Aid in Latin America*. Madison: University of Wisconsin Press.

Geertz, Clifford. 1983. *Local Knowledge: Further Essays in Interpretive Anthropology*. New York: Basic.

Geiger, Roger L. 1986. *To Advance Knowledge: The Growth of American Research Universities, 1900–1940*. New York: Oxford University Press.

Gellman, Irwin F. 1979. *Good Neighbor Diplomacy: United States Policies in Latin America, 1933–1945*. Baltimore: Johns Hopkins University Press.

Gerschenkron, Alexander. 1962. *Economic Backwardness in Historical Perspectives: A Book of Essays*. Cambridge, Mass.: Harvard University Press.

Gibson, Charles, and Benjamin Keen. 1957. "Trends in United States Studies in Latin American History." *American Historical Review* 62.4: 855–77.

Gilbert, Jess. 2001. "Agrarian Intellectuals in a Democratizing State." In *The Countryside in the Age of the Modern State: Political Histories of Rural America*, ed. Catherine McNicol Stock and Robert D. Johnston, 213–39. Ithaca: Cornell University Press.

Gilderhus, Mark T. 1986. *Pan American Visions: Woodrow Wilson in the Western Hemisphere 1913–1921*. Tucson: University of Arizona Press.

———. 2000. *The Second Century: U.S.-Latin American Relations since 1889*. Wilmington, Del.: Scholarly Resources.

Goldin, Claudia, and Lawrence Katz. 1999. "The Shaping of Higher Education: The Formative Years in the United States, 1890 to 1940." *Journal of Economic Perspectives* 13.1: 37–62.

Goodman, Edward J. 1972. *The Explorers of South America*. Norman: University of Oklahoma Press.

Goodman, Jordan. 2009. *The Devil and Mr. Casement: One Man's Battle for Human Rights in South America's Heart of Darkness*. New York: Farrar, Straus and Giroux.

Goodwying, Lawrence. 1978. *The Populist Movement: A Short History of the Agrarian Revolt in America*. New York: Oxford University Press.

Gosh, Durba. 2012. "Another Set of Imperial Turns?" *American Historical Review* 117.3: 772–93.

References

Green, David. 1971. *The Containment of Latin America: A History of the Myths and Realities of the Good Neighbor Policy.* Chicago: Quadrangle.

Gross, Matthias. 2003. "Sociologists of the Unexpected: Edward A. Ross and Georg Simmel on the Unintended Consequences of Modernity." *American Sociologist* (winter): 40–57.

Grover, Mark L. 1988. "Latin American History: Concerns and Conflicts." *History Teacher* 21.3: 349–65.

Guy, Donna. 1998. "The Politics of Pan-American Cooperation: Material Feminism and the Child Rights Movement, 1913–1960." *Gender and History* 10.3: 449–69.

Haglund, David G. 1984. *Latin America and the Transformation of U.S. Strategic Thought, 1936–1940.* Albuquerque: University of New Mexico Press.

Haines, Gerald K. 1989. *The Americanization of Brazil: A Study of U.S. Cold War Diplomacy in the Third World, 1945–1954.* Wilmington, Del.: SR Books.

Hanke, Lewis. 1947. "The Development of Latin-American Studies in the United States, 1939–1945." *Americas* 4.1: 32–64.

———, ed. 1964. *Do the Americas Have a Common History?* New York: Alfred A. Knopf.

———. 1967. "Studying Latin America, the Views of an 'Old Christian.'" *Journal of Inter-American Studies* 9.1: 43–64.

Hardt, Michael, and Antonio Negri. 2000. *Empire.* Cambridge, Mass.: Harvard University Press.

Haskell, Thomas L. 1977. *The Emergence of Professional Social Science.* Urbana: University of Illinois Press.

Heaney, Christopher. 2010. *Cradle of Gold: The Story of Hiram Bingham, a Real-Life Indiana Jones, and the Search for Machu Picchu.* New York: Palgrave Macmillan.

Hertzler, J. O. 1951. "Edward Allsworth Ross: Sociological Pioneer and Interpreter." *American Sociological Review* 16.5: 597–613.

Hietala, Thomas R. 2003 [1985]. *Manifest Design: American Exceptionalism and Empire.* Ithaca: Cornell University Press.

Hill, Roscoe. 1947. "Leo S. Rowe 1871–1946." *Hispanic American Historical Review* 27.2 (May): 187–88.

Hirschman, Albert O. 1997 [1977]. *The Passions and the Interests: Political Arguments for Capitalism before Its Triumph.* Princeton: Princeton University Press.

Hispanic American History Group. 1927. "Notes and Comment." *Hispanic American Historical Review* 7.2: 220–28.

Holmes, W. H. 1909. "The First Pan-American Scientific Congress, Held at Santiago, Chile." *Science* 29.742: 441–48.

Hopkins, A. G. 1999. "Back to the Future: From National History to Imperial History." *Past and Present* 164: 198–243.

Horowitz, Louis. 1967. *The Rise and Fall of Project Camelot: Studies in the Relationship between Social Science and Practical Politics.* Cambridge: Massachusetts Institute of Technology Press.

Horwitz, Howard. 1998a. "Always with Us." *American Literary History* 10.2: 317–34.

———. 1998b. "Maggie and the Sociological Paradigm." *American Literary History* 10: 606–38.

Hunnicutt, Benjamin Kline. 1988. *Work without End: Abandoning Shorter Hours for the Right to Work.* Philadelphia: Temple University Press, 1988.

Hunter, Lynette. 1999. *Critiques of Knowing: Situated Textualities in Science, Computing, and the Arts.* London: Routledge.

Hyam, Ronald. 1999. "Bureaucracy and 'Trusteeship' in the Colonial Empire." In *The Oxford History of the British Empire,* vol. 4, *The Twentieth Century,* ed. Judith M. Brown and W. Roger Louis, 255–79. Oxford: Oxford University Press.

Hyam, Ronald, and Ged Martin. 1975. *Reappraisals in British Imperial History.* London: Macmillan.

Inman, Samuel Guy. 1942. *Latin America. Its Place in World Life.* Freeport, N.Y.: Books for Library Presses, 1970 reprint.

Immerman, Richard H. 1980–1981. "Guatemala as Cold War History." *Political Science Quarterly* 95.4 (winter): 629–53.

Jaksic, Iván. 2007. *Ven conmigo a la España lejana: Los intelectuales norteamericanos ante el mundo hispánico, 1820–1880.* Mexico City: Fondo de Cultura Económica.

Jarausch, Konrad H., ed. 1983. *The Transformation of Higher Learning, 1860–1930.* Chicago: Chicago University Press.

Jessup, Philip C. 1938. *Elihu Root.* New York: Dodd, Mead.

Johnson, Courtney. 2009. "Understanding the American Empire: Colonialism, Latin Americanism, and Professional Social Science, 1898–1920." In *Colonial Crucible: Empire in the Making of the Modern American State,* ed. Alfred W. McCoy and Francisco A. Scarano, 175–90. Madison: University of Wisconsin Press.

Johnson, Harvey L. 1961. "Latin American Area Programs." *Hispania* 44.2: 304–7.

Johnson, John J. 1985. "One Hundred Years of Historical Writing on Modern Latin America by United States Historians." *Hispanic American Historical Review* 65.4: 745–65.

———. 1990. *A Hemisphere Apart: The Foundations of United States Policy toward Latin America.* Baltimore: Johns Hopkins University Press.

Joseph, Gilbert M., Catherine LeGrand, and Ricardo Salvatore, eds. 1998. *Close Encounters of Empire: Writing the History of U.S.-Latin American Cultural Relations.* Durham: Duke University Press, 1988.

Joseph, Gilbert M., and Daniela Spencer, eds. 2008. *In from the Cold: Latin America's New Encounter with the Cold War.* Durham: Duke University Press.

Julien, Catherine. 2000. *Reading Inca History.* Iowa City: University of Iowa Press.

Kagan, Richard, ed. 2002. *Spain in America: The Origins of Hispanism in the United States.* Urbana: University of Illinois Press.

Kaplan, Amy. 2002. *The Anarchy of Empire in the Making of U.S. Culture.* Cambridge, Mass.: Harvard University Press.

Kaplan, Amy, and Donald E. Pease, eds. 1993. *Cultures of United States Imperialism.* Durham: Duke University Press.

Karem, Jeff. 2001. "On the Advantages and Disadvantages of Postcolonial Theory for Pan-American Study." CR: *The New Centennial Review* 1.3: 87–116.

Karnes, Thomas L. 1979. "Hiram Bingham and His Obsolete Shibboleth." *Diplomatic History* 3.1: 39–58.

References

303

Kaulicke, Peter, ed. 1998. *Max Uhle y el Perú Antiguo*. Lima: Pontificia Universidad Católica del Perú.

Kazin, Michael, and Joseph A. McCartin, eds. 2006. *Americanism: New Perspectives on the History of an Ideal*. Chapel Hill: University of North Carolina Press.

Keen, Benjamin. 1985. "Main Currents in United States Writings on Colonial Spanish America, 1884–1984." *Hispanic American Historical Review* 65.4: 657–82.

Kloppenberg, James T. 1986. *Uncertain Victory: Social Democracy and Progressivism in European and American Thought, 1870–1920*. New York: Oxford University Press.

Kuklick, Henrika. 1976. "The Organization of Social Science in the United States." *American Quarterly* 28.1: 124–41.

Laclau, Ernesto. 1972. *Feudalismo y capitalismo en América Latina*. Barcelona: A. Redondo Editor.

Langley, Lester D. 2005. *The Americas in the Modern Age*. New Haven: Yale University Press.

Latour, Bruno. 1987. *Science in Action: How to Follow Scientists and Engineers through Society*. Cambridge, Mass.: Harvard University Press.

———. 1990. "Drawing Things Together." In *Representation in Scientific Practice*, ed. Michael Lynch and Steve Woolgar, 19–68. Cambridge: Massachusetts Institute of Technology Press.

———. 1999. *Pandora's Hope: Essays on the Reality of Science Studies*. Cambridge, Mass.: Harvard University Press.

Latour, Bruno, and Steve Woolgar. 1986. *Laboratory Life: The Social Construction of Scientific Facts*. Princeton: Princeton University Press.

Leavitt, Sturgis E. 1941. "Pan-Americanism at the University of Florida." *Hispanic American Historical Review* 21.1: 129–32.

Leonard, Thomas C. 2003. "More Merciful and Not Less Effective: Eugenics and American Economics in the Progressive Era." *History of Political Economy* 35.4: 687–712.

Leonard, Thomas M. 1999. "United States–Latin American Relations: Recent Historiography." *Journal of Third World Studies* 16.2: 163–79.

Leuchtenburg, William E. 1952. "Progressivism and Imperialism: The Progressive Movement and American Foreign Policy, 1898–1916." *Mississippi Valley Historical Review* 39.3: 483–504.

Levin, N. Gordon. 1968. *Woodrow Wilson and World Politics: America's Response to War and Revolution*. New York: Oxford University Press.

Livingston, James. 1994. *Pragmatism and the Political Economy of Cultural Revolution, 1850–1940*. Chapel Hill: University of North Carolina Press.

Lopez Lenci, Yazmín. 2004. *El Cusco, paqarina moderna: Cartografía de la modernidad e identidades en los Andes peruanos (1900–1935)*. Lima: Fondo Editorial de la Universidad Nacional Mayor de San Marcos.

Lord, Everett W. 1921. "Professional Training for Leadership in Foreign Trade." *Proceedings of the Academy of Political Science of the City of New York* 9.2: 167–74.

Lutz, Catherine A., and Jane L. Collins. 1993. *Reading National Geographic*. Chicago: University of Chicago Press.

Manchester, Alan K. 1933. "Descriptive Bibliography of the Brazilian Section of the Duke University Library." *Hispanic American Historical Review* 13.2: 238–66.

Manela, Erez. 2007. *The Wilsonian Moment: Self-Determination and the International Origins of Anticolonial Nationalism.* New York: Oxford University Press.

Martin, Geoffrey. 1980. *The Life and Thought of Isaiah Bowman.* Hamden, Conn.: Shoe String Press.

———. 1986. "Bowman's New World and the Council on Foreign Relations." *Geographical Review* 76.4: 438–60.

Martz, John D. 1966. "Characteristics of Latin American Political Thought." *Journal of Inter-American Studies* 8.1: 54–74.

Matienzo, José Nicolás. 1917 [1910]. *El gobierno representativo federal en la República Argentina.* Madrid: Editorial América.

Mato, Daniel. 2008. "No hay saber 'universal,' la colaboración intercultural es imprescindible." *Alteridades* 18.35: 101–16.

Maxwell, David. 2008. "The Soul of the Luba: W. F. P. Burton, Missionary Ethnography and Belgian Colonial Science." *History and Anthropology* 19.4: 325–51.

McCoy, Alfred W., and Francisco A. Scarano, eds. 2009. *Colonial Crucible: Empire in the Making of the Modern American State.* Madison: University of Wisconsin Press.

McGerr, Michael. 2003. *A Fierce Discontent: The Rise and Fall of the Progressive Movement in America, 1870–1920.* Oxford: Oxford University Press.

McMahon, Sean H. 1999. *Social Control and the Public Intellect: The Legacy of Edward A. Ross.* New Brunswick: Transaction.

McPherson, Alan. 2003. *Yankee No!: Anti-Americanism in U.S.-Latin American Relations.* Cambridge, Mass.: Harvard University Press.

Means, Philip Ainsworth. 1931. *Ancient Civilizations of the Andes.* New York: Charles Scribner's Sons.

Meléndez, Edgardo. 1993. *Movimiento anexionista en Puerto Rico.* Rio Piedras: Editorial de la Universidad de Puerto Rico.

Menand, Louis. 2001. *The Metaphysical Club: A Story of Ideas in America.* New York: Farrar, Straus and Giroux.

Messer-Davidow, Ellen, David Shumway, and David Sylvan, eds. 1993. *Knowledges: Historical and Critical Studies in Disciplinarity.* Charlottesville: University Press of Virginia.

Mignolo, Walter D. 2000. *Local Histories/Global Designs: Coloniality, Subaltern Knowledges and Border Thinking.* Princeton: Princeton University Press.

———, ed. 2001. *Capitalismo y geopolítica del conocimiento.* Buenos Aires: Ediciones del Signo.

———. 2005. *The Idea of Latin America.* Oxford: Blackwell.

Miller, Nicola. 1999. *In the Shadow of the State: Intellectuals and the Quest for National Identity in Twentieth-Century Spanish America.* London: Verso.

Mirsepassi, Ali, Amrita Basu, and Frederick Weaver, eds. 2003. *Localizing Knowledge in a Globalizing World: Recasting the Area Studies Debate.* Syracuse, N.Y.: Syracuse University Press.

References

Moore, Barrington. 1978. *Injustice: The Social Bases of Obedience and Revolt*. White Plains, N.Y.: M. E. Sharpe.

Moraña, Mabel, Enriqué Dussel, and Carlos A. Jáuregui, eds. 2008. *Coloniality at Large: Latin America and the Postcolonial Debate*. Durham: Duke University Press.

Moreiras, Alberto. 2001. *The Exhaustion of Difference: The Politics of Latin American Cultural Studies*. Durham: Duke University Press.

Mould de Pease, Mariana. 2000. "The Formation of Permanent Collections in the United States: The Role of E. G. Squier as Collector within Peru." Paper presented at the 65th Annual Meeting of the Society for American Archaeology, Philadelphia.

———. 2008. *Machu Picchu, antes y después de Hiram Bingham: Entre el saqueo de "antigüedades" y el estudio científico*. Lima: Centro de Estudios Históricos Luis A. Valcárcel.

Murphy, Gretchen. 2005. *Hemispheric Imaginings: The Monroe Doctrine and Narratives of U.S. Empire*. Durham: Duke University Press.

Naylor, Robert, Leon Helguera, and Thomas McGann. 1962. "Research Opportunities in Modern Latin America." *Americas* 18.4: 352–79.

Nelson, Adam R. 2005. "The Emergence of the American University: An International Perspective." *History of Education Quarterly* 45.3: 427–37.

Newfield, Christopher. 2003. *Ivy and Industry: Business and the Making of the American University, 1880–1980*. Durham: Duke University Press.

"A New Inter-American Center." 1934. *Hispanic American Historical Review* 14.3: 355–58.

Ninkovich, Frank A. 1977. "The Currents of Cultural Diplomacy: Art and the State Department." *Diplomatic History* 1.3 (July): 215–38.

———. 1981. *The Diplomacy of Ideas: U.S. Foreign Policy and Cultural Relations, 1938–1950*. Cambridge: Cambridge University Press.

Normano, J. Frank. 1931. *The Struggle for South America: Economy and Ideology*. Boston: Houghton Mifflin.

Nugent, David. 2010. "Knowledge and Empire: The Social Sciences and United States Imperial Expansion." Special issue of *Identities* 17.1: 2–44.

O'Brien, Thomas F. 1993. "The Revolutionary Mission: American Enterprise in Cuba." *American Historical Review* 98.3 (June): 765–85.

Ogilvie, A. G. 1950. "Isaiah Bowman: An Appreciation." *Geographic Journal* 115.4–6: 226–30.

Osorio Tejeda, Nelson. 2007. "Estudios Latinoamericanos y la nueva dependencia cultural." *Revista de Crítica Literaria Latinoamericana* 33.66: 251–78.

Pagden, Anthony. 1990. *Spanish Imperialism and the Political Imagination*. New Haven: Yale University Press.

Page, Charles Hunt. 1969. *Class and American Sociology: From Ward to Ross*. New York: Octagon.

Palti, Elías José. 2010. "From Ideas to Concepts to Metaphors: The German Tradition of Intellectual History and the Complex Fabric of Language." *History and Theory* 49.2: 194–211.

Parsons, James. 1996. "Carl Sauer's Vision of an Institute of Latin American Studies." *Geographic Review* 86.3: 377–84.

Patterson, Jerry. 1957. "Hiram Bingham, 1875–1956." *Hispanic American Historical Review* 37: 131–37.

Paul, Harry W. 1985. *From Knowledge to Power: The Rise of the Science Empire in France, 1860–1939*. Cambridge: Cambridge University Press.

Peers, Douglas. 2005. "Colonial Knowledge and the Military in India, 1780–1860." *Journal of Imperial and Commonwealth History* 33.2: 157–80.

Pérez, Louis A. 2008. *Cuba in the American Imagination*. Chapel Hill: University of North Carolina Press.

Perkins, Whitney T. 1981. *Constraint of Empire: The United States and Caribbean Interventions*. Westport, Conn.: Greenwood.

Perry, Edward. 1920. "Anti-American Propaganda in Hispanic America." *Hispanic American Historical Review* 3.1: 17–40.

Phelps, Dudley M. 1936. *Migration of Industry to South America*. New York: McGraw-Hill.

Pike, Frederick B. 1992. *The United States and Latin America: Myths and Stereotypes of Civilization and Nature*. Austin: University of Texas Press.

Pletcher, David M. 1998. *The Diplomacy of Trade and Investment: American Economic Expansion in the Hemisphere, 1865–1900*. Columbia: University of Missouri Press.

Podgorny, Irina. 2008. "Antigüedades portátiles: Transportes, ruinas y comunicaciones en la arqueología del siglo 19." *História, Ciências, Saúde–Manguinhos* 15.3: 577–95.

Poovey, Mary. 1998. *A History of the Modern Fact: Problems of Knowledge in the Sciences of Wealth and Society*. Chicago: University of Chicago Press.

Prieur, Annick, and Mike Savage. 2011. "Updating Cultural Capital Theory: A Discussion Based on Studies in Denmark and in Britain." *Poetics* 39.6 (December): 566–80.

Prisco, Salvatore. 1973. *John Barrett, Progressive Era Diplomat: A Study of a Commercialist Expansionist, 1887–1920*. Tuscaloosa: University of Alabama Press.

Quesada, Ernesto. 1926 [1898]. *La época de Rosas*. Buenos Aires: Artes y Letras.

Rabe, Stephen G. 1988. "Historic Patterns of Intervention: U.S. Relations with Latin America." *Latin American Research Review* 23.2: 206–13.

Radway, Janice. 2004. "Research Universities, Periodical Publication, and the Circulation of Professional Expertise." *Critical Inquiry* 31.1: 203–28.

Rafael, Vicente L. 2000. *White Love and Other Events in Filipino History*. Durham: Duke University Press.

Ramos Mejía, Francisco. 1889. *El federalismo argentino: Fragmentos de la historia de la evolución argentina*. Buenos Aires: F. Lajouane.

Randall, Stephen J. 2003. "The Tragedy of American Diplomacy Revisited: U.S. Relations with Latin America and the Caribbean." *Latin American Research Review* 38.2: 167–79.

Ratliff, William. 1989–1990. "Latin American Studies: Up from Radicalism?" *Academic Questions* 3.1: 60–74.

Reich, Cary. 1996. *The Life of Nelson A. Rockefeller*. New York: Doubleday.

"Report of a Committee of the Pan American Union on the Teaching of Latin-American History in Colleges, Normal Schools, and Universities in the United States." 1927. *Hispanic American Historical Review* 7.3: 352–85.

References

———

Rippy, J. Fred. 1931. *The Capitalists and Colombia*. New York: Vanguard.

———. 1934. "The British Bondholders and the Roosevelt Corollary of the Monroe Doctrine." *Political Science Quarterly* 49.2 (June): 195–206.

Rivarola, Rodolfo. 1908. *Del régimen federativo al unitario: Estudio sobre la organización política de la Argentina*. Buenos Aires: J. Peuser.

Riviale, Pascual. 2000. *Los viajeros franceses en busca del Perú antiguo (1821–1914)*. Lima: Editorial de la Pontificia Universidad Católica del Perú.

Robertson, William S. 1923. *Hispanic-American Relations with the United States*. New York: Oxford University Press.

Rogers, Daniel T. 1982. "In Search of Progressivism." *Reviews in American History* 10.4: 113–32.

Roorda, Eric P. 1998. *The Dictator Next Door: The Good Neighbor Policy and the Trujillo Regime in the Dominican Republic, 1930–1945*. Durham: Duke University Press.

Rosenberg, Emily S. 1975. "Economic Pressures in Anglo-American Diplomacy in Mexico, 1917–1918." *Journal of Interamerican Studies and World Affairs* 17.2 (May): 123–52.

———. 1982. *Spreading the American Dream*. New York: Hill and Wang.

———. 2003. *Financial Missionaries to the World: The Politics and Culture of Dollar Diplomacy, 1900–1930*. Durham: Duke University Press.

Rosenberg, Emily S., and Norman L. Rosenberg. 1987. "From Colonialism to Professionalism: The Public-Private Dynamic in United States Foreign Financial Advising, 1898–1929." *Journal of American History* 74.1 (June): 59–82.

Ross, Dorothy. 1978. "Professionalism and the Transformation of American Social Thought." *Journal of Economic History* 38.2: 494–99.

———. 1992. *The Origins of American Social Science*. Cambridge: Cambridge University Press.

Rothblatt, Sheldon. 1997. "The Place of Knowledge in the American Academic Profession." *Daedalus* 126.4: 245–64.

Rothery, Agnes. 1930. *South America: The West Coast and the East*. Boston: Houghton Mifflin.

Rowe, John Carlos. 2000. *Literary Culture and U.S. Imperialism: From the Revolution to World War 2*. Oxford: Oxford University Press.

Sable, Martin H. 1989. *Guide to the Writing of Pioneer Latin Americanists in the United States*. New York: Haworth.

Sadlier, Darlene J. 2012. *Americans All: Good Neighbor Cultural Diplomacy in World War 2*. Austin: University of Texas Press.

Said, Edward W. 1979. *Orientalism*. New York: Vintage.

Salvatore, Ricardo D. 1996. "North American Travel Narratives and the Ordering/Othering of South America (c. 1810–1860)." *Journal of Historical Sociology* 9.1 (March): 85–110.

———. 1998a. "Ansiedades y prácticas culturales de comerciantes norteamericanos a mediados del siglo 19." *Prismas* (Buenos Aires), no. 2: 43–73.

———. 1998b. "The Enterprise of Knowledge: Representational Machines of Informal Empire." In *Close Encounters of Empire: Writing the History of U.S.-Latin American*

Cultural Relations, ed. Gilbert M. Joseph, Catherine LeGrand, and Ricardo Salvatore, 69–104. Durham: Duke University Press, 1988.

———. 1999. "Re-Discovering Spanish America: Uses of Travel Literature about South America in Britain." *Journal of Latin American Cultural Studies* 8.2: 199–217.

———. 2002. "Early American Visions of a Hemispheric Market in South America." In *Transnational America: The Fading of Borders in the Western Hemisphere*, ed. Berndt Ostendorf, 45–64. Heidelberg: C. Winter.

———. 2003. "Local versus Imperial Knowledge: Reflections upon Hiram Bingham and the Yale Peruvian Expedition." *Nepantla* 4.1 (February): 67–80.

———, ed. 2005a. *Culturas imperiales: Experiencia y representación en América, Asia y África, 1850–1960.* Rosario, Argentina: Beatriz Viterbo Editora.

———. 2005b. "Library Accumulation and the Emergence of Latin American Studies." *Comparative American Studies* 3.4 (December): 415–36.

———. 2005c. "Panamericanismo práctico: Acerca de la mecánica de la penetración comercial norteamericana." In *Culturas Imperiales: Experiencia y representación en América, Asia y África, 1850–1960*, ed. Ricardo D. Salvatore, 269–300. Rosario, Argentina: Beatriz Viterbo Editora.

———. 2005d. "Yankee Advertising in Buenos Aires: Reflections on Americanization." *Interventions: International Journal of Postcolonial Studies* 7.2: 216–35.

———. 2006a. *Imágenes de un imperio: Estados Unidos y las formas de representación de América Latina.* Buenos Aires: Editorial Sudamericana.

———. 2006b. "Imperial Mechanics: South America's Hemispheric Integration in the Machine Age." *American Quarterly* 58.3: 662–91.

———, ed. 2007a. *Los lugares del saber: Contextos locales y redes transnacionales en la formación del conocimiento moderno.* Rosario, Argentina: Beatriz Viterbo Editora.

———. 2007b. "Saber hemisférico y disonancias locales: Leo S. Rowe en Argentina, 1906–1919." In *Los lugares del saber: Contextos locales y redes transnacionales en la formación del conocimiento moderno*, ed. Ricardo D. Salvatore, 327–67. Rosario, Argentina: Beatriz Viterbo Editora.

———. 2008a. "Libraries and the Legibility of Hispanic America: Early Latin American Collections in the United States." In *Hybrid Americas: Contacts, Contrasts and Confluences in New World Literatures and Cultures*, ed. Josef Raab and Martin Butler, 191–211. Münster, Germany: LIT / Bilingual Publishers.

———. 2008b. "The Unsettling Location of a Settler Colony: Argentina, from Settler Economy to Failed Developing Nation." *South Atlantic Quarterly* 107.4: 755–90.

———. 2010a. "The Making of a Hemispheric Intellectual-Statesman: Leo S. Rowe in Argentina (1906–1919)." *Journal of Transnational American Studies* 2.1. https://escholarship.org/uc/item/92m7b409.

———. 2010b. "The Postcolonial in Latin America and the Concept of Coloniality: A Historian's Point of View." *A Contra Corriente* 8.1: 332–47.

———. 2013. "Imperial Revisionism: U.S. Historians of Latin America and the Spanish Colonial Empire (ca.1915–1945)." *Journal of Transnational American Studies* 5.1. http://escholarship.org/uc/item/30m769ph.

References

———. 2014. "Progress and Backwardness in Book Accumulation: Bancroft, Basadre, and Their Libraries." *Comparative Studies in Societies and History* 56.4: 1–32.

Sarfatti Larson, Magali. 1977. *The Rise of Professionalism: A Sociological Analysis.* Berkeley: University of California Press.

Scarano, Francisco. 2009. "Censuses in the Transition to Modern Colonialism: Spain and the United States in Puerto Rico." In *Colonial Crucible: Empire in the Making of the Modern American State*, ed. Alfred W. McCoy and Francisco A. Scarano, 210–19. Madison: University of Wisconsin Press.

Scarfi, Juan Pablo. 2009. "James Brown Scott y la propagación del derecho internacional norteamericano en las Américas, 1900–1939." Master's thesis, Departamento de Historia, Universidad Torcuato Di Tella.

———. 2014. *El imperio de la ley.* Buenos Aires: Fondo de Cultura Económica.

Schäfer, Axel A. 2000. *American Progressives and German Social Reform, 1875–1920.* Stuttgart: Franz Steiner.

Scheller, William. 1994. *Amazing Archaeologists and Their Finds.* Minneapolis: Oliver Press.

Schmidt-Nowara, Christopher. 2007. *The Conquest of History: Spanish Colonialism and National Histories in the Nineteenth-Century.* Pittsburgh: University of Pittsburgh Press.

Schoultz, Lars. 1998. *Beneath the United States: A History of U.S. Policy toward Latin America.* Cambridge, Mass.: Harvard University Press.

Schultz, Theodore W. 1964. *Transforming Traditional Agriculture.* New Haven: Yale University Press.

———. 1980. "Nobel Lecture: The Economics of Being Poor." *Journal of Political Economy* 88.4: 639–51.

Scifres, Diana. 1964. "Consideration of Edward A. Ross as a Progressive in the 1920s." Master's thesis, Department of History, University of Wisconsin, Madison.

Scott, James C. 1998. *Seeing Like a State: How Certain Schemes to Improve the Human Condition Have Failed.* New Haven: Yale University Press.

Seidel, Robert N. 1973. *Progressive Pan Americanism: Development and United States Policy towards South America, 1906–1931.* Ithaca: Cornell University Press.

Sheinin, David, ed. 2000a. *Beyond the Ideal: Pan Americanism in Inter-American Affairs.* Westport, Conn.: Praeger.

———. 2000b. " 'Its Most Destructive Agents': Pan American Environmentalism in the Early Twentieth Century." In *Beyond the Ideal: Pan Americanism in Inter-American Affairs*, ed. David Sheinin, 115–32. Westport, Conn.: Praeger.

———. 2006. *Argentina and the United States: An Alliance Contained.* Athens: University of Georgia Press.

Shepherd, William R. 1933. "Brazil as a Field for Historical Study." *Hispanic American Historical Review* 13.4: 427–36.

Shohat, Ella. 1991. "Imagining Terra Incognita: The Disciplinary Gaze of Empire." *Public Culture* 3.2 (spring): 41–70.

Simpson, Christopher, ed. 1998. *Universities and Empire: Money and Politics in the Social Sciences during the Cold War.* New York: New Press.

References

Simpson, Lesley Byrd. 1949. "Thirty Years of the *Hispanic American Historical Review*." *Hispanic American Historical Review* 29.2: 188–204.

Sloan, John W. 1978. "United States Policy Responses to the Mexican Revolution: A Partial Application of the Bureaucratic Politics Model." *Journal of Latin American Studies* 10.2 (November): 283–308.

Smith, Neil. 2003. *American Empire: Roosevelt's Geographer and the Prelude to Globalization.* Berkeley: University of California Press.

Smith, Peter H. 1996. *Talons of the Eagle: Dynamics of U.S.–Latin American Relations.* New York: Oxford University Press.

Smith, Robert Freeman. 1963. "The Formation and Development of the International Bankers Committee on Mexico." *Journal of Economic History* 23.4 (December): 574–86.

Solberg, Carl. 1969. "Immigration and Urban Social Problems in Argentina and Chile, 1890–1914." *Hispanic American Historical Review* 49.2 (May): 215–32.

Solovey, Mark. 2001. "Project Camelot and the 1960s Epistemological Revolution: Rethinking the Politics-Patronage-Social Science Nexus." *Social Studies of Science* 31.2: 171–206.

Spenser, Daniela, ed. (2004). *Espejos de la guerra fría: México, América Central y el Caribe.* Mexico City: CIESAS.

Steers, J. A. 1957. "South America as a Field for Geographical Research." *Geographical Journal* 123.3: 329–41.

Stein, Stanley J., and Barbara H. Stein. 1970. *The Colonial Heritage of Latin America: Essays on Economic Dependence in Perspective.* New York: Oxford University Press.

Steward, Julian H. 1943. "Acculturation Studies in Latin America: Some Needs and Problems." *American Anthropologist* 45.2: 198–206.

Stocking, George W., ed. 1991. *Colonial Situations: Essays on the Contextualization of Ethnographic Knowledge.* Madison: University of Wisconsin Press.

Streeby, Shelley. 2002. *American Sensations: Class, Empire, and the Production of Popular Culture.* Berkeley: University of California Press.

Stromquist, Shelton. 2006. *Reinventing "The People": The Progressive Movement, the Class Problem, and the Origins of Modern Liberalism.* Urbana: University of Illinois Press.

Tannenbaum, Frank. 1934. *Whither Latin America?: An Introduction to Its Economic and Social Problems.* New York: Thomas Y. Crowell.

Tax, Sol. 1953. *Penny Capitalism: A Guatemalan Indian Economy.* Chicago: University of Chicago Press.

Tenorio, Mauricio. 1991. "Viejos gringos: Radicales norteamericanos en los años treinta y su visión de México." *Secuencia* 21 (September–December): 95–116.

Terán, Oscar. 2000. *Vida intelectual en el Buenos Aires de fin-de-siglo (1880–1910).* Buenos Aires: Fondo de Cultura Económica.

Thomas, Nicholas. 1994. *Colonialism's Culture: Anthropology, Travel and Government.* Cambridge: Polity Press.

Thompson, I. Eric. 1936. *Archaeology of South America.* Anthropology Leaflet 33. Chicago: Field Museum of Natural History.

References

Tota, Antonio Pedro. 2009. *The Seduction of Brazil: The Americanization of Brazil during World War 2*. Translated from the Portuguese by Lorena B. Ellis. Foreword by Daniel J. Greenberg. Austin: University of Texas Press.

Turnbull, David. 1993–1994. "Local Knowledge and Comparative Scientific Traditions." *Knowledge and Policy* 6.3–4: 29–54.

Valcárcel, Luis E. 1938. *The Latest Archaeological Discoveries in Peru*. Lima: National Museum of Lima.

———. 1981. *Memorias*. Lima: Instituto de Estudios Peruanos.

van Bath, B. H. Slicher. 1974. "Feudalismo y capitalismo en América Latina." *Boletín de Estudios Latinoamericanos y del Caribe*, no. 17: 21–41.

Van Buren, Mary. 1996. "Rethinking the Vertical Archipelago: Ethnicity, Exchange, and History in the South Central Andes." *American Anthropologist* 98.2: 338–51.

Van Cleave, James W. 1907. "What Americans Must Do to Make an Export Business." *Annals of the American Academy of Political and Social Science* 29 (May): 30–37.

Vessey, Lawrence R. 1965. *The Emergence of the American University*. Chicago: University of Chicago Press.

Warner, Charles D. 1896. "Our Foreign Trade and Consular Services." *North American Review* 162.472: 274–86.

Webber, Irving L. 1981. "Sociology: Parochial or Universal?" *Social Forces* 60.2: 416–31.

Weinberg, Julius. 1972. *Edward Allsworth Ross and the Sociology of Progressivism*. Madison: State Historical Society of Wisconsin.

Welles, Sumner. 1947. "In Memoriam: Dr. Leo S. Rowe." *Americas* 3.3 (January): 363–67.

Werking, Richard H. 1981. "United States Consular Reports: Evolution and Present Possibilities." *Business History* 23.3: 300–304.

West, Nancy Martha. 2000. *Kodak and the Lens of Nostalgia*. Charlottesville: University Press of Virginia.

Wexler, Laura. 2000. *Tender Violence: Domestic Visions in an Age of U.S. Imperialism*. Chapel Hill: University of North Carolina Press.

Wiebe, Robert H. 1967. *The Search for Order, 1877–1920*. New York: Hill and Wang.

Wilkins, Mira. 1970. *The Emergence of Multinational Enterprise: American Business Abroad from the Colonial Era to 1914*. Cambridge, Mass.: Harvard University Press.

Wood, Bryce. 1967. *The Making of Good Neighbor Policy*. New York: W. W. Norton.

Wrigley, Gladys M. 1951. "Isaiah Bowman." *Geographical Review* 41.1: 7–65.

Zulawski, Ann. 2007. *Unequal Cures: Public Health and Political Change in Bolivia, 1900–1950*. Durham: Duke University Press.

References

INDEX

American Geographic Society, 30, 161, 268n58; Bowman and, 42, 43; mapping of South America by, 5, 11; mapping projects in Latin America and, 62–63

American Historical Association, 31, 68–69, 120–21

Americanization, South American scholarship and, 10–16

American Museum of Natural History, 99

American Society of International Law, 215

American Sociological Association, 31, 188

Amundsen, Roald, 87

anarchy, in Haring's historical research, 115–16

Ancient Civilizations of the Andes (Means), 27

Andean nations: archaeological research in, 7, 19; Bowman's research in, 44, 71–72, 162–64; comparative history and, 69–70; mapping projects in, 61–63; peasant class in, 197–99; Ross's research on, 47, 67–68; Ross's sociological research on, 189, 206–8; social anthropology of, 5, 9, 267n44; Yale Peruvian Expedition and, 26–28, 60–61

The Andes of Southern Peru (Bowman), 43, 167–70, 173–77, 218–19

Anglo-American history, Hispanic American history and, 68–70

anthropology: expansion of Latin American studies and, 29, 267n52; Mexico-U.S. research collaboration in, 26

anti-Americanism: economic imperialism and, 221–25; Haring's research on, 46, 123, 222–25, 245; Rowe's analysis of, 146–47; U.S. hegemony, 63–65, 247–48, 287n14

antiquarians: commerce in antiquities and, 95–98, 104; conflicts with YPE and, 91–95; cultural legacy of, 101–4

archaeology: armature of scientific conquest and, 77–80; Bingham's contributions to, 40–42; commerce in antiquities and, 95–98; in Ecuador, 19–20; imperiality of, 61, 270n3; penetration of U.S. capital and, 103–4; Yale Peruvian Expedition and, 26–28, 59–60

Archeological Institute of America, 77–78, 268n58

area studies, influence on South American scholarship, 18–20

Argentina: Bowman's geographical research in, 43–44, 165–67, 181–82, 282n8; economic and political structure of, 108–9, 280nn32–33; European research on, 285n17; federalism in, 10, 49, 135–37, 150–54; Haring's assessment of, 46, 123–27; military coup in, 121–23; in Ross's research, 46, 68, 189, 192–94, 199–201, 206, 286n4; in Rowe's research, 49–51, 135–36, 141–42, 147–50, 232, 251–52

Argentina and the United States (Haring), 46

Argentine Confederation, 66

Atacama Desert: Bowman's research in, 44, 71–72, 162–64, 177–86, 237–38, 241–42; mapping projects in, 43, 62–63

"The Awakening of Bolivia" (Rowe), 134

ayllus (Indian communities), 97–98, 253

Ballivian, Manuel, 253

Balmaceda, José Manuel, 125

Bandelier, Adolphe, 77

bandos, 97

banking industry: cultural engagement in South America and, 22–24; expansion in South America of, 32, 264n15; Spanish American resistance to, 223–25

Barnard, Luther, 267n49

Barrett, John, 4, 78, 145, 261n6, 282n6

Basadre, Jorge, 121

Belli, Carlos, 98

bibliographical projects in Latin American studies, 34–35; Bingham's contributions to, 40

Big Stick diplomacy, U.S. hegemony in South America and, 6

Billinghurst, Guillermo, 85–87

Bingham, Hiram, 2, 5, 8, 264n5; colonialism and research of, 237–40; commerce in antiquities and, 96–98; explorations of Machu Picchu by, 40–42, 59–61, 75–104, 269n4; indigenista conflict with, 85–90, 215, 251, 253–54; interdisciplinarity in research of, 70–72; Monroe Doctrine criticized by, 106, 213–15, 258; Panama Canal criticized by, 218; at Pan-American Scientific Congress, 25; Peruvian intelligentsia conflicts with, 83–90, 215; promotion of South American research by, 26, 243–44, 266nn39–41; scholarly legacy of, 39, 99–104, 212, 236–59, 268n3, 269n5; transdisciplinary implications in research of, 59–61; transnational research and, 52–53

birth rates, Ross's discussion of, 191–92

Blaine, James G., 3, 36, 261n3

Bolivar, Simón, 41

Bolivia: agriculture in, 197, 282n9; in Bingham's research, 41; in Bowman's research, 44, 165–67, 172–73; ethnological research in, 77; gold smuggling through, rumors of, 94–95; military coup in, 121–23; mining industry in, 79–80; in Ross's research, 48, 189, 192, 197–99, 206; in Rowe's research, 142–43; Yale Peruvian Expedition and, 87–91

Bolton, Eugene, 68–70

Bolton, Herbert, 68–70

border disputes, mapping projects in Latin America and, 62–63

Bowman, Isaiah, 2, 5, 8, 10, 15; colonialism and research of, 170–73, 237–40; on commercial and capital penetration in South America, 218, 246–48; comprehensive visibility and work of, 164–67; desertic research of, 44, 71–72, 162–64, 177–82; geographic research in South America by, 42–44, 241–42; informal empire theory of, 225–27; interdisciplinarity in research of, 70–73; labor exploitation and slavery in work of, 173–77, 195; local encounters and research of, 249–54; Machu Picchu explorations by, 41–42, 60; mapping projects in Latin America and, 61–63, 73; scholarly legacy of, 39, 160–64, 182–86, 212, 236–59; on subalternity and economic progress, 173–77; transnational research and, 52–53; view of South America, 160–86; Yale Peruvian Expedition and, 26–28, 43, 79–80, 83

Braden Company, 79, 180

Brandt, Anthony, 40

Brazil: in Bowman's research, 165–67, 182, 282n7; geography of, 30, 264n9; in Haring's research, 46, 107, 123–27; historical research in, 27, 266n36; military coup in, 121–23; in Rowe's research, 49–51, 142–43

British imperialism: in Africa, 287n18; comparative study of empires and, 227–30; cultural engagement in South America and, 22–23; in Haring's historical research, 110–16, 223–25; Rowe's assessment of, 145; scholarship on South America and, 237–40; settler colonies of, 14, 263n26

Bryan, William Jennings, 259

Burgin, Miron, 106

business expansion in South America: Bowman's warnings concerning, 183–86; Haring's analysis of, 222–25; regional knowledge production and, 22–24; Ross's criticism of, 192, 285nn7–8; Rowe's analysis of, 145–50; scholarship and research on, 28–30, 70–72; in South America, 30–33; Summer Round Tables on Latin America and, 117–20; U.S. hegemony and, 63–65, 287n14; Yale Peruvian Expedition and, 79–80, 100–104

Calancha, Antonio de la, 42

Canal Zone, creation of, 48, 214, 231–32

capital penetration in South America: archaeological research and, 103–4; in Atacama desert, 178–82; expansion of, 31–33; Rowe's criticism of, 221; scholarly absolution of, 220–21; Yale Peruvian Expedition and, 78–80

Caribbean region: economic internationalism in, 63–65; Haring's opposition to U.S. imperialism in, 45, 115–17, 224, 229–30, 248–49; piracy in, 106; Rowe's criticism of U.S. policy in, 135, 140–41, 150, 221; U.S. hegemony in, 58–59, 65–67, 211, 215, 270n6

Carnegie, Andrew, 269n18

Carranza, Venustiano, 49

cartographic analysis, Bowman's contributions to, 161–64

Casa de Contratación, 111, 239, 243

Castro, Fidel, 34

"The Causes of Race Superiority" (Ross), 190

cédulas, 97

Central America: corporate expansionism in, 31–32; Haring's criticism of U.S. intervention in, 107, 224, 229–30; U.S. hegemony in, 20–21, 211, 215. See also specific countries and regions

Central American Court of Justice, 49

Centro de Arte e Historia de Cuzco, 91

Cerro de Pasco Mining, 79–80, 220–21

Changing America (Ross), 47, 188, 191–92, 220

Chile: Atacama Desert in, 177–82; in
Bowman's research, 44, 165–67, 181–82,
282n8; copper mining in, 32; Haring's
assessment of, 46, 123–27; military coup
in, 121–23; mining industry in, 79–80,
180–82; political transition in, 66; in Ross's
research, 48, 189, 192, 196–200, 204, 206,
220; in Rowe's research, 49–51, 142–44;
Spanish conflict with, 286n2

China: Ross's research in, 188–89; uprising
of 1910 in, 48

Chinese labor: in Peru, 194, 217; in U.S.
railroad industry, 188

Chirgwin, Enrique, 121–22

Choqqeqirau ruins, 41

Chuquicamata mining company, 180

Circum-Caribbean protectorates: Haring's
discussion of, 225; Rowe's views on,
136–37, 157–58, 288n30

class structure in South America: coloniality and, 112–14, 202–4; Ross's criticism of,
191–92, 199–202, 206–7

Clemenceau, George, 244, 285n17

Cline, Howard, 106

Close Encounters of Empire, 6

Colby, Charles C., 160–61

Cold War politics: informal empire of U.S.
and, 226–27; Latin American studies and,
15–16, 34–35, 262n9

colleges and universities: curriculum in U.S.
of, 265n27; South Cone universities
compared with, 10. *See also* academic
knowledge

Colombia: Bingham's research in, 41;
Bowman's research in, 44; Canal Zone
and, 48, 214; Haring's assessment of,
123–27; political climate in, 122; in Ross's
research, 48, 189, 196–97, 206, 219

The Colonial Heritage of Latin America
(Stein), 286n31

colonialism: European, 17; of agriculture,
181–82; in Amazon region, 170–73;
Bowman's geographical analysis of,
164–67; governance under, 5, 54, 57–59;

in Haring's research, 45–46, 106–14;
Haring's research on, 127–29; historical
scholarship on, 5, 9–10; imperiality of
knowledge and, 53–57; labor conditions in
South America linked to, 196–99; "rediscovery" of South American and influence
of, 237–40; Ross on South American
character and, 202–8, 286n31; Rowe's
experiences with, 49–51; study of, 9, 54

Comentarios Reales de los Incas (Garcilaso),
92, 167

Commentaries (Story), 151

commercial conquest: cultural engagement
in South America and, 22–24; Ross's discussion of, 219–20; Rowe's criticism of, 221

Committee on Latin American History
(CLAH), 120–21

Committee on Latin American Studies, 70

commodities: indigenous commodity exchange and production, 179, 183, 219; Latin
American production of, 116, 165, 175, 222;
markets for U.S. goods, 17–18, 166, 183,
220–22; Peruvian antiquities as, 104

Commons, John R., 284n2

Compañía del Salitre de Chile, 122

comparative history: comparative study of
empires and, 227–30; development of,
68–70; Haring's contributions so, 68–70,
127–29, 242; Rowe's contributions to, 49

comparative international sociology: formation of, 189; in Ross's South American
research, 204–8

comprehensive visibility: in Bowman's work,
164–67; Haring's historical research and,
127–29; of Latin American studies, 4, 11

conditional conquest: in Atacama desert,
179–82; Bowman's concept of, 170–73,
182–86; commercial and capital penetration and, 218–20

conquest: Machu Picchu explorations as part
of, 99–104; scientific inquiry and armature
of, 77–80

constitutional government: federalism and,
10; intellectual conquest and Eurocentric
ideas of, 8; in Mexico, 32; neocolonial
governance and, 57–59; Rowe's analysis of,
49–51, 73, 137–41, 147–50, 157–59; in South
America, 25, 48–49

Index

Index

Dominican Republic: Columbus Lighthouse in, 155; U.S. receivership in, 214
Dom Pedro II (Emperor of Brazil), 125–26
Downes v. Bidwells, 138
Downey, James E., 265n28
Dumbarton Oaks Conference, 257
Durkheim, Émile, 47, 188

East India Company, 54
Eaton, George F., 96
economic conditions in South America: in Atacama desert, 178–82; Bowman on geography and capital penetration, 162–64, 170–73, 181–86, 218–20; Caribbean region policies and, 63–65; commercial and capital penetration in, 218–20; enclave economies and, 220–21; Haring's research on, 45–46, 107–9, 112–14, 121–23, 222–25; imperiality of knowledge and, 53–57; indigenous subalternity and, in Bowman's research, 170–77; influence on U.S. economy of, 115–16; integration in global economy and, 211–12; political structure and, 232–34; regional history and, 106; research design and, 70–72; Rowe's discussion of, 221, 232, 252; scholarship and, 28–30; South American attitudes concerning, 221–25; Summer Round Tables on Latin America and, 117–20; U.S. hegemony and, 2–16, 218–20, 246–49, 287n9; Yale Peruvian Expedition and, 26, 243–44, 266nn39–41. *See also* banking industry; business enterprises; trade relations
Ecuador: Bowman's research in, 44; military coup in, 121–23; in Ross's research, 48, 189, 192, 194–95, 197, 206, 220; U.S. research in, 18–20
Eighth American Scientific Congress, 45
El Comercio (Cuzco) newspaper, 83
El Comercio (Lima) newspaper, 85–88, 91
elite stratification: attitudes to economic imperialism and, 221–25; colonial failure and, 112–14; Ross's criticism of, 191–92, 199–202, 206–7
El Sol (Cuzco) newspaper, 85, 88, 91
Ely, Richard, 46, 284n2
empire, questions of. *See* imperialism; imperial visibility

Empire in Brazil: A New World Experiment with Monarchy (Haring), 107
enclave economies, scholarly absolution of, 220–21, 247–48
enganchadores (planters' recruiters), 173
enganche indentured-labor system, 221
enhanced visibility: cartography and, 161–64; of South American studies, 4, 10–11, 14, 261n9
enticement, U.S. policy of, 13–16
environmental-human interaction, Bowman's research on, 166–82, 184–86
Erving, William G., 42, 83
eugenics, Ross and, 284n2
European–South American trade: First World War and decline of, 32, 65; Haring's research on, 222–25; Spanish colonization and, 113–16
excavation permits, Yale Peruvian Expedition and conflicts over, 84–90, 92
exceptionalism, South American scholarship and influence of, 8–16
expanded visibility, imperiality of knowledge and, 55–57
expansionism: knowledge enterprises in context of, 30–33; in United States, 160–64
expert knowledge: constructive Pan-Americanism and, 231–32; expanding prestige of, 31–33; imperiality of, 12, 15, 55–57
extraterritoriality, imperiality of knowledge and, 55–57

Fabian, Johannes, 197
fake artifacts, commerce in antiquities and, 96
family structure in South America, Ross's analysis of, 199–202
Farabee, William C., 77
federalism: in Argentina, 10, 49, 135–37, 150–54; Rowe's analysis of, 150–54
Federalist Papers, 151
The Federal System of the Argentine Republic (Rowe), 49, 135–36, 150–54, 158
Ferro, Mariano, 98
feudalism: colonialism linked to, 203–4; South American labor conditions compared to, 196–99
Foote, Harry W., 41, 59–60, 83, 270n8

Index

Index

Hague International Court, 240

Haiti, U.S. intervention in, 49, 224

Handbook of Latin American Studies, 34–35, 107

Hanke, Lewis, 36–37, 106

Hardy, Osgood, 100–101

Haring, Clarence H., 2, 5, 8; academic prestige, 120–21; on Caribbean region policies, 45, 63–65, 115–17, 229–30, 248–49, 287n12; comparative history and, 68–70, 127–29, 227–30, 242; on economic conditions in South America, 107–9, 112–14, 121–23, 222–25; Hispanic American history and, 44–46, 105–33; interdisciplinarity in research of, 70–72, 74; on Latin American history, 27–28, 34–35, 267n46; local encounters and research of, 250–51, 253–54; scholarly legacy of, 39, 129–33, 212, 236–59; on South American attitudes toward U.S., 45–46, 107, 116–17, 287n11; on Spanish colonization, 45–46, 106–14, 237–40, 243, 288n8; Summer Round Tables on Latin America and, 117–20; transnational research and, 52–53

Harper's Weekly, 81

Harvard Bureau of Economic Research on Latin America, 65, 72, 107, 271n19

Harvard College Observatory, 79

Harvard University: Haring's career at, 44–46; Hispanic American history at, 105–33; Latin American studies at, 29

Hastings, Warren, 54

Haya de la Torre, Raúl, 93–94

hegemonic politics: anti-Americanism in South America and, 221–25; Bowman's analysis of, 161–64, 166–67; colonial history linked to, 113–14; comparative study of empires and, 227–30; constructive Pan-Americanism and, 230–32; economic development in South America and, 2–16; Haring's view of, 116–17, 128–29, 131–33; informal empire of U.S. and, 211–35; Monroe Doctrine and, 216–17; Ross's scholarship and, 209–10; Rowe's intellectual cooperation and, 144–47; scholarship and, 246–49, 255–59; U.S. diplomacy and, 6

Hendriksen, Kai, 41, 60, 83

Hertzler, J. O., 188

Hiram Bingham Highway, 101

Hispanic American Historical Review, 44, 107, 120

Hispanic American history: compatibility of imperialism with, 114–16; diplomatic history and, 2–3; Haring's academic gatekeeping concerning, 120–21; Haring's contributions to, 44–46, 105–33, 245; inclusion of U.S. in, 68–70; U.S. scholarship in, 7, 9, 34, 264n5, 267n48

Hispanic American History Group, 27–28

Hispanic-American Relations with the United States (Robertson), 28

Hispanic Society of America, 81

historical convergence in North and South America, Haring's theory of, 105–33

Honduras, U.S. imperialism in, 20–21, 214

Horwitz, Howard, 284n6

Hrdlička, Aleš, 78

Huaina Capac, 97–98

Huanca people, 96

huaqueros, Peruvian denunciation of YPE scholars as, 91–95, 253–54; commerce in antiquities and, 95–98, 104

Huayna Kenti ruins, rival explorations of, 90

Huerta, Victoriano, 155–56

humanities: expanding prestige of, 31–33; regional knowledge production and, 24–28

Humboldt, Alexander von, 171–73, 183

Huntington, Samuel, 259

immigration: in Bowman's geographic analysis, 166–67; Bowman's research on agricultural pioneering and, 181–82; Monroe Doctrine and policies on, 217; Ross's criticisms concerning, 46–47, 188, 190, 192, 194

imperialism: comparative study of empires and, 109–14, 227–30; cultural nationalism as critique of, 93–95, 103–4; desert geography and economy and, 177–82; of disciplinary knowledge, 13–16; formal and informal empire and, 13; Haring's historical research as service of empire, 109–10, 130–33; imperial engagement ideology, 12–16; imperiality of knowledge and, 53–57; influence of, in South American scholarship, 6–16, 202–4; intellectual conquest of South America and, 11–16;

regional history and visibility of, 105–33; Ross's race generalizations and, 190; Rowe on governance and, 137–41; South American attitudes concerning, 221–25; teaching history in context of, 114–16; U.S. scholarship and question of empire, 211–35

imperial visibility, Hispanic American history and, 120–21

Inca history and culture: Bingham's research on, 40–42, 269n4, 270n10; Bowman's discussion of, 167; commerce in antiquities and, 95–98; cultural nationalism about, 92–95; fake Incaica production and, 96; governance in, 282n16; interdisciplinary research on, 70–72; local resistance to YPE appropriation of, 83–90; transdisciplinary research on, 60–61; Yale Peruvian Expedition and, 27

Inca Land (Bingham), 40, 101–2

"Inca metallurgy" discourse, 79–80

Inca Mining Company, 79

Indian rebellions in Peru (1922–1923), 93–94

Indian Removal Act, 217

indigenismo movement, 102–4, 249–54

indigenistas: conflicts with Yale Peruvian Expedition, 85–90, 215; cultural legacy of, 101–4; politics and nationalist ideology of, 90–95

indigenous cultures: archaeological research on, 27; in Atacama Desert, 177–82; Bowman's interaction with, 166–77, 170–73; commerce in antiquities and, 97–98; conflicts with Yale Peruvian Expedition, 90–95; elite disregard of, 217; labor exploitation of, 221; resistance to archaeological research by, 42; in Ross's research, 189, 194–96; scholarship in South America and influence of, 9–10, 14–16, 19–21, 249–54, 268n60; scientific inquiry vs., 268n60; slavery in, 174–77

industrial development: early U.S. initiatives in South America for, 17; informal empire of U.S. and, 226–27; Ross's criticism of, 192, 284n5

informal empire of U.S.: comparative study of empires and, 227–30; formation of theory concerning, 225–27; in Haring's research, 113–14; imperiality of knowledge

and, 54–57; Machu Picchu explorations in context of, 76–104; print-photo-capitalism and, 82–83; situated knowledge and, 8; South American scholarship and, 211–35

Ingeniería Internacional, 118

Instituto Histórico de Cuzco, 85–86, 88–89, 91

intellectual conquest of South America, U.S. scholarship and, 10–16

intellectual cooperation: comparative history and, 69–70; Rowe's policy of, 49–51, 134–35, 144–47, 156–58

intelligence activities of Haring, 45–46, 121–23, 131–33, 245

intelligentsia of Peru. *See* cuzqueñistas; indigenistas

Inter-American Affairs, 20

inter-American cooperation: foreign policy transitions and, 51; Haring's scholarship on, 45–46; intellectual entente and, 12, 144–47; Long's Ecuador proposal and, 18–20; Monroe Doctrine and, 213–15; in Ross's scholarship, 201–2; Rowe's promotion of, 49–51, 134–37, 230–32

interdisciplinary approach to South American scholarship, 24–28, 264n12; legacy of, 240–43; research design for, 70–74

International Bureau of the American Republics, 4, 17–18, 261n6; cultural engagement and, 22–24

International Congress of Americanists, 102

International School at Panama, proposal for, 265n28

interventores, Peruvian nationalism and, 89–90

investment opportunities: Bowman's analysis of, 162–64; expansion in South America of, 32–33, 37; Haring's research on, 46, 222–25; informal empire of U.S. and, 226–27; traveling scholars and, 39–40

Irving, Washington, 17

Jackson, William K., 118

James, Preston, 282n1

Jefferson, Mark, 282n1

Jenks, Leland, 118

Jivaros people, 19

Johns Hopkins University, Bowman at, 42, 244

Johnson, John J., 35

Index

Jones, Clarence E., 282n1
Journal of Social Forces, 67

Kemmerer, Edwin, 287n9
Ketchua peoples, 177
Kinley, David, 28
knowledge: armature of conquest and, 77–80; business and diplomatic discourse and, 18; commerce in antiquities and, 95–98; expansionism and promotion of, 30–33; foreign policy and, 28–30; geography as, 162–64; imperial hemispheric hegemony and, 2–16; imperiality of, 53–57, 63–65; informal empire of U.S. and, 212–13; scholarship on South America as harvesting of, 243–46; Summer Round Tables on Latin America and, 117–20; universality vs. locality in, 268n60; wealth equated with, 94–95
Kodak Company, 42; Yale Peruvian Expedition supported by, 78–81, 99–100
Kroeber, Alfred, 251, 269n4
Kubler, George, 269n4

labor issues: Bowman's analysis of, 163–64, 167–77, 183–86, 284n39; colonialism linked to, 202–4; in mining industry, 220–21; Ross's discussion of, 192, 196–99, 206–8, 250; slavery and, 175–77; for Yale Peruvian Expedition, 90–95
Land Claims Commission (Panama), 135
landlordism, Ross's research on, 196–99
language competency, cultural engagement in South America and, 22–24
Lanius, Paul B., 42
Lanning, John Tate, 70
La Prensa newspaper, 92
La Razón newspaper, 223–25
Latin American studies: compatibility of imperialism with, 114–16; origins of, 2, 33–35
Latour, Bruno, 6, 8–9
League of Nations, 43, 225, 232, 240
Le Bon, Gustave, 188
Leguía, Augusto B., 84–86, 123
Leonard, Irving, 70
Letelier, Valentín, 253
Leuchtenburg, William E., 267n56
Levene, Ricardo, 46

The Limits of Land Settlement (Bowman), 43
Listas de Toros, 97
local landowners, conflicts with Yale Peruvian Expedition, 90–95
locally-based knowledge: Haring's research and, 46; of indigenistas and cuzqueñistas, 90–95; research on Inca cultures and, 41–42; Ross's use of, 285n117; scientific universalization vs., 83–90; South American scholarship and, 9–10, 14–16, 30–33, 249–54, 268n60
Lomellini, Cesar, 41, 84, 95
Long, Boaz W., 18–21, 36, 264nn17–18, 265n19
Longfellow, Henry W., 17
López de Gómara, Francisco, 171–72
Lost City of the Incas (Bingham), 40, 90
Luce, Henry, 162

Machiganga Indians, 174–77, 250
Machu Picchu: archaeological research on, 25, 27; Bingham's exploration of, 5, 40–42, 59–61, 75–104, 269n4; commerce in antiquities and, 98; conflicts of cultural property at, 83–90; legacy of explorations at, 99–104; news coverage of explorations in, 75–76; rival explorations of, 90; Ross's travels to, 48; transdisciplinary implications of, 59–61
Machu Picchu: A Citadel of the Incas (Bingham), 40
Madeira-Mamoré Railroad, 171
Mama Ocllo, 97–98
Manco Capac, 42
Mann, Mary T. Peabody, 17
Maphis, Charles, 119, 289n27
mapping projects in Latin America, 61–63, 242
Mapuche people, 196
Mariátegui, José Carlos, 93–94
market development: Bowman's geographical analysis of, 165–67; cultural engagement in South America and, 17, 22–24, 265n27; expansion in South America of, 32–33, 271n19; informal empire of U.S. and, 212, 226–27
Markham, Clement (Sir), 60
Matienzo, José Nicolás, 153
McKinley, William, 135–39, 138
Means, Philip A., 27, 251, 269n4

Index

Index

Nelson, Ernesto, 252–53
neocolonialism: Bowman's analysis of, 162–64, 184–86; government under, 5, 57–59; labor exploitation and, 175–77; postcolonial Pan-Americanism and, 230–32; regional knowledge production and, 15–16
neutral rights in South America, Rowe's promotion of, 135
news media: coverage of Yale Peruvian Expedition in, 77–80, 84–93, 99–104; economic imperialism of U.S. discussed in, 223–25; Machu Picchu explorations in, 75–76; Ross's support for free expression and, 192
The New World (Bowman), 161–62, 257
Nicaragua: Haring's criticism of policies in, 45; U.S. banking control in, 264n15; U.S. diplomacy in, 21
nitrate mining, 178–80
North American Review, 142, 144

object-based epistemology, Machu Picchu exploration and, 99–104
Ocampo, Baltasar de, 42
The Old World in the New (Ross), 188
Organization of American States (OAS), 48
The Outlines of Sociology (Ross), 205–8

Pacific region, U.S. colonialism in, 211
Panama: Rowe's work in, 136–37; U.S. intervention in, 211–12, 214, 224
Panama Canal: Bingham's criticism of, 218; diminished expectation concerning, 36; Rowe's discussion of, 57–58, 231–32; Yale Peruvian Expedition and politics of, 94–95
Panama-Pacific Exposition, 81
Pan-American Atlas project, 62–63
Pan-American Conference (1889–1890), 17
Pan-American Exhibition, 81
Pan American Institute of Geography and History, 45–46, 62–63
Pan-Americanism: Bowman's alternative to, 167; comparative history and, 69–70; Haring's support for, 44–46, 107–9, 117–20, 132–33, 225; mapping projects in Latin America and, 62–63; Monroe Doctrine and, 215–17; postcolonialism and, 230–32; relative failure of, 36; resource exploitation and, 78; Rowe's analysis of, 48–51, 135–37, 144–47, 154–56, 221; scholarship in South America and, 2–16, 28–30; Summer Round Tables on Latin America and, 117–20; transnational research and, 52
Pan-American Scientific Congress (1908), 25, 37, 39
Pan-American Union, 4, 14, 29, 240, 261n6; Rowe as director of, 48–51, 134–37, 154–56, 231–32
Paraguay, Bowman's geographical analysis of, 165–67
Páramos regions, 19, 264n10
Paris Peace Conference (1919), 43, 161–62, 225, 257–58
Partido Autonomista Nacional, 125
Patchin, Robert H., 118
Pax Americana, Ross's proposal for, 156, 217, 249
Peabody Museum, 42, 99
Peary, Robert, 87
Pérez de Velazco, F., 97
Peru: in Bingham's research, 41, 75–104; in Bowman's research, 43–44, 172–73; ethnological research in, 77; Haring's visit to, 46; impact of development in, 182–86; Indian rebellions in, 93–94; intelligentsia of, conflicts with Bingham, 83–90, 215; mapping projects in, 61–63; political conditions in, 122–23; reception of Yale Peruvian Expedition in, 76–77; regional fragmentation in, 161–64, 167–70; in Ross's research, 48, 189, 192, 194–95, 197–98, 200, 206, 220; in Rowe's research, 142–44
Peruvian Corporation, 79, 84, 86
Pezet, Federico Alfonso, 102
Philippines: Ross's comments on, 286n32; Rowe's discussion of, 136–37, 139–41; U.S. census in, 54
photography, Yale Peruvian Expedition and importance of, 78–81, 99–104
pioneer settlements, Bowman's study of, 43
The Pioneer Fringe (Bowman), 43, 181–82
Pizarro, Francisco, 75–76
plantation labor, Bowman's analysis of, 175–77, 184–86
"plateau Indians," Bowman's interaction with, 172–77

Platt, Robert S., 282n1

Plaza, Galo, 21, 265n20

policy making, regional-based knowledge and, 10–11

political culture in South America: Bowman's geographical analysis of, 164–67, 183–86, 243–44; colonialism and, 202–4; Haring's assessment of, 121–27, 225; regional fragmentation and, 167–70; Ross's analysis of, 199–202; Rowe's research on, 58–59, 65–67, 232–34, 242–43; Summer Round Tables on Latin America and, 117–20; U.S. hegemony and, 246–49; Yale Peruvian Expedition and, 85–95, 102–4, 243–44

politics: Andean consciousness and, 104; Argentina's political regimes, 125; Bingham enters, 42,97; Brazil's political stability, 125; Chile, political conditions, 122–23; class in contemporary politics, 108; Cold War, 20, 109; democratic, 46; German geo-politics, 63; of intellectual cooperation, 59, 69; Peru, political conditions, 85, 90, 122; political disturbances, early 1930s, 126; Puerto Rico, political disputes, 139–40; U.S. hegemonic politics, 113; world politics, 43

pongo labor system, 197

Poovey, Mary, 268n60

Porfirio Diaz, José, 26, 66, 205

Portales, Diego, 123

Posada, Adolfo, 285n17

power/knowledge dualism, South American scholarship and, 9

pre-Columbian cultures: archaeological research on, 27–28; in Bowman's geographic analysis, 166–67; commerce in antiquities and, 95–98; U.S. research on, 19

Prescott, William H., 17, 60

probanzas (colonial statements of evidence), 97

Problems of City Government (Rowe), 49, 135

professionalization: expansion of South American scholarship and emergence of, 31–33, 268n58; transnational scholarship and rise of, 39–40

progress, economic and social: in ABC powers, 4, 49, 59, 108, 135; in Copiapó, 179; in Cuzco, 84; expected impact of the Panama Canal, 219; indigenous peoples excluded of, 217; and institutional convergence, 154; of Mexican universities, 26; and modern sociability, 200; outside forces of, 170–71; pessimism over Andean progress, 218; social progress and revolutions, 46; 65–66; in South America, 73, 106, 123–27, 141–43

progressivism: expansion of South American scholarship and, 31–33, 267n56; goals of, 280n35; lack in South America of, 202–4; Ross and, 190–92, 208–10; Rowe and, 49, 137–41, 149–50

property relations in Inca culture, 97–98

public goods, 110, 115–16, 167, 204, 227–28, 234–35, 248, 285n7. *See also* economic conditions in South America

public opinion, Rowe on government of, 147–50, 152–54

Puerto Rico, Rowe's work in, 48–49, 57, 135–41, 237–40

Pukara excavation, 102

Puna de Atacama, 180–82

Putumayo massacres, 286n1

Quesada, Ernesto, 252–53

Quintanilla, Gutiérrez de, 90–92

race relations: Argentine federalism and, Rowe's analysis of, 279nn13; Bowman's analysis of, 163–64, 170–77, 183–86; in Haring's historical research, 46, 115–16, 126–27; indigenous encounters and, 102–4, 249–54; Machu Picchu explorations in context of, 75–77; Ross's research and generalizations on, 189–90, 192–96, 217, 238–40, 284n2; transnational scholarship on, 67–68

race suicide, Ross's concept of, 188

railroad industry: dependency theory and, 283n19; in Peru, 172–73, 179, 284n40; Ross's criticism of, 188; Yale Peruvian Expedition and, 78

Rand McNally Lands and Peoples series, 26–28

Ravignani, Emilio, 46

regional fragmentation, Bowman's analysis of, 161–64, 167–70, 185–86

Index

325

regional knowledge: business and economic enterprises and, 22–24; diplomatic promotion of, 20–21; evolution of Latin American studies and, 33–35; fields of study and, 24–28; geopolitics and, 29–30; limitations of, 36; regional history and imperial visibility, 105–33; Rowe's influence on development of, 158–59; sale of regional-ethnic history and, 97; South American studies and, 5–16

Reinsch, Paul, 25

religiosity, in Ross's research, 195

Report to the Congressional Immigration Commission (Ross), 188

research design: anti-Americanism in South America and, 63–65; business expansion and interdisciplinarity and, 70–72; comparative history and, 68–70; imperiality of knowledge and, 53–57, 72–73

research universities: expansion of, 31–33, 264n12; foreign service training and, 23–24, 266n32; regional knowledge production and, 24–28; South American scholarship and growth of, 7–16; transnational scholarship and transformation of, 38–40

resource exploitation: Bowman's analysis of, 166–67; corporate methods and, 10; desert geography and economy and, 180–82; early U.S. initiatives in South America for, 17; expansion in South America of, 32–33

revolutions in Caribbean and South America: Bowman's analysis of, 167–70; Rowe's research on, 65–67

Rice, Hamilton, 40–41

Rippy, J. Fred, 70, 118, 120–21

Rivarola, Roldofo, 142, 153

Rivera, Raúl O., 121

Roads to Social Peace (Ross), 47

Robertson, William Spence, 28, 118

Roca, Julio A., 125

Rockefeller, Nelson, 20

Roman Catholic Church, dominance in South American of, 286n25

Roosevelt, Franklin D., 3, 18; Bowman and, 42, 44, 257; Haring and, 45; Rowe and, 155

Roosevelt, Theodore, 50–51, 63; Roosevelt Corollary and, 65, 214; Rowe and, 144

Roosevelt Corollary to Monroe Doctrine, 65, 214–15

Root, Elihu, 7, 23–26, 32, 36–37, 236; Bingham and, 39, 214, 269n8; Carnegie and, 269n18

Rosas, Belisario, 96

Ross, Edward A., 2, 5, 8, 10; on colonialism and South American character, 202–4, 238–40; on commercial and capital penetration in South America, 218–20, 247; democratic sociability concept of, 199–202; enclave economies absolved by, 220; on indigenous encounters, 249–54; on landlordism and labor servitude, 196–99; on Monroe Doctrine, 217, 258–59; racial generalizations of, 67–68, 188–90, 192–96; research in South America by, 46–48, 73, 187–210, 240–41, 287n5; scholarly legacy of, 39, 208–10, 212, 236–59; transnational research and, 52–53

Rowe, Leo S., 2, 5, 8, 10–13; comparative history and, 70; criticism of U.S. Caribbean policy by, 135, 140–41, 288n30; of democratic transition in South America, 65–67, 137–41, 232–34; on economic conditions in South America, 221, 247–48; on elites in South America, 201; governance studies by, 57–59, 237–40, 242–43, 245–46; Haring's collaboration with, 45; intellectual cooperation policy of, 49–51, 134–35, 144–47; interdisciplinarity in research of, 70–72; on Mexico-U.S. research collaboration, 26, 264n18; on Monroe Doctrine, 215–17; Pan-Americanism of, 48–51, 116, 230–32; at Pan-American Scientific Congress, 25; Pan-American Union and, 29, 134–37, 154–56; on progress in South America, 141–44; scholarly legacy of, 39, 48–51, 156–58, 212, 236–59; transnational research and, 52–53; on U.S. interventionism in Caribbean, 65–67

rubber industry, 167–70; slavery in, 174–77, 184–86

Russia, Ross's research on, 188–89, 204–5

Russia in Upheaval (Ross), 205

Russian Revolution, 48

Sacsaywaman excavation, 41, 102

Sánchez Cerro, Miguel, 122–23

Index

326

Santo Domingo, U.S. intervention in, 224

Sartigés, Count of, 95–98

Sauer, Carl, 267n51, 282n1

scholarship on South America: harvesting of knowledge in, 243–46; impact of U.S. influence in, 63–65; interdisciplinarity in, 70–72, 240–43; international influence of, 257–59; legacy of, 236–59; local and indigenous contributions to, 249–54; overview of, 1–16; question of empire in, 211–35

School of American Research, 19

Schultz, Theodore, 166

scientific inquiry: armature of conquest and, 77–80; Bowman's belief in, 42–44, 160–64, 182–86; geography and, 163–64; indigenous knowledge vs., 268n60; legacy of YPE and, 100–104; locally based knowledge vs., 94–95; as replacement for colonialism, 238–40; South American studies and, 5–16, 261n7, 266n37; U.S. research in Ecuador and, 18–20

Scott, James Brown, 118, 241

Scramble for Africa, in Haring's historical research, 109–10

Scroggs, William, 121

Second Congress on the History of America, 46, 68–69

Second Pan-American Financial Conference (1920), 45

Second Pan-American Scientific Conference (1915–1916), 146

secularization, Ross's discussion of, 191–92

self-rule, Rowe on education in, 136–37, 157–58, 245–46

settler research, Bowman's geographic analysis and, 165–67, 177–82, 241–42, 282nn11–13

Shepherd, William, 25, 264n5; Brazilian research by, 27

Simmel, Georg, 188

situated knowledge, informal empire and, 8

slavery: Bowman's research on, 167–70, 173–77, 184–86; historical scholarship on, 9; Ross's racial generalizations concerning, 193–95

Small, Albion, 188, 284n1

Smith, Neil, 15, 161, 225–26, 269n11

Smithsonian Institution, 99

social conditions in South America: Bowman's analysis of, 172–73; Haring's assessment of, 123–27; Ross's research on, 187–210

Social Control (Ross), 47

social mobility, in Ross's research, 199

Social Psychology (Ross), 47

social sciences: expanding prestige of, 31–33, 267n49; Latin American studies and, 5, 9, 15–16; regional knowledge production and, 24–28; Ross's sociological research in South America as, 46–48, 187–210, 242–43; U.S. research in Ecuador and, 18–20

The Social Revolution in Mexico (Ross), 47, 205

The Social Trend (Ross), 47

Sociedad Geográfica (Peru), 83–84

Society for American Archaeology, 31

Society of American Geographers, 160

sociology, Ross's contributions to, 187–89, 205–10, 242–43, 258–59

"soft empire" ideology: informal empire of U.S. and, 226–27; regional knowledge production and, 36; Rowe's discussion of, 216–17

South America: early American interest in, 17; geopolitical division of, 3–4; military coups during early 1930s in, 121–23; recent scholarship on, 1–16; "rediscovery" through scholarship on, 237–40; regional and local differences in scholarship on, 254–59; Ross's research on, 188; U.S. economic and cultural influence in, 5–16. *See also specific countries and regions*

South America: A Geography Reader (Bowman), 164–67

South America Looks at the United States (Haring), 45–46, 107, 116–17, 222–25

South American Expedition, 43

South American Progress (Haring), 45, 107, 123–27

South Cone universities, Rowe's research on, 10

South of Panama (Ross), 47, 67, 187, 189, 204–5, 208–10, 217, 252–53, 289n17

sovereignty issues, Rowe's discussion of, 136–37, 139–41

Spanish-American War (1898), 17–18, 214

Index

Spanish colonialism: 5, 44–45, 67, 110;
comparative study of empires and, 227–30,
249; Haring's research on, 45–46, 106–14,
237–40, 243; imperialism in context of,
114–16; Indian character and, 195; legacy
of, 73, 184, 189, 198; policy mistakes of,
110–12; parallel histories, 128–30; Philippines, 139–41; resistance to, 75, 196; in
Ross's research, 192, 196–99; sale of artifacts from, 97–98; scholarship on South
America and, 237–40; in South America,
17–18, 45–46, 264n1

The Spanish Empire in America (Haring),
45–46, 107–8

specialized knowledge, expanding prestige
of, 31–33

State Department (U.S.): Haring's collaboration with, 45–46; Latin American
division of, 20–21; Rowe's career with,
134–37; scholarship on South America
and, 257–59

Steers, J. A., 29–30

Stein, Stanley and Barbara, 128–29, 286n31

Steward, Julian, 29–30, 267n52

Story, Joseph, 151

subalternity: in Bowman's environmental research, 166–77; colonialism and,
203–4; scholarship in South America and
influence of, 246–54; in South American
scholarship, 254–59

Summer Round Tables on Latin America,
117–20

Sumner, William, 188

Sundt, Alfredo, 79

Supreme Court (U.S.): Caribbean policies
and, 58–59; ruling on by Puerto Rico,
138–41, 279nn9–11

system building in social theory, Ross's
research and, 47, 188

Tacna-Arica dispute (1925–1926), 155, 223,
281n48

Tambayeque excavation, 102

Tarnawiecki, engineer, 80

Tax, Sol, 166

technology: Bowman's analysis of, 162–64;
expansion in South America of, 31–33,
218–20

Tello, Julio, 253

temporal displace, constructive Pan-
Americanism and, 231–32

"terra incognita," image of South America as,
17, 27, 238–40

Thompson, I. Eric, 267n43

Thompson, Wallace, 118

Ticknor, George, 17

*Trade and Navigation between Spain and the
Indies in the Time of the Habsburgs* (Haring), 45–46, 106–7, 110–11, 113, 253

trade relations: corporate expansionism and,
31–32; in desert culture, 177–82; in Haring's historical research, 112–14; informal
empire of U.S. and, 226–27; regional
knowledge production and, 22–24, 37;
traveling scholars and, 39–40

Transandine Railway, 48

transnational scholarship: Bowman's work
on rubber industry and slavery, 176–77;
imperiality of knowledge and, 53–57,
270n1; race research and, 67–68; Ross's sociological research as, 188–89, 206–8, 259;
scope and design of, 52–74; transformation of research universities and, 38–40

transportation technology in South America,
78, 171–72, 266n30; in Andean region,
182–86; in Atacama Desert, 179

traveling scholars: imperiality of knowledge
and, 56–57; transformation of research
and, 38–40

travel narratives: Bowman's geographical
work as, 164–67; South American scholarship and, 41

Tucker, Herman L., 41, 59–60

Turlington, Edgar W., 118, 289n23

Turner, Frederic J., 44, 181

Uhle, Max, 77, 86, 102

Ulloa, Luis, 97–98

United Fruit, 119; South American scholarship and, 79

United States: economic and cultural influence in South America, 5–16; expansionism in, 160–64; Haring's comparisons of
South America with, 123–27; influence on
scholarship on South America of, 63–65;
intervention in Caribbean by, 65–67; Latin

Index